Faith Reads

A Selective Guide to Christian Nonfiction

David Rainey

A Member of the Greenwood Publishing Group
Westport, Connecticut • London

Library of Congress Cataloging-in-Publication Data

Rainey, David.
  Faith reads : a selective guide to Christian nonfiction / David Rainey.
     p. cm.
  Includes bibliographical references and index.
  ISBN 978-1-59158-602-9 (alk. paper)
  1. Christian literature—Bibliography. 2. Christianity—Bibliography. I. Title.
  Z7751.R28 2008
  [BR121.3]
  016.23—dc22   2008010352

British Library Cataloguing in Publication Data is available.

Copyright © 2008 by Libraries Unlimited

All rights reserved. No portion of this book may be
reproduced, by any process or technique, without the
express written consent of the publisher.

Library of Congress Catalog Card Number: 2008010352
ISBN: 978-1-59158-602-9

First published in 2008

Libraries Unlimited, 88 Post Road West, Westport, CT 06881
A Member of the Greenwood Publishing Group, Inc.
www.lu.com

Printed in the United States of America

The paper used in this book complies with the
Permanent Paper Standard issued by the National
Information Standards Organization (Z39.48–1984).

10   9   8   7   6   5   4   3   2   1

With love and honor
to my dad, Chris Charles Rainey,
and my mom, Kathleen Ann Schuster Rainey.

Contents

Acknowledgments — xi
Introduction — xiii

Chapter 1: Life Stories — 1
Introduction — 1
Story Types and Themes — 2
  Conversion Stories — 2
  Heavenly Visions — 5
  Personal Narratives — 7
Christians from All Walks of Life — 10
  Actors — 10
  Doctors and Scientists — 12
  Military and Political Figures — 15
  Ministers and Christian Leaders — 18
  Missionaries, Martyrs, and Saints — 29
  Musicians — 35
  Sports Figures — 39
  Writers — 40

Chapter 2: Prayer, Worship, and Spiritual Growth — 47
Introduction — 47
Daily Devotionals and Prayer Books — 48
Fasting — 50
Prayer and Revival — 52
Spiritual Warfare — 64
Worship — 71
Spiritual Growth Classics — 74
Discipleship — 78

Spiritual Gifts	81
Christian Living	86
Bibliographies	97

Chapter 3: Christian Self-Help — 101

Introduction	101
Health	102
General Health	102
Nutrition	106
Fitness	108
Illness and Healing	109
House and Home	111
Men's, Women's, and Teens' Issues	113
Sex and Sexuality	117
Relationships	122
Dating and Singles	122
Marriage	124
Parenting	129
Counseling and Psychology	142
Grief and Death	150

Chapter 4: Evangelism — 155

Introduction	155
Apologetics	156
Evangelism	165
Missions	174

Chapter 5: Arts, Culture, and Education — 181

Introduction	181
The Arts	182
Visual Arts	182
Literature	185
Music	188
Culture	191
History	192
Philosophy	197
Social Issues	201
Popular Culture	209
Education	215
General Education	216
Homeschooling	221
Bibliographies	226

Chapter 6: Business and Leadership — 233

Introduction	233
Christians in the Marketplace	234

Personal Finance	239
Leadership	244
Bibliographies	249
Chapter 7: Science and Nature	251
Introduction	251
Science and Faith	251
Nature	256
The Human Body	257
Animals	258
Ecology and Environmental Protection	259
General Nature	260
Creationism and Evolution	263
Young-Earth Creation Science	264
Old-Earth Creation Science	267
Intelligent Design	269
Theistic Evolution	272
Chapter 8: Bible and Theology	275
Introduction	275
Bible	276
Bible—English Translations	276
Bible Study Tools	278
Other Books about the Bible	283
Theology	286
Reference and Bibliographies	294
Appendix A: Christian Nonfiction Book Awards	297
Appendix B: Review Sources	299
Appendix C: Christian Nonfiction Publishers	303
Author/Title Index	307
Subject Index	339

Acknowledgments

I am very glad to acknowledge my beautiful bride, Tonja, and my three wonderful children, Rebekah Joy, Alyssa Grace, and Anna Catherine. Thanks for your support and encouragement.

I would also like to acknowledge Gary Ferguson, my friend and reference mentor. Thanks for being a patient and thoughtful sounding board—and also for finding and fixing problems in the manuscript.

At the Lion's Den, I want to acknowledge Daniel Savala. Thanks for opening the door to Christian nonfiction by introducing me to the likes of Tozer, Schaeffer, Sauer, and Custance.

Thank you Kytara and State Library of Louisiana Interlibrary Loan staff (Errin, Beryl, Gussie, Kathe, and Julie) for mountains of fulfilled requests. Thank you Patrick Henry and Glen Davis for your great minds and helpful recommendations. I am also very grateful to Barbara Ittner who made this book possible, and for others at Libraries Unlimited who helped make this book better.

Finally, I would like to acknowledge God, the author of faith and the one who is called the Word. "Nothing was made without the Word." Thank you.

Introduction

One of the first books that Gutenberg printed on his newly invented printing press (circa 1450) was the source book for all Christian nonfiction: the Bible. Today, Christian nonfiction interest and publishing is stronger than it has ever been. In just 2005 alone, more than 7,000 books were published by members of the Evangelical Christian Publishers Association. In 2006, almost 6,000 titles were published.[1] So much is being published today and so much has been written over the centuries, where does a reader or a librarian start?

That is where *Faith Reads* comes into play. A quick glance at the table of contents shows that this book covers more than the typical "religious" categories of publishing, such as prayer and spiritual growth. There are whole sections devoted to topics like business, science, education, and parenting. Why? Because people's faith informs more than just their time of worship on Sunday; it also informs their work on Monday, their children's education throughout the week, and their entertainment on the weekend. Despite the great and enduring interest in Christian nonfiction publishing, guides to the literature or readers' advisory tools that cover this recent explosion of titles are virtually nonexistent. This book is an attempt to change that.

Faith Reads is an annotated bibliography of Christian nonfiction arranged by subject. Six hundred forty-six titles are annotated here. In addition, over 1,000 books have been selected to complement the annotated titles. For general readers, this is a guide for exploration and discovery. For librarians, this is a tool to assist both readers' advisory services and collection development.

Christian publishing is a unique subset of the larger publishing industry. It has its own set of authors (like Max Lucado and Beth Moore), book publishers (such as Zondervan and InterVarsity), trade associations (including the Evangelical Christian Publishers Association and the Christian Booksellers Association), and bookstore chains and shops (like Family Christian Stores and LifeWay Christian Stores) that are distinct from mainstream publishing. To make things more interesting, Catholics also have their own authors, publishers, associations, and bookstores. The Christian book industry has been around for generations, but for many years it was small and remained within well-defined borders.

In recent years, things have changed. The "big boys" of publishing and bookselling no longer ignore Christian nonfiction. What happened? *The Prayer of Jabez* by Bruce Wilkinson (Multnomah, 2000) sold more than eight million copies in 2001, and *The Purpose-Driven Life* by Rick Warren (Zondervan) has sold more than 25 million copies since it was first published in 2002. Once secular publishers witnessed the commercial success of these and other Christian nonfiction titles, large outfits like HarperCollins, Random House, and Simon & Schuster started either buying Christian publishers or creating new imprints to market Christian nonfiction books. For instance, HarperCollins bought Zondervan in 1984. Also, Random House created WaterBrook in 1996 and then bought Harold Shaw Publishers in 2000 and Multnomah Press in 2006. Another major change is that mega-retailers also started wanting a piece of the pie. Wal-Mart and Target now sell popular Christian nonfiction books.

Besides Family Christian Stores, Barnes & Noble, and Wal-Mart (not to mention Amazon.com and Christianbook.com), where else can readers satisfy their hunger for Christian nonfiction? The public library, of course, where books are plentiful and free.

Public libraries, like all in the world of books, are still adjusting to the proliferation of Christian nonfiction. Books by Christian authors with Christian perspectives on life no longer reside only in the Dewey 200s (religion and Christianity); they are spilling into many other areas such as the 300s (social sciences including everything from adolescence and education to law and social problems), the 500s (natural sciences), the 640s and 650s (family living and business/leadership), the 700s and 800s (arts and literature), and the 900s (history). Libraries are meeting the needs of readers who hunger for Christian nonfiction, and this book is here to help.

Guidance

What in the world is spiritual warfare? How do I select a homeschool curriculum? What is the difference between young-earth creation science and intelligent design? How does one define apologetics? These questions make it clear that Christian nonfiction comes with its own set of terms and trends that many readers and librarians may not be familiar with. *Faith Reads* explains these concepts and discusses these trends in both the chapter introductions and the annotations. The table of contents reveals the broad subject groupings used to organize this guide, but note also the subject index at the back of the book. This subject index gives readers the most focused access to the hundreds of titles gathered here, especially since books on a certain subject can be found in two or more different chapters (for instance, biographies can be found in several chapters besides Chapter One). Most annotations are followed by a "More" section that recommends additional titles by the same author or titles of related subject interest. Many of these additional titles are annotated elsewhere in the book. A glance at the author/title index will give the page number.

Scope

This book includes titles published by Christian publishers (or secular publishers with Christian imprints) and/or by Christian authors. The predominant perspective of the books in this guide is Protestant/evangelical because evangelical publishers are responsible for the lion's share of books available and in demand. Catholic authors and publishers come next, for there is a long and well-established history of Catholic publishing. The third main branch of Christianity is the Eastern Orthodox Church. There are a small number of Eastern Orthodox authors/titles here, which represent this small but growing area of American religion and publishing.

"Classic" titles are included (about forty are annotated) but not emphasized, because other books do this job well. Also, I was very selective here because many libraries already have books by such classic authors as Paul Tillich and Søren Kierkegaard (to use an example from philosophy). For readers and librarians who still desire to learn about classic Christian authors and titles, I have annotated several bibliographies at the end of Chapter Two; these include works such as Terry Glaspey's *Book Lover's Guide to Great Reading*, which has a forty-page section listing "great books of the Christian tradition."

For the purposes of this book, a "classic" work must have been written by an author born at least one hundred years ago (1907). However, the main focus of *Faith Reads* is on books still in print that have been first published in the last twenty or thirty years.

Titles of interest to teens are included (and noted with the phrase "Young-Adult Interest" in the "Subjects" line after the annotation), but children's books are excluded. Although fiction and children's literature are not covered in this volume, the "Bibliographies" section at the end of Chapter Five does include some excellent bibliographies that annotate and recommend these types of books.

Academic and scholarly works of Christian nonfiction comprise a vast area of interest and publishing. These titles are represented here, but very selectively since *Faith Reads* primarily addresses people working in or visiting a public library or a church library.

Publication dates generally refer to the most recent or highest quality copy, corresponding to the ISBN that appears; original publication dates appear parenthetically when that information is available. Exact original publication dates are excluded if they are not available. However, a general idea of those dates can be surmised from the authors' birth and death dates, which appear in the annotations.

Selection

How were books selected to represent the best of Christian nonfiction? Well, one book leads to another, and it was this author's fifteen years of personal exploration and discovery that led to the creation of this book. Numerous bibliographies of recommended titles from a wide variety of sources were consulted. Some entire books that helped are Scott Larsen's *Indelible Ink: Twenty-Two Prominent Christian Leaders Discuss the Books that Shape Their Faith* and Eugene Peterson's *Take and Read: Spiritual Reading: An Annotated List*. Specialized bibliographies found in the backs of certain books such as *The Transforming Vision: Shaping a Christian World View* by Brian J. Walsh and Richard Middleton were used as well. There were also Web sites like Bryon K. Borger's (owner of Hearts & Minds bookstore in Dallastown, Pennsylvania): http://www.heartsandmindsbooks.com.

In addition to articles, book reviews, and best-seller lists in magazines like *Publishers Weekly*, *Christianity Today*, and *Library Journal*, the two main book award programs that cover Christian nonfiction were considered. The Evangelical Christian Publishers Association has offered the Christian Book Awards (formerly called the Gold Medallion Book Awards) since 1978. Also, *Christianity Today* magazine has granted its Christianity Today Book Awards contest since 1990. These awards are discussed in an appendix; award winners are also tagged in the "Subject" line of each annotation.

Collection Development

Review journals and awards lists are some of the best places to start for librarians doing collection development (picking which books to buy for the library's collection). An appendix is included ("Review Sources") to help librarians with the task of selecting Christian nonfiction. This appendix lists trade and consumer journals and Web sites that will be of interest to collection-development librarians. You may also want to familiarize yourself with (and order catalogs from) the main publishers of Christian nonfiction. Another appendix lists the top fifty publishers of Christian nonfiction including their mailing and Web addresses. Also, for those books that sometimes "fly below the radar," try niche Web sites like http://www.elijahshopper.com, which specializes in small publishers of charismatic and prophetic titles. Christian Book Distributors (CBD) has been in operation since 1978, and their website is http://www.christianbook.com.

Whether for purposes of collection development, readers' advisory, or personal edification, I hope this guide opens up the way for you to explore the rich world of Christian nonfiction.

Note

1. "CBA Expo: Shrinking Attendance, Mutinous Publishers" by Lynn Garrett and Jana Riess. *Publishers Weekly* 254 no. 7 14 F 12, 2007.

Chapter 1

Life Stories

Introduction

This chapter includes autobiographies, biographies, memoirs, letters, journals, and diaries. This genre of nonfiction literature has enduring and widespread appeal. It is an interesting fact that a Christian nonfiction work, Augustine's *Confessions*, is considered to be the first autobiography in Western literature.

Unique to the Christian biography genre are conversion stories. Chuck Colson was chief counsel for President Richard Nixon and went to jail for his involvement in the Watergate scandal. Watergate led to Colson's conversion to evangelical Christianity. His autobiographical conversion story, *Born Again*, became a surprise best seller when it was published in 1976. Some conversion stories may appeal, although with quite a twist, to true-crime fans. For instance, Nicky Cruz tells about how he moved from a life of drugs, violent crime, and gangs to a life of healing and international ministry in *Run, Baby, Run*.

For those interested in true adventure, Christian biography has a lot to offer. Missionary stories are unparalleled for their thrilling and true tales. For instance, *Bruchko* tells the story of a nineteen-year-old American teenager who traveled across the world, by himself, to live with a Stone Age tribe of South American Indians. *God's Smuggler* tells the story of Brother Andrew, a Dutch minister who smuggled Bibles into the Communist countries of Eastern Europe during the Cold War years.

Life stories serve as a launching pad into the larger world of Christian nonfiction. Reading about a famous person's life and times creates interest in other famous figures of the period. For instance, John

Wesley was friends with George Whitefield, a fellow British revivalist; both lived at the same time as Jonathan Edwards, the famous colonial American minister and theologian. All three have journals, sermons, and biographies written by or about them. Now, readers may wish to cross over to other forms of nonfiction (or even fiction) because these men were also, at times, writers. For example, reading Humphrey Carpenter's *The Inklings* may spur readers on to read works by C. S. Lewis, J. R. R. Tolkien, Charles Williams, and others in that famous writers' group. Therefore, after each annotated title in this chapter (and in the others, too), additional titles are recommended, which have been selected with this increased interest in mind.

Note: Since it is sometimes difficult to distinguish between autobiographies and memoirs, all memoirs are indexed under the heading "Autobiography."

Story Types and Themes

This section groups together biographies about people who may not be rich or famous, but whose stories are nonetheless fascinating. There are several personal narratives that describe how everyday people have overcome monumental trials. Also, there are conversion stories that capture some of the most exciting, life-changing events of a person's life. Near-death experiences (NDEs) are also life-changing and exciting to read about. NDEs typically occur when a person clinically dies and is brought back to life. During these brief seconds or moments, people often report spiritual experiences that include leaving their bodies and being drawn to a light or being escorted to heaven. Other people claim to have visited heaven without any such traumatic medical circumstances. These "heavenly visions" also enable some to describe in detail what heaven is like.

Conversion Stories

Colson, Charles W.

Born Again. Chosen Books, 2004 (1976). 351 pp. ISBN 0800793773.
> Chuck Colson's conversion story surprised the nation when it came out in 1976. He was chief counsel for President Richard Nixon and went to jail for his involvement with the Watergate scandal. When Colson proclaimed his faith, it made headlines. After he was released from prison, Colson started a prison ministry called Prison Fellowship. He has written many books about his life, faith, culture, the church, and criminal justice.

Subjects: Autobiography, Charles W. Colson (1931–), Conversion Stories, Crime, Politics, Watergate

More: *Charles Colson: A Story of Power, Corruption, and Redemption* by John Perry (B&H Publishing, 2003) is a recent biography of Colson that discusses his conversion as well as what he has been doing for the last thirty years. For some of Colson's writing on faith and modern culture, try *How Now Shall We Live?* (Tyndale House Publishers, 2004), which Colson coauthored with Nancy Pearcey.

Cruz, Nicky, and Jamie Buckingham.

Run, Baby, Run. Bridge-Logos Publishers, 1988 (1968). 360 pp. ISBN 0882706306.

This book recounts the stunning story of a young man who moves from a life of drugs, crime, and gangs to a life of healing and international ministry. Nicky Cruz was born in Puerto Rico and moved to New York when he was young. His life was filled with hate and violence until he met inner-city evangelist David Wilkerson, who introduced him to Jesus Christ.

Subjects: Autobiography, Conversion Stories, Crime, Nicky Cruz (1938–), Drug Abuse, Evangelists

More: Cruz is also mentioned in David Wilkerson's best-selling biography, *The Cross and the Switchblade*, which has been turned into a film. Jim Cymbala's *Fresh Wind, Fresh Fire* (Zondervan, 2003) tells the story of a Brooklyn, New York, church where drug addicts, alcoholics, and homeless people's lives were transformed by the presence of God.

Hahn, Scott, and Kimberly Hahn.

Rome Sweet Home: Our Journey to Catholicism. Ignatius Press, 1993. 182 pp. ISBN 0898704782.

Scott Hahn and Kimberly Hahn tell how they went from dyed-in-the-wool, seminary-trained Calvinist ministers to Roman Catholic apologists. The process involved much study, prayer, and relational hardship, but it ended in harmony, joy, and this delightful and instructive book.

Subjects: Autobiography, Catholics, Conversion Stories, Kimberly Hahn (1957–), Scott Hahn (1957–)

More: Three more books about converts to Catholicism are *Surprised by Truth: 11 Converts Give the Biblical and Historical Reasons for Becoming Catholic* by Patrick Madrid (Basilica Press, 1994), *Born Fundamentalist, Born Again Catholic* by David B. Currie (Ignatius Press, 1996), and *My Life on the Rock: A Rebel Returns to the Catholic Faith* by Jeff Cavins (Ascension Press, 2000).

Michaelsen, Johanna.

The Beautiful Side of Evil. Harvest House, 1982. 222 pp. ISBN 0890813221.

The true story of a woman who was a personal assistant to a psychic surgeon. This "surgeon" actually healed many people with demonic powers. Johanna Michaelsen (1949–) believed these powers were from God, but soon learned the truth about the deceptive demonic activity she took part in for years. The author describes many hair-raising experiences, including her conversion to Christianity.

Subjects: Autobiography, Conversion Stories, Johanna Michaelsen (1949–), Occultism, Psychic Phenomena

More: For more on occult issues, see *Deliver Us From Evil* by Cindy Jacobs (Gospel Light, 2002), *Protecting Your Teen from Today's Witchcraft: A Parent's Guide to Confronting Wicca and the Occult* by Steve Russo (Baker, 2005), and *Protecting Your Home from Spiritual Darkness* by Chuck Pierce (Gospel Light, 2004).

Sheikh, Bilquis, and Richard H. Schneider.

I Dared to Call Him Father: The Miraculous Story of a Muslim Woman's Encounter with God. Chosen Books, 2003 (1978). 190 pp. ISBN 0800793242.

Bilquis Sheikh (1912–1997), a Muslim woman from a prominent family in Asia, has a series of strange dreams about Jesus. This book tells the story of how she learns to call God her father. First published in 1978, this new edition updates the story a bit (Bilquis died in 1997) and adds a section written by Synnove Mitchell, Bilquis' missionary friend.

Subjects: Autobiography, Bilqus Seitch (1912–1997) Conversion Stories, Muslims

More: For more on Muslims, try *Unveiling Islam: An Insider's Look at Muslim Life and Beliefs* by Ergun Mehmet Caner and Emir Caner (Kregel Publications, 2002), which was written by two brothers who were raised Muslim by a mosque leader and are now Christian seminary professors. Also, Shirin Taber's *Muslims Next Door: Uncovering Common Myths and Creating Friendships* (Zondervan, 2004) gives an insider's view of how North American Muslims think.

Telchin, Stan.

Betrayed! Chosen Books, 2007 (1981). Revised edition. 160 pp. ISBN 0800794230.

Testimony of how Stan Telchin, a Jew, came to accept Jesus as Messiah. When Stan was very young, he encountered hate and cruelty at the hands of "Christians." He learned that it was us versus them—Jews versus Gentiles. When Stan's daughter became a follower of Jesus, Stan felt betrayed by his own flesh and blood. Stan shows how he and his family resolved these conflicts in their own family and personal lives. This book gives insight into the Jewish mindset and culture, describing the historical background and the present tension between Jews and non-Jews in America.

Subjects: Autobiography, Conversion Stories, Jews and Judaism, Stan Telchin (1924–)

More: Telchin also wrote *Messianic Judaism Is Not Christianity: A Loving Call to Unity* (Chosen, 2004). For more on Messianic Judaism, try *Not Ashamed: The Story of Jews for Jesus* by Ruth A. Tucker (Multnomah, 2000).

Heavenly Visions

Baker, H. A.

Visions Beyond the Veil. Sovereign World, 2006 (1938). 96 pp. ISBN 1852404574.

Something unusual happened during a regular morning prayer meeting at the Adullam Rescue Mission in Yunnanfu, Yunnan Province, China. H. A. Baker and his wife, Josephine, saw this brief before-school meeting turn into a twenty-hour prayer service where young children were seeking God earnestly for the forgiveness of their wrongdoings. Many of these Chinese orphans saw angels and visions of hell and heaven. These visions recurred for quite a while among even very young children. During this amazing time, children were transported in visions to heaven where they talked to loved ones and saw angels and even animals like deer and elephants. At other times, the children saw angels in the room with them, protecting them from enemy attacks. Several different incidents included the "sensation of rain pouring down on their heads," which the author concludes was the latter rain prophesied in the Old Testament book of Joel 2:23. H. A. Baker (1881–1971) was an American missionary to Tibet, China, the Hakka people of Taiwan, and the Navajo Indians of New Mexico. He was the grandfather of present-day missionary Rolland Baker, cofounder of IRIS Ministries in Mozambique. This book was first published circa 1938.

Subjects: Angels, China, Heaven, Missions, Revival, Visions

More: In 1988, evangelist Jesse Duplantis went to heaven for five hours where he saw family members and famous Bible figures such as David and Paul. He had encounters with angels and was taken to the throne room of God. This is described in Duplantis's *Heaven: Close Encounters of the God Kind* (Harrison House, 2006).

Bennett, Rita.

To Heaven and Back: True Stories of Those Who Have Made the Journey. Zondervan, 1997. 208 pp. ISBN 031021078X.

In this hopeful account, Rita Bennett discusses the nature of NDEs, presents personal accounts of several people who had NDEs, and then discusses what the Bible says about heaven. Bennett also writes about how she dealt with the death of her husband Dennis Bennett, an American Episcopal priest who was a foundational part of the Charismatic Movement in the 1960s and 1970s.

Subjects: Death and Dying, Grief, Heaven, Near-Death Experiences

More: Robert Liardon gives his own account of going to heaven and back when he was eight years old. He then relates the stories of three others who had similar experiences in *We Saw Heaven: True Stories of What Awaits You on the Other Side* (Destiny Image, 2006), including Marietta Davis (a twenty-five-year-old New Yorker), H. A. Baker (a missionary to China), and Rebecca Springer (a poet, novelist, and the wife of an Illinois legislator). For Marietta Davis's full story (first published in 1859 as *Scenes Beyond the Grave*), read *Nine Days in Heaven: The Vision of Marietta Davis* (Creation House, 2006). For Rebecca Springer's full story (first published in 1898 as *Intra Muros*), try *My Dream of Heaven: A Nineteenth Century Spiritual Classic*, edited by Vicki Jamison-Peterson (Harrison House, 2002).

Sjogren, Steve.

The Day I Died. Regal Books, 2006. 163 pp. ISBN 0830738126.

Megachurch pastor Steve Sjogren went to the hospital for routine surgery, but something went wrong. He died. During this traumatic experience, God comforted Sjogren and spoke to him about his life. Miraculously, Sjogren survived, but his life would never be the same physically. Sjogren talks about the many valuable lessons he has learned since the day he died.

Subjects: Autobiography, Death and Dying, Disabilities, Near-Death Experiences, Steve Sjogren (1955–)

More: *90 Minutes in Heaven: A True Story of Death and Life* (Revell, 2007) by Don Piper and Cecil Murphey tells a similar story of a man who died and came back to life with a message of hope amid the reality of many painful disabilities. Also try *Falling to Heaven* by Mickey Robinson (Arrow Publications, 2003). Robinson was a skydiver involved in a plane crash that burned him and led to his NDE.

Personal Narratives

Beamer, Lisa, and Ken Abraham.

Let's Roll!: Ordinary People, Extraordinary Courage. Tyndale, 2002. 317 pp. ISBN 0842373195.

As Todd Morgan Beamer and others on United Airlines Flight 93 were ready to take on the terrorists who had highjacked their plane, Beamer uttered the famous words, "Let's roll." Sadly, this brave man left behind his wife and three children, but his courage prevented what could have been a devastating blow to the White House, the U.S. Capitol building, or some other national landmark. This book tells the story of what happened on Flight 93. It also recounts the lives of Todd's wife Lisa Beamer (1969–) and their children in the aftermath of his death on 9/11.

Subjects: Autobiography, Award Winners (ECPA), Lisa Beamer (1969–), Todd Morgan Beamer (1968–2001), Biography, September 11 Terrorist Attacks

More: The operator who took Todd Beamer's call from Flight 93 wrote *"Hello, My Name is Mrs. Jefferson, I Understand Your Plane is Being Hijacked? 9:45 AM, Flight 93, September 11, 2001* by Lisa Jefferson and Felicia Middlebrooks (Northfield, 2006).

Eller, T. Suzanne.

Real Teens, Real Stories, Real Life. Life Journey, 2002. 251 pp. ISBN 1589195000. **YA**

In thirty-nine true stories of teenagers who have faced a variety of problems in life, we hear from teens who have faced shame and failure, and those who were victims of physical abuse, self-abuse, and drug abuse. These are real stories that all end with hope, faith, and changed lives.

Subjects: Collective Biography, Conversion Stories, Teenagers, Young-Adult Interest

More: Suzanne Eller has written another book for teens called *Making It Real: Whose Faith Is It Anyway?* (Kregel, 2007).

Hall, Ron, Denver Moore, and Lynn Vincent.

Same Kind of Different as Me. W Publishing Group, 2006. 237 pp. ISBN 0849900417.

Ron Hall did not like homeless people, but his life was about to be changed by one. This is the story of how an international art dealer from Texas and his wife met a homeless black man from Louisiana (who was raised on a plantation as a modern-day slave)

and how their lives were dramatically changed. It is a story of hope and miracles in the midst of grief and loss.

Subjects: Autobiography, Cancer, Death and Dying, Grief, Ron Hall (1945–), Homeless, Denver Moore (1937–)

More: Try *Under the Overpass* by Mike Yankoski (Multnomah, 2005), in which Yankoski lives as a homeless person for five months.

Kramarik, Akiane, and Foreli Kramarik.

Akiane: Her Life, Her Art, Her Poetry. W Publishing Group, 2006. 136 pp. ISBN 0849900441.

Akiane Kramarik, a child prodigy, sold her first painting at age eight for $10,000. Her complex poetry is effortlessly written or dictated to her mother (in either English, Russian, or Lithuanian). She started having visions of God when she was four years old (although her parents had never told her about God). Akiane has appeared on *Oprah*, *Good Morning America*, and on many other shows and in articles. This book provides biographical information about her life, presents full-color reproductions of her art, and collects dozens of her poems. Akiane credits God for her inspiration, her talent, and her mission.

Subjects: Artists, Biography, Akiane Kramarik (1994–), Poets, Prodigies

Morris, Debbie, and Gregg Lewis.

Forgiving the Dead Man Walking: Only One Woman Can Tell the Entire Story. Zondervan, 1998. 251 pp. ISBN 0310231876.

Sixteen-year-old Debbie Morris was kidnapped and raped by Robert Willie in 1980. Her boyfriend was stabbed and shot. In this book, Morris describes what happened to her, and she talks about her relationship with Sister Helen Prejean, the nun (opposed to the death penalty) who wrote the book *Dead Man Walking*. Most importantly, Morris presents forgiveness as a powerful, life-changing way of life.

Subjects: Autobiography, Crime, Forgiveness, Debbie Morris (1964–), Rape

More: Two more books related to forgiveness are *Forgive and Forget: Healing the Hurts We Don't Deserve* by Lewis B. Smedes (HarperOne, 2007) and *What's So Amazing About Grace?* by Philip Yancey (Zondervan, 2002).

Ritchie, Mark Andrew.

God in the Pits: The Enron-jihad Edition. VMI Publishers, 2005 (Macmillan, 1989). 242 pp. ISBN 0974719080.

Mark Andrew Ritchie is a successful commodities trader, but he started out in poverty in Afghanistan, where his parents were missionaries. With compelling writing and penetrating observations, Ritchie shares many stories in this book: about his spiritual journey, about life in the financial services industry, and about travels and tragedies in Afghanistan. In the process, Ritchie reveals what is rotten in North American Christianity and what is beautiful in certain Islamic parts of the world, all of which applies to every human heart.

Subjects: Autobiography, Brokers, Business Ethics, Mark Andrew Ritchie (1948–)

More: Ritchie also wrote *Spirit of the Rainforest: A Yanomamo Shaman's Story* (Island Lake Press, 2000), which graphically depicts the horrors of life among a "Stone Age" tribe.

Sonnenberg, Joel, and Gregg Lewis.

Joel. Zondervan, 2004. 214 pp. ISBN 0310246938.

Joel Sonnenberg was severely burned when he was about two years old. It is a miracle that he lived, but the greatest miracle is to witness the choices that this young man made to not give up on life or God. In this inspiring book, Joel talks about what happened to him, his forty-five surgeries, his bodily disfigurements, and the many obstacles he has overcome.

Subjects: Autobiography, Disabilities, Joel Sonnenberg (1977–)

More: For another child who overcame a considerable handicap, try *Adventures in Darkness: Memoirs of an Eleven-Year-Old Blind Boy* by Tom Sullivan (Nelson, 2006).

Yankoski, Mike.

Under the Overpass. Multnomah, 2005. 224 pp. ISBN 1590524020.

For five months in 2003, Mike Yankoski and his friend Sam lived as homeless people. They slept and ate on the streets and in shelters in five different cities. Yankoski's descriptions of his experiences are striking: the other homeless people they encountered, the churches and businesses they visited in their ragged condition, the poverty, the smells—all of these are very moving and thought-provoking.

Subjects: Autobiography, Homeless, Michael Yankoski (1983–)

More: Try *Same Kind of Different as Me* by Ron Hall and Denver Moore (W Publishing, 2006), which is about how a wealthy art dealer's life was changed by a homeless man.

Christians from All Walks of Life

This section groups life stories by vocation. Hollywood may not seem a likely place for Christians, but these biographies show that actors and sports stars are people of active faith. The autobiographical writing of doctors and surgeons gives readers a rare glimpse inside the world of medicine. Moreover, the life stories of missionary doctors provide a double dose of excitement as readers travel the world to witness exotic places and intriguing people groups. Christian nonfiction biography also includes the life stories of ministers, martyrs, and saints. *Foxe's Book of Martyrs* has been a classic record of the imprisonment and torture of Christians since it was first published in 1563. Here also are real-life stories of musicians, war heroes, world leaders, and writers—indeed, Christians from all walks of life.

Actors

Baldwin, Stephen, and Mark Tabb.

The Unusual Suspect: My Calling to the New Hardcore Movement of Faith. Warner Faith, 2006. 281 pp. ISBN 0446579750. **YA**

> Stephen Baldwin is the youngest of the "Baldwin Brothers," four American brothers who became notable actors. In a very informal, chatty style, Baldwin tells readers about his entry into acting, his conversion, his family, and his passion for Jesus Christ and ministry. This book will appeal to fans of his movies, to the teen crowd, and to those familiar with Baldwin's "Livin It" extreme sports youth ministry tour.
>
> **Subjects:** Actors, Autobiography, Stephen Baldwin (1966–), Conversion Stories, Young-Adult Interest
>
> **More:** Baldwin also wrote *Livin It: Testimonies* (B&H Publishing, 2006) and *Livin It: What It Is* (B&H Publishing, 2006) about several famous skateboarding and BMX stars and other celebrities who are Christians.

Cameron, Barbara, and Lissa Halls Johnson.

A Full House of Growing Pains. Bridge-Logos Publishers, 2006. 240 pp. ISBN 0882701894.

> Barbara Cameron is the mother of two children who were successful child actors and television stars. Her son Kirk starred in *Growing Pains*, and her daughter Candace was a star on *Full House*. Cameron describes how she raised her kids in the midst of Hollywood while still keeping God as a priority.

Subjects: Actors, Autobiography, Biography, Barbara Cameron (1950–), Candace Cameron (1976–), Kirk Cameron (1970–), Mothers

More: Kirk Cameron has partnered in ministry with evangelist Ray Comfort. Comfort's autobiography is *Out of the Comfort Zone* (Bridge-Logos, 2004). Cameron and Comfort collaborated on the evangelism book, *The Way of the Master* (Bridge-Logos, 2006).

Norris, Chuck, and Ken Abraham.

Against All Odds: My Story. B&H Publishing, 2004. 246 pp. ISBN 0805431616.

Famous martial artist and movie star Carlos Ray "Chuck" Norris shares the story of his hard childhood and rise to fame. Norris is half Irish and half Cherokee. His father was an alcoholic, but his mother was a woman of strong faith. Norris describes his involvement in martial arts and his friendship with Bruce Lee. In recent times, he has starred in the TV series *Walker, Texas Ranger* and started a new life by remarrying and having twins. As the years have gone by, Norris's faith has become more and more important to him.

Subjects: Actors, Autobiography, Martial Arts, Carlos Ray "Chuck" Norris (1940–)

Rogers, Dale Evans, and Norman B. Rohrer.

Dale Evans Rogers: Rainbows on a Hard Trail. Revell, 1999. 141 pp. ISBN 0800717694.

Actress and singer Dale Evans Rogers was married to the singing cowboy, Roy Rogers. She talks about her early years in Hollywood but spends most of the book discussing the trials she faced in life, including the deaths of three of her children. She also describes her heart attack, stroke, and rehabilitation. Through all of these trials, she relied upon and took comfort in God. Rogers ends the book with a brief biography of her husband, Roy Rogers.

Subjects: Actors, Autobiography, Grief, Dale Evans Rogers (1912–2001)

More: For a more complete biography of Dale Evans and Roy Rogers, see *Happy Trails: Our Life Story* (Simon and Schuster, 1994). Dale Evans's first book, *Angel Unaware* (Revell, 1953) was a best seller. It is about her Down syndrome daughter, Robin.

Whelchel, Lisa.

The Facts of Life: And Other Lessons My Father Taught Me. Multnomah, 2001. 190 pp. ISBN 1576738582.

Lisa Whelchel is famous for her role as "Blair" on the 1980s TV show *The Facts of Life*. In this book, Whelchel describes her life as a child actress, her relationship with God, and her life as a wife and mother of three homeschooled children.

Subjects: Actors, Autobiography, Homeschooling, Mothers, Lisa Whelchel (1963–)

More: Whelchel has written other nonfiction books, including *So You're Thinking About Homeschooling: Fifteen Families Show How You Can Do It!* (Multnomah, 2003) and *Creative Correction* (Tyndale, 2000).

Doctors and Scientists

Carson, Ben, and Cecil Murphey.

Gifted Hands. Zondervan, 1996 (1990). 224 pp. ISBN 0310214696.

In this incredible story, a kid from the ghetto of Detroit ultimately becomes a famous neurosurgeon. Ben Carson begins by writing about his youth: family problems and encounters with racism and peer pressure. He tells how he became a top student in junior high, and then he goes on to discuss Yale, his wife, and medical school. Carson entered the public spotlight after he performed a surgery to separate conjoined twins. *Gifted Hands* is also available on video.

Subjects: African American Surgeons, Autobiography, Ben Carson (1951–), Doctors, Seventh-Day Adventists

More: Carson also wrote a book called *The Big Picture: Getting Perspective on What's Really Important in Life* (Zondervan, 1999). For a biography of another famous Christian surgeon, try *Ten Fingers for God: The Life and Work of Dr. Paul Brand* by Dorothy Clarke Wilson (Paul Brand Publishing, 1996).

Graves, Dan.

Doctors Who Followed Christ: Thirty-Two Biographies of Eminent Physicians and Their Christian Faith. Kregel, 1999. 255 pp. ISBN 0825427347.

Inspiring biographies of leading men and women from the history of health care. Meet and be inspired by the stories of James Ramsay (anti-slavery surgeon), Joseph Lister (father of antiseptic surgery), Clara Swain (medical missionary), Walter Reed (army surgeon who helped conquer yellow fever), and many more.

Subjects: Collective Biography, Doctors

Graves, Dan.

Scientists of Faith: Forty-Eight Biographies of Historic Scientists and Their Christian Faith. Kregel, 1996. 192 pp. ISBN 082542724X.

Broken into three sections: 1) before 1500, 2) 1500–1830, and 3) after 1830. Learn about Johannes Kepler, the man who discovered the laws of planetary motion; Robert Boyle, the founder of modern chemistry; John Ray, the father of English natural history; and many more.

Subjects: Collective Biography, Professors, Scientists

More: For a related collection, try *Christian Men of Science* by George Mulfinger (Ambassador-Emerald, 2004). Also, *Professors Who Believe: The Spiritual Journeys of Christian Faculty* by Paul Anderson (InterVarsity, 1998).

Hale, Thomas.

Living Stones of the Himalayas: Adventures of an American Couple in Nepal. Send the Light, 2000 (1993). 255 pp. ISBN 1884543359.

Thomas Hale and his wife, Cynthia, are medical missionaries in Nepal. Hale tells many interesting stories from his time as a surgeon and his travels around the country treating sick people and sharing the gospel. He encounters witch doctors, water buffaloes, and much more.

Subjects: Adventure, Autobiography, Doctors, Thomas Hale (1937–), Missions—Medical, Nepal

More: Two more titles by Hale are *On the Far Side of Liglig Mountain* (Zondervan, 1989) and *Don't Let the Goats Eat the Loquat Trees* (Zondervan, 1986).

Hamlin, Catherine, and John Little.

The Hospital by the River: A Story of Hope. Monarch Books, 2005 (2001). 308 pp. ISBN 0825460719.

Catherine Hamlin and her late husband are medical doctors. They have lived in Ethiopia for over forty years treating obstetric fistula, a condition which if untreated ruins the lives of thousands of young women. Hamlin's team has helped more than 25,000 women with successful surgeries. This book tells Hamlin's story, which takes place in the midst of the poverty and political turmoil of Ethiopia.

Subjects: Autobiography, Doctors, Catherine Hamlin (1924–), Missions—Medical

More: For another book about doctors helping in underdeveloped countries, try *Tales of a Seasick Doctor: Life Aboard a Mercy Ship* (Zondervan, 1996) by Christine Aroney-Sine. Also, *Ships of Mercy: The Remarkable Fleet Bringing Hope to the World's Forgotten Poor* by Don Stephens (Nelson Books, 2005).

Larimore, Walt, M.D.

Bryson City Tales: Stories of a Doctor's First Year of Practice in the Smoky Mountains. Zondervan, 2002. 336 pp. ISBN 0310256704.

Medical journalist and family physician Walt Larimore is known for his popular medical books like *The Highly Healthy Child*, but this book is different. First-class storytelling relays Larimore's memorable time in a small North Carolina town. Fresh from medical school in a big city, Larimore has quite a few adjustments to make and lessons to learn in Bryson City.

Subjects: Autobiography, Creative Nonfiction, Doctors, Walter L. Larimore (1952–), North Carolina

More: Larimore's stories continue in *Bryson City Seasons* (Zondervan, 2005) and *Bryson City Secrets* (Zondervan, 2007).

Perry, John.

Unshakable Faith. Multnomah, 1999. 387 pp. ISBN 1576734935.

This is a biography of two great African American educators who played important roles in the history of Tuskegee University. Booker T. Washington became the first principal of Tuskegee; and George Washington Carver famous as a botanist, inventor, and artist, was hired to head the school's agriculture department. Perry incorporates the spiritual lives and beliefs of these two famous men as well as their shortcomings and struggles.

Subjects: African American Agriculturists, African American Educators, Biography, George Washington Carver (1864–1943), Collective Biography, Tuskegee University, Booker T. Washington (1856–1915)

More: For a biography aimed at young-adult audiences, try *George Washington Carver: Man's Slave Becomes God's Scientist* by David Collins (Mott Media, 2005), which is part of the Sower series. Another book on Washington is *Then Darkness Fled: The Liberating Wisdom of Booker T. Washington* by Stephen Mansfield (Cumberland House, 2002).

Wilder-Smith, Arthur Ernest, and Beate Gottwaldt Wilder-Smith.

Fulfilled Journey: The Wilder-Smith Memoirs. The Word For Today Publishers, 1998. 544 pp. ISBN 0936728752.

This biography of A. E. Wilder-Smith (1915–1995) was begun by him and finished by his wife Beate Gottwaldt Wilder-Smith, who also includes her own autobiographical section. It is a wonderful memoir that traces the lives of A. E. (born in England) and Beate (born in Germany) through the school years (three doctorates for A. E.), through the war years, through life in various European countries, and through his experiences as a lecturer. Wilder-Smith wrote some groundbreaking books dealing with science and faith that influenced the creation science and intelligent design movements.

Subjects: Autobiography, Biography, Creation Scientists, Intelligent Design, Scientists, Arthur Ernest Wilder-Smith (1915–1995), Beate Wilder-Smith (1928–)

Wilson, Dorothy Clarke.

Ten Fingers for God: The Life and Work of Dr. Paul Brand. Paul Brand Publishing, 1996 (McGraw-Hill, 1965). 289 pp. ISBN 0964313707.

Dr. Paul Brand (1914–2003) was a world-famous hand surgeon. His parents were missionaries in India. He did pioneering work with leprosy patients in India and around the world. Brand's love for people and skill as a doctor allowed thousands of leprosy patients to find hope, work, and a future. In this book, readers learn about Brand's childhood in India and England and the future life and medical endeavors of this fascinating man. Brand wrote and cowrote several books about God and the important role that pain plays in our lives.

Subjects: Biography, Paul Brand (1914–2003), Doctors, India, Leprosy, Missions—Medical

More: With Philip Yancey, Brand cowrote a fascinating book about the wonders of the human body called *Fearfully and Wonderfully Made* (Zondervan, 1997) and a follow up to that book called *In His Image* (Zondervan, 1997).

Military and Political Figures

Aikman, David.

A Man of Faith: The Spiritual Journey of George W. Bush. W Publishing Group, 2004. 237 pp. ISBN 0849918111.

This biography traces George Bush's spiritual heritage and life from his grandfather's time through Bush's early life, governorship of Texas, and U.S. Presidency (up until 2004). Aikman is a veteran journalist, and it really shows in this well-researched, clearly written book.

Subjects: Biography, George Walker Bush (1946–), Politicians, Presidents

More: A biography of the Secretary of State under Bush is *Condi: The Condoleezza Rice Story* by Antonia Felix (Zondervan, 2005). *God and the Oval Office* by John McCollister (Thomas Nelson, 2005) discusses the religious faith of all forty-three presidents. Also, try this best-selling biography of a U.S. Senate chaplain titled *A Man Called Peter: The Story of Peter Marshall* by Catherine Marshall (Chosen, 2002).

Gordon, Ernest.

To End All Wars. Zondervan, 2002 (Harper, 1962). 232 pp. ISBN 0007118481.

Ernest Gordon spent three years in Japanese prison camps during World War II and was forced to work on the infamous Thailand–Burma "Death Railway." In the midst of such torture and suffering, Gordon converted to Christ and learned that life is not about being served but serving others. Gordon tells the whole story of his long imprisonment and life after release in this book that was originally published in 1962 with the title *Through the Valley of the Kwai*. The movie *To End All Wars* is based on this book.

Subjects: Autobiography, Conversion Stories, Ernest Gordon (1917–2002), Military, POWs, World War II

More: Try Corrie ten Boom's *The Hiding Place* (Chosen, 2006). She spent time in one of Hitler's concentration camps where her father and sister died. Like Gordon, she survived and became a minister.

Mansfield, Stephen.

Never Give In: The Extraordinary Character of Winston Churchill. Cumberland House, 1996. 234 pp. ISBN 1888952199.

Winston Churchill, the former prime minister of England, was a man of courage and leadership. This brief biography avoids his negative characteristics and discusses Churchill's early life, including his father's loathing of him and his military and political career. Mansfield writes about Churchill's love for animals, poetry, history, and writing, and shows how Churchill overcame many obstacles, failures, and disappointments in life. Churchill's courageous character is an inspiration to all.

Subjects: Biography, Winston Churchill (1874–1965), Great Britain, Leadership, Politicians

More: For another leader in time of war—and another book in the same series—try *Call of Duty: The Sterling Nobility of Robert E. Lee* by J. Steven Wilkins (Cumberland House, 2003).

Perry, John.

Sgt. York: His Life, Legend, and Legacy. B&H Publishing, 1997. 349 pp. ISBN 0805460748.

This biography of war hero and Medal of Honor recipient Alvin Cullum York starts with the incident that made him famous—an unprecedented act of bravery during World War I. York almost single-handedly captured more than 130 German soldiers during the Battle of the Argonne Forest. York gave credit to God for this stunning instance of bravery, and he returned home a hero. This book goes on to describes the rest of York's life, which included a famous 1941 movie starring Gary Cooper and, sadly, many financial struggles along the way.

Subjects: Biography, Military, World War I, Alvin Cullum York (1887–1964)

More: For other inspiring war-related stories, try *Taking the High Ground: Military Stories of Faith* by Jeff O'Leary (Chariot Victor, 2001).

Rabey, Steve.

Faith Under Fire: Stories of Hope and Courage from WWII. Thomas Nelson, 2002. 274 pp. ISBN 0785288325.

The brave men and women who fought and lived through this era are dying out. This book keeps their amazing and miraculous stories alive in tales in which separation, suffering, and death are transformed by faith in God and by God's love. Here are stories in which tortured POWs go back to minister to their former enemies, tales of behind-the-scenes rescues, and scenes of frontline combat. An inspiring read.

Subjects: Collective Biography, Military, World War II

More: Also try Alice Gray's *Stories from a Soldier's Heart: For the Patriotic Soul* (Multnomah, 2003). For a recent account of the hand of God in combat, try Marine chaplain Carey Cash's book *A Table in the Presence: The Dramatic Account of How a U.S. Marine Battalion Experienced God's Presence Amidst the Chaos of the War in Iraq* (W Publishing Group, 2004).

Struecker, Jeff, and Dean Merrill.

The Road to Unafraid: How the Army's Top Ranger Faced Fear and Found Courage Through Black Hawk Down and Beyond. W Publishing Group, 2006. 210 pp. ISBN 0849900603.

Jeff Struecker (1969–) was mentioned several times in the best-selling book and movie *Black Hawk Down*. Struecker was an Army Ranger who saw combat in Panama, Kuwait, Somalia, and Afghanistan. Still braving combat, he returned to serve as a chaplain. In this book, he recounts Black Hawk Down and other military incidents. Beyond that, Struccker talks about his family, his struggles with fear, and his faith in God.

Subjects: Autobiography, Baptists, Fear, Military, Ministers, Jeff Struecker (1969–)

More: *Bulletproof: The Making of an Invincible Mind* by Chuck Holton (Multnomah, 2005) also deals with fear from the perspective of a brave soldier. For a biography of a famous military chaplain, try *Oswald Chambers: Abandoned to God* by David McCasland (Discovery House, 1993).

Ministers and Christian Leaders

Anderson, Leith.

Jesus: An Intimate Portrait of the Man, His Land, and His People. Bethany, 2005. 363 pp. ISBN 0764202707.

This biography of Jesus Christ is a retelling of the gospels that incorporates background geographic and historic information to enhance and enlighten the context of the story. Leith Anderson, a speaker and writer, is senior pastor of Woodale Church in Minnesota.

Subjects: Biography, Jesus Christ

More: *The Master: A Life of Jesus* (Chariot Victor, 2002) by notable biographer John Pollock, who also wrote *The Apostle: A Life of Paul* (Chariot Victor, 1994). For a study on the life of Christ, try *Jesus, the One and Only* by Beth Moore (B&H Publishing, 2002).

Bainton, Roland H.

Here I Stand: A Life of Martin Luther. Abingdon Press, 1990 (1950). 336 pp. ISBN 0687168953.

This is considered by many to be a classic biography of Martin Luther. The author was a Yale professor and authority on Reformation history. Although it was first published in 1950, this book is still in print and widely read.

Subjects: Biography, Martin Luther (1483–1546), Reformers of the Church, Theologians

More: Two more biographies of reformers include *A Life of John Calvin: A Study in the Shaping of Western Culture* by Alister McGrath (Blackwell, 1993) and *For Kirk and Covenant: The Stalwart Courage of John Knox* by Douglas Wilson (Cumberland House, 2000).

Benedict XVI, Pope.

Milestones: Memoirs 1927–1977. Ignatius Press, 1998. 156 pp. ISBN 0898707021.

When this book was first published, his name was Joseph Cardinal Ratzinger, and he was Prefect of the Vatican Congregation for the Doctrine of the Faith. These autobiographical writings cover the first fifty years of the life of Pope Benedict XVI, walking the reader through his childhood in Germany, his involuntary service in the Hitler Youth and the German infantry, and his training to be a professor and a priest.

Subjects: Autobiography, Pope Benedict XVI (1927–), Catholics, Theologians

More: Also try a biography of the last pope, *Witness to Hope: The Biography of Pope John Paul II* by George Weigel (Harper Perennial, 2005). For a classic autobiography of a famous Catholic thinker, try *Apologia Pro Vita Sua* by John Henry Cardinal Newman (Everyman's Library, 1955).

Bethge, Eberhard.

Dietrich Bonhoeffer: A Biography. Revised edition. Fortress, 2000. 1,048 pp. ISBN 0800628446.

This is the authoritative biography of the famous German Lutheran pastor and theologian who was hanged for his part in a plot to kill Hitler. Dietrich Bonhoeffer's books, still in print, continue to encourage and challenge Christians around the world. Bethge was a personal friend of Bonhoeffer and was married to Bonhoeffer's niece. This new English edition includes information that was left out of an earlier, abridged English edition.

Subjects: Biography, Dietrich Bonhoeffer (1906–1945), Martyrs, Ministers, Theologians

More: For some of Bonhoeffer's writings, try *Letters and Papers from Prison* (Touchstone, 1997) and *Life Together: The Classic Exploration of Faith in Community* (HarperSanFrancisco, 1993). Also try his most popular book, *The Cost of Discipleship* (Touchstone, 1995).

Dallimore, Arnold.

Spurgeon: A New Biography. Banner of Truth, 1985. 252 pp. ISBN 0851514510.

Charles Spurgeon, the British Baptist pastor known as the "Prince of Preachers," frequently had health problems (as did his wife). These problems did not stop him from preaching to record crowds and carrying on a tremendous writing ministry through his magazine and many books.

Subjects: Biography, Baptists, Ministers, Charles Haddon Spurgeon (1834–1892)

More: To learn about another famous preacher, try *Memoir and Remains of the Rev. Robert Murray McCheyne* by Andrew Bonar (Banner of Truth, 1966). For one of Spurgeon's classic books, try *All of Grace* (Bridge-Logos, 2007).

Day, Dorothy.

The Long Loneliness. HarperOne, 1997 (1952). 288 pp. ISBN 0060617519.

Dorothy Day cofounded the Catholic Worker Movement with Peter Maurin in 1933. This movement protested war, established retreat centers, and opened "houses of hospitality" that fed the poor and homeless. In her autobiography, first published in 1952, Day writes about her childhood, her early life as a journalist, her conversion to Catholicism, and her involvement with the Catholic Worker Movement and its newspaper, *The Catholic Worker.*

Subjects: Autobiography, Catholics, Classics, Dorothy Day (1897–1980), Homeless, Social Justice

More: Day also wrote *Loaves and Fishes* (Orbis, 1997), which is a companion to her autobiography and discusses her experiences after thirty years in the Catholic Worker Movement. For more on famous Catholics, try Jesuit priest James Martin's memoir *My Life with the Saints* (Loyola Press, 2006), in which he interweaves the lives of saints and famous Catholics like Dorothy Day with his own life story.

Dudley-Smith, Timothy.

John Stott, The Making of a Leader: A Biography: The Early Years. InterVarsity, 1999. 513 pp. ISBN 0830822070.

John Robert Walmsley Stott, a British Anglican minister and author, is a well-respected, worldwide, evangelical leader. Volume one of two authorized biographies, this book covers the first forty years of Stott's life and describes his childhood, conversion, and early ministry. Dudley-Smith had access to Stott's diaries and papers and includes many of Stott's unpublished letters.

Subjects: Anglicans, Biography, Church of England, Ministers, John Robert Walmsley Stott (1921–)

More: The second biographical volume by Dudley-Smith is called *John Stott, A Global Ministry: A Biography: The Later Years* (InterVarsity, 2001). Also try some books written by Stott, such as the classic *Basic Christianity* (InterVarsity, 2007) and *The Cross of Christ* (InterVarsity, 2006). For more on evangelical British ministers, see *That Man of Granite with the Heart of a Child: A New Biography of J. C. Ryle* by Eric Russell (Christian Focus, 2001) and the two-volume set *David Martyn Lloyd-Jones* by Iain H. Murray (Banner of Truth, 1983).

Finney, Charles G.

The Original Memoirs of Charles G. Finney. Zondervan, 2002 (1989, 1876). 460 pp. ISBN 0310243351.

Charles Grandison Finney, one of the most famous revivalists in American history, was a major leader in the Second Great Awakening in New York (he was from Connecticut). Known for his powerful presence, his convincing sermons, and his theological writings, Finney moved to Ohio to become a professor at and then president of Oberlin College. This edition contains the "restored text" of Finney's memoirs, meaning that editors Garth Rosell and Richard Dupuis replaced things that were taken out and corrected errors. Scholarly annotations have been left out of this 2002 edition, but are available in the 1989 version.

Subjects: Autobiography, Award Winners (CT), Classics, Conversion Stories, Charles Grandison Finney (1792–1875), Ministers, Revival, Second Great Awakening, Theologians

More: For some of Finney's theological writings, try *Lectures on Revivals of Religion* (Alethea in Heart, 2005) or *Finney's Systematic Theology* (Bethany, 1994). For another autobiography of a contemporary revivalist, try *Autobiography of Peter Cartwright* (Abingdon, 1996).

Graham, Billy

Just As I Am: The Autobiography of Billy Graham. Revised and updated edition. HarperOne, 2007 (1997). 800 pp. ISBN 0061171069.

This autobiography of famous evangelist Billy Graham starts out by briefly discussing his youth, then covers his early years as a minister. Graham writes lovingly about his wife and eloquently chronicles his nationwide and worldwide crusades, spending many pages describing his unique friendships with nine U.S. presidents.

Subjects: Autobiography, Award Winners (ECPA, CT), Evangelists, Billy Graham (1918–), Ministers

More: *The Billy Graham Story* by John Pollock is the official biography of Rev. Graham (Vida, 2005). For some of Graham's best-selling devotional literature, try *The Journey: Living by Faith in an Uncertain World* (W Publishing, 2006).

Grubb, Norman

Rees Howells, Intercessor. Christian Literature Crusade, 1952. 283 pp. ISBN 0875081886.

This classic book on prayer, still in print after fifty-five years, tells the story of a Welsh coal miner who founded a Bible college and led a life of prayer. Rees Howells was about twenty-five years old when the Welsh revival broke out in 1904. Stirred to pray for the recent converts, his ministry of prayer grew until he went to southern Africa and saw revival break out there, too. When

Howells returned to Wales, he founded the Bible College of Wales (still in operation today). Grubb describes Howells's development as an intercessor, his times of fasting, and the many trials and triumphs of faith and healing that Howells encountered.

Subjects: Biography, Rees Howells (1879–1950), Intercessors, Intercessory Prayer, Prayer, Revival

More: *Praying Hyde,* edited by E. G. Carre (Bridge-Logos, 2004), is another stirring biography about an intercessor. For more about intercessory prayer, try Andrew Murray's classic *The Ministry of Intercession* (Bethany, 2003) or the more recent *Possessing the Gates of the Enemy* (Chosen, 1994) by Cindy Jacobs. For more information on the Welsh revival, try *I Saw the Welsh Revival* by David Matthews (Ambassador-Emerald, Intl., 2004). Also, for another well-known biography by Grubb, try *C. T. Studd: Cricketer and Pioneer* (Christian Literature Crusade, 1985).

Lawson, James Gilchrist.

Deeper Experiences of Famous Christians. Barbour, 1999 (1911). 320 pp. ISBN 1577485238.

James Lawson (1874–1946) was an author, editor, anthologist, and evangelist in America and briefly overseas. This book collects biographical information from dozens of famous people such as Fenelon, George Fox, John Bunyan, and General Booth. Although some of the individuals are not so famous anymore (the book was first published in 1911), like Christmas Evans, Lorenzo Dow, and A. B. Earle, that only adds to the charm and value of this classic work. The book is still in print, but some of the newer editions sadly omit the section "Other Early Saints and Sages."

Subjects: Collective Biography, Ministers

Marsden, George M.

Jonathan Edwards: A Life. Yale University Press, 2004. 640 pp. ISBN 0300105967.

This scholarly, readable, and award-winning biography is considered to be the definitive work on Jonathan Edwards, who was known as one of the most important thinkers in American history. A preacher during the time of revival called the Great Awakening, he was also a missionary to Native Americans. His theological and philosophical writings still educate and inspire readers today.

Subjects: Award Winners (CT), Biography, Congregationalists, Jonathan Edwards (1703–1758), Ministers, Theologians

More: Jonathan Edwards wrote a biography of his son-in-law that is now a classic: *The Life and Diary of David Brainerd* (Hendrickson, 2006). For another biography of a Great Awakening leader, try *George*

Whitefield: The Life and Times of the Great Evangelist of the Eighteenth-Century Revival by Arnold A. Dallimore (Banner of Truth, 1970).

McCasland, David.

Oswald Chambers: Abandoned to God: The Life Story of the Author of My Utmost for His Highest. Discovery House, 1993. 286 pp. ISBN 1572930500.

British teacher, minister, poet, and artist, Oswald Chambers was a remarkable man of God. His devotion to God and the ministry touched many people while he was alive; since his death, his teachings, compiled and edited by his wife for publication, continue to touch many people. He died from complications due to a burst appendix while serving as a military chaplain in Egypt.

Subjects: Award Winners (ECPA), Biography, Oswald Chambers (1874–1917), Ministers

More: Chambers's famous devotional, still popular today, is called *My Utmost for His Highest* (Discovery House, 1992). All of his teachings are collected in a 1,492-page book called *The Complete Works of Oswald Chambers* (Discovery House, 2000).

Moore, Beth.

Feathers from My Nest: A Mother's Reflection. Revised edition. B&H Publishing, 2005 (2001). 206 pp. ISBN 0805440399.

Beth Moore, a popular Bible teacher and best-selling author, reflects on the ups and downs of raising her two daughters, Amanda and Melissa. Once her children both moved away from home, Moore realized that she did not have an empty nest, but one full of good memories. This book collects some of those cherished times.

Subjects: Autobiography, Beth Moore (1957–) Mothers, Mothers and Daughters, Women

More: For another collection of personal stories by Moore, try *Things Pondered: From the Heart of a Lesser Woman* (B&H Publishing, 2004). For some of Moore's devotional writing on the Bible, see *A Heart Like His: Intimate Reflections on the Life of David* (B&H Publishing, 1999) and *The Beloved Disciple: Following John to the Heart of Jesus* (B&H Publishing, 2003).

Müller, George.

The Autobiography of George Müller. Whitaker, 1984. 237 pp. ISBN 0883681595.

This is the story of George Müller (1805–1898), an incredible man of faith who was born in Germany but lived in England. His orphanages in Bristol cared for more than 8,000 children. He never once asked for money, but God miraculously provided for Müller time and time again.

Subjects: Autobiography, Classics, Evangelists, Faith, Ministers, George Müller (1805–1898), Orphans

More: *George Müller of Bristol* (Kregel, 1999) by Arthur T. Pierson is the original "authorized" memoir. For another book written by Müller, try *Answers to Prayer* (Moody, 1984).

O'Connor, Lindsey.

Moms Make a Difference: Stories of Women Who Raised Amazing Children. Harvest House, 2001 (1999). 191 pp. ISBN 0736906169.

This book gives nine fascinating biographical sketches of mothers. Seven are mothers of famous children (John Wesley, John Ruskin, Augustine, George Washington, Moses, Constantine, and Amy Carmichael). One sketch covers "pioneer moms," and the last covers a modern-day mother. This inspiring book was formerly titled *Moms Who Changed the World*.

Subjects: Collective Biography, Mothers, Women

More: Here are full-length biographies of two moms mentioned: *Susanna Wesley: The Mother of John and Charles Wesley* by Arnold Dallimore (Baker, 1993) and *A Chance to Die: The Life and Legacy of Amy Carmichael* by Elisabeth Elliot (Baker, 1987). Also, for more on famous women, try: *Were It Not for Grace: Stories from Women After God's Own Heart; Featuring Condoleezza Rice, First Lady Laura Bush, Beth Moore & Others* by Leslie Montgomery (B&H Publishing, 2005).

Piper, John.

The Roots of Endurance: Invincible Perseverance in the Lives of John Newton, Charles Simeon, and William Wilberforce. Crossway, 2002. 175 pp. ISBN 1581348142.

In this book, John Piper, an American preaching pastor and writer, gives three brief biographies of famous British Christian leaders. John Newton was the master of a slave ship who converted to Christianity and wrote the hymn "Amazing Grace." Charles Simeon was a prominent clergyman in his day, and William Wilberforce was a politician who led the (successful) parliamentary campaign to end the slave trade.

Subjects: Abolitionists, Collective Biography, Ministers, John Newton (1725–1807), Politicians, Charles Simeon (1759–1836), William Wilberforce (1759–1833)

More: For more on Wilberforce, try *Amazing Grace: William Wilberforce and the Heroic Campaign to End Slavery* by Eric Metaxas

(HarperSanFrancisco, 2007). For another book in the series, try *The Hidden Smile of God: The Fruit of Affliction in the Lives of John Bunyan, William Cowper, and David Brainerd* by John Piper (Crossway, 2001).

Schaeffer, Edith.

L'Abri. New expanded edition. Crossway, 1992 (1969). 256 pp. ISBN 0891076689.

> This book tells the story of L'Abri ("the shelter"), a ministry started by Francis and Edith Schaeffer in a Swiss chalet. Various people started traveling to the chalet to ask serious, searching questions about life and God. The Schaeffers provided listening ears, hospitality, and solid answers. The many struggles, miracles, and changed lives that turned L'Abri into an international Christian community inspire readers.
>
> **Subjects:** Apologists, Biography, L'Abri (Organization), Ministers, Edith Schaeffer (1914–), Francis Schaeffer (1912–1984)
>
> **More:** Edith Schaeffer wrote an extensive biography/autobiography called *The Tapestry: The Life and Times of Francis and Edith Schaeffer* (Word, 1981). Also see *Letters of Francis A. Schaeffer*, edited by Lane T. Dennis (Crossway, 1986). For some of Francis Schaeffer's groundbreaking writing, try *A Francis A. Schaeffer Trilogy: Three Essential Books in One Volume* (Crossway, 1990).

Smedes, Lewis B.

My God and I: A Spiritual Memoir. Eerdmans, 2003. 178 pp. ISBN 0802822134.

> Lewis B. Smedes (1921–2002) was a preacher and a professor of theology and ethics at Fuller Theological Seminary. Philip Yancey, a well-known writer, encouraged him to write this book, and Smedes finished it just before he died. While recalling his life, Smedes (of Frisian descent) tells of his childhood and education, remembers his theological and spiritual journeys, and talks about his life as a writer.
>
> **Subjects:** Autobiography, Award Winners (CT), Professors, Lewis B. Smedes (1921–2002), Writers

Snyder, James L.

In Pursuit of God: The Life of A. W. Tozer. Christian Publications, 1991. 236 pp. ISBN 0875095623.

> Remembered for his classic devotional books, A. W. Tozer (1897–1963) was a preaching pastor in Chicago and Toronto in the Christian and Missionary Alliance. Yet Tozer was an anomaly.

He never went to high school, but was devoted to study his whole life. He was a Protestant preacher who loved the Catholic mystics. For his zealous devotion to God in prayer and study, Tozer became known as a prophet and a man of God.

Subjects: Award Winners (CT), Biography, Christian and Missionary Alliance, Classics, Ministers, Mystics, Aiden Wilson Tozer (1897–1963), Writers

More: Try some of Tozer's classic books such as *The Pursuit of God* (WingSpread, 2007) and *The Knowledge of the Holy* (HarperOne, 1978).

Tada, Joni Eareckson.

The God I Love: A Lifetime of Walking with Jesus. Zondervan, 2003. 357 pp. ISBN 0310253969.

Joni Eareckson Tada has been a quadriplegic since a diving accident in 1967. Her story became a best-selling book entitled *Joni*. In 1979, she starred in a movie of the same name. This memoir covers the same ground, but gives more information about her life and thinking, particularly before and since that first book. An inspiring woman who is a gifted artist and author and has written more than thirty books, Tada has traveled the world and started a ministry called Joni and Friends.

Subjects: Autobiography, Disabilities, Ministers, Joni Eareckson Tada (1949–), Writers

More: Besides her classic autobiography *Joni* (Zondervan, 2001), try *Heaven* (Zondervan, 2000) and *When God Weeps* (Zondervan, 1997), which deals with the problem of suffering.

Ten Boom, Corrie, John Sherrill, and Elizabeth Sherrill.

The Hiding Place. 35th Anniversary edition. Chosen, 2006 (1971). 272 pp. ISBN 0800794052.

Corrie ten Boom was born above her father's watch shop in Haarlem, Holland. She, her father, and her sister were imprisoned by the Gestapo when Holland was occupied by Nazi Germany. Their crime? Protecting Jews in the "hiding place" in their home. ten Boom's father and sister died in prison, but Corrie lived and ministered for many years afterward. This is an awesome story of faith, love, and the hand of God.

Subjects: Autobiography, Corrie ten Boom (1892–1983), Classics, Concentration Camps, Ministers, World War II

More: ten Boom's story continues with *Tramp for the Lord* (Jove, 1986). *In My Father's House* (Hodder & Stoughton, 2005), the prequel, tells her story before the war. For some of her teachings, try *Not I, but Christ* (Revell, 1997).

Thompson, Steve.

A 20th Century Apostle: The Life of Alfred Garr. Morningstar Publications, 2003. 189 pp. ISBN 1929371381.

Alfred Garr was a healing evangelist who played a part in many of the Pentecostal movements that occurred during his life. He was at the Azusa Street Revival of 1906, was elected Executive Presbyter of the newly formed Assemblies of God, and brought Pentecostalism to China and India as a missionary. Garr was also an apostle; that is, he established new churches and trained leaders to serve them.

Subjects: Apostles, Biography, Evangelists, Alfred G. Garr (1874–1944), Healing, Pentecostals

More: See *Derek Prince: A Biography* by Stephen Mansfield (Charisma House, 2005). Prince was a charismatic British Bible teacher famous for his teachings on demons and Christian Zionism.

Wesley, John.

The Journal of John Wesley. Moody Press, 1952. 438 pp. ISBN 0802443907.

John Wesley, founder of the Methodist Movement, lived a long and interesting life, traveling thousands of miles on horseback across England. Preaching in the streets when ministers would not let him inside local church buildings, Wesley continued ministering even when his life was in danger.

Subjects: Classics, Evangelists, Journals and Diaries, Methodists, Ministers, John Wesley (1703–1791)

More: Try the journal of one of Wesley's famous contemporaries: *George Whitefield's Journals* (Banner of Truth, 1960). Also see *Nothing to Do but to Save Souls: John Wesley's Charge to His Preachers* by Robert E. Coleman (Evangel, 2006).

Wilson, Julian.

Wigglesworth: The Complete Story. Authentic Media, 2004. 227 pp. ISBN 1932805141.

English healing evangelist Smith Wigglesworth had no formal education and was a plumber by trade. He came to be called "The Apostle of Faith" because of his trust in God and the miracles God worked through him. Wigglesworth prayed for people, and they were healed and even raised from the dead. His methods were unorthodox (he punched a person with a stomach ailment in the gut, and the man was healed). Many testimonies of healing fill the first part of the book, which is followed by a discussion of faith, prophecy, tongues, and other spiritual gifts.

Subjects: Biography, Evangelists, Faith, Healing, Pentecostals, Spiritual Gifts, Smith Wigglesworth (1859–1947)

More: Readers who enjoy Wigglesworth's story should enjoy his classic work *Ever Increasing Faith* (Whitaker, 2000). For another healing evangelist biography, try *Aimee Semple McPherson: Everybody's Sister* by Edith L. Blumhofer (Eerdmans, 1993). Also, Roberts Liardon has a collective biography of twelve healing evangelists and ministers called *God's Generals* (Albury, 1996).

Yaxley, Trevor.

William and Catherine: The Life and Legacy of the Booths: Founders of the Salvation Army. Bethany, 2003. 303 p. ISBN 0764227602.

William Booth and Catherine Booth (1829–1890) were filled with compassion for the poor and indignation for the evils that surrounded them in nineteenth-century England. While other Christians gave in to complacency, this couple, both preachers, founded a mission to bring Christ to the poor. Their London mission expanded into the international organization known as the Salvation Army. This book tells an exciting tale of evangelism, discipleship, and the power of God to change the world.

Subjects: Biography, Catherine Booth (1829–1890), William Booth (1829–1912), Evangelists, Ministers, Salvation Army

More: For another biography of William Booth, try *The General Next to God* by Richard Collier (Dutton, 1965). For another on Catherine, see *The Short Life of Catherine Booth, the Mother of the Salvation Army* by Frederick St. George de Lautour Booth-Tucker (Adamant Media, 2000), which is a facsimile reprint of an 1893 edition published by the Salvation Army in England.

Yun, Brother, and Paul Hattaway.

The Heavenly Man: The Remarkable True Story of Chinese Christian Brother Yun. Monarch, 2002. 347 pp. ISBN 082546207X.

In this adventurous story of Brother Yun (Liu Zhenying), a leader in the Chinese underground church, Brother Yun was imprisoned at least three times and suffered horrible torture and persecution, but his faith and bravery supported him and inspire readers. This book shows that many people are responding to the gospel as a result of such persecution in China.

Subjects: Biography, Chinese Church, Persecution of Christians, Brother Yun (1958–)

More: *Bold as a Lamb* by Ken Anderson is the true story of Chinese House church Pastor Samuel Lamb (Zondervan, 1991). Also look for *Against the Tide* by Angus Kinnear (Tyndale, 1978), which is the biography of the famous writer and Chinese leader Watchman

Nee. Hattaway also wrote about the Chinese House Movement in *Back to Jerusalem: Three Chinese House Church Leaders Share Their Vision to Complete the Great Commission* (Gabriel, 2003).

Zacharias, Ravi, and R. S. Sawyer.

Walking from East to West: God in the Shadows. Zondervan, 2006. 240 pp. ISBN 0310259150.

Ravi Zacharias has preached and lectured all over the world. In this book, he talks about what it was like to grow up in the exotic and extreme land of India. He describes his dramatic conversion (after a suicide attempt) and his call to ministry. His extensive travels began with a ministry trip to war-torn Vietnam where a revival broke out in the midst of carnage. Since then, he has addressed audiences varying from impoverished Indian pastors to university students to United Nations' ambassadors. Zacharias is an evangelist with a life-changing message that stirs the intellect and satisfies the philosophically oriented.

Subjects: Apologists, Autobiography, Evangelists, India, Ministers, Ravi K. Zacharias (1946–)

More: *Can Man Live Without God?* (Thomas Nelson, 2004) and *The Real Face of Atheism* (Baker, 2004) are two of Zacharias's popular apologetic books. Also try Os Guinness's *Time for Truth: Living Free in a World of Lies, Hype, and Spin* (Baker, 2002).

Missionaries, Martyrs, and Saints

Andrew, Brother, John Sherrill, and Elizabeth Sherrill.

God's Smuggler. 35th Anniversary edition. Chosen (Baker), 2001 (1967). 255 pp. ISBN 0800793013.

This is the adventurous story of a Dutch minister (real name: Anne van der Bijl) who smuggled Bibles into Communist European countries during the Cold War era. Best-selling authors John and Elizabeth Sherrill have helped make this story a classic missionary biography. This anniversary addition briefly reports on Brother Andrew's activities in Islamic countries since the book was first published.

Subjects: Adventure, Brother Andrew (1928–), Autobiography, Missionaries

More: Brother Andrew's story continues in the Middle East with the book *Light Force: A Stirring Account of the Church Caught in the Middle East Crossfire* by Brother Andrew and Al Janssen (Revell, 2005). Andrew also wrote *God's Call* (Revell, 2002), which tells still more stories of meeting world leaders and underground church members around the globe.

Augustine, Saint, Bishop of Hippo.

The Confessions. Knopf, 2001. 370 pp. ISBN 0375411739.

In perhaps the first autobiography in Western history, Saint Augustine (354–430) records his youth, his conversion to Christianity, and his theological reflections. Augustine, a prolific writer, is one of the most important theologians in the history of Christianity. This affordable but well-made edition by Knopf is part of the "Everyman's Library."

Subjects: Autobiography, Catholics, Classics, Conversion Stories, Saint Augustine (354–430), Saints, Theologians

More: A biography of another famous Catholic theologian is Chesterton's *Saint Thomas Aquinas: The Dumb Ox* (Image, 1974). For some classic Catholic devotional writing, try *The Imitation of Christ* by Thomas à Kempis (Penguin Classics, 1952).

Chesterton, G. K.

St. Francis of Assisi. Image, 1987 (1924). 160 pp. ISBN 0385029004.

This is a brief biography by the famous writer G. K. Chesterton of a man who gave up all to follow Christ. Known for embracing poverty and nursing the outcast lepers in his area, Francis claimed that the voice of God told him to "repair My house." Saint Francis of Assisi established the Franciscan order of Friars in 1209.

Subjects: Biography, Catholics, Classics, Monks, Mystics, Saint Francis of Assisi (1182–1226), Saints

More: Another famous biography by Chesterton is *Saint Thomas Aquinas: The Dumb Ox* (Image, 1974). For more about life and faith during Francis's time, try *Francis of Assisi and His World* by Mark Galli (InterVarsity, 2002).

Companjen, Anneke.

Singing Through the Night: Courageous Stories of Faith from Women in the Persecuted Church. Revell, 2007. 304 pp. ISBN 0800731980.

These are moving stories of women from all over the world who have lost their husbands because of persecution against Christians. Some husbands were jailed, some were murdered, but all of these women bear the burden of suffering for Christ in this often-forgotten way.

Subjects: Collective Biography, Martyrs, Martyrs—Wives, Persecution of Christians, Wives

More: *Daughters of Hope: Stories of Witness and Courage in the Face of Persecution* by Kay Marshall Strom and Michele Rickett (InterVarsity, 2003).

Cunningham, Loren, and Janice Rogers.

Is That Really You, God?: Hearing the Voice of God. YWAM, 2001 (1984). 203 pp. ISBN 1576582442. **YA**

The story of YWAM (Youth With A Mission), a worldwide interdenominational youth missions movement, is an exciting and miraculous one. It starts with a vision that Loren Cunningham, YWAM's founder, had of waves of young people washing onto the shores of the world. The idea to send out teenagers all over the world was unheard of, but Cunningham persisted in trusting God until he saw the fulfillment of that vision.

Subjects: Adventure, Autobiography, Loren Cunningham (1936–), Missionaries, Young-Adult Interest, YWAM (Organization)

More: Cunningham also wrote *Daring to Live on the Edge: The Adventure of Faith and Finances* (YWAM, 1992) and *Making Jesus Lord: The Dynamic Power of Laying Down Your Rights* (YWAM, 1989).

Elliot, Elisabeth.

A Chance to Die: The Life and Legacy of Amy Carmichael. Revell, 2005 (1987). 384 pp. ISBN 0800730895.

This is the inspiring story of Amy Carmichael, an Irish missionary to South India who founded the Dohnavur Fellowship, a refuge for young girls involved in cult prostitution in Hindu temples.

Subjects: Biography, Amy Carmichael (1867–1951), India, Missionaries

More: Some of Carmichael's own writings are collected by editor David Hazard in a forty-day devotional titled *You Are My Hiding Place* (Bethany, 1991).

Elliot, Elisabeth.

Through Gates of Splendor. Tyndale, 1981 (1957). 274 pp. ISBN 0842371524.

In this classic missionary biography told by a widow of one of the characters, Elisabeth Elliot tells the story of five young missionaries (Nate Saint, Roger Youderian, Ed McCully, Pete Fleming, and Jim Elliot) who were massacred by the Auca Indians (also called Waodani or Waorani) they were trying to minister to in the Amazon basin during the 1950s.

Subjects: Collective Biography, Jim Elliot (1927–1956), Pete Fleming (1928–1956), Martyrs, Ed McCully (1927–1956), Missionaries, Nate Saint (1923–1956), Roger Youderian (1924–1956)

More: Elliot also wrote a book about her husband, Jim Elliot, called *Shadow of the Almighty: The Life and Testament of Jim Elliot* (HarperCollins, 1989). Also, in the book *End of the Spear* (Tyndale, 2005), Steve Saint (son of Nate Saint) wrote about his experience going back to live with the Waodani people—some of the same people who killed his father. Two films have come from Saint's story: *Beyond the Gates of Splendor* (2002) and *End of the Spear* (2005).

Foxe, John, and Harold J. Chadwick.

The New Foxe's Book of Martyrs. Bridge-Logos Publishers, 2001. 442 pp. ISBN 0882708759.

This book has been an inspirational classic since British writer John Foxe (1516–1587) first published it in 1563. It records the sufferings, imprisonments, and tortures of Christians from the Roman persecutions to the Inquisition and Foxe's own day. Harold Chadwick, senior editor of Bridge-Logos, revised the language and updated the stories to the present time using accounts gathered by an organization called the Voice of the Martyrs.

Subjects: Classics, Collective Biography, Martyrs, Persecution of Christians

More: In *Tortured for Christ* (Hodder & Stoughton, 2004), first published more than thirty years ago, Richard Wurmbrand tells of his involvement in the underground church of Romania. For stories about Muslims who have converted to Christianity and have paid with their lives, read *The Costly Call: Modern-Day Stories of Muslims Who Found Jesus* by Emir Fethi Caner and H. Edward Pruitt (Kregel, 2005).

Grubb, Norman.

C. T. Studd: Cricketer and Pioneer. Christian Literature Crusade, 1985 (1936). 241 pp. ISBN 0875082025.

C. T. Studd, a famous cricket player in England during the late 1800s, gave up his wealth and fame to become a missionary with Hudson Taylor's China Inland Mission. Studd also traveled to India and finally to Africa where he founded WEC International (still in operation today). First published in 1933, this classic missionary biography is still in print. The author, Norman Grubb, was also a missionary and married Studd's fourth daughter, Pauline.

Subjects: Adventure, Africa, Biography, China, Cricket, India, Missionaries, Sports, Charles Thomas Studd (1860–1931)

More: Try *Hudson Taylor's Spiritual Secret* (Moody, 1955) by Howard and Geraldine Taylor to find out more about the China Inland Mission. Another biography of a famous sports figure of the time who became a missionary is *Eric Liddell: Pure Gold* (Discovery House, 2004) by David McCasland. The 1981 film *Chariots of Fire* is about Liddell.

Muggeridge, Malcolm.

Something Beautiful for God: Mother Teresa of Calcutta. HarperOne, 1986 (1971). 156 pp. ISBN 0060660430.

This brief biographical work was written by the famous British journalist Malcolm Muggeridge. Mother Teresa of Calcutta, an Albanian Roman Catholic nun who founded the Missionaries of Charity in India, devoted her life to ministering to the country's poor and sick outcasts. For her work, she received the Nobel Peace Prize as well as many other awards. Muggeridge includes an interview with Mother Teresa.

Subjects: Biography, Catholics, Classics, Missionaries, Mother Teresa of Calcutta (1910–1997), Nuns

More: Another biography of a nun is *Mother Angelica: The Remarkable Story of a Nun, Her Nerve, and a Network of Miracles* by Raymond Arroyo (Doubleday, 2005). Also try *Molokai: The Story of Father Damien* by Hilde Eynikel (Alba House, 1999); it is about another priest who served people whom others shy away from—in this case, lepers.

Olson, Bruce.

Bruchko: The Astonishing True Story of a 19-Year-Old American, His Capture by the Motilone Indians and His Adventures in Christianizing the Stone Age Tribe. Charisma House, 2006 (1973). 192 pp. 159185993X. **YA**

This book tells the story of Bruce Olson, a nineteen-year-old American teen who went to live with the Motilone tribe of South American Indians in 1961. Olson did not try to or need to westernize these people in order to tell them about Christ. He suffered torture, disease, and discouragement, but eventually the good news of Jesus Christ transformed the Motilone Indians. The story of their transformation is truly amazing. This book was first published in 1973 under the title *For This Cross I'll Kill You.*

Subjects: Adventure, Anthropology, Autobiography, Missionaries, Motilone Indians, Bruce Olsen (1941–), South America, Young-Adult Interest

More: Olson extends his account to relate what has happened to the Motilone people in recent years and his own story of capture and torture by guerrilla soldiers in his new book, *Bruchko and the Motilone Miracle* (Charisma House, 2006).

Richardson, Don.

Peace Child. 4th Edition. Regal, 2005 (1974). 256 pp. ISBN 0830737847.

In 1962, Don Richardson traveled across the world to share the gospel with the Sawi people of New Guinea, a cannibalistic jungle tribe who had never heard of Christianity. With his young wife and infant son, Richardson lived with this tribe and learned their language and customs. He was shocked to find that betrayal was a virtue among these people. When he told them the gospel, they honored Judas instead of Christ! Not until he discovered the ancient custom of the peace child was he able to communicate their need for Christ and transform the tribe. Murder, revenge, and treachery among these people was replaced by forgiveness, peace, and love. Besides being a missions classic, this book offers a vital lesson in cross-cultural ministry. This new fourth edition adds an epilogue entitled "Thirty Years Later: An Update on the Sawi Tribe."

Subjects: Adventure, Autobiography, Missionaries, New Guinea, Don Richardson (1935–), Sawi (Indonesian People)

More: *Eternity in Their Hearts* (Regal, 2006) is another classic missions book by Richardson. Richardson also wrote *Lords of the Earth* (Regal, 1979), which is also about Irian Jaya's Stone Age tribes.

Rockness, Miriam Huffman.

A Passion for the Impossible: The Life of Lilias Trotter. Discovery House, 2003 (Shaw, 1999). 368 pp. ISBN 1572931086.

John Ruskin, the famous art critic, tried to convince Lilias Trotter to stick with art; but Trotter ended up a missionary to North African Muslims in Algeria. In addition to describing her life and mission work, this book includes selections from her devotional writings.

Subjects: Algeria, Biography, Missionaries, Muslims, Lilias Trotter (1853–1928)

More: A Muslim convert to Christianity tells her story in *I Dared to Call Him Father: The Miraculous Story of a Muslim Woman's Encounter with God* by Sheikh Bilquis (Chosen Books, 2003).

Stier, Jim.

Against All Odds. 2nd Edition. YWAM, 2000 (1994). 179 pp. ISBN 0927545446.6

This is the story of how Jim Stier became a believer and, with this wife Pam, a missionary to Brazil. Jim's church would not allow him to be a minister because he was divorced, but YWAM (Youth with A Mission) would. Jim tells story after story of trying circumstances, discouragements, miraculous provisions, healings, and ministry. Stier is now the chairman of YWAM.

Subjects: Adventure, Autobiography, Brazil, Missionaries, Jim Stier (1950–), YWAM (organization)

More: Other titles in the International Adventures series include: *The Man With the Bird on His Head: The Amazing Fulfillment of a Mysterious Island Prophecy* by John Rush and Abbe Anderson (YWAM, 1999) and *Living on the Devil's Doorstep: From Kabul to Amsterdam* by Floyd McClung (YWAM, 1999).

Taylor, Howard, and Geraldine Taylor.

Hudson Taylor's Spiritual Secret. Moody, 1955 (1932). 256 pp. ISBN 0802400299.

This classic, inspiring biography tells the story of the man who founded the China Inland Mission. James Hudson Taylor (1832–1905), a physician, pioneered missions in China by 1) going inland, 2) dressing like the natives, and 3) depending totally on God. Taylor did not ask people for money or workers, but through faith was supplied both. The authors of this book are Frederick Howard Taylor (1862–1946) and Mary Geraldine Guinness Taylor (1865–1949). Howard was the second son of Hudson Taylor.

Subjects: Adventure, Biography, China, Classics, James Hudson Missionaries, Taylor (1832–1905)

More: For the story of another missionary to China, try *Gladys Aylward: The Little Woman* (Moody, 1970) by Christine Hunter. For one about another pioneering missionary (to India), see *William Carey* by Basil Miller (Bethany, 1985).

Van Braght, Thieleman J.

Martyrs Mirror: The Story of Seventeen Centuries of Christian Martyrdom, from the Time of Christ to A.D. 1660. Herald, 2002 (1660). 1,158 pp. ISBN 083611390X.

This huge volume (a *Foxe's Book of Martyrs* for those in the Anabaptist tradition) records the martyrdom of more than 4,000 people. T. J. van Braght (1625–1664), a Dutch Mennonite, first published this book in 1660, but it was not translated into English until the 1800s.

Subjects: Anabaptists, Collective Biography, Martyrs

More: Try *The New Encyclopedia of Christian Martyrs* by Mark Waters (Baker, 2001), which includes Catholic martyrs (which Protestant martyr books omit!).

Musicians

Gaither, Bill, and Ken Abraham.

It's More Than the Music: Life Lessons on Friends, Faith, and What Matters Most. WarnerFaith, 2003. 308 pp. ISBN 0446692875.

A singer/songwriter of southern gospel and contemporary Christian music, William J. Gaither, along with his wife, is responsible for such songs as "Because He Lives," "He Touched Me," and hundreds of others. Gaither founded the Bill Gaither Trio and the Gaither Vocal Band. In this book, Gaither writes about his life, family, and long music career, including the Gaither Homecoming series of videos and concerts.

Subjects: Autobiography, William J. Gaither (1936–), Music—Southern Gospel, Musicians

More: *Homecoming: The Story of Southern Gospel Music Through the Eyes of Its Best-Loved Performers* by Bill Gaither and Jerry Jenkins (Zondervan, 1997). Gloria Gaither talks about some of the songs she and her husband have written in *God Gave the Song: Glimpses into the Inspiration Behind the Songs of Bill and Gloria Gaither* (Zondervan, 2000). For a book about another famous gospel group, try *The Cathedrals: The Story of America's Best-Loved Gospel Quartet* by Glen Payne and George Younce (Zondervan, 1998).

Green, Melody and David Hazard.

No Compromise: The Life Story of Keith Green. Harvest, 2000 (1989). 389 pp. ISBN 0736903194.

Keith Green (1953–1982), a singer/songwriter, died in a plane crash when he was only twenty-eight years old. Green was known for his passionate devotion to God in his life and music. This popular biography traces Green's conversion to Christianity and his involvement with the secular and religious contemporary music world.

Subjects: Biography, Conversion Stories, Keith Green (1953–1982), Music—Contemporary Christian, Musicians

More: One of Green's friends and neighbors was Matthew Ward of the Jesus Music band, 2nd Chapter of Acts. Ward's autobiography is titled *My Second Chapter: The Matthew Ward Story* (WaterBrook, 2006). *Rich Mullins: An Arrow Pointing to Heaven* by James Bryan Smith (B&H Publishing, 2002) is the story of another Christian musician who died young. Green was closely associated with the ministers Leonard Ravenhill, who wrote *Why Revival Tarries* (Bethany, 2004), and Winkie Pratney, who wrote *Ultimate CORE: Church on the Radical Edge* (Bethany, 2004).

Jones, Bobby, and Lesley Sussman.

Touched by God: Black Gospel Greats Share Their Stories of Finding God. Pocket Books, 1998. 296 pp. ISBN 067102003X.

Grammy and Dove award winner Bobby Jones tells the stories of nineteen gospel music stars such as Shirley Caesar, Kirk Franklin,

Dottie Peoples, and Vickie Winans. Their stories are filled with both trials and testimonies of God's faithfulness. Through Jones, we learn about their family lives, their struggles, and their rise to success.

Subjects: African American Musicians, Collective Biography, Music—Gospel, Musicians

More: Here are three books on individual singers: *The Lady, The Melody, and the Word: The Shirley Caesar Story* by Shirley Caesar (Thomas Nelson, 1998); *Church Boy* by Kirk Franklin (Word, 1998); and *On a Positive Note* by CeCe Winans (Pocket Books, 1999). For more on African American spiritual music, try *Ev'ry Time I Feel the Spirit: 101 Best-Loved Psalms, Gospel Hymns, and Spiritual Songs of the African-American Church* by Gwendolin Sims Warren (Henry Holt, 1999).

Smith, James Bryan.

Rich Mullins: An Arrow Pointing to Heaven. B&H Publishing, 2000. 224 pp. ISBN 0805421351.

Here is the biography of a uniquely talented singer/songwriter who died in a car accident when he was only forty-one years old. Rich Mullins (1955–1997) was a successful contemporary Christian musician who refused to give in to the temptations of fame and wealth. For instance, Mullins hired an accountant and asked him to give him a monthly allowance equal to the average workingman's wage. Much of the extra money was given away to needy people and ministries. This edition comes with a CD including ten songs performed by Mullins. (A paperback edition issued after this one has an additional section with writings by Mullins.)

Subjects: Biography, Rich Mullins (1955–1997), Music—Contemporary Christian, Musicians

More: *The World as I Remember It: Through the Eyes of a Ragamuffin* (Multnomah, 2004) is a collection of articles that Mullins wrote for *Release* magazine. Read about another famous Christian singer/songwriter who died young in *Hammers and Nails: The Life and Music of Mark Heard* by Matthew Dickerson (Cornerstone Press, 2003).

Smith, Jane Stuart, and Betty Carlson.

The Gift of Music: Great Composers and Their Influence. Third edition. Crossway, 1995 (1978). 317 pp. ISBN 089107869X.

This biographical study of great composers is not limited to Christian musicians. Rather, it examines the cultural influences, beliefs, and worldviews that shaped the people and their music. About forty-five composers are covered; there are also brief sections on the Psalms, on Shakespeare's influence on music, and on

Christmas carols. Each composer's chapter ends with recommended reading and listening selections.

Subjects: Collective Biography, Composers, Music—Classical

More: Readers should also enjoy Patrick Kavanaugh's *Spiritual Lives of the Great Composers* (Zondervan, 1996).

Trapp, Maria Augusta.

The Story of the Trapp Family Singers. Harper, 2001 (Lippincott, 1949). 320 pp. ISBN 0060005777.

Maria Augusta Trapp wrote at least six books; this one was the basis for *The Sound of Music*, the Rodgers and Hammerstein Broadway musical and the 1965 motion picture starring Julie Andrews. First published in 1949 by Lippincott, the book tells the story of (Baroness) Maria and Baron Georg Ritter von Trapp, from their romance in Austria and their escape from the Nazis to their life in America.

Subjects: Autobiography, Music, Maria Augusta Trapp (1905–1987), Trapp Family

More: Maria writes more about her life in *Maria* (Creation House, 1972) and more about her family's spiritual life in *Yesterday Today and Forever* (New Leaf Press, 1998).

Turner, Steve.

The Man Called Cash: The Life, Love, and Faith of an American Legend. W Publishing Group, 2005. 298 pp. ISBN 0849908159.

This is the "authorized" biography of Johnny Cash (1932–2003), the country music singer/songwriter famous for such songs as "I Walk the Line" and "The Man in Black." Turner describes the ups and downs of Cash's life, including his music, drug addiction and recovery, and adultery. Turner also delves into Cash's spirituality. The author, Steve Turner, is a noted music journalist and biographer.

Subjects: Biography, Johnny Cash (1932–2003), Music—Country, Music—Rock and Roll, Musicians

More: Cash's second wife's son, John Carter Cash, wrote a biography of her titled *Anchored in Love: An Intimate Portrait of June Carter Cash* (W Publishing, 2007). For another country musician biography, try *Forever and Ever, Amen: The Heart-Warming Stories Behind the Music of Paul Overstreet*, written by Paul Overstreet (Treasure House, 2001). Yet another biography of a Christian musician involved with secular rock music is *Pat Boone: The Authorized Biography: April Love, the Early Days of Rock 'n' Roll* by Paul Davis (Zondervan, 2002).

Sports Figures

Dravecky, Dave, and Tim Stafford.

Comeback. Zondervan, 1990. 252 pp. ISBN 031052881X.

All-Star baseball player (and left-handed pitcher) Dave Dravecky was a rising star in major league baseball—until cancer in his arm changed everything. Dravecky shares his moving story, which involves life in the big leagues, family, cancer, and faith. Later books by Dravecky and his wife describe in depth the struggles of depression, burnout, and discouragement that they endured—and the grace and faith that helped them throughout.

Subjects: Autobiography, Award Winners (ECPA, CT), Baseball Players, Cancer, Dave Dravecky (1956–), Sports

More: For more on baseball, All-Star catcher Gary Carter writes about life in the major leagues in *The Gamer* (Word, 1993). Dravecky and his wife have written more about facing life's trials in *When You Can't Come Back* (Zondervan, 1992) and *A Joy I'd Never Known: One Woman's Triumph over Panic Attacks and Depression* by Jan Dravecky (Zondervan, 1996).

Maravich, Pete, and Darrel Campbell.

Pistol Pete: Heir to a Dream. Thomas Nelson, 1987. 234 pp. ISBN 0840776098.

Basketball Hall of Famer Pete Maravich became legendary as a college player at Louisiana State University, where his father was coach. In this book, Maravich tells his story from childhood through his professional basketball career, which ended early due to a leg injury. This led to Maravich's salvation as he turned over his life to Christ. Maravich writes about his faith and how it sustained him through disappointments and trials, including his father's death from cancer.

Subjects: Award Winners (ECPA), Autobiography, Basketball Players, Pete Maravich (1947–1988), Sports

More: *Pete Maravich: Magician of the Hardwood* by Mike Towle (Cumberland House, 2000) is another biography of Pistol Pete. Another sports figure who died in his forties and was coached by his father was golfer Payne Stewart. His wife, Tracey Stewart, tells his story in *Payne Stewart: The Authorized Biography* (B&H Publishing, 2000).

Warner, Kurt, and Michael Silver.

All Things Possible: My Story of Faith, Football, and the Miracle Season. Zondervan, 2000. 269 pp. ISBN 006251718X.

Football quarterback Kurt Warner led the St. Louis Rams to a Super Bowl victory in 2000. This book tells about that miracle season and the story of his life, faith, and family.

Subjects: Autobiography, Football Players, Sports, Kurt Warner (1971–)

More: *Winning* (Regal, 1990) by football star Rosey Grier collects the inspirational stories of thirty-eight different Christian athletes from a variety of sports. For another football biography, try the NFL's MVP Shaun Alexander's *Touchdown Alexander: My Story of Faith, Football and Pursuing the Dream* (Harvest House, 2006).

Writers

Buechner, Frederick.

The Eyes of the Heart: A Memoir of the Lost and Found. HarperSanFrancisco, 1999. 183 pp. ISBN 0062516396.

In Frederick Buechner's fifth volume of memoirs, the reader is brought into the author's office and library, which he calls the magic kingdom. As Buechner points out various volumes on the shelf or photos on the wall, we learn about his life. He discusses painful family secrets, including his father's suicide, and he remembers close family members and friends, especially James Merrill, the Pulitzer Prize-winning poet. Buechner is a Presbyterian minister and an acclaimed author of novels, poetry, short stories, and nonfiction.

Subjects: Autobiography, Frederick Buechner (1926–), Ministers, Writers

More: Buechner's first memoir is *The Sacred Journey: A Memoir of Early Days* (HarperSanFrancisco, 1991).

Carpenter, Humphrey.

Tolkien: A Biography. Houghton Mifflin, 2000 (1977). 304 pp. ISBN 0618057021.

This is the authorized biography of the man who wrote *The Hobbit* and *The Lord of the Rings*. J. R. R. Tolkien was an Oxford professor and friend of C. S. Lewis. This book takes readers through Tolkien's life from his childhood (at twelve years old he was an orphan) to his professorship, through his writing and publishing experiences, and his eventual fame.

Subjects: Biography, Catholics, Professors, J. R. R. Tolkien (1892–1973), Writers

More: Carpenter also wrote *The Inklings: C. S. Lewis, J. R. R. Tolkien, Charles Williams and Their Friends* (Houghton Mifflin, 1978). Also try *The Letters of J. R. R. Tolkien* (Houghton Mifflin, 2000).

Tolkien fans will also want to know about *J. R. R. Tolkien: Artist and Illustrator* (Houghton Mifflin, 2000), edited by Wayne Hammond and Christina Scull, which has more than 200 reproductions of Tolkien's paintings and drawings.

de Vinck, Christopher.

The Power of the Powerless: A Brother's Legacy of Love. Crossroad, 2002 (Doubleday, 1988). 176 pp. ISBN 0824519744.

This book shows readers how Christopher de Vinck's life was touched by his brother Oliver, who could not see or talk or walk. Oliver, severely handicapped, was a great blessing to his family. To this beautiful story, de Vinck adds the story of others, like Lauren, Anthony, and Paul, boys and girls who posed challenges familiar to many parents with handicapped children.

Subjects: Autobiography, Catholics, Disability, Christopher de Vinck (1951–), Writers

More: Here are two more books by de Vinck: *Only the Heart Knows How to Find Them: Precious Memories for a Faithless Time* (Viking, 1991) and *The Book of Moonlight: Why Life Is Good and God Is Generous and Kind* (Zondervan, 1998).

Eble, Diane.

Behind the Stories: Christian Novelists Reveal the Heart in the Art of Their Writing. Bethany, 2002. 288 pp. ISBN 0764224638.

Great reading and inspiring tales can be found in these "behind the scenes" glimpses of forty Christian fiction authors, including Randy Alcorn, Robin Jones Gunn, Janette Oke, Lawana Blackwell, Angel Elwell Hunt, Bodie Thoene, Francine Rivers, Jan Karon, Jane Kirkpatrick, Gilbert Morris, Liz Curtis Higgs, Jerry B. Jenkins, and Diana Noble.

Subjects: Christian Fiction Authors, Collective Biography, Writers

More: For more about Christian fiction authors, see *Contemporary Christian Authors: Lives and Works* by Janice DeLong and Rachel Schwedt (Scarecrow Press, 2000).

Elie, Paul.

The Life You Save May Be Your Own: An American Pilgrimage. Farrar, Straus and Giroux, 2004. 576 pp. ISBN 0374529213.

This book pulls together the biographies of four famous Catholic writers: Flannery O'Connor, Thomas Merton, Walker Percy, and Dorothy Day. Paul Elie, an editor at Farrar, Straus and Giroux, shows what these authors shared in their writings and in their expressions of faith.

Subjects: Catholics, Collective Biography, Dorothy Day (1897–1980), Literature, Thomas Merton (1915–1968), Flannery O'Connor (1925–1964), Walker Percy (1916–1990), Writers

More: For more on O'Connor, try *Flannery O'Connor: Spiritual Writings* by Robert Ellsberg, ed. (Orbis Books, 2003) and *Habit of Being: Letters of Flannery O'Connor* by Sally Fitzgerald, ed. (Farrar, Straus and Giroux, 1979). For Merton's autobiography, see *The Seven Storey Mountain* (Harvest/HBJ, 1978). For Day's memoirs, try *The Long Loneliness* (HarperCollins, 1997).

Kirkpatrick, Jane.

Homestead: A Memoir of Modern Pioneers Pursuing the Edge of Possibility. WaterBrook Press, 2005 (Word, 1991). 374 pp. ISBN 1400070619.

In 1979, Jane Kirkpatrick, a licensed clinical social worker and an award-winning author of inspirational Christian fiction, bought 160 acres of undeveloped land in Starvation Point, in eastern Oregon. She describes her and her husband's many struggles to tame this land so they could at least live there and maybe even operate a ranch.

Subjects: Autobiography, Homesteading, Jane Kirkpatrick (1946–), Writers

More: *Assault on Eden* (Baker, 1995) by Virginia Stem Owens, tells of Owens's life in an intentional community (commune) during the 1970s in the New Mexico desert.

Lamott, Anne.

Traveling Mercies: Some Thoughts on Faith. Anchor, 2000. 288 pp. ISBN 0385496095.

Anne Lamott confesses her troubled and tangled past (drugs, alcohol, abortion, adultery, and bulimia) and describes how Christianity and her son bring hope into her life. Although Lamott is famous for her articulate, witty, and raw memoirs and her unconventional faith, some readers might be put off by her frequent use of curse words and her graphic confessions.

Subjects: Autobiography, Conversion Stories, Anne Lamott (1954–), Writers

More: *Plan B: Further Thoughts on Faith* by Anne Lamott (Riverhead Trade, 2006). If you like Lamott, you might also like *Blue Like Jazz: Nonreligious Thoughts on Christian Spirituality* by Donald Miller (Nelson, 2003).

Lewis, C. S.

Surprised by Joy: The Shape of My Early Life. Harvest, 1984 (1956). 238 pp. ISBN 0156870118.

In this autobiography of the famous writer, Christian apologist, and scholar C. S. Lewis, the author traces his life from his childhood in Ireland and his early school experiences to his atheism and eventual conversion to Christ. Lewis is famous for such books as *Mere Christianity* and *The Lion, the Witch, and the Wardrobe*.

Subjects: Autobiography, Classics, Conversion Stories, C. S. Lewis (1898–1963), Professors, Writers

More: Other autobiographical materials by Lewis, in the form of diaries and journals, include: *All My Road Before Me: The Diary of C. S. Lewis, 1922–1927* (Harvest, 2006) and *A Grief Observed* (HarperSanFrancisco, 2001).

Lewis, C. S., and Walter Hooper, editor.

The Collected Letters of C. S. Lewis, Volume 1: Family Letters, 1905–1931. HarperOne, 2004. 1,072 pp. ISBN 0060727632.

This first of three comprehensive volumes of C. S. Lewis's correspondence has many letters to his family, especially his father and brother, and to his friend Arthur Greeves. Editor Walter Hooper includes a helpful biographical appendix to describe the people that were a part of Lewis's life. This first volume ends right about the time of Lewis's conversion to Christianity.

Subjects: Correspondence, C. S. Lewis (1898–1963), Professors, Writers

More: Volume 2 of the *Collected Letters* covers the years 1931–1949 and volume 3 covers 1950–1963. Even though these books, in effect, replace the previous collections of letters, readers may still appreciate some of the earlier collections like the small volume called *Letters to Children*, edited by Lyle Dorsett and Marjorie Lamp Mead (B&H Publishing, 2000), or the large volume called *Letters of C. S. Lewis*, edited and with a memoir by W. H. Lewis (Lewis's brother) and Walter Hooper, editor (Harvest Books, 2003).

Merton, Thomas.

The Seven Storey Mountain. Harvest, 1999 (1948). 496 pp. ISBN 0156010860.

Thomas Merton (1915–1968) was a Trappist monk and famous spiritual writer. This classic autobiography, which inspired many to enter the priesthood, was completed when Merton was thirty-one years old and first published in 1948. In it, he talks about his early life, education, conversion to Catholicism, and commitment to life as a monk in the Abbey of Gethsemani in Kentucky.

Subjects: Autobiography, Catholics, Conversion Stories, Thomas Merton (1915–1968), Monks, Mystics, Writers

More: For more writing by Merton, try *No Man Is an Island* (Harvest, 2002). For those interested in monastic life, see Kathleen Norris's *The Cloister Walk* (Riverhead, 1996), in which she describes her years in a Benedictine monastery.

Sayer, George.

Jack: A Life of C. S. Lewis. Crossway Books, 2005 (Harper & Row, 1986). 464 pp. ISBN 1581347391.

George Sayer studied under C. S. Lewis at Oxford and was a personal friend (for almost thirty years) of the famous writer and Oxford scholar. This is one of the very few biographies written by someone who personally knew C. S. Lewis, who is famous for writing books like *Mere Christianity* and *The Chronicles of Narnia*.

Subjects: Biography, C. S. Lewis (1898–1963), Professors, Writers

More: Douglas Gresham, Lewis's stepson, wrote two books of interest, *Lenten Lands: My Childhood with Joy Davidman and C. S. Lewis* (HarperSanFrancisco, 1994) and *Jack's Life: A Memory of C. S. Lewis* (B&H Publishing, 2005). Also Walter Hooper and Roger Lancelyn Green knew Lewis and wrote the biography *C. S. Lewis: A Biography* (HarperSanFrancisco, 2002). An award-winning recent biography by someone who did not know Lewis is *The Narnian: The Life and Imagination of C. S. Lewis* by Alan Jacobs (HarperSanFrancisco, 2005).

Timmerman, John H.

Jane Kenyon: A Literary Life. Eerdmans, 2002. 246 pp. ISBN 0802863264.

Jane Kenyon was an American poet who died of leukemia in 1995. Faith was not the main focus of her poetry; nonetheless, it was an important part of her life. Kenyon was New Hampshire's poet laureate when she died. Her husband, Donald Hall, became the U.S. poet laureate in 2006. Timmerman, professor of English at Calvin College, offers here a literary biography in which he examines Kenyon's life, literary influences, and poetry.

Subjects: Biography, Jane Kenyon (1947–1995), Literature, Poets, Writers

More: Another biography of an American poet is Roger Lundin's *Emily Dickinson and the Art of Belief* (Eerdmans, 2004).

Vanauken, Sheldon.

A Severe Mercy. HarperOne, 1987 (1980). 240 pp. ISBN 0060688246.

Sheldon Vanauken and his wife were atheists before they met C. S. Lewis. In this book, Vanauken recounts his conversion to Christ, the love story of his relationship with his wife, his wife's untimely death, and the grief with which he had to struggle. Vanauken includes eighteen letters that C. S. Lewis wrote to him.

Subjects: Anglicans, Autobiography, Award Winners (ECPA), Conversion Stories, Grief, Sheldon Vanauken (1914–1996), Writers

More: Try C. S. Lewis's own book about grappling with the death of his wife in *A Grief Observed* (HarperSanFrancisco, 2001).

Winner, Lauren, F.

Girl Meets God: On the Path to a Spiritual Life. Random House, 2003. 320 pp. ISBN 0812970802.

This is a spiritual memoir of a young woman with a Jewish father and Baptist mother. Lauren F. Winner became an Orthodox Jew but was attracted to Christianity. This book records her conversion to Christ and shows how Judaism continues to give deep meaning to her faith. Winner has written articles, essays, and reviews for *Christianity Today*, *New York Times Book Review*, and *Publishers Weekly*.

Subjects: Autobiography, Conversion Stories, Lauren Winner (1975–), Writers

More: Try *Mudhouse Sabbath* (Paraclete, 2003), in which Winner writes about her spiritual life and the Jewish rituals that she misses—and talks about them in light of Christianity.

Chapter 2

Prayer, Worship, and Spiritual Growth

Introduction

Prayer, worship, and spiritual growth are ancient subjects. Through the millennia, countless books have been written on these themes; a number of the books in this chapter are considered classics. For example, *The Imitation of Christ* has been called the most famous religious work of the Christian world. This book was written centuries ago in medieval Latin by a Catholic monk who lived from 1380–1471 named Thomas à Kempis. It is still relevant, insightful, and inspiring today.

While Christianity is an old religion, it is also current and living. There is much that is new and exciting in Christian publishing in the areas of prayer, worship, and spiritual growth, especially subjects like spiritual warfare, healing, deliverance, worshipful dance, and Christian living.

This chapter is divided into nine sections: 1) "Daily Devotionals and Prayer Books," 2) "Fasting," 3) "Prayer and Revival," 4) "Spiritual Warfare," 5) "Worship," 6) "Spiritual Growth Classics," 7) "Discipleship," 8) "Spiritual Gifts," and 9) "Christian Living."

Of course, there are many more Christian devotional books and authors than can be covered in this chapter or this guide. This section gives just a small sample to acquaint readers with some standard "classic" authors and to introduce some of the newest names in Christian nonfiction publishing. See the bibliography at the end of this chapter to get more recommendations for classic Christian nonfiction.

Daily Devotionals and Prayer Books

Daily devotionals are "devotional" books designed to be read daily, so the chapters are brief—usually only a page or two in length. These books are often dated on each page, so readers can open up to the day's selection—December 19, for instance—and enjoy that day's reading. Other books are not dated but still lend themselves to daily use. For a full list of all such books in this chapter and others, please refer to the subject index entry for daily devotionals. Prayer books are somewhat similar to daily devotionals in that their content is arranged by date (or by occasion). Some prayer books, like the Episcopalian *Book of Common Prayer*, are used to guide church members through a service.

Chambers, Oswald.

My Utmost for His Highest. Discovery House Publishers, 1992 (Dodd, Mead and Company, 1935). 395 pp. ISBN 0929239571.

> This is probably one of the most popular daily devotionals in print. It has been in print continuously since it was first published in America in 1935 (and still appears on Christian best-sellers' lists). This classic book has 365 one-page devotionals known for their penetrating, thoughtful, and biblical insights. Oswald Chambers (1874–1917) was a British (born in Scotland) teacher, minister, poet, and artist. His wife, Gertrude "Biddy" Hobbs Chambers, spent her life compiling and editing his lecture notes into various books, including *My Utmost for His Highest*. This particular edition was edited by James Reimann to update the language. Chambers used the New King James for Bible references, and this edition has been approved and authorized by the Oswald Chambers Publications Association.
>
> **Subjects:** Classics, Daily Devotionals
>
> **More:** David McCasland has written a popular biography of Chambers called *Oswald Chambers: Abandoned to God: The Life Story of the Author of My Utmost for His Highest* (Discovery House, 1993). All of Chambers' teachings are collected in a 1,492-page book called *The Complete Works of Oswald Chambers* (Discovery House, 2000).

Cowman, L. B.

Streams in the Desert. Zondervan, 1997 (Oriental Missionary Society, 1925). 384 pp. ISBN: 0310210062.

> First published in 1925, this classic devotional features 366 daily one-page readings selected from dozens of famous writers such as

F. B. Meyer, Charles Spurgeon, and A. B. Simpson. L. B. Cowman was a missionary in Japan and China from 1901 to 1917. This edition was revised by James Reimann to update the language. It uses the New International Version of the Bible.

Subjects: Classics, Daily Devotionals

More: Another classic year-round devotional is *Morning and Evening* by Charles Spurgeon (Hendrickson, 1995). This one actually has 732 devotionals, one for every morning and evening of the year. A more recent, award-winning devotional that gathers the writings of famous authors is *In His Presence: Daily Devotionals Through the Gospel of Matthew*, compiled and edited by Lance Wubbels (Emerald Books, 1998).

Episcopal Church.

The Book of Common Prayer. Church Hymnal Corporation, 1979. 1,001 pp. ISBN 0898690617.

The Book of Common Prayer 1979 (BCP) is the name of the current liturgical book in the Episcopal Church of America (other churches use it, too). It is in the public domain, so various publishers have printed it. The edition listed here is a sturdy hardback copy suitable for libraries. Previous editions of the American *Book of Common Prayer* were issued in 1789, 1892, and 1928. The full title is *The Book of Common Prayer and Administration of the Sacraments and Other Rites and Ceremonies of the Church: Together with the Psalter or Psalms of David According to the Use of the Episcopal Church.* The American *Book of Common Prayer* descended from the first *English Prayer Book* of 1549 by Archbishop Thomas Cranmer for the Church of England (Anglican Church).

Subjects: Classics, Episcopal Church, Liturgy, Prayer Books

More: The 1928 *Book of Common Prayer* (Oxford University Press, 1993) is still very popular for its King James-style language (and because many 1979 revisions were controversial).

Tickle, Phyllis.

The Divine Hours: Prayers for Summertime. Doubleday, 2000. 672 pp. ISBN 0385492863.

A book of hours, or the divine offices, refers to the sixth-century Benedictine Rule of fixed-hour prayer. In this book, Phyllis Tickle draws upon the *Book of Common Prayer* and the writings of famous Christian authors, paired with many scripture readings from the New Jerusalem Bible, to guide Christians day by day and month by month in prayer, praise, and devotion. For instance, there are prayers for the morning office (between 6:00 and 9:00 A.M.), the midday office (between 11:00 A.M. and 2:00 P.M.), and the vespers office (between 5:00 and 8:00 P.M.). Some of the reading selections come from authors such as Isaac Watts, Francis of Assisi, Charles Wesley, Frederick Faber, Fenelon, Fanny Crosby, and Bernard of Clairvaut. This book is part one of a trilogy. The other books are *The Divine Hours: Prayers for Autumn and Wintertime* (Doubleday, 2000) and *Divine Hours: Prayers for Springtime* (Doubleday, 2001). Tickle is an author and religion editor for *Publishers Weekly*.

Subjects: Daily Devotionals, Prayer Books

More: A fourth book by Tickle covers nighttime, *The Night Offices: Prayers for the Hours from Sunset to Sunrise* (Oxford, 2006). Scot McKnight has written *Praying with the Church: Following Jesus Daily, Hourly, Today* (Paraclete Press, 2006) for people who wish to understand and enrich their prayer life with fixed-hour prayer methods used in Anglican, Orthodox, and Catholic traditions. McKnight's book serves as a great introduction to Tickle's book for evangelicals who are wary of saying prayers that are not spontaneous.

Fasting

Fasting is a particular spiritual discipline that involves abstaining from food. The concept may seem unusual to many North Americans, but the word appears in our daily language. The word "breakfast" refers to the meal where people "break" their nightly "fast." One can fast for one meal, a week of meals, or some other time period, but the practice of fasting is usually associated with prayer. The Bible records several types of fasts, and some people apply fasting principles to activities like watching TV. There are spiritual and physical benefits to fasting; the books gathered here discuss both areas. Some of the books in the "Nutrition" section of Chapter 3 touch on fasting.

Chavda, Mahesh.

The Hidden Power of Prayer and Fasting. Destiny Image, 2007 (1998). 207 pp. ISBN 0768424100.

Mahesh Chavda started fasting one day at a time in 1971. In 1972, he fasted for three days, and then seven and then fourteen days at a time. By 1974, Chavda had completed a forty-day fast. This veteran of more than twenty-five forty-day fasts says he has learned that fasting is an important part of a New Testament lifestyle for today's Christians. Chavda gives many stirring testimonials of healings and answers to prayer that he has seen in his ministry. He saw a sixteen-year-old boy healed of polio. He even witnessed the resurrection of Katshinyi, a boy who had died of malaria in Zaire. Chavda urges believers to be willing to fast and pray so that people can be freed from sin, sickness, and bondage. He writes about people who fasted in the Bible and the various kinds of fasts they observed. He also gives advice for fasting and breaking a fast.

Subjects: Fasting, Prayer

More: Two books that Bible teacher Derek Prince has written on fasting are *How to Fast Successfully* (Whitaker House, 1995) and *Shaping History Through Prayer and Fasting* (Whitaker House, 2002).

Piper, John.

A Hunger for God: Desiring God Through Fasting and Prayer. Crossway, 1997. 239 pp. ISBN 0891079661.

When people fast (don't eat), they get hungry. Pastor John Piper says that fasting is about hungering and yearning for God. Piper examines the practice of fasting in the Bible and in church history. He discusses the nature and purpose of fasting, right and wrong reasons for fasting, and how fasting can bring breakthrough and righteousness concerning various social issues.

Subjects: Fasting, Prayer

Towns, Elmer L.

Fasting for Spiritual Breakthrough. Gospel Light, 1996. 252 pp. ISBN 0830718397.

Elmer Towns encourages readers to return to the discipline of fasting. He discusses what the Bible says about the subject and then focuses on various kinds of fasts. The Disciple's fast (Matthew 17) is a fast to break addiction. The Ezra fast (Ezra 8) is a fast to seek solutions to a specific problem. There are also fasts to succeed in evangelism (the Samuel fast), to find freedom from fear and mental problems (the Elijah fast), to provide for the needy (the Widow's fast), and to receive wisdom in decision-making (the Saint Paul fast). Towns promotes fasting for health and spiritual deliverance. Appendices list scriptures relating to fasting and show readers how to keep a fasting journal.

Subjects: Fasting, Prayer

More: *The Transforming Power of Fasting and Prayer: Personal Accounts of Spiritual Renewal* by Bill Bright (New Life Publications, 1997).

Wallis, Arthur.

God's Chosen Fast. Christian Literature Crusade, 1986 (1968). 154 pp. ISBN 0875085547.

Arthur Wallis examines the different kinds of fasts and the spiritual benefits of fasting. He discusses fasting for personal sanctity, fasting to be heard on high, fasting to change God's mind, fasting to free captives, fasting to buffet the body, and fasting for health and healing. He describes how to begin and end a fast, and includes a diary of one of his twenty-one-day fasts that contains notes on his activities, prayer times, and physical discomforts. An appendix gives answers to common questions. Some of the health advice is dated since this book was first published in 1968.

Subjects: Fasting, Prayer

More: For more recent information on the health aspects of fasting, try medical doctor Don Colbert's *Fasting Made Easy* (Siloam, 2004).

Prayer and Revival

The word "prayer" etymologically means "to make an earnest request." In Christian practice, prayer also refers to worship of God and communion with God. There are many types of prayer. This section includes general books on the topic as well as books on intercession, a specific type of prayer that refers to the act of praying for—or on behalf of—another person or situation. Books on intercessory prayer are found in the next section as well because intercession is also an element of spiritual warfare. Revival is the other topic included here. Revival, which is usually associated with prayer, refers to an extraordinary time of spiritual renewal in a certain geographical region. For instance, the First Great Awakening was a time of revival that hit New England in the 1720s. Jonathan Edwards, one of America's most famous preachers and theologians, is associated with this revival. The Great Awakening, as well as other revivals, was marked by mass conversions, healings, societal transformation, and other miraculous events. Revival is, for Christians, a tangible expression of the saying "prayer changes things."

Bevington, G. C.

Remarkable Miracles. Bridge-Logos, 1991. 296 pp. ISBN 0882707035.

G. C. Bevington, an itinerant holiness preacher from Ohio, tells the story of his life and ministry, focusing on incidents that demonstrate the fact that God still heals people in the modern age. While seeking direction from God, Bevington frequently fasted and prayed inside of hollow logs in the forest—sometimes for days at a time. Bevington saw drunks, homeless people, and even hardened religious people transformed by the power and love of Christ. He refused medical treatment for himself and saw his own broken ribs and cancerous lesions heal. Bevington says scores of others also were healed as he prayed—men, women, and children (once even a horse). This book was first published in the 1920s as *Remarkable Incidents and Modern Miracles Through Prayer and Faith*.

Subjects: Autobiography, Guy Carlton Bevington (1849–1938) Healing, Prayer

More: *Answers to Prayer* by George Mueller (Moody, 1984) records Mueller's work with thousands of orphans in England and the many incredible stories of faith and answered prayer that kept the orphanages going.

Billheimer, Paul E.

Destined for the Throne: How Spiritual Warfare Prepares the Bride of Christ for Her Eternal Destiny. Bethany, 2005 (Christian Literature Crusade, 1975). 144 pp. ISBN 0764200356.

Paul Billheimer (1897–1984), a minister and Christian educator, says that romance is at the heart of the universe because the fulfillment and consummation of all history is the wedding supper of the Lamb—Jesus Christ and his bride, the Church. Billheimer goes on to discuss the mystery, purpose, and privilege of prayer in this context. He talks about the authority of the believer, the victory of Christ, and the power of praise to inspire faith. This book was first published in 1975.

Subject: Prayer

Bounds, E. M.

Power Through Prayer. Whitaker, 2005 (1902). 143 pp. ISBN 0883688115.

"The church is looking for better methods; God is looking for better men." So opens this brief but famous book on prayer. In it, Edward McKendree Bounds inspires preachers—and readers in general—to pray. Preaching without prayer, he writes, kills. Bounds' simple writing, urgent and entreating tone, and the interesting stories and quotes of famous ministers and men of prayer make this an inspiring read. Bounds (1835–1913), a pastor, evangelist, and writer from Missouri, gave up a promising legal career to be a Methodist Episcopal preacher just in time to minister during the Civil War. This book was first published in 1902 as *Preacher and Prayer*.

Subjects: Classics, Prayer

More: Bounds wrote other books on prayer. They are collected in *The Complete Works of E. M. Bounds on Prayer* (Baker, 2004). Lyle Dorsett wrote a biography of Bounds called *E. M. Bounds, Man of Prayer* (Zondervan, 1991).

Bunyan, John.

Prayer. Banner of Truth, 1999. 172 pp. ISBN 0851510906.

John Bunyan (1628–1688) was a Puritan writer and preacher from England famous for his allegorical novel *Pilgrim's Progress* (first published in 1678). This book is a collection of two short works on prayer. The first (written in jail) is called *Praying in the Spirit* and was originally published in 1662. The second book is called *The Throne of Grace* and was published in 1692.

Subjects: Classics, Prayer

More: For more Puritan writings on prayer, try *The Valley of Vision: A Collection of Puritan Prayers and Devotions*, edited by Arthur Bennett (Banner of Truth, 1999). The prayers are taken from the writings of Thomas Shepard, Thomas Watson, Richard Baxter, John Bunyan, Isaac Watts, David Brainerd, Spurgeon, and others. Classic works on prayer of similar interest are P. T. Forsyth's *The Soul of Prayer* (Regent College Publishing, 1997) and Alexander Whyte's collection of sermons called *Lord, Teach Us to Pray* (Regent College Publishing, 2001). A recent book that may appeal to the same crowd is J. I. Packer's *Praying: Finding Our Way Through Duty to Delight* (cowritten with Carolyn Nystrom; Inter-Varsity Press, 2006).

Carre, E. G., editor.

Praying Hyde. Third edition. Bridge-Logos, 2004 (1982). 166 pp. ISBN 0882705415.

John Hyde (1865–1912) was an American missionary to India who saw little fruit during his early years as a minister. But then he caught a vision for intercessory prayer and experienced revival. Hyde was called "Praying Hyde" because he rarely ate or slept, frequently spending whole nights in prayer. By faith, he claimed one soul a day, then two, and then four. "Give me souls or I die!" was his cry. This book is a collection of three short biographies of Hyde. The first is called *Praying Hyde* and was written by Francis McGaw. It was the first biography of Hyde, authored by a personal friend of Hyde's family. The second biography is called *A Vessel Unto Honor* and was written by Rev. J. Pengwern Jones. The third biography is *A Master Fisher of Souls* by Rev. R. M'Cheyne Paterson. After the biographies, there are ten pages of letters by Hyde.

Subjects: Biography, Classics, India, Intercessory Prayer, Missionaries, Prayer, Revival

More: For another classic biography of a man of prayer, try *Rees Howells, Intercessor* by Norman Grubb (CLC, 1997).

Crabb, Larry.

The PAPA Prayer. Thomas Nelson, 2006. 202 pp. ISBN 1591454247.

The PAPA prayer is about relational prayer. This book focuses on getting God, not getting something from God. Larry Crabb's goal is to provide "a plan for restoring relationship with God to its place at the center or your life." "Relational prayer," he says, "is the center of all true prayer." Asking for things (petitionary prayer) is important, he suggests, but it comes after relational prayer. Crabb encourages Christians to consider how they think about God. Can a believer really say to God, "I see You as more eager to be close to me than I am to be close to You"? With healing words, Crabb helps readers present themselves to God and remove any blocks that stand in the way of their relationship with God. Crabb is a well-known psychologist, writer, and director of NewWay Ministries.

Subject: Prayer

More: Larry Crabb has also written *The Pressure's Off: There's a New Way to Live* (WaterBrook, 2004).

Eastman, Dick.

No Easy Road: Discover the Extraordinary Power of Personal Prayer. 30th Anniversary revised edition. Chosen, 2003 (Baker, 1971). 158 pp. ISBN 0800793366.

In this book, designed to inspire readers to pray, Dick Eastman tells stories and quotes the words of famous praying men and women such as Billy Bray, John "Praying Hyde" Hyde, Mary Slessor, and George Müller. Eastman also describes the challenges and the rewards of persisting in prayer. He shares many tales of godly people who chose holiness and intercession instead of comfort and unbelief. Eastman is president of Every Home for Christ, an evangelism ministry based in Colorado Springs. This book was first published in 1971.

Subject: Prayer

More: Eastman has also written *The Hour That Changes the World* (Chosen Books, 2002), which provides a step-by-step plan for guiding people through sixty minutes of prayer. Another inspiring and instructional book on prayer is *The Kneeling Christian* (Zondervan, 1986), which was written sometime before the 1930s by an "unknown Christian."

Finney, Charles G., and Louis Gifford Parkhurst.

Principles of Prayer. Revised edition. Bethany, 2001 (1980). 128 pp. ISBN 076422476X.

This book is a collection of Charles Finney's writings on prayer. There are forty short (one- or two-page) chapters making it fit for a daily devotional. Finney (1792–1875) was one of America's most famous revivalists; he was a leader in the Second Great Awakening in America. Louis Gifford Parkhurst, Jr., compiled and edited the selections.

Subjects: Classics, Daily Devotionals, Prayer

More: *How to Pray* by R. A. Torrey (Whitaker House, 1983) is another brief and straightforward guide to prayer. Torrey (1856–1928) was an American evangelist who worked alongside D. L. Moody and became superintendent of Moody Bible Institute and pastor of the Moody Church in Chicago.

Foster, Richard.

Prayer: Finding the Heart's True Home. HarperSanFrancisco, 1992. 288 pp. ISBN 0060628464.

God invites us, says Richard Foster, to come home to His heart. Foster shows readers how to do this as he examines various kinds of prayer, including formation prayer, covenant prayer, adoration, rest, sacramental prayer, meditative and contemplative prayer, petitionary prayer, intercessory prayer, and several others. Foster, a Quaker, writer, and teacher, is the founder of Renovaré, a Christian renewal organization.

Subjects: Award Winners (ECPA, CT), Prayer

Greig, Pete, and Dave Roberts.

Red Moon Rising: How 24-7 Prayer Is Awakening a Generation. Relevant Books, 2003. 255 pp. ISBN 0972927662.

Pete Greig is the founder of 24-7 Prayer, a prayer movement that began in 1999 in England and has spread to sixty-five nations. In this book, Greig discusses the 24-7 movement—how it started and how it grew. He also talks about the people whose lives have been changed by prayer, including orphans, drug addicts, and prostitutes. Greig writes about setbacks, discouragement, and failure, as well as new beginnings, successes, and miracles.

Subject: Prayer

Guyon, Madame.

Experiencing the Depths of Jesus Christ. Seedsowers, 1981. 160 pp. ISBN 0940232006.

Jeanne-Marie Bouvier de la Motte-Guyon (1648–1717) was a French Catholic mystic whose works have been enjoyed by Catholics and Protestants. This classic book, originally titled *A Short and*

Easy Method of Prayer, caused Madame Guyon to be jailed, as Catholic leaders of the day considered it heretical. Guyon shows readers how to experience uninterrupted prayer. "Nothing is so easily obtained," says Guyon, "as the possession and enjoyment of God. He is more present to us than we are to ourselves. He is more desirous of giving Himself to us than we are to possess Him."

Subjects: Catholics, Classics, Mystics, Prayer

More: *The Autobiography of Jeanne Guyon* (Seedsowers, 2002). Readers may also enjoy *The Practice of the Presence of God* by Brother Lawrence (Whitaker House, 1982). Brother Lawrence (1611–1691) was a Carmelite monk in Paris.

Hayford, Jack W., and S. David Moore.

The Charismatic Century: The Enduring Impact of the Azusa Street Revival. Warner Faith, 2006. 313 pp. ISBN 0446578134.

This is a readable history of the Pentecostal and Charismatic movements in America that spanned the twentieth century. Hayford, a well-known leader in the Charismatic Movement and the founder of Church on the Way in California and of Kings' Seminary, chronicles the three "waves" of renewal. The first wave started with the Azusa Street Revival at the turn of the twentieth century in Los Angeles, when a group of people were baptized in the Holy Spirit and started speaking in tongues. The second wave, known as the Charismatic Renewal, came after World War II and blossomed in the 1960s. Church members from many denominations (Catholics, Presbyterians, Episcopalians, etc.) were baptized in the Holy Spirit and also began speaking in tongues. The third wave became apparent during the 1980s, with the Vineyard Movement and the Toronto Blessing.

Subjects: Charismatic Renewal, Church History, Pentecostalism, Revival

More: Another excellent study of the same subject is Vinson Synan's *Century of the Holy Spirit: 100 Years of Pentecostal and Charismatic Renewal, 1901–2001* (Nelson, 2001). Synan traces the roots of Pentecostalism in *The Holiness-Pentecostal Tradition: Charismatic Movements in the Twentieth Century* (Eerdmans, 1997).

Hybels, Bill.

Too Busy Not to Pray: Slowing Down to Be with God. 10th Anniversary revised and expanded edition. InterVarsity, 1998 (1988). 191 pp. ISBN 0830819711.

Bill Hybels, pastor of the noted Willow Creek Community Church near Chicago, writes about the presence and power of God, forming good prayer habits, and learning how to listen to and be led by God. He also discusses hindrances to prayer and unanswered prayer. In clear and direct prose, Hybels addresses those who are somewhat new to prayer, offering guidance and support. His pastoral wisdom, years of experience, and interesting storytelling make this a practical and useful guide.

Subject: Prayer

More: Another classic book on prayer written by a pastor is *Prayer Is Invading the Impossible* by Jack Hayford (Bridge-Logos, 2002). Hayford's book (first published in 1977) shows readers how every desperate and seemingly hopeless situation can be changed by prayer.

Johnstone, Patrick, and Jason Mandryk.

Operation World: When We Pray God Works. 6th Edition. Paternoster, 2001 (Dorothea Mission, 1974). 798 pp. ISBN 1850783578.

This guide to praying for every nation on the planet, arranged alphabetically by country, lists key background information, including geography, population, economy, politics, religion, and missionary statistics. The authors specify what God is doing in each country and their urgent prayer needs. The book also includes a prayer calendar that makes it easy to pray through the world in a year. One source for statistical information is the landmark reference work, *World Christian Encyclopedia*.

Subjects: Award Winners (ECPA), Geography—Christianity, Missions, Prayer, Statistics—Christianity

More: There are two similar books for children and teens. *Window on the World: Prayer Atlas for Children* by Daphne Spraggett and Jill Johnstone (Authentic, 2007) is a full-color guide to praying for about 100 countries and people groups. It has a beautiful layout, interesting facts, and prayer ideas. *A Call to Prayer: For the Children, Teens, and Young Adults of the 10/40 Window* by Beverly Pegues and Nancy Huff (YWAM, 2002) includes engaging narratives, basic geographic facts, and helpful prayer suggestions for sixty-six nations from "West Africa through the Middle East to Eastern Asia." For more statistical information related to Christianity and world religion, see the impressive *World Christian Encyclopedia: A Comparative Survey of Churches and Religions in the Modern World* by David B. Barrett, George T. Kurian, and Todd M. Johnson (Oxford University Press, 2001).

Kreeft, Peter.

Prayer: The Great Conversation: Straight Answers to Tough Questions About Prayer. Ignatius Press, 1991. 178 pp. ISBN 0898703573.

For those who are new to prayer, Peter Kreeft's book gives a practical and down-to-earth introduction. The book is in the format of a dialogue between Chris and Sal (a conversation that began in Kreeft's book *Yes or No?: Straight Answers to Tough Questions About Christianity* (Ignatius Press, 1991). In the beginning of the book, Chris says, "The essence of Christianity is a lived relationship with God, a love affair with God." Kreeft goes on to show how readers can pursue this relationship through prayer. Peter Kreeft is a writer and a professor of philosophy at Boston College.

Subjects: Catholics, Prayer

More: Rosalind Rinker's *Learning Conversational Prayer* (Liturgical Press, 1992) would be a great companion to Kreeft's book. Another simple but excellent book on prayer is Catherine Marshall's *Adventures in Prayer* (Chosen, 2002).

Lewis, C. S.

Letters to Malcolm: Chiefly on Prayer. Harvest Books, 2002 (1964). 132 pp. ISBN 0156027666.

This is a collection of twenty-two letters to an imaginary friend about prayer and theological issues like heaven, the Resurrection, and liturgy. Lewis discusses different types of prayer, deals with practical concerns like when and where to pray, and offers food for thought for the philosophically minded.

Subjects: Prayer, Theology

Lockyer, Herbert.

All the Prayers of the Bible. Zondervan, 1990 (1959). 304 pp. ISBN 0310281210.

Herbert Lockyer (1886–1984), a British minister associated with the Keswick Higher Life Movement, lived in the United States for about the last forty years of his life. In this book, which is part of the All Series, Lockyer discusses every mention of prayer in the Bible, starting in Genesis and going through to Revelations. He presents the text of the scripture (King James Version) and follows that with his brief teaching.

Subject: Bible, Prayer

More: This book is part of a series of twenty-one books that started in 1958 with *All the Men in the Bible* (Zondervan, 1988). Other titles include *All the Parables of the Bible* (Zondervan, 1988), *All the Promises of the Bible* (Zondervan, 1990), and *All the Messianic Prophecies of the Bible* (Zondervan, 1988).

Maxwell, John.

Partners in Prayer: How to Revolutionize Your Church with a Team Prayer Strategy. Thomas Nelson, 1996. 179 pp. ISBN 0785274391.

Pastor, leadership expert, and founder of INJOY, John Maxwell describes personal prayer, praying for others, and prayer for church and leadership. Using examples from history and his own life, Maxwell says that behind every great leader or church there are praying people—intercessors and prayer teams. He shows how to build prayer teams for local churches and includes sample letters, charts, and calendars. He also includes practical information for planning prayer-partner retreats and breakfasts.

Subjects: Prayer Teams

More: C. Peter Wagner goes more in-depth about how churches can harness the power of prayer in his book *Churches That Pray: How Prayer Can Help Revitalize Your Congregation and Break Down the Walls Between Your Church and Your Community* (Regal, 1993). Wagner also wrote a book dealing specifically with praying for pastors and leaders: *Prayer Shield: How to Intercede for Pastors, Christian Leaders, and Others on the Spiritual Frontlines* (Regal, 1992). Also try *The Prayer Saturated Church: A Comprehensive Handbook for Prayer Leaders* by Cheryl Sacks (NavPress, 2007).

Meyer, Joyce.

The Power of Simple Prayer: How to Talk with God about Everything. FaithWords, 2007. 299 pp. ISBN 0446531960.

Joyce Meyer is a well-known Charismatic Bible teacher who gets her message out through speaking, writing, and radio and television shows. Her books have been *New York Times* best sellers. In *The Power of Simple Prayer*, Meyer shows readers that prayer is not meant to be difficult or mysterious. Simple prayers, she says, can be effective. She describes prayer as an unfolding relationship with God and a powerful weapon to defeat the enemy; and she discusses praise, worship, and thanksgiving. In addition, Meyer explains to readers what it means to commit oneself to God's ways. As with many of her books, the author includes wisdom for emotional healing concerning anxiety, worry, complaining, destructive attitudes, and interpersonal relationships.

Subject: Prayer

More: For more books by Meyer on similar topics, try *How to Hear from God: Learn to Know His Voice and Make the Right Decisions* (FaithWords, 2003) and the best-selling *Battlefield of the Mind* (FaithWords, 2002).

Murray, Andrew.

With Christ in the School of Prayer. Hendrickson, 2007 (Revell, 1895). 288 pp. ISBN 1598561707.

Andrew Murray (1828–1917), a Scottish pastor and devotional writer who resided in South Africa, wrote on many topics, including Christ and prayer, the Holy Spirit, unbelief, persevering in prayer, obedience, boldness, and more. First published in 1895, this classic book on prayer can be used as a daily devotional since it is arranged into thirty-one readings—each about five or six pages long. An appendix contains a section called "George Müller and the Secret of His Power in Prayer."

Subjects: Classics, Daily Devotionals, Prayer

More: For those who are put off by Murray's antiquated language, try *Teach Me to Pray* (Bethany, 2002). This is the same book as *With Christ in the School of Prayer*, but the language is updated for modern readers. For more by Murray on prayer, try *The Ministry of Intercession* (Bethany, 2003).

Nee, Watchman.

Let Us Pray. Christian Fellowship Publishers, 1977. 87 pp. ISBN 0935008268.

In this short book, Watchman Nee (1903–1972) explores praying according to God's will and the impact of prayer on Satan's kingdom. Nee was a House Church minister in China; translations of his writings and messages have become popular in the United States. In 1952, he was imprisoned by the Chinese government for his faith. He remained jailed until his death twenty years later.

Subject: Prayer

More: *Crafted Prayer: The Joy of Always Getting Your Prayers Answered* by Graham Cooke (Chosen, 2004) shows readers how to find God's will for a particular situation and then "craft" a faith-building prayer. Another book by Nee, *The Release of the Spirit* (Christian Fellowship Publishers, 2000), shows readers the need for the "outer man" (that is, the soul) to be broken so believers can walk with the Holy Spirit.

Omartian, Stormie.

The Power of a Praying Husband. Harvest House, 2007 (2001). 224 pp. ISBN 0736919767.

This practical book for men is intended to inspire and guide them to pray for their wives. In each of the twenty brief chapters, readers will find a prayer relevant to that chapter's subject. Omartian shows readers how to pray for their spouse's spirit, emotions, motherhood, moods, sexuality, purpose, fears, and so on. She includes advice and personal stories from well-known men like Neil T. Anderson, Steven Curtis Chapman, Jack Hayford, and others.

Subject: Award Winners (ECPA), Marriage—Prayer, Prayer

More: Omartian wrote a similar book (which actually came out first) for women called *The Power of a Praying Wife* (Harvest, 1997).

Also try *Loving Your Spouse Through Prayer: How to Pray God's Word into Your Marriage* by Cheri Fuller (Thomas Nelson, 2007).

Pratney, Winkie.

Revival: Principles to Change the World. Christian Life Books, 2002 (Whitaker, 1983). 288 pp. ISBN 1931393036.

In this book (first published in 1983), author, speaker, and youth minister Winkie Pratney sweeps through the fascinating history of revival. He describes various historical time periods like the Reformation, the Great Awakenings, and the Welsh revival, offering mini-biographies of people like Martin Luther, Ulrich Zwingli, John Calvin, John Wesley, Jonathan Edwards, Charles Finney, D. L. Moody, and Evan Roberts. Pratney also touches on the healing revival of the 1950s and the charismatic renewal of the 1960s. Throughout the book, he examines history and asks questions about how and why revival comes, leaves, and returns again.

Subjects: Church History, Revival

More: For a whole book on the famous Welsh revival, try *The Great Revival in Wales* by Solomon Benjamin Shaw (Christian Life Books, 2002). This book, first published in 1905, includes photographs and contemporary testimonies from people like F. B. Meyer, G. Campbell Morgan, and R. A. Torrey. Also try Charles Finney's *Lectures on Revivals of Religion* (Alethea in Heart Ministries, 2005).

Ravenhill, Leonard.

Why Revival Tarries. Bethany House, 2004 (1959). 176 pp. ISBN 0764229052.

Leonard Ravenhill (1907–1994) was a British evangelist and author who moved to America around 1950. In this stirring and searing book (first published in 1959), Ravenhill issues a wake-up call to a pleasure-loving church filled with drowsy ministers. Says Ravenhill, "Bible schools don't teach 'tears.' They really cannot, of course. This is Spirit-taught; and a preacher, however weighed down with degrees and doctorates, has not gotten far unless he knows soul-bitterness over the sin of this day." Why does revival tarry? A lack of prayer has something to do with it. Another quote from Ravenhill: "At the judgment seat the most embarrassing thing the believer will face will be the smallness of his praying."

Subjects: Classics, Prayer, Revival

More: For more by Ravenhill, try *Revival Praying: An Urgent and Powerful Message for the Family of Christ* (Bethany, 2005).

Sheets, Dutch.

Authority in Prayer: Praying with Power and Purpose. Bethany, 2007. 192 pp. ISBN 0764204068.

Dutch Sheets, a speaker, writer, and pastor in Colorado Springs, says there is a power struggle over who will spiritually govern the people and events in this world. According to Sheets, Satan has staked his claim and seeks to influence people with his evil intent; but God has other plans. Jesus came to destroy the power of the enemy, Sheets says, and we can stand in that authority to do God's will to bring life and truth and freedom to the people God sends us to. Sheets shows how—in the name of the King of kings—believers have kingly authority.

Subjects: Prayer, Spiritual Warfare

More: For another book on the believer's authority in Christ, try *Praying with Authority* by Barbara Wentroble (Regal, 2003). Sheets has written other books on prayer, including *Intercessory Prayer* (Regal, 1996) and *Releasing the Prophetic Destiny of a Nation*, cowritten with Chuck D. Pierce (Destiny Image, 2005), and *How to Pray for Lost Loved Ones* (Gospel Light, 2001).

Sittser, Jerry.

When God Doesn't Answer Your Prayer: Insights to Keep You Praying with Greater Faith and Deeper Hope. Zondervan, 2007 (2003). 216 pp. ISBN 0310272688.

Although he had prayed that very day for their protection, Gerald Sittser lost his daughter, his wife, and his mother in one car wreck. What happened? Why does God not answer prayers? Sittser shares many stories from his own life, the Bible, and history, as he deals with this difficult subject. The message he offers is not simplistic, but it is full of hope and faith.

Subjects: Award Winners (ECPA), Grief, Prayer

More: *God on Mute: Engaging the Silence of Unanswered Prayer* by Pete Greig (Regal, 2007) was written after Greig struggled for his wife's life after a diagnosis of a debilitating brain tumor.

Smith, Alice.

Beyond the Veil: Entering into Intimacy with God Through Prayer. Gospel Light, 1997. 201 pp. ISBN 0830720707.

This is a book for intercessors and for those wondering if they are called to intercession. Focusing on the believer's personal and intimate relationship with God, Alice Smith offers personal stories and foundational Bible teaching about intercessory prayer. She is the prayer coordinator of the U.S. Prayer Track of the A.D. 2000 & Beyond Movement and Mission America.

Subjects: Intercessory Prayer, Prayer

Yancey, Philip.

Prayer: Does It Make Any Difference? Zondervan, 2006. 351 pp. ISBN 0310271053.

Philip Yancey, award-winning Christian writer and editor-at-large for *Christianity Today* magazine, explores the mystery of prayer. Even though Yancey was raised as a Christian, he does not approach the subject as an expert, but as an investigator who earnestly and honestly wants to know God and learn more about prayer. He shares the personal prayer experiences and cultural encounters he has had in his international travels. Asking hard questions about unanswered prayers and requests for physical healing, Yancey discusses the nature of prayer, the practice of prayer, and the difference that prayer makes.

Subjects: Award Winners (CT), Prayer

More: *Deepening Your Conversation with God: Learning to Love to Pray* by Ben Patterson (Bethany, 2001) explores prayer, fasting, and spiritual growth with a down-to-earth and welcoming style. It is geared toward pastors but can be helpful to anyone.

Spiritual Warfare

This section covers a relatively new area of interest and Christian publishing called spiritual warfare. What is spiritual warfare? Spiritual warfare has to do with the conflict between God's kingdom and enemy (demonic) forces. Many Christians believe that sickness, poverty, and other societal ills are often caused by sinful human choices and demonic activity. Spiritual warfare, therefore, involves seeking God's forgiveness for sinful human choices and His assistance in destroying the work of the enemy, Satan. Much of the battle in spiritual warfare is accomplished through prayer and worship.

The phrase "spiritual warfare" comes from one of Paul's letters in the New Testament—2 Corinthians 10:4—which says "for the weapons of our warfare are not of the flesh, but divinely powerful for the destruction of fortresses." Paul explains more in his letter to the Ephesians (Chapter 6, verses 11–12) when he says, "Put on the full armor of God so that you can take your stand against the devil's schemes. For our struggle is not against flesh and blood, but against the rulers, against the authorities, against the powers of this dark world and against the spiritual forces of evil in the heavenly realms."

In the gospels, there is a passage where Jesus cast out demons that were causing disease in people. Jesus gave authority to his followers to do the same. Even today, people "war" with spiritual forces; lately there have been many books written and published on this subject, which includes deliverance (that is, casting out demons or exorcism) and divine healing. This subject even appears in fiction. Frank E. Peretti's bestselling 1986 novel, *This Present Darkness,* was a landmark in Christian fiction publishing; its main theme, like many of his books, is spiritual warfare.

Alves, Elizabeth.

Becoming a Prayer Warrior: A Guide to Effective and Powerful Prayer. Revised edition. Regal, 2003 (1998). 216 pp. ISBN 0830731288.

Elizabeth Alves, founder and president of Intercessors International, discusses different kinds of prayer (confession, petition, intercession, etc.), how to hear God's voice (what do people mean when they say "God spoke to me?"), and journaling. The last portion of the book focuses on spiritual warfare, discussing the nature of the battle, the tactics of the enemy, and the Christian weapons of warfare (faith, obedience, prayer, fasting, praise, the Word of God, and so on).

Subjects: Intercessory Prayer, Prayer, Spiritual Warfare

More: *A Woman's Guide to Spiritual Warfare* by Quin Sherrer and Ruthanne Garlock (Vine, 2004).

Dawson, John.

Taking Our Cities for God: How to Break Spiritual Strongholds. Revised and updated edition. Charisma House, 2001 (1989). 224 pp. ISBN 0884197646.

This is a landmark book that shows people how to transform their communities and cities for Christ. John Dawson lived for decades in a neighborhood infamous for gang violence and mass arrests. What creates such an atmosphere of despair and hopelessness? Dawson says the problem and the solution are spiritual. Claiming that each city has a God-given purpose for being, he says, "Determining your city's redemptive gift is even more important than discerning the nature of evil principalities." To this end, Dawson writes about spiritual mapping, identificational repentance and reconciliation, prayer walking, and more. Dawson (son of well-known Bible teacher Joy Dawson) helped found the International Reconciliation Coalition. He is currently the international president of YWAM.

Subjects: Community Transformation, Spiritual Warfare, Urban Missions

More: For more on identificational repentance, try *Father Forgive Us* by Jim Goll (Destiny Image, 1999) and John Dawson's *Healing America's Wounds* (Regal, 1994).

Jackson, John Paul.

Needless Casualties of War. Streams Publishing House, 1999. 147 pp. ISBN 158483000X.

Jackson warns readers that presumptuous spiritual warfare prayers can be harmful. Several female intercessors—all from a certain church—approached Jackson wondering why they were miscarrying their babies. It turns out that these ladies had taken it upon themselves to proclaim spiritual war over demonic principalities relating to abortion in a certain city. Jackson sought God for an answer and learned that "to attack principalities and powers over a geographical area can be as useless as throwing hatchets at the moon. And it can leave you open to unforeseen and unperceived attacks." These intercessors proclaimed their own battle and lost—they attacked a spirit of abortion and lost their own unborn children to miscarriage. This book is an eye-opening corrective for today's intercessors.

Subject: Spiritual Warfare

Jacobs, Cindy.

Possessing the Gates of the Enemy: A Training Manual for Militant Intercession. 2nd Edition. Chosen, 1994 (1991). 271 pp. ISBN 0800792238.

This book is a classic on the subject of intercessory prayer. Cindy Jacobs gives practical guidelines for intercession and helpful explanations of different concepts like breaking yokes, tearing down strongholds, binding and loosing, supplication, travailing, and more. She discusses various types of intercession like prophetic intercession, intercessory praise, corporate intercession, personal prayer partners, prayer watches, and prayer walks. She also warns readers against some unhealthy types of intercession that she has encountered in her experience.

Subjects: Intercessory Prayer, Prayer, Spiritual Warfare

More: For another book on this topic, try *Intercession, Thrilling and Fulfilling* by Joy Dawson (YWAM, 1997).

Kraft, Charles H.

Defeating Dark Angels: Breaking Demonic Oppression in the Believer's Life. Vine, 1992. 254 pp. ISBN 0830734120.

In this book about finding emotional and spiritual freedom for Christians, Charles Kraft rejects showmanship and dramatic exorcisms. Instead, he believes that "getting rid of demons is a normal part of the Christian life." Kraft, a professor at Fuller Theological Seminary, explains how people become demonized and how they can break free. Freedom involves more than just getting rid of demons; it also involves inner healing. Kraft also talks about the spiritual authority and power that Christians have—and often don't utilize. In a helpful question-and-answer section at the end of the book, Kraft reveals specifics about how he handles deliverance ministry.

Subjects: Deliverance, Inner Healing

More: Charles Kraft has a more recent book titled *I Give You Authority* (Baker, 1997), which shows believers how to walk in spiritual authority. For instance, fathers and mothers have authority over their homes—that often goes unused—to protect and bless their children and property. For more information about inner healing, try *Transforming the Inner Man: God's Powerful Principles for Inner Healing and Lasting Life Change* by John Loren Sandford and Paula Sandford (Charisma House, 2007).

MacNutt, Francis.

Healing. Revised and expanded silver anniversary edition. Ave Maria Press, 1999 (1974). 268 pp. ISBN 0877936765.

Francis MacNutt brings a balanced view and a lifetime of experience to the subject of divine healing—both physical and emotional. In fact, this is a classic book on the subject (first published in 1974). While sharing many stories of healing (bladder hernia, back pain, drug addiction, eczema, and more), MacNutt teaches what the Bible says about salvation and healing, faith, forgiveness, inner healing, and deliverance. He also examines twelve reasons why people are not healed. MacNutt's theology is favorable to Catholics (he is a former priest) and Protestants alike. Francis and Judith MacNutt are directors of Christian Healing Ministries in Jacksonville, Florida.

Subjects: Deliverance, Healing

More: For a much shorter book on the topic of healing, which also serves as a great introduction to the subject, try Francis MacNutt's *The Prayer That Heals: Praying for Healing in the Family* (Ave Maria, 2000). For more about deliverance by MacNutt, see *Deliverance from Evil Spirits: A Practical Manual* (Chosen, 1995). *The Healing Reawakening: Reclaiming Our Lost Inheritance* by Francis MacNutt (Chosen, 2006) talks about divine healing in Christianity throughout world history. For the first 300 years of church history, healing was "normal," but at other times healing has almost disappeared and has even been rejected by Christians. Today, MacNutt says, healing is on the rise again.

Malone, Henry.

Shadow Boxing: The Dynamic 2-5-14 Strategy to Defeat the Darkness Within. Vision Life Ministries, 1999. 175 pp. ISBN 1888103167.

As a young pastor, Henry Malone tired of hiding the many sins that beset him—anger, jealousy, and lust. He cried out to God to be delivered and his prayers were answered. In this book, Malone discusses his thirty years of experience in helping people find freedom. He shares his "2-5-14 strategy," which refers to the two general ways Satan has access to people's lives (invasion and invitation), the five specific doors through which Satan gains legal access, or permission, to people's lives (ancestral curses, disobedience, unforgiveness, emotional trauma, and inner vows/judgments), and the fourteen evil spirits that the Bible names specifically (including infirmity, fear, divination, lying, error, and so on). This book contains stories of people set free from abuse, fear, murder, suicide, seizures, accidents, multiple personality disorder, adultery, scoliosis, and more. Malone desires to see every person come to know what Jesus said in Luke 4:18: "The spirit of the Lord is upon me, because he anointed me to preach the gospel to the poor. He has sent me to proclaim release to the captives, and recovery of sight to the blind, to set free those who are oppressed."

Subjects: Deliverance, Spiritual Warfare

More: *How to Minister Freedom: Helping Others Break the Bonds of Sexual Brokenness, Emotional Woundedness, Demonic Oppression and Occult Bondage* edited by Doris Wagner (Regal, 2005). This book is a collection of short chapters written by several authors on topics like: "Can a Christian have a demon?," spiritual housecleaning, deliverance and revival, rejection, bitter-root judgments, fear, trauma, and more. Also by Doris Wagner is *How to Cast Out Demons: A Guide to the Basics* (Renew Books, 2000).

Moore, Beth.

Praying God's Word: Breaking Free from Spiritual Strongholds. B&H Publishing, 2000. 352 pp. ISBN 0805423516.

This topical prayer guide is intended to help people overcome a variety of issues like unbelief, pride, insecurity, rejection, addiction, food issues, loss, unforgiveness, depression, sexual problems, and other issues. Beth Moore briefly discusses each topic, gives appropriate scriptures, and guides the reader through actual prayers. Moore is a well-known writer and popular Bible teacher from Houston, Texas.

Subjects: Bible, Deliverance, Prayer, Spiritual Warfare

More: This book is a companion to Moore's *Breaking Free* (B&H Publishing, 2007). A similar book by Moore is *Get Out of That Pit:*

Straight Talk about God's Deliverance (Thomas Nelson, 2007). Another well-known book on this subject is Neil T. Anderson's *The Bondage Breaker: Overcoming Negative Thoughts, Irrational Feelings, and Habitual Sins* (Harvest House, 2006).

Otis, George, Jr.

Informed Intercession. Renew, 1999. 276 pp. ISBN 0830719377.

How do you transform a community through prayer? In this book, George Otis, Jr., explains the innovative concept of spiritual mapping, which can aid in such a community transformation. Spiritual mapping uses geographic and historic research to provide intercessors with "spiritual intelligence." For example, suppose a group of people get together to pray for Eritrea. Their prayer time would not get very far unless they know something about Eritrea (it is a country in East Africa with two dominant religions: Sunni Islam and Oriental Orthodox Christianity). But spiritual mapping goes deeper; it seeks to identify the spiritual forces and demonic strongholds at work in a community's midst. This information, collected through prayer-walking profiles, special briefings, neighborhood and regional reports, helps the prayer team understand prevailing social bondages of the area and how they happened. In short, spiritual mapping shows intercessors how to pray.

Subjects: Community Transformation, Intercessory Prayer, Spiritual Mapping, Spiritual Warfare

More: George Otis, Jr., wrote a book on a similar topic dealing with territorial spirits called *The Twilight Labyrinth: Why Does Spiritual Darkness Linger Where It Does?* (Chosen, 1997). He also made a series of documentary videos (*Transformations* and *Transformations II* are the first two) showing actual communities and cities that have been radically transformed by the gospel and successful spiritual warfare. For another notable book on spiritual mapping and community transformation, try *Taking Our Cities for God: How to Break Spiritual Strongholds* by John Dawson (Charisma, 2001).

Pierce, Chuck D., and Rebecca Wagner Sytsema.

Protecting Your Home from Spiritual Darkness. Regal, 2004. 111 pp. ISBN 0830736379.

Chuck Pierce and Rebecca Sytsema show how the things brought into the home can affect lives spiritually. For example, a woman named Cathy was continually plagued by gloom and depression. A prayerful investigation of her house led the authors to a certain book on Cathy's shelf—a handbook for thirty-second-degree Masons. Once this book was destroyed and Masonic curses in her family were dealt with, the authors say, Cathy experienced freedom from the gloom and depression. Pierce and Sytsema also discuss land and property like buildings, which can harbor evil spirits that bring darkness and calamity. The authors show readers how to pray through each room of their house.

Subjects: Deliverance, Houses—Prayer, Spiritual Warfare

More: Two other books on this topic are *Protect Your Home and Family from Spiritual Pollution* by Alice and Eddie Smith (Regal, 2003) and *Portals to Cleansing* by Henry Malone (Vision Life Ministries, 2002). For a more thorough treatment of the principles involved here, try Charles Kraft's *I Give You Authority* (Baker, 1997).

Sherman, Dean, and Bill Payne.

Spiritual Warfare for Every Christian. YWAM Publishing, 1995. 216 pp. ISBN 0927545055.

More than twenty years of experience as a missionary fighting spiritual battles went into this practical and balanced book on spiritual warfare. Dean Sherman takes the mystery and fear out of this sometimes-unbalanced topic. He reminds readers that they are in the battle whether they like it or not. He explains the battleground, the tactics of the enemy, and how to use God-given authority. One of the main reasons for spiritual warfare is evangelism—freeing souls from death, darkness, and destruction so they can live in God's light and life. Sherman encourages readers that "Jesus in us does not shrivel up when confronted by oppression." When it comes to Satan versus God, Satan doesn't have a chance. A twelve-episode video series of Sherman's teachings on spiritual warfare is available. He has worked with YWAM since 1967. He serves as the international dean for the College of Christian Ministries in YWAM's University of the Nations.

Subject: Spiritual Warfare

More: For a more in-depth study on this subject, Ed Murphy has a comprehensive, 626-page manual titled *The Handbook for Spiritual Warfare* (Thomas Nelson, 2003).

Smith, Alice.

Delivering the Captives: Overcoming the Strongman and Finding Victory in Christ. Bethany, 2006. 192 pp. ISBN 076420291X.

Alice Smith asserts the ministry of deliverance as valid for all Christians. Discussing her many experiences in helping people find freedom from demonic oppression and possession, she explains how demonic strongholds are built and how they are torn down. She also writes about curses, yokes, and false covenants. Smith says that spirits often come in groups; therefore, she includes an appendix that lists apparent demonic groupings to aid those involved with ministering deliverance. Other appendices give sample prayers for renouncing freemasonry, false religion, and other possibly demonic influences.

Subjects: Spiritual Warfare, Deliverance

More: British author and Bible teacher Derek Prince shares biblical teaching and decades of personal experience ministering deliverance in *They Shall Expel Demons: What You Need to Know About Demons—Your Invisible Enemies* (Chosen, 1998).

Worship

The root of the word "worship" means "worth." Worship refers to giving God, the being of all "worth," one's honor, devotion, and reverence. Christians worship God by living their lives according to the Bible. They also worship God by offering prayers, singing songs, playing musical instruments, and even dancing. A Christian "worship service," therefore, usually includes music.

Included in this section are books that give advice on leading worship services, books that tell stories of favorite hymns, and books on worshipful dance (an often overlooked or neglected way to praise and worship God). Several inspirational books by popular contemporary worship songwriters such as Matt Redman and Tim Hughes are also annotated in this section.

Hughes, Tim.

Here I Am to Worship. Regal, 2004. 166 pp. ISBN 0830733221.

Tim Hughes, an award-winning songwriter from England, and the worship director at Holy Trinity Brompton in London, addresses other musicians, worship leaders, and worshipers. He gives practical tips for leading a band, creating a song list, small-group worship, and song writing. He reminds readers that worship is their highest calling, and it isn't about music or songs—it's about Jesus. Quoting John Wimber, Hughes says, "The difficulty will not be so much in the writing of new and great music; the test will be in the godliness of those who deliver it." Hughes also leads worship for Soul Survivor events.

Subjects: Worship, Worship Leading

More: Mike Pilavachi is the cofounder and leader of Soul Survivor. One of his books is *For the Audience of One* (Regal, 2005). Readers also may be interested in *The Worship God Is Seeking: An Exploration of Worship and the Kingdom of God* by David Ruis (Regal, 2005).

Osbeck, Kenneth.

101 Hymn Stories. Kregel, 1982. 288 pp. ISBN 0825434165.

This book is a collection of inspiring biographical stories about the lives of the men and women who wrote and composed popular hymns. For instance, the hymn "What a Friend We Have in Jesus" was written by Joseph Scriven—not for publication—but as a poem to comfort his seriously ill mother. Scriven was no stranger to grief—his fiancée accidentally drowned the night before their wedding. Scriven did not lose heart, but became a generous man, frequently giving away his possessions and helping those in need around him. For "What a Friend We Have in Jesus" and 100 other hymns, Osbeck gives the full text and musical score along with the names and dates of the authors and composers/arrangers and the tune name and the meter for each hymn.

Subjects: Collective Biography, Hymns, Music, Worship

More: Robert Morgan has a similar collection of hymn stories called *Then Sings My Soul: 150 of the World's Greatest Hymn Stories* (Thomas Nelson, 2003). For Christmas carols and music, try *Stories Behind the Best-Loved Songs of Christmas* by Ace Collins (Zondervan, 2001).

Park, Andy.

To Know You More: Cultivating the Heart of the Worship Leader. InterVarsity, 2004. 272 pp. ISBN 0830832211.

"Becoming a worship leader isn't about the pursuit of a ministry or a career; it's about the pursuit of a person." That's how Andy Park begins his book in which he talks about how he got involved in worship ministry and what it means to be a part of a church community in leadership (including working with pastors). He discusses songwriting, as well as leading a worship service and leading a worship team. Park has been a worship leader for more than twenty-five years. He is a songwriter and a worship leader at North Langley Vineyard Church in Canada.

Subjects: Worship, Worship Leading

More: Kevin Navarro has two books about worship leading: *The Complete Worship Leader* (Baker, 2001) and its follow-up, *The Complete Worship Service: Creating a Taste of Heaven on Earth* (Baker, 2005).

Pierce, Chuck D., and John Dickson.

The Worship Warrior: Ascending in Worship: Descending in War. Regal, 2002. 288 pp. ISBN 0830730567.

Explaining the relationship between worship and spiritual warfare, the authors call upon readers to abandon lifeless traditions and hear the call of God to an intimate and transforming relationship through personal and corporate worship. Christians, they say, have access to the throne room of God. Chuck Pierce and John Dickson urge readers to go up to the throne room through worship; there they will be empowered to do the work and warfare they are called to do on earth.

Subjects: Spiritual Warfare, Worship

More: Chuck Pierce has also written (with Rebecca Wagner Systema) *The Future War of the Church: How We Can Defeat Lawlessness and Bring God's Order to the Earth* (Regal, 2nd ed., 2007).

Redman, Matt.

The Unquenchable Worshipper: Coming Back to the Heart of Worship. Regal, 2001. 126 pp. ISBN 0830729135.

Matt Redman, a British worship leader and songwriter, shares the cry of his heart to love and worship God through hard trials and without reserve. Some of Redman's well-known songs are "Heart of Worship," "Let Everything That Has Breath," "Once Again," "Undignified," "Blessed Be Your Name," and "You Never Let Go." This book is part of a series of books called the Worship Series.

Subject: Worship

More: For more like this, try *The Air I Breathe: Worship As a Way of Life* by Louie Giglio (Multnomah, 2006). Redman has also written *Facedown* (Regal, 2004). For another book in the Worship Series, try *He Knows My Name* by Tommy Walker (Regal, 2004).

Scheer, Greg.

The Art of Worship: A Musician's Guide to Leading Modern Worship. Baker, 2006. 223 pp. ISBN 080106709X.

Greg Scheer, a composer, a choir and music director, and a music associate with the Calvin Institute of Christian Worship, bridges the gap from traditional music ministry to contemporary worship. Stating that the "praise-and-worship" style of church service is here to stay, Scheer shows readers how to assemble and train a worship team. Scheer addresses a host of pertinent issues, including planning a worship service, finding new songs, incorporating hymns, rehearsing, and leading a service. He discusses the role and effective use of vocalists, guitar, piano, bass, drums, keyboards, and more.

Subjects: Music, Worship, Worship Leading

More: Bob Sorge has a well-known book for worship leaders called *Exploring Worship: A Practical Guide to Praise & Worship*

(Oasis House, 1987). Also try *The Worship Leader's Handbook: Practical Answers to Tough Questions* by Tom Kraeuter (Emerald Books, 1999).

Stevenson, Ann.

Restoring the Dance: Seeking God's Order. Destiny Image, 1998. 143 pp. ISBN 1560433051.

Asserting that God created dance, Ann Stevenson discusses the original purpose of dance and the scriptural foundation for dance in worship. In 1987, Stevenson, a licensed minister, dancer, and instructor, started Restored to Glory Dance Ministry and School of Worship. Today, with more than 200 dedicated Christian dancers, it is one of the largest Christian dance ministries in the nation.

Subjects: Dance, Liturgical Dance, Worship

More: Stevenson's newest book is *Dance!* (Destiny Image, 2007). Also try *Dancing into the Anointing: Touching the Heart of God Through Dance* by Aimee Kovacs (Treasure House, 1997). For an introduction to Messianic dance worship, try *Dancing for Joy: A Biblical Approach to Praise & Worship* by Murray Silberling (Messianic Jewish Publishers, 1995). Here are two more titles: *Dance with a Purpose: Dancing in the Church or Dancing in God's Presence* by Sabrina McKenzie (Dance International, 2005) and *Embodied Prayer: Harmonizing Body and Soul* by Celeste Snowber Schroeder (Liguori Publications, 1995).

Tozer, A. W., and Gerald B. Smith, editor.

Whatever Happened to Worship?: A Call to True Worship. WingSpread, 2006 (Christian Publications, 1985). 128 pp. ISBN 1600660169.

This book is taken from a series of messages that A. W. Tozer preached in 1962 called "Worship: The Chief End of Man." Tozer desired to write a book on this subject, but he died before he could do it. Fortunately, the audiotapes from his sermon series were preserved, transcribed, and edited into this book by Gerald B. Smith.

Subject: Worship

More: Readers will want to know about Tozer's most famous books, *The Pursuit of God* (WingSpread, 2007) and *The Knowledge of the Holy* (HarperOne, 1978).

Spiritual Growth Classics

This section gathers classic Christian devotional literature. A number of these titles date back to the fifteenth, sixteenth, and seventeenth centuries. For example, *The Imitation of Christ* has been called the most famous religious work of the Christian world. Written in medieval Latin by a Catholic monk named Thomas à Kempis (1380–1471), it encourages believers to forsake the attractions of this world and to give themselves wholly to God. More recent classics include books by authors such as the Scottish writer who ministered in South Africa, Andrew Murray (1828–1917), C. S. Lewis (1898-1963), and the American preacher A. W. Tozer (1897–1963).

John of the Cross, Saint.

Dark Night of the Soul. Image, 1959. 224 pp. ISBN 0385029306.

    Saint John of the Cross (1542–1591), one of the thirty-three Doctors of the Church, was a Spanish mystic and cofounder (with St. Teresa of Avila) of the Discalced Carmelite Order. In this book, he writes about a union with God that can occur after a purging of the soul that includes times when God seems far away. This type of "dark night," he asserts, is part of the process that leads us closer to God.

    Subjects: Catholics, Classics, Mystics, Spiritual Growth

    More: Iain Matthew examines and helps readers to understand the writings of St. John of the Cross in *The Impact of God: Soundings from St. John of the Cross* (Hodder Headline, 1995). For a book by St. John's contemporary and fellow mystic and Doctor of the Church, St. Teresa of Avila, try *Interior Castle* (Image, 1972). Another classic mystic work (written by an anonymous English monk) is *The Cloud of Unknowing* (Penguin Classics, 2003).

Law, William.

A Serious Call to a Devout and Holy Life. Vintage, 2002. 352 pp. ISBN 0375725636.

    "He, therefore, is the devout man, who lives no longer to his own will, or the way and spirit of the world, but to the sole will of God." This is a quote from the first chapter of this classic book. William Law (1686–1761) was an Anglican priest who had a big impact on the lives of figures in the Great Awakening, including John and Charles Wesley and George Whitefield.

    Subjects: Classics, Spiritual Growth

    More: For more writing by British ministers of this period, try *A Plain Account of Christian Perfection* by John Wesley (Relevant Books, 2006) and *George Whitefield's Journals* (Banner of Truth, 1986).

Lawrence, Brother.

The Practice of the Presence of God. Whitaker House, 1982. 96 pp. ISBN 0883681056.

Brother Lawrence (1611–1691), a Carmelite monk in Paris where he served as a kitchen worker, led a simple life and had an intimate and trusting relationship with God that inspires today's readers. For many years, Brother Lawrence struggled to become wholly God's. This short, classic work is a collection of four conversations and fifteen letters in which Nicholas Herman of Lorraine, better known as Lawrence of the Resurrection, reveals how he turned his life over to God.

Subjects: Classics, Mystics, Spiritual Growth

More: *The Sacrament of the Present Moment* by Jean-Pierre de Caussade (HarperOne, 1989), translated by Kitty Muggeridge, also discusses communion with God in daily life. Jean Pierre de Caussade (1675–1751) was a French Jesuit priest and spiritual director. Also try *Experiencing the Depths of Jesus Christ* by Madam Guyon (Seedsowers, 1981).

Lewis, C. S.

The Weight of Glory. HarperOne, 2001 (Macmillan, 1949). 208 pp. ISBN 0060653205.

This book gathers nine essays that C. S. Lewis delivered as sermons during World War II. In the title essay, Lewis reminds readers that people are immortal and that "the dullest and most uninteresting person you talk to may one day be a creature which, if you saw it now, you would be strongly tempted to worship." Other topics covered in the collection deal with war, pacifism, friendship, and forgiveness.

Subjects: Classics, Essays

More: Another collection of essays by Lewis is called *God in the Dock: Essays on Theology and Ethics* (Eerdmans, 1994). Two more well-known books by Lewis are *The Great Divorce* (HarperOne, 2001), which is an allegorical dream of heaven and hell, and *Miracles* (HarperOne, 2001), which makes room for divine intervention in today's world.

Murray, Andrew.

Abiding in Christ. Bethany, 2003. 192 pp. ISBN 0764227629.

This is one of popular devotional writer Andrew Murray's better-known works. In it, he invites readers to accept all that "Jesus the Vine" has for those who abide in Him. Arranged in thirty-one short chapters, this book is suitable for a daily devotional. Andrew Murray (1828–1917) was a Scottish pastor and devotional writer from South Africa.

Subjects: Classics, Daily Devotionals, Spiritual Growth

More: Murray also wrote *Absolute Surrender* (Bethany, 2003), *Humility* (Bethany, 2001), and *The Blood of Christ* (Bethany, 2001).

Scougal, Henry.

The Life of God in the Soul of Man. Christian Focus, 1996. 159 pp. ISBN 1857921054.

Famous revivalist George Whitefield claimed that this book changed his life. The author, Henry Scougal (1650–1678), was a Puritan minister who died at the young age of twenty-eight. In this short book, Scougal urges people to examine their religion and see if it is true Christianity: "Men are unwilling to quarrel with the religion of their country, and since all their neighbors are Christians, they are content to be so too." He reminds the reader that salvation cannot be purchased with money or good works, but God is loving and willing to save. Scougal writes, "There can be no treaty of peace till once we lay down these weapons of rebellion wherewith we fight against heaven; nor can we expect to have our distempers cured if we be daily feeding on poison." This edition also includes *Rules and Instructions for a Holy Life* by the archbishop of Glasgow, Robert Leighton (1611–1684).

Subjects: Classics, Spiritual Growth

More: For more classic works by Puritans, try *The Doctrine of Repentance* by Thomas Watson (Banner of Truth, 1987). This book, first published in 1668, shows the six ingredients of repentance: sight of sin, sorrow of sin, confession of sin, shame for sin, hatred for sin, and turning from sin. Also see *The Saints' Everlasting Rest* by Richard Baxter (Sovereign Grace Publishers, 2000).

Thomas, à Kempis.

The Imitation of Christ. Penguin Classics, 1952. 217 pp. ISBN 0140440275.

This book has been called the most famous religious work in the Christian world. Written in medieval Latin by a Catholic monk, it encourages believers to forsake the attractions of this world and to give themselves wholly to God. Thomas à Kempis (1380–1471) was born in Germany and died in the Netherlands. Here are some quotes from this classic work: "I would far rather feel contrition than be able to define it." "If you knew the whole Bible by heart, and all the teachings of the philosophers, how would this help you without the grace and love of God?" "Strive to withdraw your heart from the love of visible things, and direct your affections to things invisible." This Penguin edition was translated into English by Leo Sherley-Price, who also wrote the introduction.

Subjects: Catholics, Classics, Mystics, Spiritual Growth

More: *Devotional Classics: Selected Readings for Individuals and Groups*, edited by Richard Foster and James Bryan Smith (HarperOne,

2005), includes fifty-two selections from famous devotional writers old and new like Thomas à Kempis, C. S. Lewis, Thomas Merton, Bernard of Clairvaux, Frank Laubach, Julian of Norwich, Dallas Willard, Charles Spurgeon, and Jeremy Taylor. Another collection by Foster is called *Spiritual Classics: Selected Readings for Individuals and Groups on the Twelve Spiritual Disciplines* (HarperOne, 2000).

Tozer, A. W.

The Pursuit of God. WingSpread, 2007 (Christian Publications, 1948). 121 pp. ISBN 1600660541.

In this classic book, A. W. Tozer explains, "we pursue God because, and only because, He has first put an urge within us that spurs us to the pursuit." Tozer inspires Christians to continue this pursuit because they have been created for this adventure that will bring them into conformity with the likeness of Jesus Christ. Tozer (1897–1963) was a writer, editor, and pastor in Chicago and Toronto.

Subject: Classics, Mystics, Spiritual Growth

More: Another classic by Tozer is *The Knowledge of the Holy* (HarperOne, 1978). Also try Tozer's *The Root of the Righteous* (WingSpread, 2007). *The God Chasers* by Tommy Tenney (Destiny Image, 1999) is a more recent book similar to *The Pursuit of God*. Tenney urges readers not to seek revival but to seek Him.

Discipleship

The word "disciple" literally means "student." In the New Testament, the followers of Jesus were called disciples. Today, discipleship refers to the process by which a Christian seeks to become like Christ by believing and obeying Christ's teachings. Spiritual disciplines are a means to that end; therefore, books on spiritual disciplines (like prayer, fasting, worship, study, etc.) are included in this section.

Bonhoeffer, Dietrich.

The Cost of Discipleship. Touchstone, 1995 (Macmillan, 1959). 320 pp. ISBN 0684815001.

This classic work begins by contrasting costly grace and cheap grace. Cheap grace, a mere mental assent to the love of God and the forgiveness of sins, requires no true repentance or renunciation of the world. Costly grace calls people to give up all to follow Christ. It cost God the life of His son, and it requires our lives as well. That, says Dietrich Bonhoeffer, is the cost of discipleship. The heart of this book is a study of the Sermon on the Mount found in Matthew (Chapters 5–7). Bonhoeffer discusses the call to Christ, the cross, the community of believers, prayer, baptism, and other topics concerning Christian life. Bonhoeffer (1906–1945), a German Lutheran pastor, theologian, and writer, was hanged just before the end of World War II for his involvement in a plot to assassinate Adolf Hitler.

Subjects: Classics, Discipleship, Spiritual Growth

More: Bonhoeffer also wrote *Life Together: The Classic Exploration of Faith in Community* (HarperOne, 1978) and *Letter and Papers from Prison* (Touchstone, 1997), in which he puts forth the idea of "religionless Christianity." The definitive biography of Bonhoeffer, by Eberhard Bethge, is called *Dietrich Bonhoeffer: A Biography* (Fortress, Revised edition, 2000). Also try Gregory Boyd's *Repenting of Religion: Turning from Judgment to the Love of God* (Baker, 2004), which is based on some of Bonhoeffer's ideas about the knowledge of good and evil as found in the book of Genesis.

Cunningham, Loren.

Making Jesus Lord: The Dynamic Power of Laying Down Your Rights. YWAM, 1989. 160 pp. ISBN 1576580121.

One of the main precepts of Christianity is that we have nothing that we have not first received from God. In God's economy, He gives us rights—to family, reputation, ownership of material things, health, and everything else—and then asks us to relinquish them. In this way, we find freedom and a vibrant relationship with God as we learn to trust in Him. Loren Cunningham shares many stories that exemplify these principles from his own life, a life filled with faith, adventures, and miracles of provision. Cunningham is the founder of Youth With A Mission, one of the world's largest missions organizations.

Subjects: Discipleship, Spiritual Growth

More: Cunningham has also written *Is That Really You, God?: Hearing the Voice of God* (YWAM, 2001) and *Daring to Live on the Edge: The Adventure of Faith and Finances* (YWAM, 1992). His most recent book is *The Book That Transforms Nations: How the Bible Can Change Any Country* (YWAM, 2007).

Foster, Richard J.

Celebration of Discipline: The Path to Spiritual Growth. 25th Anniversary edition. HarperOne, 1998 (1978). 256 pp. ISBN 0060628391.

In this classic Christian work, first published almost thirty years ago, Richard Foster explores the spiritual disciplines. "Inward" disciplines include prayer, meditation, fasting, and study. "Outward" disciplines include simplicity, solitude, submission, and service. The "corporate" disciplines include confession, worship, guidance, and celebration. Foster, a Quaker, is the founder of Renovaré, an organization designed to bring renewal to the church.

Subjects: Spiritual Disciplines, Spiritual Growth

More: Foster has also written books that focus on specific disciplines: *Prayer: Finding the Heart's True Home* (HarperOne, 1992) and *Freedom of Simplicity* (HarperOne, 2005). Also try Dallas Willard's *The Spirit of the Disciplines: Understanding How God Changes Lives* (HarperOne, 1991).

Ortberg, John.

The Life You've Always Wanted: Spiritual Disciplines for Ordinary People. Expanded edition. Zondervan, 2002 (1997). 272 pp. ISBN 0310246954.

With down-to-earth language, humorous style, and moving stories, John Ortberg shows readers how to grow spiritually as Christians. God, he says, is calling us to His kingdom and to spiritual transformation. Spiritual disciplines are a conduit of this transformation, so Ortberg writes about the need for joy and gratitude, and the need for solitude and an undivided life. He talks about living a life of servanthood; he shows readers the importance of the confession of sin and forgiveness; and he discusses enduring through times of testing and suffering. Ortberg is the senior pastor of Menlo Park Presbyterian Church in Menlo Park, California.

Subjects: Spiritual Disciplines, Spiritual Growth

More: Ortberg has also written *If You Want to Walk on Water, You've Got to Get Out of the Boat* (Zondervan, 2001), which is about faith and trust in God, and *God Is Closer Than You Think* (Zondervan, 2005), which is about experiencing the presence of God in everyday life.

Pratney, Winkie.

Ultimate CORE: Church on the Radical Edge. Bethany, 2003. 298 pp. ISBN 076422803X. **YA**

This book, aimed at high school/college age readers (although applicable to any believer), answers the question, "What does it mean to be a follower of Jesus?" The overarching goal of the book is to provide foundational, "core" truths for living life as a Christian. Winkie Pratney covers such concepts as being a learner (disciple), hearing God's voice, repentance and restitution, prayer, sexuality, living in today's culture, Bible study, and more. This practical book deals with issues and attitudes that today's teens face: music, media, persecution, purity, forgiveness, pride—it's all here. (*Ultimate CORE* is almost identical in its goal to Pratney's previous book, *Youth Aflame*.)

Subjects: Discipleship, Spiritual Growth, Young-Adult Interest

More: Pratney also wrote *Revival: Principles to Change the World* (Christian Life Books, 2002). Other similar books on discipleship are *Basic Discipleship* by Floyd McClung (InterVarsity, 1992) and *Intimate Friendship with God: Through Understanding the Fear of the Lord* by Joy Dawson (Chosen, 2008).

Willard, Dallas.

The Divine Conspiracy: Rediscovering Our Hidden Life in God. HarperOne, 1998. 448 pp. ISBN 0060693339.

What does it mean to be a disciple of Christ? Is God relevant to people in today's world? Philosopher and theologian Dallas Willard shows readers that conformity to Christ is the forgotten secret to meaning and life—not just for those who died long ago, but for us today; not just for church on Sunday, but in all areas of life. Willard says, "The divine conspiracy refers to God's plan to overcome evil with good on earth—without force—by enlisting people through the ages to build His kingdom among men."

Subjects: Award Winners (CT), Discipleship, Spiritual Growth

More: Dallas Willard has also written *The Spirit of the Disciplines: Understanding How God Changes Lives* (HarperOne, 1991), *Hearing God: Developing a Conversational Relationship with God* (InterVarsity, 1999), and *The Great Omission: Reclaiming Jesus' Essential Teachings on Discipleship* (HarperOne, 2006).

Spiritual Gifts

Spiritual gifts, mentioned in several books of the Bible including 1 Corinthians, include—among other things—healing, prophecy, and speaking in tongues (unknown languages). Many Christians believe that these "gifts of the Spirit" are still given by God to Christians today in order to minister to both believers and unbelievers in times of need. Since the Charismatic Renewal Movement of the 1960s, which spread across Christian denominational lines in North America and Europe, more and more books have been written that give personal testimonies and biblical instruction about spiritual gifts. Books on dreams and Christian dream interpretation are also included in this section.

Bennett, Dennis J., and Rita Bennett.

The Holy Spirit and You: A Study Guide to the Spirit-Filled Life. Revised edition. Bridge-Logos, 2001 (1971). 250 pp. ISBN 0882706233.

Dennis Bennett (1917–1991), an Episcopal priest, started the Charismatic Movement when he announced in 1960 that he had been baptized in the Holy Spirit. In this classic book, first published in 1971, Bennett discusses what the scriptures say concerning the baptism and gifts of the Holy Spirit. He also explains how to receive the Baptism of the Holy Spirit, describing each of the gifts of the spirit individually—tongues and interpretation, prophecy, healing, miracles, discerning of spirits, word of knowledge, and word of wisdom.

Subjects: Charismatic Movement, Speaking in Tongues, Spiritual Gifts

More: *Your Spiritual Gifts Can Help Your Church Grow* by C. Peter Wagner (Regal, 2005) is a guide that includes a well-developed questionnaire to help readers identify and understand their spiritual gifts. Also try *The Gifts of the Spirit* by Derek Prince (Whitaker House, 2007) and *The Gifts and Ministries of the Holy Spirit* by Lester Sumrall (Whitaker House, 2005).

Cooke, Graham.

Developing Your Prophetic Gifting. Chosen, 2003 (Sovereign World, 1994). 288 pp. ISBN 0800793269.

Graham Cooke asserts that prophecy, a gift from the Holy Spirit, can be used to bring healing, encouragement, and correction into people's lives. Prophecy, he says, can bolster evangelism, provide direction, and strengthen spiritual warfare. This book was written for Christians with prophetic giftings and those who have received prophecies and want to know how to handle them properly. Cooke believes that prophets should not just blow into a city, "do their thing," and then depart. Because prophecy can shift the whole direction of a person or a church, he says prophets should stay around to offer guidance, teach, and help build the local church body. Cooke explains how prophets can work with church leadership to calm fears and work with greater effectiveness, and he shows how to judge and weigh prophecy and how to handle wrong prophecy. Cooke leads schools of prophecy in England and the United States.

Subject: Prophecy

More: For two pioneering books on personal prophecy and prophetic gifting, try *The Elijah Task* by John Loren Sanford and Paula Sanford (Charisma House, 2007), first published in 1977, and *Prophets and Personal Prophecy* by Bill Hamon (Destiny Image, 1987). Also see these two more recent authors: *Secrets of the Prophetic* by Kim Clement (Destiny Image, 2005) and *The Seer* by James "Jim" W. Goll (Destiny Image, 2004).

Dawson, Joy.

Some of the Ways of God in Healing: How to Get Answers and Direction When You're Suffering. YWAM, 1991. 138 pp. ISBN 0927545144.

Joy Dawson claims she has seen many miracles of healing in her own family and others. She points out the proper perspective of this issue when she says, "God is working out a plan that will be for our good in *all* our circumstances." In this balanced book on divine healing, Dawson explains the many biblical purposes for illness, and suggests that sometimes sickness is due to Satan and sometimes sickness is due to sin. Dawson (mother of YWAM president John Dawson) is a missionary, intercessor, and Bible teacher. She is originally from New Zealand but now lives in California.

Subject: Healing

More: For a book that shows readers how to pray for people to be healed, try Che Ahn's *How to Pray for Healing* (Regal, 2003).

Deere, Jack.

Surprised by the Power of the Spirit: Discovering How God Speaks and Heals Today. Zondervan, 1996. 302 pp. ISBN 0310211271.

Jack Deere, an associate professor at Dallas Theological Seminary, did not believe in the gifts of the spirit (for example, healing and speaking in tongues); he believed such miracles ceased after the death of the apostles. But when he began to witness amazing things, his way of thinking changed, and so did his life! Deere discusses why people choose not to believe in the miraculous gifts, explaining that they are not scriptural reasons. He also discusses why some people get healed and others don't.

Subjects: Healing, Miracles, Spiritual Gifts

More: Deere also wrote *Surprised by the Voice of God* (Zondervan, 1998), in which he explains how God speaks today through prophecies, dreams, and visions.

Dueck, Murray.

If This Were a Dream, What Would It Mean? Discovering the Spiritual Meaning Behind Everyday Events. Fresh Wind Press, 2006. 265 pp. ISBN 097335867X.

Murray Dueck says that God uses current events in life to speak to people today. Dueck gives the example of an agitated horse that belonged to the prince of Jordan. In 1992, the agitated horse broke free from its master and crossed water to end up in an Israeli city. The horse became peaceful once it arrived on "enemy" turf. This horse turned out to be a prophetic symbol—or a sign from God—because (although no one knew it at the time) peace between Jordan and Israel was only two years away. Dueck discusses many instances in the Bible where God uses signs to confirm or foreshadow what He is doing. For instance, did you ever wonder why

God used a rooster as a sign to mark Peter's denial of Jesus? Roosters are symbolic of pride ("cocky"), and Peter needed to depend upon God—not his flesh. Through examples from his personal life, Dueck shows that God still speaks to individuals personally and that He still has plans and purposes for people, communities, and nations. Dueck leads Samuel's Mantle, a prophetic school associated with Langley Vineyard Church in Canada.

Subjects: Dream Interpretation, Signs (Miraculous)

More: Readers may also enjoy *When Heaven Invades Earth: A Practical Guide to a Life of Miracles* by Bill Johnson (Treasure House, 2003) and *Expecting Miracles: True Stories of God's Supernatural Power and How You Can Experience It* by Heidi and Rolland Baker (Chosen, 2007).

Hamon, Jane.

Dreams and Visions: Understanding Your Dreams and How God Can Use Them to Speak to You Today. Regal, 2000. 176 pp. ISBN 0830725695.

Jane Hamon suggests that God has a purpose for dreams today. Some dreams are natural and some are spiritual, she says, and God can use both. Through examples of her own dreams, Hamon shows how to (and how not to) interpret them. She also discusses various Bible stories that contain dreams.

Subjects: Dream Interpretation, Visions

More: Three more books on the subject are *Dream Language: The Prophetic Power of Dreams* by James W. and Michal Ann Goll (Destiny Image, 2006), *Understanding the Dreams You Dream* by Ira Milligan (Treasure House, 1997), which is basically a dream-interpretation dictionary, and *When God Speaks* by Chuck D. Pierce and Rebecca Wagner Sytsema (Regal, 2005), which covers dreams, visions, and prophecy.

Jacobs, Cindy.

The Supernatural Life. Regal, 2006. 189 pp. ISBN 0830729615.

Cindy Jacobs, the founder of Generals International, a worldwide prayer ministry, recounts her spiritual journey, which involves many supernatural events. She discusses speaking and singing in the spirit, the laying on of hands, visions, angels, discernment, healing, and creative miracles. Jacobs also writes about some of the great healing evangelists that she studied while learning about the supernatural life, people like Aimee Semple McPherson and Smith Wigglesworth who saw thousands of miracles. Jacobs says she wrote this book because she has seen an increase in this kind of supernatural activity all over the world.

Subject: Spiritual Gifts

More: Jacobs has another book called *The Voice of God: How God Speaks Personally and Corporately to His Children Today* (Regal, 2004). In *Surprised by the Voice of God* (Zondervan, 1998), Jack Deere explains how God speaks today through prophecies, dreams, and visions.

Sherrill, John L.

They Speak with Other Tongues. 40th Anniversary edition. Chosen, 2004 (McGraw-Hill, 1964). 192 pp. ISBN 0800793595.

This is a brief, fascinating, and articulate introduction to the baptism of the Holy Spirit, or speaking in tongues. John Sherrill, who did not believe in speaking in tongues, was given an assignment to investigate this phenomenon. This writer got more than he bargained for as he sought the truth about the gift of the Holy Spirit!

Subjects: Speaking in Tongues, Spiritual Gifts

More: *Nine O'Clock in the Morning* by Dennis J. Bennett (Bridge-Logos, 1970) tells of how Episcopalian priest Bennett was baptized in the Holy Spirit and kicked off the Charismatic Movement of the 1960s and '70s. Bennett also wrote *How to Pray for the Release of the Holy Spirit* (Bridge-Logos Publishers, 1985). For two more books on speaking in tongues, try *The Hidden Power of Speaking in Tongues* by Mahesh Chavda (Destiny Image, 2003) and *The Beauty of Spiritual Language* by Jack Hayford (Thomas Nelson, 1996).

Wimber, John, and Kevin Springer.

Power Healing. HarperCollins, 1991. 320 pp. ISBN 0060695412.

John Wimber (1934–1997), one of the founders of the Vineyard Movement of churches, describes how he came to believe in and be used by God in the ministry of healing and deliverance. This book includes not only Wimber's personal story (he saw many incredible healings during his Christian ministry), but also a scriptural study on healing and deliverance, as well as a practical, "how-to" training guide. The authors show how physical, emotional, and spiritual problems are interconnected, and how they can be discerned and healed through God's guidance. The testimonies of many people are included here, ranging from physical healings of every kind to emotional healings and deliverance from various forms of bondage.

Subjects: Deliverance, Healing

More: Another classic on the subject is *Healing* by Francis MacNutt (Ave Maria Press, 1999). For more on deliverance and inner healing, try Charles Kraft's *Deep Wounds, Deep Healing: Discovering* *the Vital Link Between Spiritual Warfare and Inner Healing* (Vine Books, 2004).

Christian Living

"Christian Living" is a somewhat broad category. This section includes everything from new and upcoming authors such as Alicia Britt Chole (author of *Anonymous* and *Sitting in God's Sunshine ... Resting in His Love*) to mega-best-selling writers such as Rick Warren and Joel Osteen. Readers will also find books by beloved authors such as Max Lucado and Beth Moore, not to mention jewels such as Joy Dawson's *Intimate Friendship with God* and Thomas Merton's *No Man Is an Island*.

Bell, Rob.

Velvet Elvis: Repainting the Christian Faith. Zondervan, 2005. 194 pp. ISBN 031026345X.

Rob Bell is a pastor of Mars Hill Bible Church in Grand Rapids, Michigan. In this brief book, he challenges the reader to rethink what Christianity is all about and move away from stiff, lifeless, and irrelevant religion. He addresses a variety of topics (biblical interpretation, pastoral ministry, sin, burnout, cultural involvement, and more), but all from the same perspective, that of a revitalizing gospel that delivers love, grace, and truth to real people in today's world. Bell is associated with the Emerging Church Movement.

Subjects: Emerging Church Movement, Spiritual Growth

More: One of the most well-known books representing the Emerging Church Movement is *A New Kind of Christian: A Tale of Two Friends on a Spiritual Journey* by Brian D. McLaren (Jossey-Bass, 2001).

Bevere, John.

The Bait of Satan: Living Free from the Deadly Trap of Offense. 10th Anniversary edition. Charisma House, 2004 (1994). 255 pp. ISBN 59185413X.

The bait of Satan, says John Bevere, is offense; when Christians become offended by other people, they are falling into a trap of the enemy. He continues, "Our response to an offense determines our future." Throughout the book, he relates many stories from the Bible and from people he has met that demonstrate the destructive outcome of offense, including bitterness and unfruitfulness. They also show the restorative, healing power of forgiveness and reconciliation.

Subject: Forgiveness

More: Two more titles by Bevere are *Breaking Intimidation* (Charisma House, 2006) and *Driven by Eternity: Making Your Life Count Today & Forever* (FaithWords, 2006).

Bickle, Mike.

Passion for Jesus: Cultivating Extravagant Love for God. Revised edition. Charisma House, 2007 (1993). 205 pp. ISBN 1599790602.

Mike Bickle shows readers how they can experience a passionate love for God in their own lives. This love, he says, does not come from natural human zeal, because human enthusiasm is not enough. To illustrate his principles, Bickle shares his story of how he became a Christian and a worshipper of God. Although his own zeal had failed him, he eventually found "a secret life with God hidden from the eyes of others." Bickle, director of the International House of Prayer in Kansas City (IHOP-KC), is also the president of the Forerunner School of Ministry (FSM) in Kansas City, Missouri.

Subjects: Intimacy with God, Spiritual Growth

More: Bickle wrote a follow-up book titled *After God's Own Heart: Becoming a David Generation* (Charisma House, 2004). Also try John Bevere's *Drawing Near: A Life of Intimacy with God* (Thomas Nelson, 2006). Dale Fife desired to walk with God like Enoch did. God answered his prayer, and Fife shares the resulting visions, revelations, and experiences in his book *The Secret Place* (Whitaker, 2001). Yet another book on this subject is *Enjoying Intimacy with God* by well-known writer and Christian leader J. Oswald Sanders (Discovery House, 2001).

Buchanan, Mark.

The Holy Wild: Trusting in the Character of God. Multnomah, 2005. 269 pp. ISBN 1590524489.

Is God really good? Can we trust Him with our lives when there is so much turmoil in the world? Mark Buchanan, a writer and the pastor of New Life Community Baptist Church on Vancouver Island in British Columbia, Canada, says "yes." Buchanan encourages readers to seek this wise and creative, wrathful and merciful, holy and faithful God. God may not be as "safe" as some would wish, but He is the only one we can trust and the only one for whom we were created.

Subjects: Attributes of God, Spiritual Growth

More: Buchanan also wrote *Hidden in Plain Sight: The Secret of More* (Thomas Nelson, 2007) and *The Rest of God: Restoring Your Soul by Restoring Sabbath* (Thomas Nelson, 2007).

Chole, Alicia Britt.

Anonymous. Thomas Nelson, 2006. 183 pp. ISBN 1591454212.

Pointing to Jesus's life as an example, Alicia Britt Chole gives encouragement to those whose dreams and gifts seem to be in limbo. For the first twenty-nine years of Christ's life, he was hidden. Chole shows readers that these anonymous years are not wasted and don't need to be filled with despair or regret.

Subject: Spiritual Growth

More: Chole also wrote *Sitting in God's Sunshine ... Resting in His Love* (Thomas Nelson, 2005) and *Pure Joy* (Thomas Nelson, 2003). Chole's writing has been compared to Max Lucado's work. Lucado wrote *It's Not About Me: Rescue from the Life We Thought Would Make Us Happy* (Thomas Nelson, 2004) and *Traveling Light: Releasing the Burdens You Were Never Intended to Bear* (Thomas Nelson, 2006).

Crabb, Larry.

The Pressure's Off. WaterBrook, 2002. 231 pp. ISBN 1578564530.

In this book, Larry Crabb presents a new way to live—a way that is not based on following detailed rules to ensure God's blessings. Instead, this new way involves forgetting about trying to be in control of life and happiness and instead focusing on God. Crabb says the new way, which is about trusting in God no matter life's circumstances, leads to freedom and intimacy with God. Crabb is a Christian author, a psychologist, and the founder of New Way Ministries.

Subject: Spiritual Growth

More: Crabb's recent book, *The PAPA Prayer: The Prayer You've Never Prayed* (Thomas Nelson, 2006), goes right along with the concepts in *The Pressure's Off.*

Dawson, Joy.

Intimate Friendship with God: Through Understanding the Fear of the Lord. 2nd Revised edition. Chosen, 2008 (1986). 176 pp. ISBN 0800794419.

International Bible teacher Joy Dawson explains what it means to "fear the Lord," which is a common phrase in the Bible. Dawson shows Christians how to live out the fear of the Lord in today's world, discussing topics such as obedience to God, release from the fear of man, God's holiness, sin, repentance, our thought lives, and sex. She also lists the rewards that the Bible promises for those who fear God; it is quite a surprising list.

Subjects: Fear of the Lord, Intimacy with God, Spiritual Growth

More: For more books by Dawson, try *The Fire of God: Discovering Its Many Life Changing Purposes* (Destiny Image, 2005) and *Jesus, the Model: The Plumb Line for Christian Living* (Charisma, 2007). For another book on the fear of the Lord, see *The Fear of the Lord: Discover the Key to Intimately Knowing God* by John Bevere (Creation House, 1997).

Edwards, Gene.

A Tale of Three Kings: A Study in Brokenness. Tyndale, 1992. 111 pp. ISBN 0842369082.

This is a classic Christian work on authority, unfair treatment by authority, and proper response to spiritual authority. The three kings mentioned in the title are Saul, David, and Absalom. The book is brief and engaging in style—it's easy to read in one sitting. It especially appeals to those who have dealt with overbearing leaders, rebellious attitudes, offenses, and hurts from being a part of a church or ministry.

Subjects: Authority, Spiritual Authority, Spiritual Growth

More: Another book by Edwards on abuse of spiritual authority is *Letters to a Devastated Christian* (Seedsowers, 2000). For more on other aspects of spiritual authority, try Watchman Nee's *Spiritual Authority* (Christian Fellowship Publishers, 1972) and John Bevere's *Under Cover: The Promise of Protection Under His Authority* (Thomas Nelson, 2001).

Eldredge, John.

Desire: The Journey We Must Take to Find the Life God Offers. Thomas Nelson, 2007. 224 pp. ISBN 0785288422.

Many Christians kill their desire in the name of godliness, but John Eldredge suggests that desire is at the very heart of Christianity. The church doesn't need more nice, moral people. It needs passionate people, alive with adventure and desire. In this book, Eldredge presents a stirring alternative to lifeless religion. This book was originally published as *The Journey of Desire*.

Subject: Spiritual Growth

More: This book is the companion to an earlier work called *The Sacred Romance: Drawing Closer to the Heart of God* (Thomas Nelson, 1997). Eldredge also wrote *Waking the Dead* (Nelson, 2006).

Guinness, Os.

The Call: Finding and Fulfilling the Central Purpose of Your Life. Thomas Nelson, 2003. 292 pp. ISBN 0849944376.

Using anecdotes from history and literature, Os Guinness probes the great questions of meaning and vocation. He writes for those "who long to find and fulfill the purpose of their lives" and seeks to dismantle confusion and false ideas about what "calling" really is. One of these false ideas says that only religious "callings" are truly admirable; secular "callings," such as farming or business, are less worthy. The truth is, says Guinness, we are not called to some*thing* so much as we are called to some*one*—to God. To know God is our primary calling. Being a lawyer or a pastor or a homemaker is important, but it is secondary. Guinness is an internationally known speaker, thinker, and writer who combines faith and cultural analysis with an intellectually stimulating style.

Subjects: Award Winners (CT), Spiritual Growth, Work

More: Guinness also wrote *Long Journey Home: A Guide to Your Search for the Meaning of Life* (WaterBrook, 2003). Readers who like Guinness may also enjoy these three authors: Malcolm Muggeridge, whose autobiography is called *Chronicles of Wasted Time* (Regent College, 2006); Francis Schaeffer, author of *True Spirituality* (Tyndale, 1979); and Nancy Pearcey, who wrote *Total Truth: Liberating Christianity from Its Cultural Captivity* (Crossway, 2005).

Hsu, Albert Y.

The Suburban Christian: Finding Spiritual Vitality in the Land of Plenty. InterVarsity, 2006. 220 pp. ISBN 083083334X.

Albert Hsu, associate editor at InterVarsity Press, writes about the nature and evolution of life in the suburbs. He talks about the spiritual dimensions of prosperity, materialism, and simplicity, and discusses the impact of suburban living on our individual lives and our community, including our churches. Hsu says that prosperous suburban Christians can choose to be more than purposeless consumers; they can become connected to their community and practice hospitality and self-sacrifice. They can use their share of power and wealth responsibly and strategically.

Subjects: Materialism, Suburban Life

More: For more on materialism, try *Money, Possessions, and Eternity* by Randy Alcorn (Tyndale, 2003).

Johnson, Bill.

When Heaven Invades Earth. Destiny Image, 2005. 190 pp. ISBN 0768429528.

Bill Johnson takes a look at the Bible and concludes that miracles should be a normal part of a Christian's life today. Why? Because the Bible shows that miracles go along with the kingdom of God. Johnson shows from the Bible and from contemporary experience that the presence and power of God is a part of the believer's life. From this perspective, Johnson presents his biblical teaching on faith, prayer, identity, the anointing, and the great commission.

Subjects: Faith, Kingdom of God, Miracles

More: Johnson also wrote *The Supernatural Power of a Transformed Mind: Access to a Life of Miracles* (Destiny Image, 2005) and *Dreaming with God* (Destiny Image, 2006).

Keller, Phillip.

A Shepherd Looks at Psalm 23. Zondervan, 2006 (1970). 144 pp. ISBN 0310607043.

Phillip Keller, an agricultural researcher, ranch developer, journalist, wildlife photographer, and shepherd, examines the nature of sheep and helps readers to see sheep and Psalm 23 in a new light based on his firsthand experience. This book was first published in 1970.

Subjects: Psalm 23, Spiritual Growth

More: Keller has also written *Lessons from a Sheep Dog* (Thomas Nelson, 2002).

Lucado, Max.

He Chose the Nails: What God Did to Win Your Heart. Thomas Nelson, 2005 (2000). 240 pp. ISBN 0849905702.

This book examines the elements of Christ's crucifixion—such as the sign placed over His head, the two crosses next to Him, the wine-soaked sponge lifted up to Him, and the blood and water that flowed from His side. Each of these elements are gifts and promises, reminding Christians of God's love and forgiveness. Lucado's simple, conversational, storytelling style and strong message have made his many books best sellers. He is the senior pastor of the Oak Hills Church in San Antonio, Texas.

Subjects: Award Winners (ECPA), Crucifixion, Jesus Christ, Spiritual Growth

More: Another book by Lucado on the crucifixion is *Six Hours One Friday: Living in the Power of the Cross* (Thomas Nelson, 2005). Three more of Lucado's books that have won ECPA Christian Book Awards are *Just Like Jesus* (Word, 1998), *In the Grip of Grace* (Thomas Nelson, 2004), and *When God Whispers Your Name* (Thomas Nelson, 1999).

McClung, Floyd.

The Father Heart of God: Experiencing the Depths of His Love for You. Harvest House, 2004 (1985). 144 pp. ISBN 0736912150.

For many people, says Floyd McClung, "to speak of a loving Father God only evokes pain and anger." In this book, McClung shows how to overcome such emotional wounds. He also shows that God himself knows all about broken hearts. While discussing this topic, McClung explains the difference between dominating fathers and godly fathers, as well as the difference between sin, wounds, and bondage. Those in sin need to be forgiven, those who are wounded need to be healed, and those in bondage need to be set free.

Subjects: Inner Healing, Spiritual Growth

More: McClung also has written *Basic Discipleship* (InterVarsity, 1992), which shows readers how to follow Christ wholeheartedly. For more information about inner healing, try these two books by John and Paul Sandford: *Transforming the Inner Man: God's Powerful Principles for Inner Healing and Lasting Life Change* (Charisma House, 2007) and *Choosing Forgiveness: Turning from Guilt, Bitterness, and Resentment Toward a Life of Wholeness and Peace* (Charisma House, 2007).

Marshall, Paul A., and Lela Gilbert.

Heaven Is Not My Home: Learning to Live in God's Creation. Word, 1998. 269 pp. ISBN 0849990408.

Speaker and writer Paul Marshall and award-winning author Lela Gilbert say that although the world that God has made is fallen, it is not evil or unredeemable. Christians should not "check out" from life and wait until they die so they can go to heaven; escapism and fear are not Christian. Earth is not the problem; sin is. Christians, the authors say, need to be "salt and light." The authors demonstrate how believers should approach work and rest, and learning and play. They discuss nature, ecology, technology, and the arts. There will be a new earth, not because this one is bad, Marshall and Gilbert say, but because it is good and because God is a redeemer.

Subject: Worldview

More: *Heaven Is a Place on Earth: Why Everything You Do Matters to God* by Michael E. Wittmer (Zondervan, 2004).

Merton, Thomas.

No Man Is an Island. Harvest, 2002 (1955). 288 pp. ISBN 0156027739.

This collection of sixteen essays covers a variety of topics such as hope, prayer, sincerity, mercy, solitude, being and doing, vocation, and more. Thomas Merton (1915–1968), a Trappist monk in the Cistercian Abbey of Gethsemani in Kentucky, became famous after he published his autobiography, *The Seven Storey Mountain* (Harvest, 1999), in 1948.

Subjects: Catholics, Essays, Mystics, Spiritual Growth

More: Also try Merton's *New Seeds of Contemplation* (New Directions, 1972), which deals with contemplative prayer, and *Wisdom of the Desert* (New Directions, 1970), Merton's collection of sayings from the desert fathers (Christian hermits and monks from third- and fourth-century Egypt). Henri Nouwen stayed for seven months at a Trappist monastery (Thomas Merton was a Trappist monk), and his journal is *The Genesee Diary: Report from a Trappist Monastery* (Image, 1981). Another related book by Nouwen is *Reaching Out* (Image, 1986).

Meyer, Joyce.

Battlefield of the Mind. FaithWords, 2002 (1995). 288 pp. ISBN 0446691097.

According to Joyce Meyer, a popular Bible teacher and author with her own television and radio programs, all Christians are engaged in a war. The enemy is Satan, and the battlefield is the mind. Meyer tells Christians how to overcome strongholds and such conditions as confusion, doubt, unbelief, anxiety, worry, judgmental and critical thinking, and passivity. For each of these conditions, Meyer uses Bible passages to demonstrate how God's truth cuts through the enemy's lies.

Subject: Spiritual Growth

More: Meyer has also written *Managing Your Emotions: Instead of Your Emotions Managing You* (FaithWords, 2002) and *In Pursuit of Peace: 21 Ways to Conquer Anxiety, Fear, and Discontentment* (FaithWords, 2004).

Moore, Beth.

Believing God. B&H Publishing, 2004. 272 pp. ISBN 0805431896.

In this book, Bible teacher Beth Moore encourages readers to believe God with words like these: "Beloved, God has made us promises. Real Ones. Numerous ones. Promises of things like all-surpassing power, productivity, peace, and joy while still occupying these jars of clay. Few of us will argue the theory, but why aren't more of us living the reality?" Moore emboldens Christians to believe that not only is God who He says He is, but also that He can do what He says He can do. And Christians, as His children, can live victoriously because they can do all things through Christ. Moore is a well-known writer and Bible teacher from Houston, Texas.

Subject: Spiritual Growth

More: Moore also wrote *Get Out of That Pit: Straight Talk about God's Deliverance* (Thomas Nelson, 2007) and *To Live Is Christ: Embracing the Passion of Paul* (B&H Publishing, 2001). Readers who like her may also enjoy *Experiencing God: Knowing and Doing the Will of God* by Henry Blackaby and Claude King (B&H Publishing, 2004) and *How to Hear from God: Learn to Know His Voice and Make the Right Decisions* by Joyce Meyer (FaithWords, 2003).

Nee, Watchman.

The Release of the Spirit. Christian Fellowship Publishers, 2000 (1965). 126 pp. ISBN 0935008837.

Watchman Nee (1903–1972) was a well-known writer and Chinese church leader who spent twenty years in prison for his faith. He writes about the need for the outer man (that is, the soul) to be broken so that believers can live by the Spirit. It is through this brokenness that God ministers to us and through us as we live with and serve others.

Subjects: Classics, Mystics, Spiritual Growth

More: Another classic work by Nee is *The Normal Christian Life* (Tyndale, 1977), which examines part of the book of Romans, explaining that God has given one answer to every human need: Jesus Christ. Another book by Nee is *Sit, Walk, Stand* (Tyndale, 1977), which is a study of Ephesians.

Piper, John.

Desiring God: Meditations of a Christian Hedonist. Revised and expanded edition. Multnomah, 2003 (1996). 358 pp. ISBN 1590521196.

Hedonism is living for pleasure. John Piper, a writer and the pastor for preaching at Bethlehem Baptist Church in Minneapolis, Minnesota, suggests that people should not try to deny or resist a longing for happiness and pleasure. Instead, they should seek to intensify and satisfy this longing. Since God is the only source of true and enduring happiness, Christians should abandon lesser and false pleasures that will only disappoint. They should find delight in God. Piper says, "God is most glorified in me when I am most satisfied in him."

Subject: Spiritual Growth

More: Piper also has written *What Jesus Demands from the World* (Crossway, 2006) and *Battling Unbelief: Defeating Sin with Superior Pleasure* (Multnomah, 2007).

Swindoll, Charles R.

David: A Man of Passion & Destiny. Thomas Nelson, 1997. 226 pp. ISBN 0849913829.

Charles "Chuck" Swindoll examines the life of David, considers the strengths and failures of this famous musician, soldier, and king, and offers practical application to modern Christians. This is volume one of the Great Lives from God's Word Series of books about the lives of famous biblical characters such as Esther, Joseph, Elijah, and Paul. Swindoll (1934–) is an evangelical pastor, author, educator, and founder of Insight for Living, a popular radio program.

Subjects: Biography, David (King of Israel), Spiritual Growth

More: Beth Moore also has several books about famous Bible characters, including a study of David called *A Heart Like His* (B&H Publishing, 1999) and a study of John called *The Beloved Disciple* (B&H Publishing, 2003). British pastor F. B. Meyer also has a similar series, including *The Life of Abraham: The Obedience of Faith* (YWAM, 1996) and *The Life of Moses: The Servant of God* (YWAM, 1996). For other books by Charles Swindoll, try *The Grace Awakening* (Thomas Nelson, 2006) and *Improving Your Serve* (Thomas Nelson, 2004).

ten Boom, Corrie.

Not Good If Detached. Christian Literature Crusade, 1966. 127 pp. ISBN 0875080227.

Corrie ten Boom (1892–1983) was imprisoned during World War II for hiding Jews from Hitler's forces. When she was released, she traveled all over the world preaching and teaching. In this book, with simple but powerful writing, she shares some of the touching experiences she had and some of the inspiring lessons she learned. The title of the book refers to the fact that abiding in Christ is the source of love, hope, and strength. The chapters are only a page or two long, making this a good daily devotional.

Subjects: Daily Devotionals, Spiritual Growth

More: For more of ten Boom's teachings, try *He Cares for You* (Revell, 1998) and *Not I, but Christ* (Revell, 1997). Her most famous book is called *The Hiding Place* (Chosen, 2006).

Thomas, Gary L.

Sacred Pathways. Zondervan, 2002. 240 pp. ISBN 0310242843.

In this book, Gary Thomas explains that so many Christians have dry and anemic devotional lives because they have been led into a false religious paradigm of what spirituality must be. Thomas suggests it is ok for one person to connect with God in the midst of nature and for another to reach God through intellectual stimulation. He identifies nine different pathways to God: naturalists, sensates, traditionalists, ascetics, activists, caregivers, enthusiasts, contemplatives, and intellectuals. Thomas is a writer and the founder of the Center for Evangelical Spirituality, which integrates scripture, church history, and the Christian classics.

Subject: Spiritual Growth

More: Thomas also has written *Authentic Faith: The Power of a Fire-Tested Life* (Zondervan, 2003) and *The Glorious Pursuit: Embracing the Virtues of Christ* (NavPress, 1998).

Warren, Rick.

The Purpose-Driven Life: What on Earth Am I Here For? Zondervan, 2002. 334 pp. ISBN 0310205719.

In this best-selling (and record-breaking) book, the author's goal is to help readers "discover the life he (God) created you to live—here on earth, and forever in eternity." Rick Warren talks about what it means to worship and serve God. He writes about being a part of God's family (which has to do with living in community with other people). He also explains what it means to become like Christ and to fulfill your mission. The book is divided into forty daily readings. Warren is the pastor of Saddleback Church in Lake Forest, California—one of the largest churches in the United States.

Subjects: Award Winners (ECPA), Daily Devotionals, Spiritual Growth

More: Two more record-breaking best sellers by notable American ministers are *The Prayer of Jabez: Breaking Through to the Blessed Life* (Multnomah, 2000) by Bruce Wilkinson which challenges Christians to tap into the blessings of a generous God, and *Your Best Life Now: 7 Steps to Living at Your Full Potential* by Joel Osteen (FaithWords, 2004), which is a Christian successful-living title. *Prayer of Jabez* was such a hit that the publishers issued a fifth-anniversary edition in 2005. *Your Best Life Now* was so successful that Free Press (a secular imprint of Simon & Schuster) offered Osteen $13 million for the sequel.

Weaver, Joanna.

Having a Mary Heart in a Martha World: Finding Intimacy with God in the Busyness of Life. WaterBrook, 2007 (2000). 288 pp. ISBN 1400074037.

When Jesus went to Martha's house, Martha was busy waiting on Jesus. Martha's sister, Mary, however, sat at Jesus' feet listening to what he had to say. Martha became upset that Mary would not help do the work that needed to be done, but Jesus told Martha, "Mary has chosen what is better, and it will not be taken away from her." In this book, Joanna Weaver addresses women who live in today's hectic world and shows them how to live a balanced and spiritually rewarding life.

Subjects: Spiritual Growth, Women's Issues

More: Weaver has written a follow-up to this book called *Having a Mary Spirit: Allowing God to Change Us from the Inside Out* (WaterBrook, 2006).

Yancey, Philip.

What's So Amazing About Grace? Zondervan, 2002 (1997). 304 pp. ISBN 0310245656.

Notable author Philip Yancey writes about what he calls the summation of the gospel in one word: grace. Yancey says, "Grace comes free of charge to people who do not deserve it." But what about child abusers? What about murderers? Is grace available to these people? Yancey faces these tough issues head on. Often the church fails to offer grace, he says, but God never flounders. As he writes about grace and forgiveness, Yancey tells many stories of real people whose lives have been transformed by grace or ruined by the lack thereof. He puts his finger on an issue that tests the mettle of a person's spirituality and searches the depth of God's love. Yancey is a well-known evangelical writer whose books have won numerous awards, including twelve ECPA Christian Book awards. He serves as editor-at-large for *Christianity Today*.

Subjects: Award Winners (ECPA, CT), Forgiveness, Grace, Spiritual Growth

More: Brennan Manning has written powerfully about the unconditional love of God in his book *The Ragamuffin Gospel* (Multnomah, 2005). For another book on the subject of grace, see Randy Alcorn's *The Grace and Truth Paradox* (Multnomah, 2003). For more award-winning books by Philip Yancey, try *The Jesus I Never Knew* (Zondervan, 2002), *Where Is God When It Hurts?* (Zondervan, 2002), and *The Bible Jesus Read* (Zondervan, 2002).

Bibliographies

The bibliographies gathered here are annotated lists of books selected by and for Christians. Many of the titles have been selected because they helped the authors grow spiritually. Each contains Christian nonfiction, but some also include other genres of literature such as poetry, children's literature, and fiction.

Edwards, David, Margaret Feinberg, Janella Griggs, and Matthew Paul Turner.

Twenty Things You Should Read. Tyndale, 2006. 196 pp. ISBN 1414305958.

This book introduces readers to twenty famous Christian thinkers and devotional writers. For each classic writer, the authors present a brief two-page biography followed by a six- to eight-page excerpt from that writer's work. The compilers have placed explanatory notes in the margins of these excerpts. Some of the authors include St. Augustine, Thomas à Kempis, Martin Luther, Brother Lawrence, John Bunyan, William Law, Frederick Douglass, Andrew Murray, Charles H. Spurgeon, G. K. Chesterton, Karl Barth, and A. W. Tozer.

Subjects: Best Books, Spiritual Growth

Ford, Marcia.

God Between the Covers: Finding Faith Through Reading. Crossroad Publishing, 2005. 222 pp. ISBN 0824522907.

Author, journalist, book reviewer (for *Publishers Weekly*), and bibliophile Marcia Ford recommends and discusses the books that shaped her life and faith. More than 100 different fiction, nonfiction, and children's authors are included.

Subjects: Best Books, Children's Literature, Literature

Glaspey, Terry.

Book Lover's Guide to Great Reading: A Guided Tour of Classic & Contemporary Literature. InterVarsity Press, 2001. 237 pp. ISBN 0830823298.

Glaspey gives annotated lists of books by categories. Besides forty pages listing "great books of the Christian tradition," Glaspey also has sections for classics, poetry, books for spiritual growth, contemporary fiction, and children's literature. He includes a one-year reading plan for the classics. He also writes a few pages about reading groups. Glaspey ends the book with an essay answering the question, "Why read books by non-Christians?"

Subjects: Best Books, Literature—Classic, Spiritual Growth

Hardon, John A.

The Catholic Lifetime Reading Plan. Updated edition. Grotto Press, 1998 (Doubleday, 1989). 299 pp. ISBN 1581880006.

The author lists 104 authors, working his way chronologically from the age of persecution (for example, Ignatius, Justin Martyr), to the patristic age (for example, John Chrysostom, Augustine, Bede), then on to medieval times (for example, Bernard of Clairvaux, Francis of Assisi, Thomas a Kempis), to the Catholic reformation (for example, Thomas More, Ignatius Loyola, Teresa of Avila), and finally through more than sixty authors of the modern age (including Frederic William Faber, John Henry Newman, G. K. Chesterton, Edith Stein, Evelyn Waugh, and Christopher

Dawson). For each author, Hardon gives a brief biography and recommends one or more books. A bibliography at the end lists all titles by each author.

Subjects: Best Books, Catholics, Spiritual Growth

More: Georgetown professor of political philosophy, James Schall, S. J., has written an interesting book of essays that includes dozens of book lists. The title (with its long subtitle) is *Another Sort of Learning: Selected Contrary Essays on the Completion of Our Knowing, or, How to Finally Acquire an Education While Still in College, or Anywhere Else: Containing Some Belated Advice About How to Employ Your Leisure Time When Ultimate Questions Remain Perplexing in Spite of Your Highest Earned Academic Degree, Together with Sundry Book Lists Nowhere Else in Captivity to Be Found* (Ignatius Press, 1988).

Hunt, Gladys.

Honey for a Woman's Heart: Growing Your World Through Reading Great Books. Zondervan, 2002. 208 pp. ISBN 0310238463.

This book is a collection of essays from a Christian perspective about books and reading with many lists of volumes scattered throughout. There are sections covering the classics, mysteries, historical fiction, westerns, fantasy, and poetry. Hunt also recommends nonfiction "genres" such as autobiography, history, travel, and parenting. There are also lists and essays for poetry, reading the Bible, prayer, and spiritual growth.

Subjects: Best Books, Literature, Spiritual Growth, Women

Larsen, Scott, editor.

Indelible Ink: 22 Prominent Christian Leaders Discuss the Books That Shape Their Faith. WaterBrook Press, 2003. 321 pp. ISBN 1578565545.

This book collects twenty-two bibliographic essays by the likes of Charles Colson, Joni Eareckson Tada, Dallas Willard, John Stott, Edith Schaeffer, Ravi Zacharias, Josh McDowell, Larry Crab, J. I. Packer, and more. Lasen also includes more than 130 annotated book lists from other Christian leaders such as George Barna, Henry Blackaby, Marva Dawn, Elisabeth Elliot, Wayne Grudem, Jack Hayford, Phil Keaggy, Peter Kreeft, Sir John Polkinghorne, Dennis Rainey, Hugh Ross, Charles Swindoll, and many, many more. Philip Yancey wrote the foreword to this bibliographic feast.

Subjects: Best Books, Essays

More: *Reading for Life* by Jeffry Davis, Thomas Martin, and Leland Ryken (Xlibris, 2002) is subtitled *100 Christian College Teachers Reflect on the Books That Shaped Their Lives.*

McKenna, David.

How to Read a Christian Book: A Guide to Selecting and Reading Christian Books As a Christian Discipline. Baker, 2001. 143 pp. ISBN 0801063590.

> David McKenna discusses how to choose and evaluate books and plan a personal Christian library. He offers a three-year reading plan and gives some lists of books (mostly not annotated). McKenna is a retired educator and seminary president.
>
> **Subjects:** Best Books, Books and Reading

Peterson, Eugene H.

Take and Read: Spiritual Reading: An Annotated List. Eerdmans, 2000. 122 pp. ISBN 0802840965.

> In this book, Eugene Peterson lists and annotates the books that have become a part of his own life. He arranges them in twenty categories including: basics, classics, the psalms, prayer, spiritual formation, North American spirituality, novelists, poets, pastors, Jesus, mysteries, commentaries, place, history, and more. It is an eclectic collection full of old and new classics. Peterson is a retired theology professor and translator of *The Message*, a version of the Bible in contemporary English.
>
> **Subjects:** Best Books, Spiritual Growth

Chapter 3

Christian Self-Help

Introduction

Purportedly, the first book entitled *Self-Help* was written by Samuel Smiles in 1859. It opens by quoting the adage, "Heaven helps those who help themselves." Since that time, the number of self-help books being published has grown significantly. The same is true for Christian self-help books, which seek to offer wisdom for living based on biblical principles. The heart of such wisdom is found in the book of Proverbs, which opens with these ancient and famous lines:

> *The proverbs of Solomon son of David, king of Israel: for attaining wisdom and discipline; for understanding words of insight; for acquiring a disciplined and prudent life, doing what is right and just and fair; for giving prudence to the simple, knowledge and discretion to the young—let the wise listen and add to their learning, and let the discerning get guidance—for understanding proverbs and parables, the sayings and riddles of the wise. The fear of the LORD is the beginning of knowledge, but fools despise wisdom and discipline.*

In the publishing world, self-help is an imprecise term. For the purposes of this chapter, it refers to books that are intended to help readers improve themselves. These books fall under the following categories: health care; nutrition; fitness; house and home; men's, women's, and teens' issues; sex and sexuality; dating; being single; marriage; parenting; counseling and psychology; and grief and death. Legal self-help is not included. For business self-help, see Chapter Six on business and leadership, which also includes books on personal finance.

Health

This section begins with books about nutrition. So what is Christian about nutrition? Well, the Bible has a lot to say about food. The Law of Moses clearly distinguishes between clean and unclean animals. Some Christians take Jewish dietary laws seriously, saying the ancient writings still offer sound medical wisdom for today. Also, with alternative medicine growing in popularity, Christians may want to know if practices such as acupressure, aromatherapy, chelation therapy, and magnet therapy are 1) endorsed by the medical/scientific community and 2) spiritually sound. Donal O'Mathuna's *Alternative Medicine: The Christian Handbook* has many answers for everything from herbal remedies to tai chi.

Fitness is of similar interest to nutrition. Although not commonly known, the father of aerobics, Kenneth Cooper, is a Christian and a medical doctor who advocates disease prevention through aerobic exercise. Several of his books have been published by Christian publishers. Other topics covered in this section include cancer, medical ethics, nursing, caregiving, infertility, and more.

General Health

Carter, Carrie.

A Woman's Guide to Good Health. Revised and updated edition. Spire, 2006 (Bethany, 2003). 202 pp. ISBN 0800787404.

> Carrie L. Carter, a board-certified primary care physician for sixteen years, was forced to give up her medical practice due to chronic illness (Meniere's disease and lupus). From the perspective of a doctor and a patient, Carter writers about stress, nutrition, weight gain and loss, exercise, medical screening tests, and heart disease.

Subjects: Health Care, Stress, Women—Health

More: Two more books related to women's health include *A Woman's Body Balanced by Nature: Great Health for the Rest of Your Life* by Janet Maccaro (Strang, 2006) and *Total Heart Health for Women: A Life-Enriching Plan for Physical and Spiritual Well-Being* by Ed and Jo Beth Young, Dr. Michael Duncan, and Dr. Richard Leachman (Thomas Nelson, 2007).

Doornbos, Mary Molewyk.

Transforming Care: A Christian Vision of Nursing Practice. Eerdmans, 2005. 211 pp. ISBN 0802828744.

Divided into theory and practice, this book shows how to balance the many roles that nurses play, including that of caregiver, teacher, client advocate, and hospital employee. Addressing both practicing nurses and nursing students, Mary Molewyk Doornbos answers the question, "What does it mean to be a Christian nurse?" Providing real stories from nurses' experiences, the author discusses such types of nursing as psychiatric-mental health nursing, acute care nursing, and community health nursing. She also covers such issues as justice and care, and health and environment.

Subjects: Caregivers, Health Care, Nursing

More: Judith Shelly has two books on nursing and spiritual care: *Called to Care: A Christian Theology of Nursing* (InterVarsity, 1999) and *Spiritual Care: A Guide for Caregivers* (InterVarsity, 2000).

Focus on the Family Physicians Resource Council.

Focus on the Family Complete Guide to Caring for Aging Loved Ones. Tyndale, 2002. 558 pp. ISBN 141430160X.

Dozens of medical doctors and other professionals contributed to this practical book, which shows Christian readers how to cope with health issues that aging people face. It also deals with financial matters, legal issues, choosing housing, preventing fraud, and preparing for death. A substantial resource directory lists health, medical, and social services.

Subject: Caregivers, Health Care—Older People

More: Also try *Caring for Your Aging Parents: When Love Is Not Enough* by Barbara Deane (NavPress, 1989). For those dealing with dementia-related issues, try Pastor Robert Davis's account of his struggle with Alzheimer's, *My Journey into Alzheimer's Disease* (Tyndale, 1989). On the lighter side, try *The Beauty of Aging* by popular speaker and writer Karen O'Connor (Regal, 2006).

Glahn, Sandra L., and William R. Cutrer.

The Infertility Companion: Hope and Help for Couples Facing Infertility. Zondervan, 2004. 317 pp. ISBN 0310249619.

Sandra Glahn and William Cutrer write about myths and facts concerning infertility, discussing marital issues, emotional dynamics, and biblical examples. They ask questions like, "Is infertility a curse?" and "Why did God create sex?" They describe what is involved with male and female medical evaluations and discuss high-tech treatments, moral issues, third-party reproduction, donor eggs, and more. Endorsed by the Christian Medical Association.

Subject: Infertility

Larimore, Walt, and Traci Mullins.

God's Design for the Highly Healthy Person. Zondervan, 2005 (2003). 304 pp. ISBN 0310262798.

Medical doctor Walt Larimore writes about the essentials of good health, which include everything from nutrition and disease prevention to stress-free living, good relationships, and spiritual health. This book was formerly titled *10 Essentials of Highly Healthy People.*

Subjects: Health Care, Nutrition

More: Another health book by a Christian physician is *Complete Guide to Family Health, Nutrition & Fitness* by Paul C. Reisser (Focus on the Family, 2006).

Larimore, Walt, Sherri Flynt, and Steve Halliday.

SuperSized Kids: How to Rescue Your Child from the Obesity Threat. Center Street, 2005. 306 pp. ISBN 044657760X.

Overweight children tend to be overweight adults. Today, often because of weight issues, young people are facing heart disease, diabetes, kidney disease, and other maladies that typically are associated with adults. What's going wrong? The authors show how to deal with this epidemic. Some of the common American habits that are killing kids include television instead of exercise, sodas instead of water, lack of sleep, and filling up on foods that have no nutritional value. The authors say the solution requires a whole family effort. Walt Larimore is a Christian family physician and a medical journalist. Sherri Flynt is a registered and licensed dietitian.

Subjects: Health Care—Children, Nutrition—Children

More: Larimore also has written *God's Design for the Highly Healthy Child* (Zondervan, 2005) and *God's Design for the Highly Healthy Teen* (Zondervan, 2005). For another book on children's health, which also deals with childhood obesity, try *The No-Gimmick Guide to Raising Fit Kids* by medical doctor Robert S. Andersen (Focus on the Family Publishing, 2007).

Paris, Jenell Williams.

Birth Control for Christians: Making Wise Choices. Baker, 2003. 217 pp. ISBN 0801064376.

This book deals with basic information and the moral issues surrounding birth control methods. Jenell Williams Paris covers every form of birth control in common use today, offering up-to-date medical information and describing how each method works, its effectiveness, advantages, disadvantages, and cost. Methods covered include barrier methods, hormonal methods, IUDs, sterilization, natural family planning, and more. The author is an associate professor of anthropology at Bethel College in St. Paul, Minnesota, and a fertility awareness instructor.

Subject: Birth Control

Swanberg, Dennis, Diane Passno, and Walt Larimore.

Why A.D.H.D. Doesn't Mean Disaster. Focus on the Family, 2006. 170 pp. ISBN 1589973062.

Dennis Swanberg is a Christian minister and humorist with ADHD (attention deficit/hyperactivity disorder). Diane Passno, executive vice president of Focus on the Family, has a daughter with ADHD. Together with physician Walt Larimore's medical contributions, these authors offer hope and answers to families facing ADHD Swanberg and Passno give real stories about kids and parents who have dealt with this issue. Larimore discusses various medical treatments. He does not believe that sugar and/or dye intake is a factor in ADHD and says that the Feingold diet has not been proven to work.

Subjects: Attention-Deficit Hyperactivity Disorder, Parenting

More: Ted Broer writes from the opposite viewpoint as Larimore. Broer, a nutrition expert, talks about treating hyperactive children from a nutrition perspective. He believes that sugar/dye intake and vaccines are indeed factors in ADHD. His book is titled *Maximum Solutions for ADD, Learning Disabilities and Autism: Natural Treatments for ADD, ADHD, and Autism* (Siloam, 2002). A related book, more for adults with ADD, is *The Link Between A.D.D. and Addiction: Getting the Help You Deserve* by Wendy Richardson (NavPress, 1997).

Tada, Joni Eareckson, and Nigel M. de S. Cameron.

How to Be a Christian in a Brave New World. Zondervan, 2006. 224 pp. ISBN 0310259398.

Joni Eareckson Tada and Nigel Cameron discuss designer babies, human cloning, euthanasia, disabilities, and other bioethics issues that people face in today's world. What is wrong, and what is right? How should Christians think and act in this confusing time of embryo research and assisted reproduction? Tada, a quadriplegic, is a famous speaker and writer who founded a ministry that reaches out to the disabled community worldwide. Cameron is research professor of bioethics at the Illinois Institute of Technology.

Subject: Medical Ethics

More: *Whatever Happened to the Human Race?* by Francis Schaeffer and former surgeon general C. Everett Koop (Crossway, 2003)

deals with abortion, infanticide, and euthanasia. Also try *Human Dignity in the Biotech Century: A Christian Vision for Public Policy* by Charles Colson and Nigel Cameron, editors (InterVarsity, 2004), which presents twelve essays dealing with the ethical and legal issues on topics such as biotechnology, genetic engineering, nanotechnology, cybernetics, transhumanism, cloning, and human embryos. For still more, try *Does God Need Our Help?: Cloning, Assisted Suicide, & Other Challenges in Bioethics* by John F. Kilner and C. Ben Mitchell (Tyndale, 2003).

Taylor, Daniel, and Ronald Hoekstra.

Before Their Time: Lessons in Living from Those Born Too Soon. InterVarsity, 2000. 202 pp. ISBN 0830822658.

Daniel Taylor and Ronald Hoekstra tell the stories of real men, women, and babies who have experienced the traumas and joys of premature birth. They discuss life, death, and faith, asserting that God is found in the midst of hospitals, doctors, machines, and babies and their parents. Taylor is an English professor, and Hoekstra is a neonatologist at the Children's Hospital and Clinics of Minneapolis, specializing in the care of sick and premature newborns.

Subjects: Health Care—Children, Parenting, Premature Infants

Nutrition

Broer, Ted.

Maximum Energy: Top Ten Health Strategies to Feel Great, Live Longer, and Enjoy Life. Siloam, 2006. 380 pp. ISBN 1591858763.

Ted Broer, a motivational speaker on health and nutrition issues, shows why pure water, dietary fiber, antioxidants, healthy fats, exercise, and reduced stress are important for good health. Broer also lists ten foods that readers should avoid if they want to be healthy. These include shellfish, pork, caffeine, preserved meats, artificial sweeteners, junk food, and Olestra.

Subject: Nutrition

More: Broer's wife Sharon has three cookbooks: *The Maximum Energy Cookbook* (B & A Publications, 1999), *Healthy Country Cooking* (B & A Publications, 2005), and *Train Up Your Children in the Way They Should Eat* (Siloam, 1999).

Colbert, Don.

What Would Jesus Eat?: The Ultimate Program for Eating Well, Feeling Great, and Living Longer. Nelson, 2005. 256 pp. ISBN 0785273190.

Don Colbert, a medical doctor, discusses the foods that were available to Jesus in the Middle East 2,000 years ago—foods such as whole grains, fish, cheese, butter, onions, and so forth. He describes the Levitical law in regards to food and presents an eating plan. His conclusion, based on experience, the Bible, and research, is that Americans should adopt a Mediterranean diet.

Subject: Nutrition

More: Readers will naturally want to know about Colbert's companion cookbook, *The What Would Jesus Eat Cookbook* (Nelson, 2002). Three other books by Colbert are *Toxic Relief: Restore Health and Energy Through Fasting and Detoxification* (Siloam, 2003), *The Seven Pillars of Health* (Siloam, 2007), and *Stress Less* (Siloam, 2005).

Egan, Hope, and D. Thomas Lancaster.

Holy Cow!: Does God Care About What We Eat? First Fruits of Zion, 2005. 161 pp. ISBN 189212419X.

Hope Egan is a Jewish believer in Jesus. In this book, she talks about Jewish dietary laws and how they impact Christians. Of course, these laws are not requirements for salvation, she says, but they contain timeless wisdom for our health. Egan discusses eating meat, keeping kosher, mixing dairy and meat, blood, pork, birds, and more, and explains the scientific reasons why eating "unclean" animals is not a good idea. The second portion of the book—*Man Alive! There's More!*—was written by D. Thomas Lancaster, and deals with scriptural issues of Jewish dietary law and today's Christians. He talks about Peter's vision of the sheet in Acts 10 and other New Testament scriptures that address dietary issues, such as Galatians 2, 1 Corinthians 8–10, Mark 7, and Romans 14.

Subject: Nutrition

More: Rex Russell, who wrote the foreword for Egan's book, has published on this subject under the title *What the Bible Says About Healthy Living* (Regal, 2006).

O'Mathuna, Donal, and Walt Larimore.

Alternative Medicine: The Christian Handbook. Updated and expanded edition. Zondervan, 2007 (2001). 544 pp. ISBN 0310269997.

Two Christian medical professionals write about herbal remedies, supplements, and alternative therapies that are on the market. They discuss those that are beneficial and those that may be harmful. Acupressure, aromatherapy, biofeedback, chelation therapy, chiropractic, diets, homeopathy, magnet therapy, massage therapy, Reiki, yoga, tai chi, herbs, vitamins, and more are discussed.

They also talk about supernatural healing and the facts about ancient medical legends. Donal O'Mathuna is a bioethics and chemistry professor and Walt Larimore is a medical doctor.

Subjects: Alternative Medicine, Nutrition

More: Another book on the same topic is *The Biblical Guide to Alternative Medicine* by Neil T. Anderson and Michael Jacobson (Regal, 2003).

Rubin, Jordan, and David Remedios.

The Great Physician's Rx for Health and Wellness. Nelson Books, 2005. 370 pp. ISBN 078521352X.

Jordan Rubin is a nutritionist and a practitioner of naturopathic medicine. After recovering from serious health problems, Rubin wrote the best-selling *The Maker's Diet*. This more recent book gives information on dietary supplements, hygiene, exercise, toxins, and deadly emotions. Rubin believes these principles, along with prayer and biblical living, will lead to health and wellness. Many sample menus and recipes are included as well as a twenty-nine-page resource guide that lists companies that sell recommended food and cosmetic products.

Subject: Nutrition

More: Rubin writes about healing for Crohn's disease, colitis, irritable bowel syndrome, gluten and lactose intolerance, yeast infections, food allergies, and more in his book *Restoring Your Digestive Health: How the Guts and Glory Program Can Transform Your Life* (Twin Streams, 2003). Rubin also has written *The Maker's Diet: The 40-Day Health Experience That Will Change Your Life Forever* (Siloam, 2004). Readers may also be interested in Don Colbert's *Toxic Relief: Restore Health and Energy Through Fasting and Detoxification* (Siloam, 2001).

Fitness

Cooper, Kenneth H.

Faith-Based Fitness: The Medical Program That Uses Spiritual Motivation to Achieve Maximum Health and Add Years to Your Life. Thomas Nelson, 1997 (1995). 248 pp. ISBN 0785271376.

Medical doctor Kenneth Cooper, the father of aerobics (he coined the word), advocates disease prevention through aerobic exercise. Cooper begins by discussing the link between faith and fitness. He goes on to offer programs for stretching, calisthenics, walking, jogging, cycling (both outdoors and on stationary bikes), and swimming. Much of the book provides workout schedules for an exercise program that allows people to increase their endurance, flexibility, and strength. He also discusses fitness issues for women and the elderly.

Subject: Fitness

More: Cooper wrote another book for children's exercise and fitness called *Fit Kids!: The Complete Shape-Up Program from Birth through High School* (B&H Publishing, 1999).

Willis, Laurette.

BASIC Steps to Godly Fitness: Strengthening Your Body and Soul in Christ. Harvest House, 2005. 232 pp. ISBN 0736915656.

Laurette Willis, a certified personal trainer and a women's fitness specialist (IFPA), presents her fitness plan, which includes Praise-Moves (her Christian alternative to yoga), nutrition advice with recipes, the Gimme Ten Workout (her ten-minute daily workout routine involving light aerobics and light weights), and advice on stress, faith, and prayer for mental and spiritual health. DVDs are available for both the PraiseMoves workout and the Gimme Ten Workout.

Subjects: Fitness, Nutrition, Yoga

More: For a book on stretching/yoga from a Christian perspective that comes with a DVD, try *Yoga for Christians: A Christ-Centered Approach to Physical and Spiritual Health Through Yoga* by Susan Bordenkircher (Thomas Nelson, 2006).

Illness and Healing

Fintel, William A., and Gerald R. McDermott.

Cancer: A Medical and Spiritual Guide for Patients and Their Families. Baker Books, 2004. 351 pp. ISBN 0801065011.

In this hefty, information-packed book, the authors explain what cancer is and what causes it. They talk about breast cancer, lung cancer, skin cancer, prostate cancer, colon and rectal cancer, ovarian cancer, testing and diagnosis, surgery, radiation, chemotherapy, alternative therapy, cancer and God's plan, coping, suicide, hospice, and more. William Fintel is a practicing oncologist, and Gerald McDermott is a professor of religion and philosophy.

Subjects: Cancer, Health Care

More: Amy Givler is a Christian and a medical doctor who was diagnosed with Hodgkin's lymphoma. In *Hope in the Face of Cancer* (Harvest House, 2003), she wrote the book she wished she had when she found out she had cancer. Hematologist and oncologist Al B. Weir writes about what to do when faced with a troubling diagnosis in *When Your Doctor Has Bad News: Simple Steps to Strength, Healing, and Hope* (Zondervan, 2003).

Fountain, Daniel E.

God, Medicine, and Miracles: The Spiritual Factor in Healing. Harold Shaw, 1999. 265 pp. ISBN 0877883211.

When Daniel Fountain talks about the medical profession, he does so from the inside. Fountain is a medical doctor (currently working for the Christian Medical and Dental Society). Too often, he says, medical science and medical doctors ignore the reality of the spiritual and emotional life—they view people simply as collections of tissue and organs. Fountain shows readers how faith and medicine go hand in hand. When the soul and the spirit are healed, the body is also affected. For instance, Fountain tells the story of a twenty-eight-year-old woman who was dying from a serious infection and related heart trouble. The woman had rejected God and prayer years before. During this crisis, she requested prayer from her doctor and forgiveness from God. Once this spiritual and emotional healing took place, the medicines in her body were able to do their job, and she recovered physically. Fountain's point is that since we are emotional, spiritual, and physical beings, doctors, counselors, and ministers need to work together in bringing life and healing to the people they serve.

Subjects: Healing, Health Care

More: Charles Kraft explores some of these issues of inner healing in his book *Deep Wounds, Deep Healing: Discovering the Vital Link Between Spiritual Warfare and Inner Healing* (Regal, 2004). Fountain recommends books by William Backus, who wrote the foreword to Fountain's book. Two more books by Backus are *Telling Yourself the Truth* (Bethany, 2000) and *The Healing Power of a Christian Mind* (Bethany, 1998).

Knox, Sally M., and Janet Kobobel Grant.

The Breast Cancer Care Book: A Survival Guide for Patients and Loved Ones. Zondervan, 2004. 248 pp. ISBN 0310248701.

Breast cancer surgeon Sally Knox walks the reader through the journey of breast cancer, from receiving the diagnosis to choosing surgery options to life after cancer. Knox explains medical tests to detect cancer and shows the reader how to prepare for the long list of doctors, procedures, and records that must be dealt with when cancer is detected. She clearly describes surgery, therapy options, and medical terms. Special sections show how a spouse can be supportive, how children can cope, and how patients can restore fitness and well-being.

Subjects: Cancer—Breast Cancer, Health Care—Women, Women—Health

House and Home

This section annotates books with a Christian perspective of various domestic interests, such as home decorating, organizing, hospitality, and even knitting and quilting.

Hanby-Robie, Sharon.

The Simple Home: A Faith-filled Guide to Simplicity, Peace, and Joy in Your Home. GuidepostsBooks, 2006. 200 pp. ISBN 0824947029.

Sharon Hanby-Robie, the home-decor expert for QVC, the home shopping network, gives advice for interior decoration and home organization from her thirty years of experience as an interior designer. Here is her mission statement for her own home: "I want my home to be ordered in such a way that it reflects the beauty and depth of our Lord's creation. I want it to be functional, provide safety and comfort, and yet remain gracious enough to soothe the senses and inspire dreams."

Subjects: Home Decorating, Organization

More: Hanby-Robie wrote another book (with Deb Strubel) called *Beautiful Places and Spiritual Spaces: The Art of Stress-Free Interior Design* (Northfield, 2004). For a book on the home focusing on hospitality, try *A Life That Says Welcome: Simple Ways to Open Your Heart & Home to Others* by Karen Ehman (Revell, 2006).

Jorgensen, Susan S., and Susan S. Izard.

Knitting into the Mystery: A Guide to the Shawl-Knitting Ministry. Morehouse, 2003. 147 pp. ISBN 0819219673.

Knitting and knitting ministries are on the rise. It is a way for women to enjoy friendship and express love through handiwork. Susan Jorgensen, a retreat leader, and Susan Izard, a United Church of Christ minister, write about knitting and shawl-knitting ministry. They give practical advice for selecting yarn and knitting shawls, and discuss various topics like knitting alone, knitting with others, and keeping a knitting journal. They also offer several prayers for specific life situations.

Subjects: Knitting, Quilting

More: Two related books are *What I Learned from God While Quilting* by Ruth McHaney Danner and Cristine Bolley (Barbour, 2000) and *Fabric of Faith: A Guide to the Prayer Quilt Ministry* by Kimberly Winston (Morehouse, 2006).

Mains, Karen.

Open Heart, Open Home: The Hospitable Way to Make Others Feel Welcome and Wanted. Revised edition. InterVarsity, 2002 (1976). 216 pp. ISBN 083082300X.

Karen Mains takes hospitality to a practical and spiritual level. Our homes are places where Christian ministry can happen, she says. Mains distinguishes between mere entertaining and hospitality, which is really servanthood. At the end of each chapter she offers practical ways to apply teachings. Mains is a pastor's wife and comes from the perspective of such a person; however, this book is also valuable for people who are not in full-time ministry.

Subject: Hospitality

More: Another book on the subject, which includes recipes and ideas for entertaining, is *Simple Hospitality* by Jane Jarrell (Thomas Nelson, 2005). Also try *A Life That Says Welcome: Simple Ways to Open Your Heart & Home to Others* by Karen Ehman (Revell, 2006). For books that are more of a study of the nature and importance of hospitality, try *Untamed Hospitality: Welcoming God and Other Strangers* by Elizabeth Newman (Brazos, 2007), *Making Room: Recovering Hospitality As a Christian Tradition* by Christine Pohl (Eerdmans, 1999), and *Radical Hospitality: Benedict's Way of Love* by Daniel Homan and Loni Collins Pratt (Paraclete Press, 2002).

Porter, Kathryn.

Too Much Stuff: De-cluttering Your Heart and Home. Beacon Hill, 2006. 167 pp. ISBN 0834122561.

Kathryn Porter describes how a messy home robbed her family of health and love and, eventually, her mother's life. To say the least, a messy house is an emotional burden. In this book, Porter shows readers how to become emotionally and physically free of clutter. She explains how to determine what to keep and what to say goodbye to. She demolishes excuses for keeping stuff. Offering hard-earned and life-changing wisdom, she outlines a practical plan of attack and addresses specific issues such as laundry, kitchens, paper items, bedrooms and bathrooms, and even the yard and the car.

Subjects: Clutter, Housekeeping, Materialism, Organization

More: Sandra Felton is one of the classic writers on this subject. Two of her books are *Organizing Magic: 40 Days to a Well-Ordered Home and Life* (Revell, 2006) and *The Messies Manual: A Complete Guide to Bringing Order and Beauty to Your Home* (Revell 25th anniversary edition, 2005). Also try *The One-Minute Home Organizer: Making Your Home Beautiful and Your Life Clutter Free* by Emilie Barnes (Harvest House, 2007) and *All in Good Time: Real Life Organization Strategies for Christian Work-at-Home Moms* by Debbie Williams (Let's Get It Together, 2005).

Men's, Women's, and Teens' Issues

Men, women, and teens each face issues unique to their situation. Here are books on body image, virtue, modesty, and other topics of particular interest. A subsection on sex and sexuality covers subjects including sex education, sex instruction, homosexuality, abstinence, and pornography.

Courtney, Vicky.

TeenVirtue. B&H Publishing, 2005. 150 pp. ISBN 0805430563. **YA**

In short one- or two-page articles formatted like those in a teen girls' magazine, Vicky Courtney addresses a host of issues including modesty, eating disorders, body piercing, tattoos, beauty, emotions, popularity, homosexuality, abortion, abstinence, friendship, parents, and boys.

Subjects: Award Winners (ECPA), Teenage Girls, Virtue, Young-Adult Interest

More: Courtney wrote another book with a magazine-type cover for nine- to twelve-year-old girls called *Between: A Girl's Guide to Life* (B&H Publishing, 2006). Danae Dobson has a book for girls ages eleven to fifteen called *Let's Talk!: Good Stuff for Girlfriends About God, Guys, and Growing Up* (Tyndale, 2003). Teens may also want to read *A Young Woman After God's Own Heart: A Teen's Guide to Friends, Faith, Family, and the Future* by Elizabeth George (Harvest House, 2003).

DeMoss, Nancy Leigh.

Lies Women Believe and the Truth That Sets Them Free. Moody, 2002. 284 pp. ISBN 0802472966.

Nancy Leigh DeMoss examines common women's issues and provides biblical solutions. She discusses lies about God, about identity and self-worth, about sin, about priorities, about marriage and children, about emotions, and about life circumstances. DeMoss covers a host of issues including submission in marriage, abuse, hormones and depression, suffering, women and careers, rebellion in children, body image, bondage to sin, and more.

Subjects: Marriage, Parenting, Women's Issues

More: Other books on women's issues include *Feminine Appeal* by Carolyn Mahaney (Crossway, 2004), *The Confident Woman: Knowing Who You Are in Christ* by Anabel Gillham (Harvest House, 2003), and *Let Me Be a Woman* by Elisabeth Elliot (Tyndale, 1999). For a helpful explanation of what goes on physiologically in a woman's body (from endocrine glands and hormones to premenstrual syndrome and menopause), try *Emotional Phases of a Woman's Life* by Jean Lush and Patricia Rushford (Revell, 1990).

Dobson, James.

Preparing for Adolescence. Gospel Light, 2005 (1978). 163 pp. ISBN 0830738266. **YA**

Although it is addressed to readers ages nine to fourteen, Christian parents will also benefit from this book. Dobson (a popular psychologist and the founder of Focus on the Family) talks about crucial issues that his readers are going to face: inferiority and self-esteem, conformity, puberty and body changes, identity, drug abuse, sex, and more. Dobson is straightforward, but does shock readers with dreadful stories of sexually transmitted diseases and ruined lives.

Subjects: Preteens, Teenagers, Young-Adult Interest

More: *So You Want to Be a Teenager?: What Every Preteen Must Know About Friends, Love, Sex, Dating, and Other Life Issues* by Dennis and Barbara Rainey, with their children Samuel and Rebecca (Thomas Nelson, 2002). For a book addressing older teens, such as high school seniors about to face life on their own, try *Life on the Edge: A Young Adult's Guide to a Meaningful Future* by James Dobson (Word, 1995).

Eldredge, John.

Wild at Heart: Discovering the Secret of a Man's Soul. Thomas Nelson, 2001. 224 pp. ISBN 0785268839.

John Eldredge believes that men need to get their hearts back—their sense of adventure and passion and risk. Many men have lost this freedom and motivation for life because they were wounded by their fathers and others that they loved and admired. Whatever the cause, Eldredge gives men permission to be alive again. He says that when a man's life becomes an adventure, "the whole thing takes on a transcendent purpose when he releases control in exchange for the recovery of the dreams in his heart."

Subjects: Award Winners (ECPA), Men's Issues

More: Eldredge also has written *The Journey of Desire: Searching for the Life We've Only Dreamed Of* (Thomas Nelson, 2001). Two more books somewhat in the spirit of Eldredge's book are *No More Christian Nice Guy: When Being Nice—Instead of Good—Hurts Men, Women and Children* by Paul Coughlin (Bethany, 2005) and *6 Rules Every Man Must Break* by Bill Perkins (Tyndale, 2007). For a book dealing with father issues (or fatherless issues), try *To Own a Dragon: Reflections on Growing Up Without a Father* by Donald Miller and John MacMurray (NavPress, 2006).

Feldhahn, Shaunti.

For Women Only: What You Need to Know About the Inner Lives of Men. Multnomah, 2004. 189 pp. ISBN 1590523172.

Shaunti Feldhahn writes to women about what makes guys tick. She spoke with more than 1,000 men, and the results of her interviews matched a recent national survey. Feldhahn was surprised at what she learned. In this book she shares the results of her interviews and shows women how to understand men when it comes to love, romance, sex, respect, insecurity, and more.

Subjects: Man–Woman Relationships, Women's Issues

Graham, Michelle.

Wanting to Be Her: Body Image Secrets Victoria Won't Tell You. InterVarsity Press, 2005. 169 pp. ISBN 0830832661.

In this book, addressed to Christian adults, Michelle Graham exposes false ideas that our society embraces concerning beauty and body image. She includes a chapter on ethnicity and the problems that Asian, Jewish, and African American women face in today's culture. She also discusses when a desire to be accepted or to please others becomes sinful. Graham writes about how to have a balanced view of beauty, and distinguishes between looking beautiful and being beautiful.

Subjects: Beauty, Body Image, Women

More: *Why Beauty Matters* is a book by Karen Lee-Thorp and Cynthia Hicks (NavPress, 2006) that discusses why women want to look good and where things go wrong for them in the process. Also try *You Are Not What You Weigh: End Your War with Food and Discover Your True Value* by Lisa Bevere (Siloam, 2007).

Gresh, Dannah.

Secret Keeper: The Delicate Power of Modesty. Moody, 2005. 96 pp. ISBN 0802439721. **YA**

Dannah Gresh discusses a woman's power of allure and shows that modesty increases that power in a good way, but immodesty only does harm. She describes from a man's point of view what happens when girls or women dress immodestly.

Subjects: Modesty, Purity, Teenage Girls, Women, Young-Adult Interest

More: For mothers with young girls (ages eight to twelve), Gresh has published the *Secret Keeper Girls Kit* (Moody, 2004), which includes an audio CD and an agenda of monthly mother/daughter dates.

Morley, Patrick.

The Man in the Mirror: Solving the 24 Problems Men Face. Zondervan, 1997 (Wolgemuth & Hyatt, 1989). 336 pp. ISBN 0310217687.

> Patrick Morley writes about identity issues, relationship issues, and money issues from a Christian perspective. He also addresses pride, fear, anger, significance and purpose in life, job contentment, time management, and more.
>
> **Subjects:** Award Winners (ECPA), Friendship, Marriage, Men's Issues, Parenting
>
> **More:** Four well-known books on men's issues are *The Measure of a Man* by Gene Getz (Regal, 2004), *Maximized Manhood: A Guide to Family Survival* by Edwin Louis Cole (Whitaker House, 2001), *He-Motions: Even Strong Men Struggle* by T. D. Jakes (Putnam, 2004), and *Disciplines of a Godly Man* by R. Kent Hughes (Crossway, 2001). To understand the purpose of being a husband and father, try *Husbands and Fathers: Rediscover the Creator's Purpose for Men* by Derek Prince (Chosen, 2000).

Osaigbovo, Rebecca Florence.

Chosen Vessels: Women of Color, Keys to Change. Revised edition. InterVarsity, 2002 (DaBar, 1992). 236 pp. ISBN 0830823808.

> This is a book written by an African American woman for other African American women. Rebecca Florence Osaigbovo suggests that although women of color are hated by Satan, they are loved by God. When these women learn of God's love and commit themselves to God's way of living, she says, communities and cities will be changed. African American women are vessels chosen by God to reverse the damage of the enemy. As this book unfolds, Osaigbovo addresses problems and hurts specific to African American women, and she presents keys to heal the pain and bring about real, Christian, spirit-led change.
>
> **Subjects:** African American Women, Women's Issues
>
> **More:** Osaigbovo also has written *It's Not About You—It's About God* (InterVarsity, 2003).

Spangler, Ann.

She Who Laughs, Lasts!: Laugh-Out-Loud Stories from Today's Best-Known Women of Faith. Zondervan, 2000. 240 pp. ISBN 0310228980.

> This is a collection of funny stories from well-known Christian women writers such as Barbara Johnson, Patsy Clairmont, Luci Swindoll, Sheila Walsh, Marilyn Meberg, Thelma Wells, Chonda Pierce, and more. The stories are grouped around themes like

friendship, men, marriage, parenting, and kids. Becky Freeman talks about a glass of tea she enjoyed that had one of her son's live worms at the bottom. Kathy Peel writes about the art of potty training. Liz Curtis Higgs writes about the wrinkles that come with age. These authors are associated with Women of Faith, a women's organization that encourages women to grow in faith and spiritual maturity. It hosts nondenominational Christian women's conferences throughout the United States.

Subjects: Humor, Women's Issues

More: Three more humorous titles for women are *Help! I'm Turning into My Mother ... With a Few Quirks of My Own* by Becky Freeman and her mother, Ruthie Arnold (Harvest House, 2002), *Second Row Piano Side* by Chonda Pierce (Beacon Hill Press, 1996), and *Just Hand Over the Chocolate and No One Will Get Hurt* by Karen Scalf Linamen (Baker, 1999). Also, two books by well-known women's writers that deal with serious issues like grief and depression are *If Mama Ain't Happy, Ain't Nobody Happy!: Making the Choice to Rejoice* by Lindsey O'Connor (Harvest House, 2006) and *Splashes of Joy in the Cesspools of Life* by Barbara Johnson (Thomas Nelson, 2005).

Sex and Sexuality

Arterburn, Steve, Fred Stoeker, and Mike Yorkey.

Every Man's Battle: Winning the War on Sexual Temptation: One Victory at a Time. WaterBrook, 2000. 229 pp. ISBN 1578563682.

Married men, Christian men, men in ministry—all struggle with thoughts and images, desires and circumstances that can easily rage out of control and destroy their marriages, children, business, and ministry. Sexual purity is possible, say the authors, and this book gives practical help for overcoming sexual addiction, be it mild or severe.

Subjects: Men's Issues, Pornography, Sexual Sin, Temptation

More: For women dealing with their husband's sexual sin, try *Every Heart Restored: A Wife's Guide to Healing in the Wake of a Husband's Sexual Sin* by Stephen Arterburn, Fred and Brenda Stoeker, and Mike Yorkey (WaterBrook, 2004).

Arterburn, Stephen, Fred Stoeker, and Mike Yorkey.

Preparing Your Son for Every Man's Battle: Honest Conversations About Sexual Integrity. WaterBrook, 2003. 256 pp. ISBN 1578566894.

This incredible book is really two books in one. Book one is for the parent to read. Book two is for the parent and child to read together. The authors recommend doing this when your children are nearing puberty (somewhere around eleven or twelve years old). This is not a clinical, cold description of physiological changes. This is a way for the Christian parent to connect in a significant way with his or her son and to help him understand—without fear or confusion—what is happening to him physically (puberty) and socially (peer pressure, dating, etc.). This book equips sons for sexual purity. This book is not just for dads; mothers and single moms will also find it very valuable.

Subjects: Award Winners (ECPA), Fathers and Sons, Parenting, Puberty, Sex Education, Sexual Abstinence

More: Shannon Ethridge wrote a similar book for mothers and daughters called *Preparing Your Daughter for Every Woman's Battle: Creative Conversations about Sexual and Emotional Integrity* (WaterBrook, 2005).

Comiskey, Andrew.

Pursuing Sexual Wholeness: How Jesus Heals the Homosexual. Creation House, 1989. 207 pp. ISBN 0884192598.

Andrew Comiskey, the founder and director of Desert Stream Ministries, shares his personal story and then discusses a biblical understanding of sexuality. He shows readers how to find gender wholeness and how to break sexual addiction. He discusses relational issues concerning parents, "woundedness," and healing.

Subject: Homosexuality, Sexual Addiction

More: Comiskey has a more recent book for men and women that covers broader topics: *Strength in Weakness: Overcoming Sexual and Relational Brokenness* (InterVarsity, 2003). Joe Dallas has written a book for men about homosexuality called *Desires in Conflict: Hope for Men Who Struggle with Sexual Identity* (Harvest House, 2003).

Eden, Dawn.

The Thrill of the Chaste: Finding Fulfillment While Keeping Your Clothes On. W Publishing Group, 2006. 212 pp. ISBN 084991311X.

This is a book on chastity for grown-ups. Journalist and music historian Dawn Eden knows the New York City sex scene. She realized that sex never brought her the relationship she wanted. In fact, it seemed to be distancing her from the ability to have a loving relationship. She describes how she started saying no to casual sex and how she struggled to get in touch with her emotions that had been blunted time and again. Fear of intimacy and fear of rejection did not keep her from sex, but kept her from love.

Subjects: Chastity, Sexual Abstinence, Sexual Sin, Single Women, Women

More: *Sex and the Soul of a Woman: The Reality of Love & Romance in an Age of Casual Sex* by Paula Rinehart (Zondervan, 2004). Also try *Real Sex: The Naked Truth About Chastity* by Lauren Winner (Brazos, 2005).

Ethridge, Shannon.

Every Woman's Battle: Discovering God's Plan for Sexual and Emotional Fulfillment. WaterBrook, 2003. 193 pp. ISBN 1578566851. **YA**

Shannon Ethridge describes from the Christian perspective female sexuality and common pitfalls women face that threaten purity and health. She shares personal stories from her own life as she discusses emotional affairs, renegade thoughts, and restoration.

Subject: Girls, Purity, Sexuality, Sexual Sin, Teenage Women, Women, Young-Adult Interest

More: Ethridge also has a volume on the same topic geared toward young women called *Every Young Woman's Battle* (WaterBrook, 2004).

Gresh, Dannah.

And the Bride Wore White: Seven Secrets to Sexual Purity. Moody, 2004. 192 pp. ISBN 0802483445. **YA**

Dannah Gresh, founder of Pure Freedom Retreats, writes about purity, defining its characteristics and describing its development. She exposes lies about sex and talks about how to break off sinful relationships. In a friendly, conversational style, Gresh explains the potential wonders and dangers of sex and relationships from a Christian perspective.

Subjects: Purity, Sexual Abstinence, Teenage Girls, Women, Young-Adult Interest

More: Another book on purity—this one for both men and women—is Randy Alcorn's *The Purity Principle* (Multnomah, 2003). Also, readers who like Gresh's books might also want to read *I Kissed Dating Goodbye: A New Attitude Toward Romance and Relationships* by Joshua Harris (Multnomah, 2003).

Gross, Craig, and Carter Krummrich.

The Dirty Little Secret: Uncovering the Truth Behind Porn. Zondervan, 2006. 176 pp. ISBN 031027107X.

Craig Gross, the founder of Fireproof Ministries and XXXchurch.com, a Web site that reaches out to the church and the porn industry, saw porn destroy many lives. In this book, Gross says that people, especially Christians, need to stop ignoring the problem of porn. It is an issue for both men and women. It is a problem for Christians and Christian pastors. Gross talks about the porn industry and porn stars. Gross also writes about various ways to escape this bondage and lifestyle. For these people, pornography promises pleasure and joy, but leaves them empty and miserable.

Subjects: Addiction to Sex, Pornography, Pornography Industry, Sexual Sin

Herman, Doug.

Time for a Pure Revolution. Tyndale, 2004. 238 pp. ISBN 0842383573. **YA**

Sixth graders are having sex parties before their parents come home from work. Sexually transmitted diseases (STDs) are rampant among today's youth. The stage is set for ruined lives. International speaker and author Doug Herman describes the drastic need for a revolution. Herman's mission is to stop young people from throwing away their futures. This book discusses how society reached this point of crisis, how kids can be a part of a pure revolution, and how Christian parents can help their children in making good choices. Herman also talks about what love and intimacy are. There is a section on STDs.

Subjects: Chastity, Sexual Abstinence, Sexually Transmitted Diseases, Teenagers, Young-Adult Interest, Youth Culture

More: For more books on youth culture, try *Hurt: Inside the World of Today's Teenagers* by Chap Clark (Baker, 2004), *Sex, Lies, and the Media* by Eva Marie Everson and Jessica Everson (Life Journey, 2005), and *Youth Culture 101* by Walt Mueller (Zondervan, 2007).

Leman, Kevin.

Sheet Music: Uncovering the Secrets of Sexual Intimacy in Marriage. Tyndale, 2003. 246 pp. ISBN 0842360247.

Well-known psychologist Kevin Leman is no prude when it comes to sex. In a lighthearted and sometimes humorous style, he talks about positions, turnoffs, sex for older couples, and other issues using clear and frank writing. Leman also discusses sex for new couples and addresses issues like oral (ok) and anal (not good) sex.

Subjects: Intimacy, Marriage, Sex in Marriage

More: For a book focusing on women's sex issues, try *Intimate Issues: Answers to 21 Questions Women Ask About Sex* by Linda Dillow and Lorraine Pintus (WaterBrook, 1999). Two classic books on sex, still in print after thirty years, are *The Act of Marriage* by Tim and Beverly LaHaye (Zondervan, 1998) and *Intended for Pleasure: Sex Technique and Sexual Fulfillment in Christian Marriage* by Ed and

Gaye Wheat (Revell, 3rd Ed., 1997). Ed Wheat is a physician, and this book gives more of a medical perspective.

Leman, Kevin, and Kathy Bell.

A Chicken's Guide to Talking Turkey with Your Kids About Sex. Zondervan, 2004. 214 pp. ISBN 031025096X.

Kevin Leman and Kathy Bell discuss when and how to talk to your children about sex, how to be a positive influence in your children's life at the time of puberty, peer pressure, and abstinence. They also describe the physiological changes that will take place in your child's body during puberty. In this well-written book, Leman and Bell tell many stories from their experience as Christian parents and counselors that will help parents and their children navigate this touchy subject with confidence and grace.

Subjects: Parenting, Puberty, Sex Education, Sexual Abstinence

More: Stan and Brenna Jones have a series of books (the God's Design for Sex series) written for children of various ages to read. For instance, for kids ages eight to eleven, they wrote *What's the Big Deal? Why God Cares About Sex* (NavPress, 2007).

MacNutt, Francis.

Can Homosexuality Be Healed? Chosen, 2006 (2001). 112 pp. ISBN 0800794095.

Francis MacNutt suggests that most homosexuals did not choose to have a same-sex attraction. He then poses hard questions like, "How can heterosexuals demand that homosexuals repent over a matter in which there seems to be no choice whatsoever?" and, "In asking homosexuals to change, aren't we asking the impossible?" MacNutt responds that we should not condemn people for their sexual orientation (since it seems to be involuntary), but that we should not approve of unbiblical sexual activity. He asserts that homosexuals, even though they didn't ask for this orientation, can be healed. The need for same-sex affection can and should be met in a healthy, healing way. The strength of this book is in the fact that MacNutt directs readers to both the emotional healing and the spiritual deliverance that people need in order to be truly healed.

Subjects: Deliverance, Homosexuality, Inner Healing

Thompson, Chad W.

Loving Homosexuals As Jesus Would: A Fresh Christian Approach. Brazos, 2004. 183 pp. ISBN 1587431211.

All Christians could benefit from this book, not just those struggling with homosexuality. Chad Thompson tells his personal story and then discusses—in very clear and plain language—

homophobia, science and homosexuality, causes of homosexuality, and overcoming homosexual attraction. For heterosexual Christians, Thompson shows how to understand and affirm fellow believers struggling with homosexuality. A resource section lists helpful books and Web sites/organizations.

Subject: Homosexuality

More: For those who have just discovered that a friend or family member is gay, try *When Homosexuality Hits Home: What to Do When a Loved One Says They're Gay* by Joe Dallas (Harvest House, 2004).

White, John.

Eros Defiled: The Christian and Sexual Sin. InterVarsity, 1977. 172 pp. ISBN 0877847819.

John White presents a nonjudgmental, nonlegalistic view of sexuality. He discusses major sexual sins such as premarital sex, adultery, homosexuality, and more. The last section shows how the local church could deal with sexual sin and discipline as a healing community of love and forgiveness.

Subject: Sexual Sin

More: *Fatal Attractions: Why Sex Sins Are Worse Than Others* by Jack Hayford (Gospel Light, 2004).

Relationships

Christian views about dating vary widely. Some Christians advocate the replacement of dating with the practice of courting. Others feel that it is healthy for Christians to date. These and other views are represented in the section on dating and singles. Marriage self-help books are wildly popular. Christian authors such as Gary Smalley (*Hidden Keys of a Loving, Lasting Marriage*) and Gary Chapman (*The Five Love Languages*) have written several best-selling books. Divorce-related books are also included. Parenting is another hot topic. Every Christian presumably wants to raise his or her children according to the Bible in a wise and loving way. This section covers the basics of raising children, including stepparenting, single parenting, discipline (spanking), and even grandparenting.

Dating and Singles

Cloud, Henry, and John Townsend.

Boundaries in Dating: Making Dating Work. Zondervan, 2000. 280 pp. ISBN 0310200342.

In answer to Joshua Harris's *I Kissed Dating Goodbye*, Cloud and Townsend say that Christians should not feel compelled to give up dating. They say that dating is not the problem, but that dating in unhealthy ways is. Cloud and Townsend list several benefits of dating and show the reader how to establish healthy relationship boundaries to help dating work.

Subjects: Dating, Single People

More: Dick Purnell, director of Single Life Resources with Campus Crusade for Christ, was single for forty-two years. He writes about finding a mate in *Finding a Lasting Love* (Harvest House, 2003). Women may also want to read *Finding Mr. Right (and How to Know When You Have)* by Stephen Arterburn and Meg J. Rinck (Thomas Nelson, 2001).

Harris, Joshua.

I Kissed Dating Goodbye: A New Attitude Toward Romance and Relationships. Updated edition. Multnomah, 2003 (1997). 238 pp. ISBN 1590521358.

Written by a young man "just out of his teen years" for teenagers or anyone wanting 1) to preserve purity during singleness and 2) to be prepared for biblical romance. Joshua Harris points out the problems with traditional dating and offers his alternative: courtship.

Subject: Dating

More: Harris also wrote *Boy Meets Girl: Say Hello to Courtship* (Multnomah, 2005) in which he talks about his own courtship with the woman who became his wife. Fans of Harris will also like the classic *Passion and Purity: Learning to Bring Your Love Life Under Christ's Control* by Elisabeth Elliot (Revell, 2002). Older singles may prefer another book with the courtship perspective called *Choosing God's Best* by Don Raunikar (Multnomah, 1998). For a totally different perspective on dating, try *How to Get a Date Worth Keeping* by Henry Cloud (Zondervan, 2005).

Hsu, Albert Y.

Singles at the Crossroads: A Fresh Perspective on Christian Singleness. InterVarsity, 1997. 194 pp. ISBN 0830813535.

Singleness is not a problem, says Albert Hsu. In this book, Hsu presents what he calls a "practical theology" of singleness. He gives a short history of singleness and then discusses such notions as the so-called "gift of singleness," the will of God, and the "perfect partner." He talks about loneliness, temptation, romance, and community. The book ends with an interview on singleness with John Stott, the noted Anglican writer and minister.

Subject: Single People

More: Another book for singles is *They Were Single Too: 8 Biblical Role Models* by David M. Hoffeditz (Kregel, 2005).

Whelchel, Mary S.

Common Mistakes Singles Make. Expanded edition. Revell, 1999 (1989). 159 pp. ISBN 0800757114.

This is a book for singles and for married people who know singles. Mary Whelchel describes mistakes involving attitudes toward marriage and the opposite sex, problems in dating and friendship, issues in dealing with married people and family members, aspects of finance and career, and more. She also discusses common mistakes that married couples (including family, friends, ministers, and church staff) make in regard to single people.

Subjects: Dating, Single People

More: For single women, try *Lady in Waiting: Becoming God's Best While Waiting for Mr. Right* by Jackie Kendall and Debby Jones (Destiny Image, 2005). Heather Arnel Paulsen has written a book dealing with one specific issue that singles face: *Emotional Purity: An Affair of the Heart* (Winepress, 2005).

Yancey, George A., and Sherelyn Whittum Yancey.

Just Don't Marry One: Interracial Dating, Marriage, and Parenting. Judson, 2002. 235 pp. ISBN 081701439X.

Articles in this book come from many different contributors and deal with topics such as transracial adoption, interracial dating, pastoring multiracial families, an Asian American Christian perspective of interracial marriage, and children of interracial couples. George Yancey is assistant professor of sociology at the University of North Texas. He and his wife, Sherelyn, are cofounders of Reconciliation Consulting (and are themselves an interracial couple). Appendix A is a resource guide listing many helpful organizations, Web sites, books, and articles. Appendix B is called "Assessment Guide: Capabilities of Persons Who Parent Cross-Racially or Cross-Culturally."

Subjects: Adoption—Interracial, Dating—Interracial, Marriage—Interracial, Parenting

Marriage

Chapman, Gary.

The Five Love Languages: How to Express Heartfelt Commitment to Your Mate. Northfield, 1995. 209 pp. ISBN 1881273156.

This best-selling book tells people how to express love. The five "languages" are words of affirmation, quality time, receiving gifts, acts of service, and physical touch. Gary Chapman helps the reader determine their primary love language and how to "speak" these "languages." He is a pastor, writer, and seminar speaker.

Subject: Marriage

More: *Love Talk: Speak Each Other's Language Like You Never Have Before* by Les and Leslie Parrott (Zondervan, 2004). Another best-selling book on communication in marriage is *Love & Respect: The Love She Most Desires; The Respect He Desperately Needs* by Emerson Eggerichs (Thomas Nelson, 2004). Chapman has several related books, including *The Five Love Languages of Children* (Moody, 1997) and *The Five Love Languages for Singles* (Moody, 2004).

House, H. Wayne.

Divorce and Remarriage: Four Christian Views. InterVarsity, 1990. 267 pp. ISBN 0830812830.

In this book, four different Christian perspectives are offered concerning whether divorce and remarriage should be allowed according to the Bible. The four views are: 1) No divorce and no remarriage by J. Carl Laney; 2) Divorce, but no remarriage by William A. Heth; 3) Divorce and remarriage for adultery or desertion by Thomas R. Edgar; and 4) Divorce and remarriage under a variety of circumstances by Larry Richards. After each view is presented, the other three authors each give a response.

Subjects: Divorce, Marriage, Remarriage

Judah, Stephen M.

Staying Together When an Affair Pulls You Apart. InterVarsity, 2006. 197 pp. ISBN 0830833994.

What causes affairs? How is the damage overcome? In this book, psychologist Stephen Judah answers these questions. He also describes different types of affairs and the stages of infidelity, which can begin during childhood. Throughout the book, Judah tells the stories of several couples who have experienced affairs and responded in various ways. This book is designed to be used by individuals and professional counselors.

Subjects: Adultery, Divorce, Marriage

Kennedy, Nancy.

When He Doesn't Believe: Help and Encouragement for Women Who Feel Alone in Their Faith. WaterBrook, 2001. 208 pp. ISBN 1578564344.

Nancy Kennedy, married to an unbeliever, wrote this book to encourage other women who face the same situation. She discusses how to build a support system and how to handle situations like when husbands tell dirty jokes or want to bring their wives to a bar; or worse, when their husbands drink or get involved with pornography. She also writes about whether divorce should be an option.

Subjects: Marriage, Wives

Parrott, Les, and Leslie Parrott.

Saving Your Second Marriage Before It Starts: Nine Questions to Ask Before (and After) You Remarry. Zondervan, 2001. 187 pp. ISBN 0310207487.

Les Parrott is a professor of clinical psychology, and his wife, Leslie, is a marriage and family therapist. In this book, they help people determine whether they are prepared to marry again. They discuss common false expectations for those who want to remarry, and give advice on communication and family matters.

Subjects: Marriage, Remarriage

Peace, Martha.

The Excellent Wife: A Biblical Perspective. Focus Publishing, 1999. 257 pp. ISBN 1885904088.

Martha Peace, a Nouthetic (Bible-centered) counselor, discusses what the Bible says about the role and responsibility of a wife. She believes that wives, motivated by a desire to honor Christ, should submit to their husbands. Peace suggests that biblical submission brings blessings, protection, and fulfillment.

Subjects: Marriage, Wives

More: *On the Other Side of the Garden: Biblical Womanhood for Today's World* by Virginia Fugate (Foundation for Biblical Research, 2004). Also try *Sacred Influence: What a Man Needs from His Wife to Be the Husband She Wants* by Gary L. Thomas (Zondervan, 2006). For a different book by Martha Peace, see *Damsels in Distress: Biblical Solutions for Problems Women Face* (P&R Publishing, 2006). Also, *Let Me Be a Woman: Notes on Womanhood for Valerie* by Elisabeth Elliot (Tyndale, 1999).

Rainey, Dennis, and Barbara Rainey.

Starting Your Marriage Right: What You Need to Know in the Early Years to Make It Last a Lifetime. Thomas Nelson, 2006. 288 pp. ISBN 078528852X.

Dennis Rainey, president of FamilyLife (a division of Campus Crusade for Christ), is a popular author and conference speaker.

In this book, the Raineys talk about how to adjust to being married and all the changes marriage brings. They also address issues such as conflict, communication, sex, money, forgiveness, having children, and vacations.

Subjects: Marriage, Newlywed Couples, Premarital Counseling

More: For books that focus more on premarital issues, try *Before You Say I Do: A Marriage Preparation Manual for Couples* by H. Norman Wright and Wes Roberts (Harvest House, 1997) and *Saving Your Marriage Before It Starts: Seven Questions to Ask Before and After You Marry* by Les and Leslie Parrott (Zondervan, 2006). For another book by Rainey on marriage, try *Staying Close: Stopping the Natural Drift Toward Isolation in Marriage* (Nelson, 2003).

Smalley, Gary.

Hidden Keys of a Loving, Lasting Marriage. Zondervan, 1993. 336 pp. ISBN 0310402913.

Popular author and marriage seminar speaker Gary Smalley addresses men and women in this book on marriage-building principles. He shows how to understand and communicate with your spouse. This book combines two earlier works, *If Only He Knew* and *For Better or For Best*.

Subject: Marriage

More: R. Paul Stevens's book, *Married for Good: The Lost Art of Staying Happily Married* (Regent College, 2001), includes a great discussion of God's covenant design in marriage. Another book that will help men with communication in marriage is *Discovering the Mind of a Woman* by Ken Nair (Thomas Nelson, 1995). Nair also shows that men need to stop blaming and making excuses and start taking responsibility for their marriages.

Stanton, Glenn T., and Bill Maier.

Marriage on Trial: The Case Against Same-Sex Marriage and Parenting. InterVarsity, 2004. 198 pp. ISBN 0830832742.

Glenn T. Stanton and Bill Maier, who work for Focus on the Family, organize this book into three sections. In the first, they address the arguments of those who desire same-sex marriage. Some of the questions they answer include: "What's wrong with letting homosexuals marry?," "Isn't this primarily an issue of justice?," "Haven't other cultures had same-sex marriage?," "How would homosexual marriage threaten other families?," and "Don't children just need loving parents?" The second section discusses how traditional marriage benefits adults and children and explains why kids need mothers and fathers. Section three addresses myths concerning homosexuality. Stanton is director of social research and cultural affairs and senior analyst for marriage and sexuality at Focus on the Family. Dr. Maier is a child and family psychologist who serves as vice president of Focus on the Family.

Subject: Marriage, Same-Sex Marriage

Thomas, Gary L.

Sacred Marriage: What If God Designed Marriage to Make Us Holy More Than to Make Us Happy? Zondervan, 2002. 304 pp. ISBN 0310242827.

In this thought-provoking book, Gary Thomas reevaluates what Christian marriage is all about. Instead of showing readers how to be happy in marriage, he directs them to God's purposes. This book restores a spiritual perspective to life and relationships and brings to light a new and deep beauty that can be found in marriage. He also shows that the trials and sufferings that come with relationships do not have to separate people from each other, but can actually bring us closer to God and one another.

Subjects: Marriage, Spiritual Growth

More: Thomas has written a similar book on parenting called *Sacred Parenting: How Raising Children Shapes Our Souls* (Zondervan, 2004).

Weintraub, Pamela, and Stephen R. Clark.

Christian Family Guide to Surviving Divorce. Alpha, 2003. 322 pp. ISBN 1592570968.

This book deals with Christian issues for those facing divorce, but it is not a philosophical book. It is practical through and through. The authors discuss legal aspects of divorce, including how to get a lawyer and understanding how lawyers work. There is also a section on settling out of court. It covers child support, custody, dividing assets, how and what to tell your children, and much more. Helpful appendices include information on divorce organizations, books and online resources, and a sample settlement agreement.

Subject: Divorce

Wright, H. Norman.

The Complete Book of Christian Wedding Vows: The Importance of How You Say "I Do." Bethany, 2001. 207 pp. ISBN 0764287222.

Christian counselor and author Norman H. Wright shows people how to create their own wedding vows. He also provides sample vows. Wright includes many ideas and words for other people and for other parts of the wedding ceremony: words for parents, in-laws, and ministers—including poems, scriptures, quotes, and prayers. There is also a reaffirmation section for those who want to renew their wedding vows.

Subjects: Marriage, Remarriage, Wedding Vows, Weddings—Planning

More: For another wedding planner, try *Goble and Shea's Complete Wedding Planner: For the Organized and Relaxed Bride* by Kathleen Goble and Cecily Shea (Multnomah, 1999).

Parenting

Arp, David, and Claudia Arp.

Answering the Eight Cries of the Spirited Child: Strong Children Need Confident Parents. Howard Publishing, 2003. 191 pp. ISBN 1582292841.

This husband-and-wife team helps parents understand their children and interpret their words and behavior from the perspective of Christian love. For instance, when a child says, "You can't make me!," parents need to know that their child is crying out for boundaries and discipline. "I hate you!" is really a cry for help in dealing with anger and frustration. David and Claudia Arp give practical advice for each of the "eight cries." The Arps (both have master's degrees in social work) are the founders of Marriage Alive International.

Subjects: Parenting, Strong-willed Children

More: James Dobson's book, *The New Strong-willed Child: Birth Through Adolescence* (Tyndale, 2004) also deals with so-called problem children. His book discusses discipline and ADHD issues. Also try *You Can't Make Me (But I Can Be Persuaded)* by Cynthia Ulrich Tobias (WaterBrook, 1999). Also see *Strong-willed Child or Dreamer?: Understanding the Crucial Differences Between a Strong-willed Child and a Creative-Sensitive Child* by Dana Spears and Ron Braund (Thomas Nelson, 1996).

Barnes, Robert G.

Winning the Heart of Your Stepchild. Zondervan, 1997 (Word, 1992). 192 pp. ISBN 0310218047.

Many stepparents have heard their stepchildren utter the words "You're not my daddy/mommy." Robert Barnes suggests that such children really do want another daddy or mommy who will love them through thick and thin. But it takes time, wisdom, and love. Explaining the situation from the child's point of view, Barnes says that a parent-child relationship is lopsided because it is all about meeting the child's needs—not the parent's. Barnes gives valuable insight for stepparents who are learning how to gain the trust of a child. He addresses issues specific to stepfathers and sons as well as daughters. There is also a chapter on being a stepmother. This book was first published in 1992 as *You're Not My Daddy*.

Subjects: Parenting, Remarriage, Stepfamilies

More: Kevin Leman has a great book on stepparenting called *Living in a Step-family Without Getting Stepped on: Helping Your Children Survive the Birth Order Blender* (Thomas Nelson, 2001). Also try Jim Smoke's *Seven Keys to a Healthy Blended Family* (Harvest House, 2004).

Beausay, Bill.

Teenage Boys! WaterBrook, 1998. 245 pp. ISBN 157856042X.

In this book about shaping teenage boys into men, speaker and psychotherapist Bill Beausay gives practical advice on topics such as teen discipline, computers, mentoring teens through hurts and difficulties, rites of passage, crisis situations, sex and girls, and more. This book offers tools to help fathers and mothers become confident parents.

Subjects: Parenting—Teenage Boys

More: Try Kevin Leman's book on adolescence called *Running the Rapid: Guiding Teenagers Through the Turbulent Waters of Adolescence* (Tyndale, 2005).

Clarkson, Clay.

Heartfelt Discipline: The Gentle Art of Training and Guiding Your Child. WaterBrook, 2003. 243 pp. ISBN 1578565839.

Clay Clarkson challenges his readers to reconsider spanking, suggesting that it is not as biblical as some Christians think. He offers much wisdom on connecting with your children by listening and understanding them and by using discernment and encouragement. Clarkson is not radically anti-spanking; he even gives guidelines for spanking if parents decide to use such measures. The book also covers other parenting issues such as protecting your child from damaging relationships, harmful appetites, and unhealthy media.

Subjects: Discipline of Children, Parenting

Clarkson, Sally.

The Mission of Motherhood: Touching Your Child's Heart for Eternity. WaterBrook, 2003. 242 pp. ISBN 1578565812.

Writer and speaker Sally Clarkson (cofounder of Whole Heart Ministries) challenges readers to rethink their attitudes toward their children and their homes. Clarkson does not focus on rules and regulations but on what really matters in parenting. She presents an inspiring vision of motherhood as a valuable Christian ministry. She also offers practical ideas for creating a nurturing home environment.

Subjects: Mothers, Parenting

More: Two more books for mothers are *And Then I Had Kids: Encouragement for Mothers of Young Children* by Susan Alexander Yates (Baker, 2002) and *The Mom I Want to Be: Rising Above Your Past to Give Your Kids a Great Future* by T. Suzanne Eller (Harvest House, 2006).

Cloud, Henry, and John Townsend.

Raising Great Kids: A Comprehensive Guide to Parenting with Grace and Truth. Zondervan, 1999. 233 pp. ISBN 0310235499.

Henry Cloud and John Townsend are clinical psychologists and best-selling authors of marriage and relationship self-help books. In this book, Cloud and Townsend say that the goal in parenting is not to raise "good" kids but to raise children of mature character. They write that it is more important for children to see themselves as being loved than it is for them to have "positive self-esteem." Once they lay down certain biblical principles for parenting, the authors give practical guidance for application. For instance, since every child will fail at some point in their life, the authors say kids need to know how to lose. They also show readers how to instill character (responsibility, reality, competence, morality, etc.) and how to prepare children for life on their own.

Subject: Parenting

More: Cloud and Townsend also coauthored *Boundaries with Kids* (Zondervan, 2001). Another book by a best-selling author is *The Key to Your Child's Heart: Raise Motivated, Obedient, and Loving Children* by Gary Smalley (W Publishing Group, 2003).

Courtney, Vicki.

Your Girl: Raising a Godly Daughter in an Ungodly World. B&H Publishing, 2004. 209 pp. ISBN 0805430539.

Vicki Courtney started Virtuous Reality, a ministry to girls and mothers. This book talks about motherhood and the kinds of temptations and trials that girls face in today's culture. Some of the topics Courtney covers include what to do about mean girls, promiscuity, self-worth, conformity, and modesty.

Subjects: Mothers and Daughters, Parenting—Daughters, Virtue

More: Another book for mothers and daughters is *Mom's Everything Book for Daughters: Practical Ideas for a Quality Relationship* by

Becky Freeman (Zondervan, 2002). For a book on parenting girls (for moms and dads), try *Girls: Helping Your Little Girl Become an Extraordinary Woman* by William and Katherine Beausay (Revell, 1998). Also see *Here for You: Creating a Mother–Daughter Bond That Lasts a Lifetime* by Susie Shellenberger and Kathy Gowler (Bethany, 2007).

Dobson, James.

Bringing Up Boys. Tyndale, 2001. 269 pp. ISBN 084235266X.

Child psychologist and founder of Focus on the Family James Dobson writes about parenting boys. He talks about the increased risk factors that they face in today's world. He explains the essential role of Christian fathers in the lives of their boys and gives helpful advice. He also counsels mothers and single parents who have boys. Dobson addresses a number of issues, including discipline, sexuality, and homosexuality.

Subjects: Award Winners (ECPA), Parenting—Boys

More: Also try *Boys! Shaping Ordinary Boys into Extraordinary Men* by William Beausay (Thomas Nelson, 2002) and *Your Boy: Raising a Godly Son in an Ungodly World* by Vicki Courtney (B&H Publishing, 2006).

Freeman, Becky.

Mom's Everything Book for Sons: Practical Ideas for a Quality Relationship. Zondervan, 2003. 168 pp. ISBN 0310242959.

With her easy-to-read and humorous style, Becky Freeman offers practical advice to Christian mothers wanting to connect with their sons. She talks about a son's need for female praise, athletics, adolescence, communication, instilling purpose, creativity, learning, and more. She shares scriptures and many stories and ideas to enable mothers and sons to bond.

Subject: Mothers and Sons, Parenting—Boys

More: *That's My Son: How Moms Can Influence Boys to Become Men of Character* by Rick Johnson (Revell, 2005).

Garrett, Ginger.

Queen Esther's Secrets of Womanhood: A Biblical Rite of Passage for Your Daughter. NavPress, 2006. 141 pp. ISBN 1576839869.

This book is designed to guide Christian mothers through twelve monthly mother/daughter "dates," in which the mom can spend a day talking and mentoring her daughter. Topics include beauty, emotions, friendships, body image, money, courage, faith, wisdom, and more. Ginger Garrett has written several novels, including one about Queen Esther called *Chosen: The Lost Diaries of Queen Esther*.

Subjects: Mothers and Daughters, Parenting—Daughters

Goyer, Tricia.

Life Interrupted: The Scoop on Being a Young Mom. Zondervan, 2004. 219 pp. ISBN 0310253160.

Tricia Goyer writes about her life as a teenage mom. She also talks about the needs that teen moms have (like finding good friends) and how to get good help and advice. Goyer addresses teens who have already had their babies (not pregnant teens).

Subjects: Single Mothers, Teenage Mothers, Teenage Pregnancy, Unplanned Pregnancy

More: For books that focus on unplanned pregnancy, try *Mom, Dad ... I'm Pregnant: When Your Daughter or Son Faces an Unplanned Pregnancy* by Jayne E. Schooler (NavPress, 2004) and *I'm Pregnant—Now What?* by Ruth Graham (daughter of Billy Graham) and Sara R. Dormon (Regal Books, 2004). Also try *Single Parenting That Works* by Kevin Leman (Tyndale, 2006).

Hersh, Sharon A.

Mom, Everyone Else Does!: Becoming Your Daughter's Ally in Responding to Peer Pressure to Drink, Smoke, and Use Drugs. WaterBrook Press, 2005. 238 pp. ISBN 0877880255.

While Sharon A. Hersh was writing this book, she discovered that her own teenage son was using illegal drugs. With her personal and professional experience as a licensed counselor, Hersh gives practical advice for mothers (and fathers) that allows them become their child's ally and know what to do when faced with issues such as smoking, drinking, drugs, and bad relationships.

Subjects: Drug Abuse, Mothers and Daughters, Parenting—Teenage Girls, Peer Pressure

More: Hersh also has a book concerning eating disorders and body image: *Mom, I Feel Fat!: Becoming Your Daughter's Ally in Developing a Healthy Body Image* (WaterBrook Press, 2001).

Kimmel, Tim.

Why Christian Kids Rebel: Trading Heartache for Hope. W Publishing, 2004. 255 pp. ISBN 0849918308.

Why do children rebel? What should parents do? Tim Kimmel says that we cannot (and should not try to) control other people, but we can control ourselves. Therefore, he suggests that the solution to rebellious children is to focus on changing the parent, not the child. He says that a child's rebellion is not the problem; it is the symptom. This book gets down to the root cause of rebellion and provides eye-opening answers and hope for parents and families.

Subjects: Parenting, Rebellion in Children

Larmoyeux, Mary, and Ethan Pope.

There's No Place Like Home: Steps to Becoming a Stay-at-Home Mom. B&H Publishing, 2001. 186 pp. ISBN 0805423761.

This book is a practical guide for working mothers who want to be stay-at-home moms. It doesn't just talk about homemaking; it shows the reader how to do it. Ethan Pope, a certified financial planner, provides financial plans and checklists to make the idea a reality. Mary Larmoyeux and Pope share many stories of people who have gone through this very issue in their lives.

Subjects: Housewives, Mothers, Parenting, Working Mothers

More: *Home by Choice* by Brenda Hunter (Multnomah, 2000) makes the case that stay-at-home moms are very important to the health and emotional security of their children.

Leman, Kevin.

Making Children Mind Without Losing Yours. 2nd Edition. Baker, 2005 (Revell, 1984). 272 pp. ISBN 0800731050.

This book has a zany title, but the wisdom found inside is first rate. Leman puts forth a practical, commonsense approach to discipline and child rearing that he calls "reality discipline." He deals with topics such as allowance, chores, discipline versus punishment, authoritarian mistakes, bedtime issues, spanking, and respect.

Subjects: Discipline of Children, Parenting

More: Two other books by Leman on parenting are *Becoming the Parent God Wants You to Be* (NavPress, 1998) and *Home Court Advantage: Preparing Your Children to Be Winners in Life* (Focus on the Family, 2005).

Leman, Kevin.

What a Difference a Daddy Makes: The Indelible Imprint a Dad Leaves on His Daughter's Life. Nelson, 2001 (2000). 256 pp. ISBN 0785266046.

Popular speaker, writer, and psychologist Kevin Leman has raised four daughters. In this book, with humor and wisdom, he shows Christian fathers how to parent their daughters with love and skill. He shares many personal stories from his own family and discusses such topics as failure, trust, sex, mother/daughter tension, God, and more. Leman's conversational style makes this book enjoyable to read.

Subjects: Fathers and Daughters, Parenting—Daughters

More: Also try *Dad's Everything Book for Daughters: Practical Ideas for a Quality Relationship* by John Trent (Zondervan, 2002) and *What a Daughter Needs from Her Dad: How a Man Prepares His Daughter for Life* by Michael Farris (Bethany, 2004). Farris is the president of Patrick Henry College and the chairman of the Home School Legal Defense Association. Two more books are *She Calls Me Daddy* by Robert Wolgemuth (Focus on the Family, 1999) and *Strong Fathers, Strong Daughters: 10 Secrets Every Father Should Know* (Regnery, 2006) by medical doctor Meg Meeker. Meeker talks about some of the disturbing things that daughters face in today's world and shows how crucial fathers are to their daughters' health and well-being.

Leman, Kevin.

The New Birth Order Book: Why You Are the Way You Are. Revell, 1998 (1985). 362 pp. ISBN 0800756797.

Psychologist and best-selling author Kevin Leman writes about birth order in this classic and best-selling book on the subject. Being the first-born child may have something to do with a person's perfectionism and inclination to leadership. Besides the first-born child, Leman also talks about the middle child, the youngest, and the only child. Leman also writes about birth-order marriages and disciplining children in regards to birth order.

Subjects: Birth Order, Parenting, Psychology

Leman, Kevin.

Single Parenting That Works: Six Keys to Raising Happy, Healthy Children in a Single-Parent Home. Tyndale, 2006. 274 pp. ISBN 1414303343.

Popular writer and psychologist Kevin Leman shows single parents how to be the best parents they can be. He talks about what kids need and how to provide it; he shows readers how to build a team for support; and he answers hard questions. Leman admits that it is a hard job, but says there is hope! He promises that it will be worth it in the end.

Subjects: Parenting, Single Mothers

Lewis, Robert.

Raising a Modern-Day Knight. Revised edition. Tyndale, 2007. 192 pp. ISBN 1589973097.

In this book, a knight refers to an honorable, godly man. How does a father raise a boy to become a man? How does the transition take place? Robert Lewis answers these questions by laying out a vision for manhood and giving several concrete examples of "initiation" ceremonies. These ceremonies mark major milestones in a young man's life (puberty, graduation, etc.) and provide lifelong memories of bonding and blessing that will help orient and establish a modern-day knight.

Subjects: Fathers and Sons, Parenting

More: Steve Farrar wrote a book that helps fathers give direction to their sons: *King Me: What Every Son Wants and Needs from His Father* (Moody, 2005). Another father-and-son book is *Dad's Everything Book for Sons: Practical Ideas for a Quality Relationship* by John Trent and Greg Johnson (Zondervan, 2003). *You Have What It Takes: What Every Father Needs to Hear* by John Eldredge (Thomas Nelson, 2004) is a brief book that talks to fathers about sons, daughters, manhood, and fatherhood. Also try *Boyhood and Beyond: Practical Wisdom for Becoming a Man* by Bob Schultz (Great Expectations Book Company, 2004).

McDonald, Stacy.

Raising Maidens of Virtue: A Study of Feminine Loveliness for Mothers and Daughters. Books on the Path, 2005. 224 pp. ISBN 0974339016. **YA**

In this book, Stacy McDonald, a homeschooling mother of nine children and the editor-in-chief of *Homeschooling Today* and *Family Reformation* magazines, uses stories, allegories, and projects to discuss topics and moral traits such as idleness, guarding the tongue, contentment, modesty, purity, feminine beauty, honoring parents, getting along with siblings, and more. Christian mothers could use it as a tool to help train their daughters, or teenage girls could use it on their own to learn what it means to be a truly beautiful, godly woman. Some of the practical projects include suggestions and instructions for scrapbooks, heirloom cookbooks, family traditions, journals, and hosting a literary luncheon for mothers and daughters. Appendices include recommended Web sites that sell modest clothing (including swimwear) and a recommended reading list.

Subjects: Femininity, Mothers and Daughters, Parenting, Teenage Girls, Virtue, Young-Adult Interest

More: Readers may also enjoy *Beautiful Girlhood* by Mabel Hale (reprinted by Barbour, 2001). Hale's book for young teens was first published in 1922. The language is old-fashioned, but the wisdom is timeless. *So Much More: The Remarkable Influence of Visionary Daughters on the Kingdom of God* (Vision Forum, 2005) is, in today's world, a radical expression of biblical "daughterhood" written by two teenage sisters, Anna Sophia and Elizabeth Botkin. These sisters are not ashamed to confess their respect and devotion to their father, saying he is their source of protection and power.

MacNutt, Francis, and Judith MacNutt.

Praying for Your Unborn Child. Image, 1989. 162 pp. ISBN 0385232829.

Christian parents can start praying for their child even in the womb. Francis and Judith MacNutt show how this is a biblical thing to do. They also show that the womb is a very important formative time in a child's emotional life. The authors explain how to make pregnancy a time of blessing for parents and unborn children. They also teach readers how to find healing from damaging experiences (for both adults and children) that occurred before birth. For example, resentful mothers can negatively affect the physical and mental health of their unborn children. The MacNutts progress through each trimester, dealing with things like stress, depression, bonding, labor, and delivery. There is an appendix discussing miscarriage and abortion. Francis MacNutt, a former priest, was one of the first Roman Catholics to become involved in the Charismatic Renewal Movement during the late 1960s. He and his wife Judith direct Christian Healing Ministries in Jacksonville, Florida.

Subjects: Childbirth, Inner Healing, Parenting, Prayer, Pregnancy

More: For more by Francis MacNutt on healing, try *The Prayer That Heals: Praying for Healing in the Family* (Ave Maria Press, 2000).

Prince, Derek.

Husbands and Fathers: Rediscover the Creator's Purpose for Men. Chosen, 2000. 160 pp. ISBN 0800792742.

Well-known Bible teacher Derek Prince shows men what it takes to become the leaders in their homes that they are meant to be. He explains the marriage covenant, and describes what it means to be a father. Suggesting that a man has to pray for his family so he can hear from God, Prince asserts that once he has heard from God, a man has authority to teach and lead his family in the right direction. Fatherlessness, he claims, is the cause of much devastation in our country. Prince shows readers how to reverse the curse of fatherlessness.

Subjects: Fatherhood, Marriage, Parenting

Priolo, Lou.

The Heart of Anger: Practical Help for the Prevention and Cure of Anger in Children. Calvary Press, 1998. 201 pp. ISBN 1879737280.

Lou Priolo gives biblical, general parenting advice as well as specific suggestions for dealing with anger in children. Not only does he show how to diagnose and solve anger problems, he also teaches parents how to avoid provoking their children to anger and how to deal with disrespect and manipulation. Priolo's methods do not merely deal with symptoms; he clearly explains how to get to the heart of the matter and to discern and correct the thoughts and intents of a child's heart.

Subjects: Anger in Children, Parenting

Rainey, Dennis, Barbara Rainey, and Bruce Nygren.

Parenting Today's Adolescent: Helping Your Child Avoid the Traps of the Preteen and Teen Years. Nelson, 2002. 361 pp. ISBN 0785265104.

This book is packed with information on parenting teens and preteens as Christians. The Raineys, parents of six children, discuss sex, dating, spiritual growth, drugs, grades, music, jobs, cars, clothes, and more. Dennis Rainey helped found FamilyLife ministry, which is associated with Campus Crusade for Christ.

Subjects: Adolescence, Parenting, Preteens, Teenagers

More: For another book on parenting teenagers, try *Age of Opportunity: A Biblical Guide to Parenting Teens* by Paul David Tripp (P&R Publishing, 2001). For a book that deals with common psychological problems that teenagers face, from anger and anxiety to eating disorders and stuttering, see *Helping Your Struggling Teenager* by psychology professor Les Parrott (Zondervan, 2000). For another parenting guide, try *The Parents' Guide to the Spiritual Mentoring of Teens: Building Your Child's Faith Through the Adolescent Years* by Joe White and Jim Weidmann (Tyndale, 2001).

Rainey, Dennis, and David Boehi.

The Tribute and the Promise: How Honoring Your Parents Will Bring a Blessing to Your Life. Thomas Nelson, 1997. 287 pp. ISBN 0785271759.

Dennis Rainey and David Boehi show readers how to restore and/or deepen their relationship with their parents by honoring them with a tribute. The authors discuss "seeing your parents through the eyes of Christ" and deal with forgiving one's parents; and they give instructions on how to write an actual tribute with pen and paper. The main focus is on obeying the fifth commandment, "Honor your father and your mother." This commandment comes with a promise, "that your days may be prolonged in the land which the Lord your God gives you." Rainey and Boehi share many stories of actual people whose lives were changed when they gave tributes to their parents.

Subjects: Adult Children, Parent and Adult Child

More: For a book on mother issues for an adult child, try *The Mom Factor: Dealing with the Mother You Had, Didn't Have, or Still Contend With* (Zondervan, 1996) and *Making Peace with Your Mom: Steps to a Healthier Mother–Daughter Relationship* by H. Norman Wright (Bethany, 2006). Also try *The Other Woman in Your Marriage: Understanding a Mother's Impact on Her Son and How It Affects His Marriage* by H. Norman Wright (Regal, 1994).

Rigby, Jill.

Raising Respectful Children in a Disrespectful World. Howard Books, 2006. 195 pp. ISBN 1582295743.

Jill Rigby has taught children across the country to have manners and respect. In this book, she cautions that parents should not focus on self-esteem with their children. Self-esteem-focused parenting can lead to kids who are greedy, self-centered, insecure, and discontent. Instead, Rigby says, parents should focus on fostering self-respect, which leads to gratitude, humility, confidence, and contentment. She shows parents how to use discipline instead of punishment and how to foster gratefulness instead of greediness, and shares many personal stories as she helps enroll people in the "school of respect."

Subjects: Manners, Parenting, Respect in Children

More: Jill Rigby also has written a book called *Manners of the Heart* (Respectfully Yours, 2002).

Savage, Jill.

Creating the Moms Group You've Been Looking For: Your How-to Manual for Connecting with Other Moms. Zondervan, 2004. 221 pp. ISBN 0310254477

Packed with helpful information, ideas, and resources, this book describes different types of groups, including playgroups, co-ops, mentoring and accountability relationships, and small and large moms' groups, as well as several child-care programming options. In Part 3, you'll find eleven chapters that deal with principles for successful leadership (develop people, not programs, etc.). Sample job descriptions, calendars, schedules, forms, and more are included in the appendices. This book is one of several in the Hearts at Home Resource series.

Subject: Mothers—Support Groups, Playgroups

Schultz, Bob.

Boyhood and Beyond: Practical Wisdom for Becoming a Man. Great Expectations Book Company, 2004. 219 pp. ISBN 1883934095.

This is a book for boys to read alone or with their fathers. It does not deal with STDs or illegal drugs or any other horrors of today's world. Instead, it offers young men sound advice for becoming men of character. With simple, clear writing, Bob Schultz introduces and explains concepts such as leadership, diligence, cheerfulness, and authority. He shows young men how to admit their wrongs and stand up for what is right. He relates how to overcome temptation, coveting, and fear, find wisdom, and build a relationship with God. Schultz also shows boys how to be self-motivated learners, servers, and friends.

Subjects: Boys, Character, Parenting

More: Schultz has also written *Created for Work: Practical Insights for Young Men* (Great Expectations Book Company, 2006).

Sears, William, and Martha Sears.

The Complete Book of Christian Parenting & Child Care: A Medical & Moral Guide to Raising Happy, Healthy Children. B&H Publishing, 1997. 608 pp. ISBN 0805461981.

This ambitious book covers many issues important to Christian parents. From pregnancy and delivery to birth and infant care, William and Martha Sears talk about what to expect and how to provide good care to children. They also write about breast-feeding, nighttime parenting, dealing with a crying baby, going back to work, weaning, solid foods, potty training, and discipline. The authors are strong advocates of attachment parenting (in fact, they coined the phrase). Attachment parenting is a parenting philosophy that seeks to ensure good parent–child bonding through breast-feeding on demand, baby-wearing, co-sleeping, and positive discipline. William Sears is a nationally known pediatrician with more than twenty-five years of experience. His wife and coauthor, Martha, is a registered nurse with experience as a childbirth educator and a lactation and parenting consultant.

Subjects: Child Birth, Child Care, Child Development, Health Care—Children, Infant Care, Parenting, Pregnancy

More: Gary Ezzo and Robert Bucknam have a very different approach to infant care and parenting that many have found helpful. Their book, *On Becoming Baby Wise: Giving Your Infant the Gift of Nighttime Sleep* (Parent-Wise Solutions, 4th Ed., 2006), has been so controversial, however, that Multnomah stopped publishing their edition in 2001. For an exhaustive manual on child care, try *The Focus on the Family Complete Book of Baby and Child Care* by Paul C. Reisser, Melissa R. Cox, and Vinita Hampton Wright (Focus on the Family, 1999).

Smalley, Gary, and John Trent.

The Blessing. Nelson Books, 2004 (1986). 320 pp. ISBN 0785260846.

The "blessing" refers to the power of a parent's approval (unconditional acceptance) for his or her children. Without "the blessing," say these authors, our lives can be devastated. Gary Smalley and John Trent discuss the five elements of the blessing and show how to give this blessing to children (and spouses and friends).

Subject: Award Winners (ECPA), Parenting

Smith, Timothy.

The Danger of Raising Nice Kids: Preparing Our Children to Change Their World. InterVarsity Press, 2006. 202 pp. ISBN 0830833757.

Many parents want their children to be "good kids." Timothy Smith says nice doesn't cut it. Parents and their children need more than nice. They need vision, discernment, empathy, contentment, and the ability to listen and to give and receive passionate love. How does a Christian parent instill such character? In this book, Smith demonstrates how to mentor children in a simple, stress-free way. He says that parents need to prepare their children to be independent adults, not merely to protect or control them so they will be nice.

Subjects: Parenting

More: A similar book that shows parents how to form a child's character and raise kids who will become morally mature adults is *On Becoming Preteen Wise: Parenting Your Child from Eight to Twelve Years* by Gary Ezzo and Robert Bucknam (Hawks Flight, 2001). Also try *Boyhood and Beyond: Practical Wisdom for Becoming a Man* by Bob Schultz (Great Expectations Book Company, 2004).

Tripp, Tedd.

Shepherding Your Child's Heart. Revised and updated edition. Shepherd Press, 2005 (1995). 215 pp. ISBN 0966378601.

Tedd Tripp teaches practical ways of speaking to the heart of a child. Behaviors or attitudes are just outward expressions of what is really in your child's heart. Dealing with outward expressions alone is merely treating the symptoms. Tripp gives insight concerning authority and how to orient a child toward God. He shows how to identify (and how to allow a child to identify) sin in his life so that he can see his need for Christ, and he helps parents confidently raise their children morally and spiritually.

Subject: Parenting

VanVonderen, Jeff.

Families Where Grace Is in Place. Bethany, 1992. 172 pp. ISBN 1556612664.

Jeff VanVonderen shows readers that it is not their job to "fix" their spouse's behavior or to make sure their children are perfect. We are not responsible for other people's behavior, he says. A spouse's/parent's job is to love and serve his or her family with God's help. VanVonderen goes against the grain of much popular thought, but his points are scriptural. He says that trying to pressure or control other people is living under a curse, and it only leads to manipulation and legalism.

Subject: Marriage, Parenting

More: Another excellent book from a similar perspective is *Grace-Based Parenting* by Tim Kimmel (W Publishing, 2004).

Wiggin, Eric.

The Gift of Grandparenting: Building a Meaningful Relationship with Your Grandchildren. Tyndale, 2001. 308 pp. ISBN 1561799246.

Fiction author Eric Wiggin writes about the importance of grandparents and grandparenting. He gives practical advice for grandparents on a variety of issues such as babysitting, setting rules for visits from older grandchildren, and connecting with the younger generation. Discussing what life is like for today's grandchildren, Wiggin addresses split-family grandparents and grandparents who must act as parents.

Subject: Grandparenting

More: How do you keep in touch with grandchildren in other states or cities? Retired teacher Janet Colsher Teitsort gives month-by-month ideas for interacting with far-off grandkids in *Long Distance Grandma: Staying Connected Across the Miles* (Howard Books, 2005). Two more books on grandparenting are *Grandparenthood* by Tim and Darcy Kimmel (Focus on the Family, 2007) and *Off My Rocker: Grandparenting Ain't What It Used to Be* by Gracie Malon (NavPress, 2003).

Counseling and Psychology

This section includes Christian self-help books that show Christians how to counsel others. It also annotates titles on a variety of topics, including abuse, depression, fear, self-esteem, addictions, and inner healing. Readers will find Christian authors do not always agree on which counseling methods are biblical and how or whether Christians should use antipsychotic drugs.

Allender, Dan B.

The Wounded Heart: Hope for Adult Victims of Childhood Sexual Abuse. Revised edition. NavPress, 1995 (1990). 255 pp. ISBN 0891092897.

How do victims of sexual abuse find understanding, healing, and forgiveness? Christian psychologist Dan Allender answers these questions. He discusses the damage that abuse does to the soul—engendering powerlessness and leading to sexual dysfunction and addiction. Allender also talks about what he calls the "unlikely route to joy" in which honesty, repentance, and bold love lead to real change and growth.

Subjects: Abuse, Child Sexual Abuse, Sexual Abuse

More: Three more books on this subject (mostly for adults looking for healing) are *Child Sexual Abuse: Hope for Healing* by Maxine Hancock and Karen Burton Mains (Harold Shaw, 1997), *Healing Victims of Sexual Abuse* by Paula Sandford (Victory House, 1988), and *Helping Victims of Sexual Abuse* by Lynn Heitritter and Jeanette Vought (Bethany, 2006). For a book that helps families deal with children who were sexually abused, try *Caring for Sexually Abused Children: A Handbook for Families and Churches* by Dr. R. Timothy Kearney (InterVarsity, 2001).

Anderson, Neil T.

The Bondage Breaker: Overcoming Darkness and Resolving Spiritual Conflicts. Harvest House, 2006 (1990). 304 pp. ISBN 0736918140.

This is a classic book on Christian counseling that incorporates spiritual warfare. Professor, pastor, and counselor Neil T. Anderson shows readers how to overcome negative thoughts, irrational feelings, and habitual sins. Anderson discusses how to get free and stay free from demonic influences that sometimes cause spiritual and mental conflicts.

Subjects: Counseling, Deliverance

More: Anderson also wrote a similar book called *Victory over the Darkness* (Regal, 2000). For a book by Anderson that focuses on psychotherapy (geared towards counselors), try *Christ Centered Therapy* by Neil T. Anderson, Terry Zuehlke, and Julianne S. Zuehlke (Zondervan, 2000).

Arterburn, Stephen, and Jack Felton.

Toxic Faith: Experiencing Healing from Painful Spiritual Abuse. Shaw, 2001 (Oliver-Nelson, 1991). 240 pp. ISBN 0877888256.

Too often people use religion to manipulate other people and to justify abuse, suggest these authors. That abuse can be mental, emotional, physical, sexual, and spiritual. Many times, misunderstanding God or the Bible leads to toxic faith. Stephen Arterburn and Jack Felton show readers how to detect spiritual abuse and how to recognize healthy Christian faith. Whether it is mainline denominations or cults, this book explains religious addiction and describes common toxic beliefs. False ideas that lead to toxic faith include: if you have the right faith, you will be wealthy; God will find you a perfect mate; you must submit to authority unquestioningly; ministers don't have problems with sin; if you have enough faith, you will be healed; God is angry with you if you are not perfect; other churches beliefs are wrong; only "our" beliefs can lead to God's approval and eternal life; and you must be faithful and give all your time to serve the church—otherwise you are a bad Christian.

Subjects: Abuse—Spiritual, Spiritual Authority—Abuse

More: For more books on this topic, see *Subtle Power of Spiritual Abuse: Recognizing and Escaping Spiritual Manipulation and False Spiritual Authority Within the Church* by David Johnson and Jeff VanVonderen (Bethany, 2005) and *Healing Spiritual Abuse: How to Break Free from Bad Church Experiences* by Ken Blue. Mary Alice Chrnalogar addresses "discipleship" abuse that is perpetuated by a false interpretation of the Bible in her book *Twisted Scriptures* (Zondervan, 2000). Also try *Letters to a Devastated Christian* by Gene Edwards (SeedSowers, 2001).

Biebel, David B., and Harold G. Koenig.

New Light on Depression: Help, Hope & Answers for the Depressed & Those Who Love Them. Zondervan and the Christian Medical Association, 2004. 318 pp. ISBN 0310247292.

This book deals with depression as a whole-person disorder. It asks, "Do real Christians get depressed?" (yes) The authors discuss myths and misconceptions like, "It is easy to tell when you are depressed," "You can beat depression with willpower," and "You're depressed because you want to be depressed." They describe mental health professionals and what they do, and examine secular and Christian counseling models and methods. There is also a chapter about antidepressant medication; the authors feel that antipsychotic drugs can be useful for Christians.

Subjects: Award Winners (ECPA), Depression

Collins, Gary. R.

Christian Counseling: A Comprehensive Guide. 3rd Edition. Nelson, 2007 (Word, 1980). 768 pp. ISBN 1418503290.

Gary R. Collins, a licensed clinical psychologist with a PhD in clinical psychology from Purdue University, has written more than forty books. This substantial tome, first published in 1980 and recently updated, covers just about every imaginable issue: AIDS, eating disorders, homosexuality, violence, multiracial issues in counseling, conflict and relationships, death and grief, alcoholism and other substance abuse, crises and trauma, counseling and terrorism, anxiety, guilt, anger, parenting, sex, singleness, vocational counseling, and more.

Subject: Counseling

More: A companion volume to this book with real-life examples is *Christian Counseling Casebook* (Thomas Nelson, 2007). Collins has also written *Christian Coaching: Helping Others Turn Potential into Reality* (NavPress, 2001). For another well-known book on counseling, try *Effective Biblical Counseling: A Model for Helping Caring Christians Become Capable Counselors* by Dr. Larry Crabb (Zondervan, 1977). For a different perspective on true biblical counseling, try *The Christian Counselor's Manual* by Jay E. Adams (Zondervan, 1986). Adams is the father of a type of biblical counseling called "Nouthetic" counseling (the word "Nouthetic" is from the Greek word meaning to admonish, correct, or instruct).

Fitzpatrick, Elyse, and Laura Hendrickson.

Will Medicine Stop the Pain?: Finding God's Healing for Depression, **Anxiety & Other Troubling Emotions.** Moody, 2006. 234 pp. ISBN 0802458025.

Fitzpatrick and Hendrickson are both Nouthetic (biblical) counselors. Hendrickson is also an MD who formerly practiced psychiatry. Nouthetic counseling, developed by Jay E. Adams, is biblical counseling designed to change a person's heart, not just their behavior. As a result, such counselors try to avoid medication. In this book, the authors explain the roots and solutions to panic attacks, fear, depression, mood swings, obsessive-compulsive disorder, self-injury, and cognitive and perceptual problems. They also discuss addiction to psychiatric medicines, which many times are prescribed when not really needed.

Subjects: Depression, Fear, Psychiatry

Fuller, Cheri.

Fearless: Building a Faith That Overcomes Your Fear. Revell, 2003 (B&H Publishing, 1986). 220 pp. ISBN 0800758544.

Cheri Fuller has much experience with various aspects of fear due to her own personal struggles with anxiety, worry, and tragedy. This is a valuable and comforting resource for those dealing with worry, fright, anxiety, and panic. Fuller discusses many fears: those about our children, finances, flying, failure, childhood fears, health, disaster, and more.

Subject: Fear

More: Also try Roger Frye's insightful book called *Conquering Fear: A Thirty-One Day Guide to Overcoming the Stronghold of Fear* (Leland Publications, 2006).

Kraft, Charles H.

Deep Wounds, Deep Healing: Discovering the Vital Link Between Spiritual Warfare and Inner Healing. Regal, 2004. 295 pp. ISBN 0830734112.

Charles Kraft says that people can be free from problems like poor self-image, depression, and abuse trauma. He explains that freedom comes when people are healed emotionally and spiritually. Although some ministers think psychology is bad, Kraft says counseling is beneficial; however, the need for spiritual deliverance is also real. Kraft shows readers how to bring these together. He discusses dealing with childhood trauma, loss, demonization, guilt, unforgiveness, and more while using the gifts of the spirit such as words of knowledge and discernment of spirits.

Subjects: Abuse, Deliverance, Depression, Inner Healing, Spiritual Gifts

More: For more on inner healing, try *Transforming the Inner Man: God's Powerful Principles for Inner Healing and Lasting Life Change* by John Loren Sandford and Paula Sandford (Charisma House, 2007). Also see Gregory Boyd's *Seeing Is Believing: Experience Jesus Through Imaginative Prayer* (Baker, 2004). For more on deliverance from demon spirits, see *How to Cast Out Demons: A Guide to the Basics* by Doris M. Wagner (Regal, 2000).

McGee, Robert S.

The Search for Significance: Seeing Your True Worth Through God's Eyes. Thomas Nelson, 2003 (McGee, 1985). 352 pp. ISBN 0849944244.

This Christian self-help classic was first published in 1985. In it, Robert McGee shows readers how to build self-worth based on the love and forgiveness of Jesus Christ. So many try to build their self-worth on the ability to please others. This leads to fear of failure, fear of rejection, fear of punishment and shame. McGee shows how to find hope and healing by dealing with these issues biblically. He is a professional counselor and the founder of Rapha, a health-care ministry to people suffering with psychiatric and substance-abuse problems.

Subjects: Psychology, Self-Esteem

More: Another psychology self-help classic is *Telling Yourself the Truth* by William Backus and Marie Chapian (Bethany reprint, 2000). In this book, the authors use what they call "misbelief therapy" to teach readers how to identify misbeliefs and replace them with the truth.

McGinnis, Alan Loy.

The Friendship Factor: How to Get Closer to the People You Care For. 25th Anniversary revised and expanded edition. Augsburg, 2004 (1979). 224 pp. ISBN 0806635711.

A classic Christian work on friendship and intimacy, this inspiring and insightful book describes five ways to deepen your relationships and five guidelines for cultivating intimacy. Alan Loy McGinnis also shows how to handle negative emotions, salvage a faltering friendship, and deal with commitment.

Subject: Friendship

Nason-Clark, Nancy, and Catherine Clark Kroeger.

Refuge from Abuse: Healing and Hope for Abused Christian Women. InterVarsity Press, 2004. 178 pp. ISBN 0830832033.

Nancy Nason-Clark, a sociology professor, and Catherine Clark Kroeger, a Bible scholar, offer wisdom and practical advice for Christian women suffering from abuse. They assert that an abused woman does not bear the responsibility for a failed marriage. Divorce is a biblical and wise option. Unfortunately, they say, many well-intentioned Christians and even ministers give misguided advice in this area. The authors seek to set the record straight and help women find help and healing. Many abusive husbands claim to have changed, but Nason-Clark and Kroeger show what true repentance looks like. They also reveal how to move on with life and restore trust in God.

Subject: Abuse—Women and Wives, Women's Issues

More: The authors also have written *No Place for Abuse: Biblical & Practical Resources to Counteract Domestic Violence* (InterVarsity Press, 2001). T. D. Jakes' best-selling book on recovering from abuse is *Woman, Thou Art Loosed!: Healing from the Wounds of the Past* (Bethany, 2004).

Parrott, Les.

The Control Freak. Tyndale, 2000. 193 pp. ISBN 0842337938.

In this book, professor of psychology Les Parrott writes about control freaks. He explains why they are the way they are (anxiety is involved), and describes how to cope with them at home and at work. Parrott also writes about how to control the control freak within.

Subjects: Control (Psychology), Fear, Psychology

Sande, Ken.

The Peacemaker: A Biblical Guide to Resolving Personal Conflict. 3rd Edition. Baker, 2004 (1991). 318 pp. ISBN 0801064856.

> Ken Sande explains when to assert your rights, how to correct others effectively, how to negotiate just and reasonable agreements, when to ask the church to intervene in a conflict, how to deal with people who refuse to be reasonable, and when it is appropriate for a Christian to go to court. Sande is a lawyer and full-time Christian conciliator who says the principles in this book have been used to prevent church splits, settle multimillion-dollar lawsuits, and even stop divorces. First published in 1991, this is the third edition.
>
> **Subject:** Conflict Management, Interpersonal Relations, Reconciliation
>
> **More:** For more on conflict management in interpersonal communication, try *Boundaries Face-to-Face: How to Have That Difficult Conversation You've Been Avoiding* by Henry Cloud and John Townsend (Zondervan, 2003).

Sandford, John Loren, Paula Sandford, and Lee Bowman.

Choosing Forgiveness: Turning from Guilt, Bitterness and Resentment Towards a Life of Wholeness and Peace. Charisma House, 2007 (Clear Stream, 1996). 224 pp. ISBN 1599790696.

> Founders of Elijah House and veteran inner-healing ministers John and Paula Sandford write about how to give and receive forgiveness. They describe the process of forgiveness, discuss four levels of wounding that need forgiveness, and show how to overcome life's bitter roots in order to live a lifestyle of forgiveness. Suggesting that even everyday irritations need to be dealt with, they reveal what happens to those who hold on to unforgiveness.
>
> **Subject:** Forgiveness
>
> **More:** Lewis Smedes wrote the following two books on forgiveness (the first is well-known): *Forgive and Forget: Healing the Hurts We Don't Deserve* (HarperSanFrancisco, 1996) and *The Art of Forgiving* (Ballantine, 1997). Also, John Bevere wrote about how to deal with offense in *The Bait of Satan: Living Free from the Deadly Trap of Offense* (Charisma House, 2004).

Sedler, Michael D.

Stop the Runaway Conversation: Take Control Over Gossip and Criticism. Chosen, 2001 (Christian Life Publications, 1999). 201 pp. ISBN 0800792890.

> Michael D. Sedler, a pastor with a master's degree in social work, explores the harmful effects of "evil reports" such as gossip and

criticism. He says that people should not even listen to negative conversation. Sedler analyzes issues such as pride, purity, and fear, and shows readers how to control the tongue and undergo a cleansing process from defiling conversation.

Subjects: Criticism, Gossip

More: Sedler also wrote: *When to Speak Up and When to Shut Up* (Baker, 2006)

Silvious, Jan.

Please Don't Say You Need Me: Biblical Answers for Codependency. Zondervan, 1989. 159 pp. ISBN 0310343917.

Counselor and Bible teacher Jan Silvious shows readers how to identify and break free from unhealthy relationships. She defines and describes the symptoms of codependency and talks about codependency in parent–child relationships, as well as in friendship, marriage, and the workplace. She also shows readers how to maintain healthy Christian relationships.

Subjects: Codependency, Relationship Addiction

Sproul, R. C.

The Hunger for Significance. P&R Publishing, 2001 (Regal, 1983). 215 pp. ISBN 0875527019.

This is a great treatise on dignity, especially dignity in the home, school, hospital, prison, and workplace. Formerly published in 1983 as *In Search of Dignity.*

Subject: Dignity

Tripp, Paul David.

Instruments in the Redeemer's Hands: People in Need of Change Helping People in Need of Change. P&R Publishing, 2002. 362 pp. ISBN 0875526071.

Paul David Tripp, a Christian counselor, says that people don't need mere psychological systems, they need redemption that is found in Christ. People need to be set free from sin, he asserts, and this hope rests on Jesus Christ. Tripp says this is the foundation for psychological and relational healing and freedom. Change is possible—and God uses broken people to help bring about this change, he says. Tripp first shows readers what they need for change in their own lives; then he shows them how to be instruments for change in other's lives.

Subject: Counseling

VanVonderen, Jeff.

Good News for the Chemically Dependent and Those Who Love Them. Bethany, 2004. 239 pp. ISBN 0764200380.

Jeff VanVonderen is a Christian counselor, college instructor, and intervention specialist. In this book, he writes about the road to addiction and the process of recovery. One section helps family and friends of the chemically dependent. He also discusses the church's (positive and negative) role in recovery. The last chapter defines various chemical substances—legal and illegal.

Subjects: Addiction, Drug Abuse

More: Wendy Richardson has a book dealing with addiction and ADHD called *When Too Much Isn't Enough: Ending the Destructive Cycle of AD/HD and Addictive Behavior* (Pinon, 2005).

Grief and Death

Christian books on grief and death all carry the hopeful note of a blissful life after death, an eternal heaven free from suffering and death. It is much easier to face suffering and death if one has the promise of a better life to come. This section annotates books that may be helpful for Christians dealing with death, dying, grief, and loss. Different losses include miscarriages, stillbirths, abortions, and relational losses that come in the wake of drug abuse and divorce. Also included here are books to guide children through grief and for those who have lost a loved one due to suicide. There are even a couple of titles to help Christians face their own inevitable passing. Of related interest are books on near death experiences and volumes that record heavenly visions; these can be found in Chapter One.

Aldrich, Sandra P.

Will I Ever Be Whole Again?: Surviving the Death of Someone You Love. WinePress, 2006. 184 pp. ISBN 1414107080.

The first two chapters of this book deal with the author's experience of having her young husband die of brain cancer, leaving her with a ten-year-old boy and an eight-year-old daughter. The rest of the book covers topics of grief such as understanding and moving through grief, talking with children about death, how to help others, abnormal grief, coping with normal depression, coping with death of a child, miscarriage and abortion, and financial decisions in the midst of grief.

Subjects: Death and Dying, Grief

More: Also try *Traveling Through Grief: Learning to Live Again After the Death of a Loved One* by Susan Zonnebelt-Smeenge and Robert C. DeVries (Baker, 2006). Marilyn Willett Heavilin, who lost three of her sons, speaks about grief and God's grace in *Roses in December: Finding Strength Within Grief* (Harvest House, 1998).

Coleman, Jan.

After the Locusts: Restoring Ruined Dreams, Reclaiming Wasted Years. B&H Publishing, 2002. 180 pp. ISBN 0805424903.

Jan Coleman tells her story and that of other women whose lives have been shattered by divorce, drug use, and other losses and regrets. In her own life, she held fast to the promise found in the book of Joel 2:25: "I will repay you for the years the locusts have eaten." Coleman, a journalist and speaker, describes her journey of healing, forgiveness, and helping others.

Subjects: Grief, Women's Issues

Fanestil, John.

Mrs. Hunter's Happy Death: Lessons on Living from People Preparing to Die. Doubleday, 2006. 261 pp. ISBN 0385516061.

John Fanestil, a Methodist pastor, became fascinated with eighteenth-century accounts of "happy deaths," especially one in particular—that of Mary Clulow Hunter (1775–1801). Although she died at the early age of twenty-six, Hunter's attitude and manner of death taught Fanestil that some ways of dying are better than others. Hunter's life and death were filled with contentment and faith in Christ. Fanestil suggests that dying is much more than a mere medical process, and in fact it is a profound emotional and spiritual part of life. Modern thinking, says Fanestil, reduces so much of life to meaningless technical terms and has overshadowed "happy dying." By telling the story of Hunter and many other Christians who have experienced "happy deaths," Fanestil shows that death can be a fulfillment and not a tragedy.

Subject: Death and Dying

More: Judson Cornwall, a minister for more than seventy years, talks about his terminal illness (inoperable spine cancer) and approaching death in his book *Dying with Grace* (Charisma House, 2003).

Hayford, Jack.

I'll Hold You in Heaven. Revised and updated edition. Regal, 2003 (1990). 117 pp. ISBN 0830732594.

This book offers hope for women who have lost a child. Jack Hayford says that the lost child still lives in heaven, even those lost through abortion. The author explains that through forgiveness, which God freely gives, you can be reunited with your precious child.

Subject: Abortion, Death and Dying, Grief, Miscarriage, Stillbirth

More: Bernadette Keaggy, wife of musician Phil Keaggy, has lost five babies (the first three were stillborn). She gives her personal story and practical advice for dealing with loss in *Losing You Too Soon: Finding Hope After Miscarriage or the Loss of a Baby* (Harvest House, 2002). For a book specifically on healing from the grief and pain after an abortion, try *Her Choice to Heal: Finding Spiritual and Emotional Peace After Abortion* by Sydna Massee and Joan Phillips (Chariot Victor, 1998).

Hsu, Albert.

Grieving a Suicide: A Loved One's Search for Comfort, Answers & Hope. InterVarsity, 2002. 182 pp. ISBN 0830823182.

The author, an editor at InterVarsity Press, lost his father to suicide. Hsu writes about the shock and turmoil that Christians face in the wake of suicide. He faces difficult questions like "Why did this happen?" and "Is suicide the unforgivable sin?" Included is an appendix with resources for suicide survivors and suicide prevention.

Subject: Death and Dying, Grief, Suicide

More: Also try *Aftershock: Help, Hope, and Healing in the Wake of Suicide* by David Cox and Candy Arrington (B&H Publishing, 2003).

Lewis, C. S.

A Grief Observed. HarperSanFrancisco, 2001 (1961). 112 pp. ISBN 0060652381.

Lewis (1898–1963), one of the most famous Christian authors of the twentieth century, composed this collection as he grieved for his wife, the American-born poet Joy Davidman. This book was first published in 1961.

Subject: Classics, Death and Dying, Grief

More: Sheldon Vanauken (a friend of C. S. Lewis) also lost his wife. He writes about his love for his wife and his grief in *A Severe Mercy* (HarperSanFrancisco reissue, 1987). The book includes eighteen letters from C. S. Lewis to Vanauken.

Marshall, Sharon, and Jeff Johnson.

Take My Hand: Guiding Your Child Through Grief. Zondervan, 2001. 192 pp. ISBN 0310238455.

This book discusses how Christians can talk to children about death and deceased relatives. Sharon Marshall and Jeff Johnson describe the grief process for kids. They answer many questions such as, "Should children attend funeral services?," "How do we help our children say goodbye?," "How can we help our children to pray?," "What do children want and need to know?," and "What is heaven like?" They also show readers how to help children who are dealing with the fear of dying. Marshall is a coordinator for a divorce and grief recovery program. She helped her preschool son deal with the death of his baby brother.

Subjects: Death and Dying, Grief in Children

More: For a Catholic perspective, try *Parenting a Grieving Child: Helping Children Find Faith, Hope, and Healing After the Loss of a Loved One* by Mary DeTurris Poust (Loyola Press, 2002).

Sittser, Jerry.

A Grace Disguised: How the Soul Grows Through Loss. Zondervan, 2005 (1996). 224 pp. ISBN 0310258952.

Though the pain is great and the darkness terrible, there is something to be gained from suffering. The same is true for many losses, like death, divorce, and illness. In a single accident, Jerry Sittser lost his mother, his wife, and a daughter. With graceful prose, Sittser tells his story and describes how he made the choice to face his loss. It was a hard choice, but the only one that led to growth and life.

Subjects: Grief, Suffering

Chapter 4

Evangelism

Introduction

Evangelism has been a concern for Christians ever since Jesus gave the "great commission" found in Matthew 28:19–20:

Therefore go and make disciples of all nations, baptizing them in the name of the Father and of the Son and of the Holy Spirit, and teaching them to obey everything I have commanded you. And surely I am with you always, to the very end of the age.

As far as books and publishing are concerned, the topic of evangelism divides itself nicely into three categories that become the sections of this chapter: apologetics, evangelism, and missions.

Apologetics has to do with proving, logically, the verity of Jesus Christ and the claims of the Bible. The work of Christian apologists has quite a history. Spanning the centuries are writers like Paul the Apostle, who wrote most of the New Testament; Saint Augustine (354–430), the North African bishop famous for writing *Confessions* and *City of God*; Thomas Aquinas (1225–1274), an Italian Catholic priest, philosopher, and theologian; and Blaise Pascal (1623–1662), the French mathematician.

The evangelism section of this chapter includes books that show readers a variety of ways to "spread the good news"—from conversational evangelism to servant evangelism. The section on missions completes this chapter. A missionary typically refers to a person (an evangelist) who is willing to learn the language and culture of a foreign people so they can travel across the globe to share the message of Christ with them.

Apologetics

The word "apologetics" comes from the Greek word *apologia*, which means "a speech in defense." Therefore, apologetics, as used in this chapter, has to do with defending, or proving, the Christian faith. Some of the most famous writers in this area are Oxford scholar C. S. Lewis, British writer G. K. Chesterton, and American theologian/philosopher Francis Schaeffer. More recent apologetics writers include Josh McDowell, Lee Strobel, and Ravi Zacharias. This section on apologetics also covers books about cults and other religions. For books on apologetics that focus on philosophy, see the philosophy section of Chapter Five (on culture). Also see Chapter Seven on science and nature. Science is a big area of interest for those studying apologetics. There is a whole branch of apologetics that seeks to answer questions like: How did God create the world? If people evolved from lower forms of life, does this disprove Christianity? How does one reconcile the Bible and science? Chapter Seven on science and nature also includes apologetics titles.

Boa, Kenneth D., and Robert M. Bowman, Jr.

Faith Has Its Reasons: An Integrative Approach to Defending Christianity. Paternoster, 2006 (NavPress, 2001). 608 pp. ISBN 1932805346.

> This ambitious and useful handbook begins with an overview of the history of apologetics. Using practical examples to illustrate, the authors describe the strengths and weaknesses of five main approaches to apologetics: 1) apologetics as proof (classical approach), 2) apologetics as defense (evidentialist approach), 3) apologetics as offense (presuppositional or reformed approach), 4) apologetics as persuasion (fideist approach), and 5) a mixture of the previous four approaches (integrative approach). Kenneth Boa and Robert Bowman also sketch the lives and thought of five proponents of each approach to defending the faith. For instance, C. S. Lewis used the classical approach, John Calvin and Van Til used the reformed approach, Blaise Pascal and Karl Barth used the fideist approach, and Francis Schaeffer used the integrative approach. Despite the size of this book and the many ideas tackled, the authors have managed to write a very clear, easy-to-read apologetics handbook. Boa is president of Reflections Ministries. Bowman is the president of the Institute for the Development of Evangelical Apologetics.
>
> **Subjects:** Apologetics, Award Winners (ECPA, CT)
>
> **More:** For another book that examines different approaches to apologetics, try *Five Views on Apologetics* edited by Steven Cowan (Zondervan, 2000).

Chesterton, G. K.

Orthodoxy. Ignatius Press, 1995 (Dodd, Mead & Co., 1908). 168 pp. ISBN 0898705525.

G. K. Chesterton (1874–1936) was a Catholic British thinker and writer famous for his Christian nonfiction as well as his detective fiction. This spiritual autobiography of Chesterton (first published in 1908) is a classic of Christian apologetics. In it, Chesterton shows how Christianity "satisfies suddenly and perfectly man's ancestral instinct for being the right way up." The word "orthodoxy" used as the title of the book refers to the basic Christian belief as found in the Apostles' Creed.

Subjects: Apologetics, Autobiography, Classics

More: *Orthodoxy* is a companion to an earlier book by Chesterton called *Heretics* (Hendrickson, 2007), which was first published in 1905. Also try Chesterton's *The Everlasting Man* (Dover, 2007), which C. S. Lewis once referred to as "the best popular apologetic I know." For more about Chesterton's life, try *The Autobiography of G. K. Chesterton* (Ignatius, 2006).

Copan, Paul.

"That's Just Your Interpretation:" Responding to Skeptics Who Challenge Your Faith. Baker, 2001. 240 pp. ISBN 0801063833.

Philosophy professor Paul Copan answers challenges related to truth, reality, and Christianity. Here are some of the slogans and questions that he deals with: "That's just your reality," "If God made the universe, who made God?," "Why would a good God send people to hell?," "How can God be three and one?," "How could a loving God command genocide?," and "Doesn't the Bible condone slavery?" Copan gives logical and biblical responses to these thorny questions.

Subjects: Apologetics, Skepticism

More: *Who Made God?: And Answers to Over 100 Other Tough Questions of Faith* edited by Ravi Zacharias and Norman L. Geisler (Zondervan, 2003), which answers questions about God, evil, science, Christ, the Bible, and about other religions, such as Hinduism, transcendental meditation, yoga, Buddhism, and Black Islam. *Handbook of Christian Apologetics* by Peter Kreeft and Ronald K. Tacelli (InterVarsity, 1994) is a thick book dealing with faith and reason and summarizing all the major arguments for important Christian teachings. *Letters from a Skeptic: A Son Wrestles with His Father's Questions About Christianity* by Gregory A. Boyd and Edward K. Boyd (Cook Communications, 1994) records a conversation between a skeptical father and a believing son, who happens to be a theologian.

D'Souza, Dinesh.

What's So Great About Christianity? Regnery, 2007. 348 pp. ISBN 1596985178.

> Dinesh D'Souza answers the critics and skeptics of Christianity with skill and clarity. D'Souza addresses a multitude of issues concerning history (the Crusades, the Galileo affair, the Inquisition), science (the Big Bang theory, Evolution, the anthropic principle), and philosophy (atheism, Pascal's Wager, the Ontological argument, Kant's ideas, etc.). D'Souza shows how evolution does not threaten Christianity and deftly handles the so-called "new atheists" like Richard Dawkins, Daniel Dennett, Sam Harris, and Christopher Hitchens. Dinesh D'Souza is a scholar at the Hoover Institution at Stanford University and a former White House domestic policy analyst.
>
> **Subject:** Apologetics, Atheism, Christianity, Evolution, Morality, Science
>
> **More:** Another best seller by D'Souza is *What's So Great About America?* (Penguin, 2003). For another book dealing with atheism, try this book by Antony Flew: *There Is a God: How the World's Most Notorious Atheist Changed His Mind* (HarperOne, 2007). For another book dealing with Darwinism, philosophy, and morality, try *Moral Darwinism: How We Became Hedonists* by Benjamin Wiker (InterVarsity, 2002).

Kreeft, Peter.

Socrates Meets Jesus: History's Great Questioner Confronts the Claims of Christ. InterVarsity, 2002 (1987). 182 pp. ISBN 0830823387.

> Peter Kreeft, a professor of philosophy at Boston College, places Socrates in a modern university divinity school. Socrates goes to several classes on subjects such as science and religion, comparative religion, and Jesus Christ. Socrates, the university students, and the professors have some very interesting conversations about Jesus, faith, truth, religion, science, and philosophy. Written in dialogue format, the book uses the Socratic method to probe these issues.
>
> **Subjects:** Apologetics, Philosophy
>
> **More:** Kreeft has another book in the "Socratic dialogue" format called *Between Heaven and Hell: A Dialog Somewhere Beyond Death with John F. Kennedy, C. S. Lewis & Aldous Huxley* (InterVarsity, 1982). Kreeft puts these three men, who all died on November 22, 1963, in the same room so they can talk about philosophic issues.

Lewis, C. S.

Mere Christianity. HarperOne, 2001 (Geoffrey Bles, 1952). 227 pp. ISBN 0060652926.

Clive Staples Lewis (1898–1963), Oxford professor, scholar, and Christian apologist, is probably the most famous Christian writer of the twentieth century. This book (first published in 1952) started as a series of popular BBC radio talks during World War II and became one of his best-known works. In this book, Lewis discusses the existence of a universal moral law (a sense of right and wrong that is shared by all humanity) and about the "law-giver," God. He also examines the basic components of Christian belief, including topics such as sin, forgiveness, faith, the trinity, pride, and sex.

Subjects: Apologetics, Classics, Moral Law, Theology

More: For another well-known book similar to *Mere Christianity*, try John Stott's *Basic Christianity* (InterVarsity, 2007). For another work by Lewis, try *The Screwtape Letters* (HarperOne, 2001). This unusual book (first published in 1942) is presented as a collection of letters giving advice from a senior demon named Screwtape to a trainee demon named Wormwood. As the demons discuss their attempts to distract and tempt a new Christian, the reader discovers many of the schemes of the enemy. For a book that discusses basic issues about God, heaven, the Bible, and Christianity in a very simple, conversational, and humorous style, try *Everything You Always Wanted to Know About God (but Were Afraid to Ask)* by Eric Metaxas (WaterBrook, 2005).

Macaulay, Susan Schaeffer.

How to Be Your Own Selfish Pig: And Other Ways You've Been Brainwashed. Summit Press, 2003 (Chariot, 1982). 123 pp. ISBN 0936163380. **YA**

In this book, aimed at high school/college students, Susan Schaeffer Macaulay introduces readers to a variety of philosophical ideas and social issues that teens face in today's world. Macaulay, daughter of renowned apologist Francis Schaeffer, incorporates stories from her own family and from people she met while living at L'Abri (the Schaeffer home that was turned into a ministry center) in Europe. The book includes well-drawn, playful illustrations; nonetheless, it faces practical issues like divorce, abortion, and drug use—as well as theoretical questions like "Who am I?," "Is God real?," and "What is the meaning of life?," directly and capably.

Subjects: Apologetics, Philosophy, Social Issues, Young-Adult Interest

McDowell, Josh.

The New Evidence That Demands a Verdict. Thomas Nelson, 1999 (Campus Crusade, 1972). 800 pp. ISBN 0785242198.

This classic reference book on apologetics, written in an outline format, covers a broad spectrum of issues related to proving the Bible, Jesus Christ, and Christianity. Is the Bible reliable? Is there proof for the resurrection of Christ? Does archaeology prove Christianity? This compilation of Josh McDowell's research (which combines the original two volumes and updates it with information about postmodernism) presents hundreds of pages of hard historical evidence for both skeptics and believers. McDowell (1939–), a writer and Christian apologist, has ministered with Campus Crusade for Christ for many years.

Subjects: Apologetics, Archaeology

More: *More Than a Carpenter* (Tyndale, 1987) is McDowell's brief but readable discussion of who Jesus Christ really is. It answers the question: Is Jesus Christ the Lord, a liar, or a lunatic? This classic book clearly argues the validity of the Bible and the life and resurrection of Christ.

Martin, Walter, author, and Ravi Zacharias, Jill Martin Rische, and Kevin Rische, editors.

The Kingdom of the Cults. Revised, expanded, and updated edition. Bethany, 2003 (1965). 704 pp. ISBN 0764228218.

This standard reference work on the subject of cults (first published in 1965) covers Jehovah's Witnesses, Christian Science, the Church of Jesus Christ of Latter-day Saints (the Mormons), spiritism, the Theosophical Society (Gnosticism), Buddhism, the Baha'i Faith, Unitarian Universalism, Scientology, Unification, Eastern religions, New Age, and Islam. It includes sections on cults of the world mission field and "how-to" information on cult evangelism. Several appendices discuss topics such as the Worldwide Church of God (which moved from a cult to Christianity), Seventh-day Adventism, Swedenborgianism, and Rosicrucianism. Jill Martin Rische and Kevin Rische, Dr. Martin's daughter and son-in-law, serve as managing editors for this edition.

Subjects: Apologetics, Cults, Evangelism

More: *Kingdom of the Cults* does not cover Freemasonry—a high-demand subject in libraries. Steven Tsoukalas has a book on the subject from a Christian perspective entitled *Masonic Rites and Wrongs* (P&R Publishing, 1995). Also, if the library's copy of *Kingdom of the Cults* cannot circulate because it is a reference book, Zondervan has a series of about fifteen small, inexpensive books that cover a range of popular topics from astrology and mind sciences to Jehovah's Witnesses and the New Age movement. The name of the series is the <u>Zondervan Guide to Cults & Religious Movements Series</u>.

Pascal, Blaise.

Pensees. Penguin Classics, 1995 (1669). 368 pp. ISBN 0140446451.

Pensees is French for "thoughts." This work by Catholic philosopher and mathematician Blaise Pascal (1623–1662) is a collection of thoughts and writing fragments that Pascal was not able to finish before his early death at the age of thirty-nine. Nonetheless, this book is a classic work on apologetics. In it you'll find Pascal's "wager," which basically says, if you bet your life that God exists and you are right, then you have everything to gain. If you turn out to be wrong, then you have nothing to lose. However, if you bet your life that God *does not* exist, then you have everything to lose if you are wrong, and if you are right (that God *does not* exist), then you have nothing to gain. Some more famous thoughts from this book are: "The heart has its reasons, of which reason knows nothing," "People are generally better persuaded by the reasons which they have themselves discovered than by those which have come in to the mind of others," and "Faith indeed tells what the senses do not tell, but not the contrary of what they see. It is above them and not contrary to them." A. J. Krailsheimer translated the text of this edition into English (from the French) and wrote the introduction.

Subjects: Apologetics, Catholics, Classics, Mystics

More: *Christianity for Modern Pagans: Pascal's Pensees* (Ignatius, 1993), edited by Peter Kreeft, includes selected portions from Pascal's *Pensees* that Kreeft has arranged and commented on in order to help modern readers. Kreeft uses Krailsheimer's translation found in the Penguin edition.

Rowe, David L.

I Love Mormons: A New Way to Share Christ with Latter-day Saints. Baker, 2005. 190 pp. ISBN 0801065224.

David Rowe clearly explains, from the evangelical Christian perspective, Mormon belief and culture. He encourages readers to love and respect Mormons as people that God loves. He shows, in a unique way, how to understand and communicate effectively the love of Christ with those in the Mormon church. Rowe tells many real-life stories that demonstrate his approach. At the back of the book, he includes a helpful glossary of Latter-day Saints terms because common theological terms have vastly different meanings for Mormons. Rowe is a professor and dean of spiritual life at Salt Lake Theological Seminary, an evangelical Protestant graduate school.

Subjects: Evangelism, Mormons

More: *The New Mormon Challenge* (Zondervan, 2002) is a collection of respectful and scholarly essays examining the history and theology of the Church of Jesus Christ of Latter-day Saints from a Christian perspective. It was edited by three authorities on Mormonism: Francis Beckwith, Carl Mosser, and Paul Owen.

Sanders, Catherine Edwards.

Wicca's Charm: Understanding the Spiritual Hunger Behind the Rise of Modern Witchcraft and Pagan Spirituality. WaterBrook, 2005. 233 pp. ISBN 0877881987.

Catherine Edwards Sanders is a journalist and a Christian who wanted to understand why Wicca attracts so many people. She spent a year researching Wicca and talking with people who practice neo-paganism. She reports on her interviews with a variety of people from teenagers to college professors who practice witchcraft, some whom were once Christians and some of whom left Wicca and became Christians. Exposing stereotypes and discussing the ways that Christians treat Wiccans and pagans, Sanders describes the roots of Wicca and Goddess worship and comments on the current popularity of witch-related books and television shows.

Subjects: Apologetics, Paganism, Wicca, Witchcraft

More: Here are two more books on Wicca and witchcraft from a Christian perspective: *Dewitched: What You Need to Know About the Dangers of Wicca & Witchcraft* by Tim Baker (Thomas Nelson, 2004) and *What's the Deal with Wicca?: A Deeper Look into the Dark Side of Today's Witchcraft* by Steve Russo (Bethany, 2005).

Schaeffer, Francis A.

He Is There and He Is Not Silent. Tyndale, 1980 (1972). 128 pp. ISBN 084231413X.

Francis Schaeffer (1912–1984), one of the most famous Christian thinkers and writers of the last century, was an American evangelical theologian, philosopher, apologist, and Presbyterian pastor who founded the L'Abri community in Switzerland. In this book he shows that the only solution to the dilemma of modern man (or postmodern man) is the Christian idea of a "God who is there, who is the infinite-personal God, who has made man in His image." Schaeffer starts this book with a basic overview of the three areas of philosophy: existence, morality, and knowing. He points out that few people are academic philosophers, but everyone has a worldview; he concludes that philosophy is important to everyone, especially if one desires to communicate the gospel in today's world. The God who is there, he asserts, solves the problem of existence (metaphysics), and the God who speaks answers the problem of knowing (epistemology).

Subjects: Apologetics, Epistemology, Philosophy

More: *He Is There and He Is Not Silent* is one of the three foundational books of all of Schaeffer's writing. These foundational books are collected in *A Francis A. Schaeffer Trilogy: Three Essential Books in One Volume* (Crossway, 1990). All of Schaeffer's books are collected in a five-volume set called *The Complete Works of Francis A. Schaeffer: A Christian Worldview* (Crossway Books, 1985).

Sire, James W.

The Universe Next Door: A Basic Worldview Catalog. 4th Edition. InterVarsity, 2004 (1976). 252 pp. ISBN 0830827803.

This is a classic handbook describing the ideas of major philosophical/religious movements, namely deism, naturalism, nihilism, existentialism, Eastern pantheistic monism, New Age, and postmodernism. James Sire (1933–), a Christian author and speaker, has experience teaching university courses in philosophy, English, and theology. He was a senior editor at InterVarsity Press.

Subjects: Apologetics, Award Winners (CT), Comparative Religion, Philosophy, Worldview

More: *Why Should Anyone Believe Anything at All?* (InterVarsity, 1994) by Sire explores the rationality of the Christian faith and the problem of evil. Sire also has written *Why Good Arguments Often Fail: Making a More Persuasive Case for Christ* (InterVarsity, 2006) and *A Little Primer on Humble Apologetics* (InterVarsity, 2006).

Strobel, Lee.

The Case for Christ: A Journalist's Personal Investigation of the Evidence for Jesus. Zondervan, 1998. 304 pp. ISBN 0310209307.

Lee Strobel, an award-winning journalist, goes across the country to interview experts in various fields to answer questions about the Bible's reliability and the historicity of Jesus. For instance, Strobel interviews John McRay, professor of New Testament and archaeology emeritus at Wheaton, about the archaeological evidence for Christ. Strobel's writing style is very clear and engaging, and this book should interest believers and skeptics.

Subjects: Apologetics, Award Winners (ECPA), Jesus Christ

More: In the same vein, Strobel has written *The Case for Faith: A Journalist Investigates the Toughest Objections to Christianity* (Zondervan, 2000). This book deals with questions such as, "Is Jesus the only way to heaven?" and "Why is there suffering in the world?" Strobel has also written a book dealing with science and faith issues called *The Case for a Creator: A Journalist Investigates Scientific Evidence That Points toward God* (Zondervan, 2005).

Thirumalai, Madasamy.

Sharing Your Faith with a Buddhist. Bethany, 2003. 208 pp. ISBN 0764227912.

Clearly written and packed with fascinating information, this book describes the historical background and basic practices and beliefs of Buddhism as practiced by people of different countries, such as Sri Lanka, Myanmar, Thailand, Cambodia, Laos, Vietnam, China, Japan, Korea, Tibet, Mongolia, Nepal, Bhutan, and India. The book also discusses Buddhism's three major divisions: Theravada (or Hinayana), Mahayana, and Vajrayana (Tibetan). Madasamy Thirumalai covers idols and relics, the influence of animism, pantheism, and polytheism, as well as magic and spirit possession. Thirumalai was born in India and brought up a Hindu, but he was influenced by Buddhism; he is now professor of world religions and linguistics at Bethany College of Missions.

Subjects: Apologetics, Buddhism, Hinduism, Missions

More: For another book dealing with Buddhism, try *The Lotus and the Cross* by Ravi Zacharias (Multnomah, 2001), in which Jesus has a conversation with Buddha. Thirumalai has written another book on Hinduism, *Sharing Your Faith with a Hindu* (Bethany, 2002).

Van Til, Cornelius, and William Edgar, editor.

Christian Apologetics. 2nd Edition. P&R Publishing, 2003 (1976). 206 pp. ISBN 0875525113.

Cornelius Van Til (1895–1987), a reformed theologian, is the father of presuppositional apologetics. "Presuppositional" means that, at the bottom of all thinking, Christians believe that God exists and the Bible is the source of truth. This book is not a "how-to" manual for doing apologetics; instead, it is more of a theological and philosophic explanation of Van Til's approach to apologetics. For Van Til, the right worldview (based on the Bible) brings meaning and value to life. All other worldviews and systems of thought, he says, will ultimately fail. Van Til was professor of apologetics at Westminster Theological Seminary until 1975. William Edgar, who wrote the introduction and explanatory notes to this book, is currently a professor of apologetics at Westminster Theological Seminary.

Subjects: Apologetics, Philosophy, Theology—Reformed Theology

More: For another book by Van Til, try *The Defense of the Faith* (P&R Publishing, 1967). For two books that examine Van Til's ideas and life, see Greg L. Bahnsen's *Van Til's Apologetic: Readings and Analysis* (P&R Publishing, 1998) and John Frame's *Cornelius Van Til: An Analysis of His Thought* (P&R Publishing, 1995). For a book on apologetics by William Edgar, try *Reasons of the Heart: Recovering Christian Persuasion* (P&R Publishing, 2003).

Zacharias, Ravi.

Deliver Us from Evil. Thomas Nelson, 1998 (1996). 256 pp. ISBN 084993950X.

Ravi Zacharias shows readers how the rejection of Christian truth by modern society degrades humanity and exposes the philosophic schemes of the enemy that pervade society today. Ideas like pluralism, he suggests, negatively affect both society and the individual. Zacharias (1946–), an international lecturer and evangelist from India, is known for his evangelism with intellectuals. In 2006, he was visiting professor at Wycliffe Hall, Oxford University in Oxford, England.

Subject: Apologetics

More: In *The Real Face of Atheism* (Baker, 2004), Zacharias examines the beliefs of atheists such as Bertrand Russell and Jean Paul Sartre. He asserts that their godless ideas do not satisfy man's deepest longings for truth and meaning, and he shows the consequences of shutting out God from life and thought. Zacharias also wrote *Can Man Live without God?* (Thomas Nelson, 2004), which won the Gold Medallion (ECPA Christian Book) Award.

Evangelism

This section includes books that show Christians how to literally "spread the good news." It also includes a few biographies of famous evangelists such as D. L. Moody; however, note that most of the biographies of evangelists are in Chapter One. Here are books that discuss Jesus' methods (*The Master Plan of Evangelism* by Robert Coleman and *The Heart of Evangelism* by Jerram Barrs), books that show readers how to incorporate prophecy and miracles into one's outreach endeavors (Che Ahn's *Fire Evangelism* and Mark Stibbe's *Prophetic Evangelism*) and books that describe how to share the love of God with people by serving them in practical ways (*Conspiracy of Kindness* by Steve Sjogren).

Ahn, Che.

Fire Evangelism: Reaching the Lost Through Love and Power. Chosen, 2006. 239 pp. ISBN 0800794109.

Che Ahn, senior pastor of Harvest Rock Church in Pasadena, California, shares his passion for evangelism. The love of God, he states, is central to evangelism. Ahn gives practical examples from his own life (including a divine appointment involving servant evangelism and the local garbage collector); he also draws examples from a variety of famous evangelists such as Bill Bright, Billy Graham, Rebecca Manley Pippert, Michael Green, Winkie Pratney,

Charles Finney, and D. L. Moody. A second point he makes is that the power of God is another major part of evangelism. Both in the early church and in modern times, miracles draw people to Christ. Ahn relates many stories about incredible healings and church growth in South America, Africa, and North America. Ahn's life and ministry demonstrates that what happened in the book of Acts is still being lived out today by Christians around the world. Besides healing, Ahn writes about prophetic evangelism, presence evangelism (as in the "presence of God"), workplace evangelism, and church planting. An appendix, "How to Plant a Church," is also included.

Subjects: Evangelism, Healing, Miracles

More: Also try Ed Silvoso's *Prayer Evangelism* (Regal, 2000). Che Ahn gives more testimonies of God's healing power for today in *How to Pray for Healing* (Regal, 2003).

Barrs, Jerram.

The Heart of Evangelism. Crossway, 2005. 288 pp. ISBN 1581347154.

Jerram Barrs, founder and resident scholar of the Francis Schaeffer Institute at Covenant Theological Seminary, discusses what the Bible has to say about evangelism. This is not a cold, hard scriptural study. Rather, the heart of God and the hand of God are revealed as Barrs examines the various means by which God draws people to himself. To explain the content of the gospel message, Barrs examines four scripture passages where the gospel is preached in the New Testament: by Jesus in Luke 24:44–47; by Peter in Acts 2:22–40; and by Paul in 1 Corinthians 15:1–5 and Acts 17:22–31. In another section, Barrs writes about the attitude Paul had toward God and the people to whom he preached. Barrs also shows readers how to understand and speak the language of the lost in today's world.

Subject: Evangelism

More: In *Learning the Language of Babylon: Changing the World by Engaging the Culture* (Xulon, 2004), Terry Crist compares our situation to Daniel's situation when he was a captive in Babylon. Daniel became proficient in understanding Babylonian culture in order to bring glory to God. Crist says, "He was willing to learn the language of Babylon without being nourished by the spirit of Babylon ... Likewise, we must learn to speak the language of the culture in which we have become exiled."

Bonnke, Reinhard.

Time Is Running Out. Regal, 1999. 257 pp. ISBN 0830724664.

Reinhard Bonnke (1940–), founder of Christ for All Nations, is a German evangelist known for large crusades in Africa and other countries where millions of people have heard the gospel and been healed from various diseases. This book is comprised of a series of lectures that Bonnke gave at Regent University in 1996 on the topic of world evangelism.

Subject: Evangelism

More: Bonnke has also written *Evangelism by Fire: Igniting Your Passion for the Lost* (Full Flame, 2002).

Carson, D. A., editor.

Telling the Truth: Evangelizing Postmoderns. Zondervan, 2002. 416 pp. ISBN 0310243343.

This book is a collection of essays by twenty-eight notable contributors, including Robert Coleman, Ravi Zacharias, Greg Ganssle, and James Sire. Kelly Monroe, leader of the Veritas Forum, writes about reaching the post-Christian university. Mark Dever discusses communicating about sin in a postmodern world. Peter Cha and Greg Jao address reaching out to postmodern Asian Americans. There are articles about campus ministry, epistemology, Christ-centric preaching, pluralism, and more. D. A. Carson is a professor at Trinity Evangelical Divinity School in Illinois.

Subjects: Evangelism, Postmodernism

More: For a book that explains postmodernism, try Heath White's *Postmodernism 101: A First Course for the Curious Christian* (Brazos, 2006). For a book that explains the impact of postmodernism in our culture and in a believer's life, try *Postmodern Times: A Christian Guide to Contemporary Thought and Culture* by Gene Edward Veith, Jr. (Crossway, 1994).

Coleman, Robert E.

Master Plan of Evangelism. Revell, 2006 (1964). 192 pp. ISBN 0800731220.

This is a classic study (first published in 1964) of the simple and effective ministry principles that Jesus Christ used to train his disciples. Rather than discussing the message of the gospel, this brief volume focuses on discipleship principles designed to fulfill the great commission. For example, readers learn how Jesus selected his disciples and what he expected of them. Robert Coleman is director of the School of World Mission and Evangelism and professor of evangelism at Trinity Evangelical Divinity School in Deerfield, Illinois.

Subjects: Discipleship, Evangelism, Jesus Christ

More: Robert Coleman has written a stirring book that examines "the character of Wesleyan evangelism." It is called *Nothing to Do but to Save Souls: John Wesley's Charge to His Preachers* (Evangel Publishing House, 2006). For more on discipleship, try *The Lost Art of Disciple Making* by Mr. LeRoy Eims (Zondervan, 1978).

Comfort, Ray, and Kirk Cameron.

The Way of the Master. Bridge-Logos, 2006 (Tyndale, 2004). 375 pp. ISBN 0882702203.

Ray Comfort and Kirk Cameron seek to prevent false conversions. They say that many people become Christians because they are told that God will give them a happy life. The truth is that the Bible shows that suffering and persecution are two things that believers can expect. Why become a Christian? The authors suggest that the truth of the matter is that we are all on a metaphorical "plane that is destined to crash." The gospel is our parachute, our only hope of survival. The Ten Commandments, they say, will direct people's attention to this reality and shows them they are sinners in need of a savior. Once people realize the true state they are in, then they will gladly receive the good news that Jesus Christ came to forgive them from their sins and to save them from hell. This book comes with an audio CD called *Hell's Best Kept Secret*. Comfort is an evangelist from New Zealand. Cameron, an actor famous for his role in the television series *Growing Pains*, works with Comfort in the Way of the Master Ministries.

Subject: Evangelism

More: Comfort and Cameron also coauthored *The School of Biblical Evangelism* (Bridge-Logos, 2004), a hefty, 782-page book including lessons on everything from open-air preaching to science apologetics. Comfort edited *The Evidence Bible* (Bridge-Logos, 2003), which has the full-text Bible (King James adaptation by Comfort) and evangelistic/apologetic notes throughout the text.

Dorsett, Lyle W.

A Passion for Souls: The Life of D. L. Moody. Moody Press, 2003 (1997). 494 pp. ISBN 0802451810.

D. L. Moody (1837–1899) went from being a barely literate, poor backwoods child to a world-renowned minister and revivalist. He ministered on the Civil War battlefield and was a contemporary of Charles Spurgeon, George Müller, G. Campbell Morgan, and many other famous men of God whom he befriended. He also started numerous bible schools and churches, some which still stand today. Although more than sixty biographies of Moody have been written, this one by Lyle Dorsett is unique because he had access to previously unpublished letters. Dorsett gives an interesting historical perspective showing Moody's strengths and weaknesses.

Subjects: Biography, Evangelism, Evangelists, Dwight Lyman Moody (1837–1899)

More: For a book written by Moody, try *Secret Power* (Bridge-Logos, 2006), which is about the working of the Holy Spirit in our lives.

Graham, Billy.

Peace with God. Revised edition. Thomas Nelson, 2000 (Doubleday, 1953). 288 pp. ISBN 0849942152.

Billy Graham, an American Baptist preacher born in 1918, is one of the most famous Christian evangelists in the world today. In this book, first published in 1953, Graham shows readers how to become children of God and followers of Jesus Christ. Graham talks about the Bible, God, sin, the devil, and death. He writes about why Jesus came, repentance, assurance of salvation, and how to live a Christian life.

Subjects: Evangelism, Gospel, Salvation

More: To learn about the life of Graham, the evangelistic campaigns he has been a part of, and the U.S. presidents he has befriended, read his life story *Just As I Am: The Autobiography of Billy Graham* (HarperOne, 2007).

Green, Michael.

Sharing Your Faith with Friends and Family: Talking About Jesus without Offending. Baker, 2005. 155 pp. ISBN 0801065259.

Well-known evangelist and scholar Michael Green wants to help people share their Christian faith naturally. He says that most people come to faith in Christ through the influence of family and friends; this is a gradual process that takes months or years. That is why Green says we should focus on building relationships and preparing ourselves for natural conversation about Christ. In this book, he shares many stories from his own experience and gives practical advice for knowing and sharing the good news and for being a "midwife" to help lead people to Christ. Green (1930–) is a British theologian, an Anglican priest, and a Christian apologist.

Subject: Anglicans, Evangelism

More: Another evangelistic title by Green is *Who Is This Jesus?* (Kingsway, 2006). For a book by Green (and Nick Spencer) dealing with apologetics, try *I'd Like to Believe, But ... Answers for Spiritual Seekers* (Baker, 2006). Also, Green has a well-known, classic study on evangelism called *Evangelism in the Early Church* (Eerdmans, 2004).

Hybels, Bill.

Just Walk Across the Room: Simple Steps Pointing People to Faith. Zondervan, 2006. 219 pp. ISBN 0310266696.

Bill Hybels shows that evangelism is as easy as walking across a room. With a simple prayer for guidance from God, and straightforward trust, anyone can be used by God to share the life-changing message of Jesus Christ. Hybels talks about his own hesitations to share his faith and about how he overcame them. He discusses how to develop friendships, explains how people can present their own life stories with others, and shows how to avoid pitfalls in this area. This clear and practical book should build confidence in even the most timid person who might think they would never be able to talk to others about God. Hybels is the pastor of Willow Creek Community Church in Illinois.

Subject: Evangelism

More: Hybels (and Mark Mittelberg) wrote another book on evangelism called *Becoming a Contagious Christian* (Zondervan, 1996). Also try *Witnessing without Fear* by Bill Bright (Thomas Nelson, 1993).

Little, Paul E.

How to Give Away Your Faith. InterVarsity, 2006 (1966). 228 pp. ISBN 0830834060.

Paul Little explains what the gospel message is, why we believe, and how Christ is relevant today. He also shows readers how to witness, how to overcome social barriers (like rude behavior or profanity on the part of people one is witnessing to), and how to be an effective ambassador for Christ. Little (1928–1975) worked with InterVarsity Christian Fellowship for more than two decades and was professor of evangelism at Trinity Evangelical Divinity School in Illinois. This classic book on personal evangelism was first published in 1966. Marie Little, the author's wife, revised and updated it in 1988 and again in 2006.

Subjects: Apologetics, Evangelism

More: Little also wrote a well-known book on apologetics called *Know Why You Believe: Connecting Faith and Reason* (Victor, 2003) in which he discusses evidence for Christ's resurrection and the Bible's authenticity, archaeological proofs, science and the Bible, other world religions, and the existence of suffering and evil.

Metzger, Will.

Tell the Truth: The Whole Gospel to the Whole Person by Whole People. 3rd Edition. InterVarsity, 2002 (1981). 216 pp. ISBN 0830823220.

Will Metzger, campus minister at the University of Delaware, distinguishes between a manipulative, human-centered gospel and the Christ-centered gospel of truth and grace. Metzger discusses personal witnessing and how to present the gospel to the "whole" person—including their minds, emotions, and wills. Suggesting that grace is the foundation for evangelism and that worship of God is the motivation for evangelism, Metzger also gives practical advice for communicating personally. This well-known book on evangelism was first published in 1981.

Subject: Evangelism

More: Readers may also enjoy *Lifestyle Evangelism* by Joe Aldrich (Multnomah, 2006), which shows readers how to build authentic, caring relationships with unbelievers.

Newman, Randy.

Questioning Evangelism: Engaging People's Hearts the Way Jesus Did. Kregel, 2004. 269 pp. ISBN 082543324X.

With the premise that questions are better than answers, Campus Crusade for Christ minister Randy Newman shows readers how to harness the power of questions for effective evangelism. To help the reader, Newman supplies sample conversations. He also discusses some of today's common issues like "Why are Christians so intolerant?," Why are Christians so homophobic?," and "Why does a good God allow evil and suffering?"

Subject: Evangelism

More: *Permission Evangelism* by Michael Simpson (Cook Communications, 2003) won the Gold Medallion (ECPA Christian Book) Award. Simpson shows readers how to effectively use conversation and their testimony to share God's love and transforming power without badgering or cornering people.

Peel, William Carr, and Walt Larimore.

Going Public with Your Faith: Becoming a Spiritual Influence at Work. Zondervan, 2003. 208 pp. ISBN 0310246091.

This book provides a model for workplace evangelism that is relational rather than confrontational. Connecting with people in authentic, caring ways, say the authors, is much more effective than "used car salesmen" techniques. They talk about earning the right to be heard and the importance of building a team and telling stories. Full of practical advice and insight.

Subjects: Award Winners (CT), Evangelism, Work and Evangelism

More: Readers may also like Regi Campbell's *About My Father's Business: Taking Your Faith to Work* (Multnomah, 2005). *Executive Influence: Impacting Your Workplace for Christ* by Christopher Crane and Mike Hamel (NavPress, 2003) describes how fifteen business executives shared their faith at work.

Pippert, Rebecca Manley.

Out of the Saltshaker and into the World: Evangelism As a Way of Life. 20th Anniversary revised and expanded edition. InterVarsity, 1999 (1979). 288 pp. ISBN 0830822208.

Rebecca Pippert, a writer and an internationally known seminar speaker on topics of evangelism and spiritual renewal, shows readers that it is not impossible to share their faith with others. After discussing what the gospel and Christ are all about, she explains how to develop a conversational style of evangelism.

Subject: Evangelism

More: *Living Proof: Sharing the Gospel Naturally* (NavPress, 1989) by Jim Peterson combines two of the author's previous books, *Evangelism and a Lifestyle* and *Evangelism for Our Generation*. There is much wisdom presented here from the author's twenty-five years of experience sharing the gospel. Greg Laurie, senior pastor of the Harvest Christian Fellowship in Riverside, California, has a brief book called *How to Share Your Faith* (Tyndale, 1999) that gives practical advice and shows readers the basics of sharing the good news.

Stibbe, Mark.

Prophetic Evangelism: When God Speaks to Those Who Don't Know Him. Authentic Media, 2004. 210 pp. ISBN 1860244572.

Mark Stibbe, Vicar of St. Andrews Church in Chorleywood, England, says prophetic evangelism is "simply God using revelatory phenomena to speak to the hearts of those who don't know Jesus." Citing the story of the woman at the well (Gospel of John, Chapter 4) and several stories in the book of Acts as New Testament examples of prophetic evangelism, he asserts that this is a biblical and effective method. Stibbe tells of many stories in which God revealed some fact (like a person's name or occupation) that believers are able to use to effectively show people that God loves them and wants to draw them to Jesus Christ. Stibbe discusses prophecy, dreams, and healing as ways that God speaks to believers and unbelievers today. He points out that "regular" people—teachers, housewives, flight attendants, etc.—can be used by God in prophetic evangelism; it's not just for full-time clergy.

Subjects: Anglicans, Evangelism, Prophecy, Spiritual Gifts

More: *Prophecy, Dreams, and Evangelism* by Doug Addison (Streams Publishing House, 2005) shows how to evangelize people without "Christianese" and without obnoxious tactics. Instead,

Addison talks about being led by the spirit to share the gospel using prophecy, words of knowledge, and dream interpretation—all biblical methods rarely used today.

Sjogren, Steve.

Conspiracy of Kindness: A Refreshing Approach to Sharing the Love of Jesus with Others. 10th Anniversary updated edition. Vine Books, 2003 (1993). 246 pp. ISBN 0830734074.

This groundbreaking book on evangelism puts forth Steve Sjogren's idea of "servant evangelism." Sjogren believes that reaching out to people in your community with acts of service and kindness can be used by God to touch people's hearts. Sjogren's strategy "operates on the premise that God is passionately in love with unbelievers." One example of servant evangelism is going out on a hot day and handing out free cold drinks "just because God loves you." There are many, many other ideas for serving a community: giving away food, cleaning and repairing neighborhood parks, etc. This is a practical way to get believers involved in working together to reach out to others and express the love of God.

Subject: Evangelism

More: Sjogren's follow-up book is *101 Ways to Reach Your Community* (NavPress, 2001). Sjogren has another book on evangelism (coauthored with Dave Ping and Doug Pollack) called *Irresistible Evangelism: Natural Ways to Open Others to Jesus* (Group Publishing, 2003).

Turner, Matthew Paul.

The Coffeehouse Gospel: Sharing Your Faith in Everyday Conversation. Relevant Books, 2004. 161 pp. ISBN 0974694282.

Matthew Paul Turner is the former editor of *CCM* magazine and leader of Jammin' Java coffeehouse in Washington, D.C. In this book, he shows readers how to share their Christian faith naturally and conversationally. There is no need to create awkward situations or to use antisocial tactics, he says. Turner records various recent conversations that he has had to provide real-life examples that illustrate these principles.

Subject: Evangelism

Wimber, John, and Kevin Springer.

Power Evangelism. 2nd Edition. Hodder Headline, 1997 (1985). 228 pp. ISBN 0340561270.

Why was Jesus so effective in evangelism? John Wimber says it is because "Jesus always combined the proclamation of the kingdom of God with its demonstration (casting out of demons, healing the sick, raising the dead, and so on)." This is power evangelism, Wimber says, and he did not always believe in it. However, when his eyes were opened to what God was doing in places like South America, Wimber reevaluated his theology and reexamined the Bible. He tested what he now believed the scriptures to teach as a pastor of a small group of fifty people. That small group grew to 40,000 people in 140 congregations around the United States and Canada. In this book, Wimber examines the teachings of Jesus on the kingdom of God and talks about his experiences with power evangelism. As the months and years went by, Wimber and his congregation began seeing hundreds of people healed every month—in church services, in hospitals, on the streets, and in homes. Wimber worked with C. Peter Wagner at the Fuller Evangelistic Association, after which he became pastor of Vineyard Christian Fellowship in California. This book was first published in 1985.

Subjects: Evangelism, Healing

More: For more about divine healing in the United States, try *Preparing the Way: The Reopening of the John G. Lake Healing Rooms in Spokane, Washington* by Cal Pierce (McDougal Publishing, 2001).

Missions

This section includes some exciting missionary tales and adventures, although most of the biographical missionary books are placed in Chapter One. There are also books to help readers get involved with missions. A number of the books found here were published by an organization called Youth With A Mission (YWAM). YWAM is one of the largest mission organizations in the world. Its people train and equip both short-term and full-time missionaries to serve in just about every country of the world. The history of dozens of mission organizations, movements, and individuals can be explored in Ruth Tucker's *From Jerusalem to Irian Jaya: A Biographical History of Christian Missions*.

Baker, Rolland, and Heidi Baker.

Always Enough: God's Miraculous Provision Among the Poorest Children on Earth. Chosen, 2003. 186 pp. ISBN 0800793617.

Civil war, famine, AIDS, and natural disasters have devastated the country of Mozambique, and the children are orphaned, diseased, abused, and starving. When Rolland and Heidi Baker reached out to these people, they found them not just hungry for food, but for God. Some of the most destitute areas were those with the most witch doctors. People now wanted a change. The Bakers saw death and destruction, but they also saw miracles.

They describe blind eyes that have been healed and cholera outbreaks that have been stopped by the hand of God. Prostitutes gave up their way of life to live with the Bakers, and scores of children came to live in the orphanage they started. These missionaries witnessed many starving people pass by food to get tracts and Bibles. This book not only describes the thousands of churches they helped to start in Mozambique but also tells the story of how the Bakers met, married, and received a call to minister to the poorest people on earth. In all the darkness, the Bakers have seen Jesus shine brightly; in all the poverty, they can testify that, with God, there is always enough.

Subjects: Autobiography, Heidi Baker (1960–), Roland Baker (1947–), Missions, Mozambique, Poverty

More: Rolland Baker's grandparents were missionaries to some of the poorest people of China. They wrote a book, first published about 1938, recording the miraculous visions that some of the children in their orphanage had. The book is called *Visions Beyond the Veil* by H. A. Baker (Sovereign World, 2006). The Bakers worked for a time with the famous Indonesian evangelist, Mel Tari, whose story is told in *Like a Mighty Wind* (New Leaf, 1995). Another famous tale of a missionary who depended upon God to provide for his orphanage is the *Autobiography of George Müller* (Whitaker, 1984).

Elliot, Elisabeth.

Shadow of the Almighty: The Life & Testament of Jim Elliot. HarperCollins, 1989 (1958). 256 pp. ISBN 006062213X.

In 1956, Jim Elliot (1927–1956), a missionary to the Auca Indians (also called the Waodani or Waorani) in Ecuador, was killed by the very people he was trying to minister to. In this classic missionary biography, Elisabeth Elliot draws from her late husband's diaries to reveal a man so committed to God that it could truly be said that his "life was hid in Christ with God." Jim Elliot's famous motto was, "He is no fool who gives what he cannot keep to gain what he cannot lose."

Subjects: Biography, Jin Elliott (1927–1956), Martyrs, Missionaries

More: *Through Gates of Splendor* by Elisabeth Elliot (Tyndale, 1986) tells the story of all five missionaries who where martyred: Jim Elliot, Nate Saint, Roger Youderian, Ed McCully, and Pete Fleming. Three years after the death of her husband, Elisabeth Elliot went back into Auca territory to minister to the people that murdered her husband. She tells the story in *The Savage, My Kinsman* (Vine Books, 1996).

Fann, Anne-Geri, and Greg Taylor.

How to Get Ready for Short-Term Missions: A Survival Guide. Thomas Nelson, 2006. 100 pp. ISBN 1418509779.

Anne-Geri Fann and Greg Taylor give practical advice for people before, during, and after they go on a short-term mission. They discuss what to pack, food situations that people might encounter, the need to be flexible in many areas, the need to understand different cultures, building relationships, and how to avoid common mistakes that short-term missionaries make. There is also a chapter for parents who are thinking about letting their kids go on a mission.

Subjects: Missions, Short-Term Missions

More: For another book on short-term missions, try *Stepping Out: A Guide to Short-Term Missions* by Tim Gibson and Steven C. Hawthorne (YWAM, 1996).

Hiebert, Paul G., R. Daniel Shaw, and Tite Tienou.

Understanding Folk Religion: A Christian Response to Popular Beliefs and Practices. Baker Books, 1999. 412 pp. ISBN 0801022193.

Many cultures and societies have two levels of belief: the formal religion and the "folk" religion, which is different and often contradictory to the formal religion. Missionaries need to study both levels in order to reach these people. Focusing on principles, this book analyzes various belief systems and religious practices of many different cultures, including topics such as luck, birth, witchcraft, gift-giving, taboos, signs, myths, and rituals. The authors are professors who have all been missionaries. Paul Hiebert served in South India, R. Daniel Shaw served in Papua New Guinea, and Tite Tienou served in Cote D'Ivoire, Africa.

Subjects: Folk Religion, Missions

Jordan, Peter.

Re-Entry: Making the Transition from Missions to Life at Home. YWAM Publishing, 1992. 150 pp. ISBN 0927545403.

Most people don't realize it, but returning home after a mission trip (short or long) can be a difficult experience emotionally, relationally, and spiritually. In fact, for some, it can be devastating. YWAM leader Peter Jordan discusses many of the issues that people face, including disorientation, guilt, culture shock, misunderstandings, pitfalls, mistakes people make, and how to prepare yourself and your kids for re-entry.

Subject: Missionaries—Reverse Culture Shock

Lai, Patrick.

Tentmaking: Business As Missions. Authentic, 2005. 432 pp. ISBN 1932805532.

Patrick Lai served for four years as a regular missionary and then for twenty-three years as a "tentmaker" (an approach to missions where the missionary uses business opportunities to be self-supporting). He writes for missionaries and tentmakers to address issues that they face in today's world. Lai says that tentmaking is a different way of doing missions and business. He describes various forms and levels of tentmaking and explains preparing for the field, church planting, and fellowship. He also discusses the tentmaker's jobs, personal life, family, home base, and difficulties.

Subject: Business and Missions

More: Also try books like *Great Commission Companies: The Emerging Role of Business in Missions* by Steve Rundle and Tom Steffen (InterVarsity, 2003) and Ed Silvoso's *Anointed for Business: How Christians Can Use Their Influence in the Marketplace to Change the World* (Regal, 2002).

McClung, Floyd.

Living on the Devil's Doorstep: From Kabul to Amsterdam. YWAM, 1999 (Word, 1988). 192 pp. ISBN 0927545454.

Floyd (1945–) and Sally McClung were missionaries to Kabul and Amsterdam for more than twenty years. In this book, McClung writes about the many adventures and miracles they experienced ministering to drugged-out hippies in Afghanistan and prostitutes of the red-light district in Amsterdam.

Subjects: Adventure, Autobiography, Missionaries

More: Other real-life adventures in this International Adventures series are *The Man with the Bird on His Head* by John Rush and Abbe Anderson (YWAM, 1999), *Tomorrow You Die* by Reona Peterson Joly (YWAM, 1996), and *Imprisoned in Iran* by Dan Baumann (YWAM, 2000).

Mallouhi, Christine A.

Miniskirts, Mothers & Muslims: A Christian in a Muslim Land. Monarch Books, 2004. 184 pp. ISBN 0825460514.

How should a Christian woman dress in a Muslim country without offending the locals? How does she understand this radically different culture? Christine Mallouhi is an Australian Christian married to an Arab Christian. Because her husband comes from a conservative Muslim family and she has lived in several Muslim countries, she is able to give insider's information. Topics include segregation, restrictions, hospitality, status, veils, stereotypes, and honor killings.

Subjects: Islamic Culture, Missions

More: Also try *Muslims Next Door: Uncovering Myths and Creating Friendships* by Shirin Taber (Zondervan, 2004) and *The Unseen Face of Islam: Sharing the Gospel with Ordinary Muslims at Street Level* by Bill Musk (Kregel, 2004). For the exciting conversion testimony of a prominent Muslim woman, try *I Dared to Call Him Father: The Miraculous Story of a Muslim Woman's Encounter with God* by Bilquis Sheikh and Richard H. Schneider (Chosen, 2003).

Miller, Darrow L., and Stan Guthrie.

Discipling Nations: The Power of Truth to Transform Cultures. 2nd Edition. YWAM, 2001 (1998). 312 pp. ISBN 1576582485.

Why are individuals, communities, and nations poor and underdeveloped? How can we bring them relief? In the introduction to this book, Darrow L. Miller says that, "the values, attitudes, culture and ethos of a people will determine whether its development is healthy, stunted, or nonexistent." The premise of this book, Miller continues, is that "there is a story that can transform poverty to bounty; there is a set of principles, a development ethic, that creates a fertile soil for development." This story is none other than the story that unfolds in the Bible, which includes the Christian gospel as its centerpiece. Miller asks and answers the question, "What is Christian development work?" Not only does the gospel have the power to transform individual lives, but it also has power to break deceptive cultural patterns that lead to poverty, hunger, and cultural devastation. Miller is the vice president of the Samaritan Strategy at Food for the Hungry International, a Christian relief and development organization. Stan Guthrie is associate news editor for *Christianity Today*.

Subjects: Economic Development, Missions, Poverty, Relief, Worldview

More*: If Jesus Were Mayor* by Bob Moffitt and Karla Tesch (Monarch, 2007) talks about the importance of the church in cultural transformation. In *The Forest in the Seed*, Scott Allen and Darrow Miller talk about the resources needed for Christian community development (Disciple Nations Alliance, 2007). *Truth and Community Transformation* (Food for the Hungry International, 2003) discusses a biblical alternative to the secular solution to community development, which views poverty as a social (not spiritual) problem.

Richardson, Don.

Eternity in Their Hearts. New edition. Regal, 2006 (1981). 224 pp. ISBN 0830738371.

In this book, missionary Don Richardson gives readers twenty-six true and fascinating stories that demonstrate how God has prepared various people groups to receive the gospel. For instance, he says, the Karen people of Burma have been waiting for hundreds of years for a "white brother" to bring them a book written by the one true God "Y'wa." Also, the Dyak people of Borneo have a strange custom almost identical to the Old Testament scapegoat. Every year, the people place their "Dosaku" (sin) in a little boat and release the boat into the river and watch, hoping it will sail out of their sight without overturning or drifting to the shore. These people have what Richardson calls "redemptive analogies," which are keys just waiting to unlock the truth of the gospel. Missionaries can tell the Dyak people that Jesus Christ is their ultimate scapegoat to remove their sins. Richardson spent fifteen years with the Sawi people in Irian Jaya.

Subjects: Anthropology, Missions

More: One of Richardson's most famous books is *Peace Child* (Regal, 2005), an autobiography in which he records his adventures in trying to share the gospel with the Stone Age Sawi people. Richardson also wrote the exciting story of Stan Dale, missionary to the Yali cannibals of Irian Jaya's mountains, in *Lords of the Earth* (YWAM, 2002).

Ritchie, Mark Andrew.

Spirit of the Rainforest: A Yanomamo Shaman's Story. Island Lake Press, 2000. 288 pp. ISBN 0964695235.

This amazing book comes with a big warning. The true stories told here are very graphic. In fact, the author couldn't get a major publishing house to publish it because of the sex and violence. The shaman named Jungleman tells in detail of atrocious, violent crimes that he and others committed, including rape and murder. Although grievous sins are described, the book is valuable because it reveals the real spirit world with which the shaman is in touch. Jungleman was filled with spirits—spirits that advised him as he led his village; spirits that led him to murder other villagers, including many children. Christian missionaries come to bring the spirit of truth to these fierce warriors, and several shamans "throw away" their evil spirits. Sadly, outsiders (including ungodly missionaries and anthropologists) sometimes bring more sin and misery to these people. This eye-opening book records both failures and victories.

Subjects: Anthropology, Deliverance, Missions, Shamans, Yanomamo Indians

Tucker, Ruth A.

From Jerusalem to Irian Jaya: A Biographical History of Christian Missions. 2nd Edition. Zondervan, 2004 (1983). 526 pp. ISBN 0310239370.

This award-winning book covers 2,000 years of Christian missionary history in a very readable style. Ruth Tucker, professor of missiology at Calvin Theological Seminary, describes the fascinating lives and adventures of pioneer missionaries all over the world. She starts with the early church and moves on to Roman Catholic missions, including such people as Boniface, Bartholomew de Las Casa, Francis Xavier, and Matthew Ricci; and then on to American Indian missions and missionaries such as John Eliot and David Brainerd. She also writes about Moravian missions and outreach efforts to south central Asia (William Carey, Adoniram and Ann Judson, Alexander Duff, etc.), Africa (David Livingston, Robert and Mary Moffat, Mary Slessor), China, the Pacific Islands, the Muslim world, and Korea and Japan. A chapter on single women missionaries such as Adele Marion Fielde, Lottie Moon, Amy Carmichael, and several chapters on twenty-first-century movements and missionaries are also included.

Subjects: Award Winners (ECPA), Missions—History

Youth With A Mission.

GO Manual: Youth With A Mission's World Guide. YWAM, 2007. 185 pp. ISBN 0927545772. **YA**

Youth With a Mission (YWAM) is a global Christian youth missions organization (with more than 800 operating locations) started by Loren Cunningham. This is YWAM's twentieth annual directory of missions trips, careers, and training. The book provides contact information and addresses for YWAM bases, school information, outreaches, seminars, and service opportunities, as well as photos and information about the many outreaches YWAM facilitates.

Subjects: Missions—Directories, Young-Adult Interest, YWAM (Organization)

More: The story of YWAM is told in Loren Cunningham's book *Is That Really You, God?: Hearing the Voice of God* (YWAM, 2001). Cunningham's newest work is called *The Book That Transforms Nations: The Power of the Bible to Change Any Country* (YWAM, 2007).

Chapter 5

Arts, Culture, and Education

Introduction

Books giving a Christian perspective on culture have been very popular in recent years. In fact, there is a word that summarizes this area of interest: worldview. According to the *American Heritage Dictionary of the English Language*, worldview means the "overall perspective from which one sees and interprets the world."

Francis Schaeffer (1912–1984) is perhaps the most well-known writer responsible for getting people to think about the forces that shape our lives and culture. Schaeffer's *Complete Works* is subtitled *A Christian Worldview*. He believed that biblical truth and the "lordship of Christ" were not confined to the church building on Sunday, but that Christianity and the Bible spoke to every area of life in a positive and liberating way. That is why he wrote about art, history, philosophy, film, theology, medical ethics, and even environmentalism. A more recent writer (who studied with Schaeffer) is Nancy Pearcey. Her book, *Total Truth: Liberating Christianity from Its Cultural Captivity*, carries on worldview thinking into the twenty-first century.

This chapter covers a broad range of topics including the arts, education, history, literature, music, philosophy, popular culture, and social issues—all with a decidedly Christian worldview.

The Arts

The number of Christian nonfiction books published on the visual arts has blossomed in the last fifteen to twenty years. Readers will find here a number of books that help Christians not only understand painting, sculpture, and modern art but also show them how to participate in the arts. A landmark book in this area is Francis Schaeffer's brief *Art and the Bible*. This section also contains books that provide a Christian understanding of literature (*The Christian Imagination* by Leland Ryken) as well as tools for Christian writers (Sally Stuart's *Christian Writers' Market Guide* and Jerry Jenkins' *Writing for the Soul: Instruction and Advice from an Extraordinary Writing Life*). Music has its own subsection in both this chapter and Chapter One. Here are books that discuss what the Bible says about music (*Selah: A Guide to Music in the Bible* by Donald Thiessen) and books that analyze the interaction between Christianity and secular rock music (*Faith, God, and Rock & Roll* by Mark Joseph).

Visual Arts

Brand, Hilary, and Adrienne Chaplin.

Art and Soul: Signposts for Christians in the Arts. 2nd Edition. Piquant, 2001 (1999). 219 pp. ISBN 0830826742.

In an effort to help people integrate their faith with their art, this handbook instructs Christians on how to interact with culture and create art. The authors discuss with clarity practical issues such as employment and new technology as well as theological and philosophic ideas like redemption and postmodernism. Profiles of individual artists and their works are found throughout the book.

Subject: Art

More: Another excellent treatment of this subject is *Imagine: A Vision for Christians in the Arts* by Steve Turner (InterVarsity, 2001).

Bustard, Ned, editor.

It Was Good: Making Art to the Glory of God. Square Halo Books, 2000. 286 pp. ISBN 0978509714.

A collection of thirteen essays written by painters, sculptors, musicians, publishers, pastors, and professors who discuss making art as a believer. Contributors include Ned Bustard, William Edgar, Makoto Fujimura, David Giardiniere, Time Keller, Edward Knippers, Charlie Peacock-Ashworth, Theodore Prescott, James Romaine, Krystyna Sanderson, Steve Scott, Gaylen Stewart, and

Gregory Wolfe. In an appendix, each contributor offers a list of suggested reading.

Subjects: Art, Essays

More: James Romaine has a collection of interviews with some of the same Christian artists in *Objects of Grace: Conversations on Creativity and Faith* (Square Halo, 2002).

Gasque, Laurel.

Art and the Christian Mind: The Life and Work of H. R. Rookmaaker. Crossway, 2005. 192 pp. ISBN 1581346948.

H. R. Rookmaaker (1922–1977) was an art history professor and a jazz critic from the Netherlands known for his Christian interpretation of modern art and his friendship with American apologist and theologian Francis Schaeffer. In this book, Laurel Gasque portrays Rookmaaker's family, career, thought, and legacy. This biography was first published as a part of *The Complete Works of H. R. Rookmaaker*, Part 4, Volume 6: "Hans Rookmaaker: An Open Life" (Piquant, 2003).

Subjects: Art, Biography, Hans R. Rookmaaker (1922–1977)

More: Another biography of Rookmaaker is *Hans Rookmaaker: A Biography* by Linette Martin (InterVarsity, 1979).

Rookmaaker, H. R.

Modern Art and the Death of a Culture. Crossway, 1994 (InterVarsity, 1970). 256 pp. ISBN 0891077995.

H. R. Rookmaaker, professor of art history at the Free University of Amsterdam, Netherlands, was one of the early advocates for Christian involvement with art and culture. First published in 1970, this book discusses modern art and modern culture in a way that helps Christians be more aware of the spirit of the age and better discern the influence and consequences of ideas upon art and culture. Rookmaaker (1922–1977) was an art and jazz critic and longtime friend of American thinker and writer Francis Schaeffer.

Subject: Art—Modern

More: Rookmaaker also has a book of essays (including a "letter to a Christian Artist") discussing art, history, and culture, called *The Creative Gift: Essays on Art and the Christian Life* (Cornerstone Books, 1981).

Schaeffer, Francis.

Art and the Bible. InterVarsity, 1973. 63 pp. ISBN 0877844437.

This brief but insightful book answers the question, "What is the place of art in the Christian's life?" The first section gives examples of art found in the Bible, including Moses' tabernacle, David's music, and Solomon's temple. The second section describes how Christians should value and evaluate art. As is true of much of Schaeffer's writing, this was a groundbreaking book.

Subject: Art

More: Philip Graham Ryken has a short book in a similar vein called *Art for God's Sake: A Call to Recover the Arts* (P&R Publishing, 2006). For a more philosophical treatment of this subject, try *Art in Action: Toward a Christian Aesthetic* by Nicholas Wolterstorff (Eerdmans, 1980). Wolterstoff, philosophy professor at Calvin College and Yale University, says that art should not be left only to museums, but it should also be appreciated in homes, businesses, and everyday public places.

Seerveld, Calvin.

Bearing Fresh Olive Leaves: Alternative Steps in Understanding Art. Piquant, 2000. 205 pp. 095357573X.

What is art? What is Christian art? Should Christians make art while others go without food or without the gospel being preached to them? Is art a necessity or a luxury? Calvin Seerveld addresses these questions in this book, which adapts a collection of his lectures. Seerveld aims to "put forward a Christian rationale for the presence of art in God's world." He encourages people to take up their calling in art, but he discourages cheap, superficial art, which he says is using the Lord's name in vain. Claiming that kitsch is evil, Seerveld argues that honest art can glorify God. The book contains sixteen color plates and seventy-one black-and-white plates.

Subject: Art

More: Seerveld's most influential book is probably *Rainbows for the Fallen World: Aesthetic Life and Artistic Task* (Tuppence, 1980). Another collection of lectures by Seerveld is *A Christian Critique of Art and Literature* (Tuppence, 1995).

Spencer, William David, and Aida Besancon Spencer.

God Through the Looking Glass: Glimpses from the Arts. Baker, 1998. 208 pp. ISBN 1900507854.

In this collection of essays on the place of the arts in Christian life, various individuals in the arts write about their specific art. Theater director Norman M. Jones writes about the dramatic arts. Painter Bruce Whitney Herman relates his personal artistic journey. Theology professor and songwriter William David Spencer writes about music. Church history professor Gwenfair Walters addresses the history of Christ in art. Bible professor Aida

Besancon Spencer writes about fiction. Dancer and professor Celeste Snowber Schroeder covers dance. Media minister Jasmin Sung writes about film. The book ends with a six-page list of recommended reading.

Subjects: Art, Art—History, Dance, Drama, Essays, Film, Literature, Theater

More: Another collection of essays on dance, literature, sculpture, music, etc., is *Beholding the Glory: Incarnation Through the Arts* by Jeremy Begbie, editor (Baker, 2000).

Veith, Gene Edward.

State of the Arts: From Bezalel to Mapplethorpe. Crossway, 1991. 256 pp. ISBN 0891076085.

Demonstrating how art reflects the worldview of artists, Gene Edward Veith walks the reader through art history, providing an interesting survey of the history of Western civilization. He also discusses what the Bible has to say about art in the stories of Bezalel and Aaron. Toward the end of the book, Veith examines the work of modern and contemporary Christian artists such as Georges Rouault, Edward Knippers, Theodore Prescott, Sandra Bowden, and Cliff McReynolds. This book is part of the Turning Point Christian Worldview Series.

Subjects: Art—History, Art—Modern

More: In the beautifully illustrated *Painters of Faith: The Spiritual Landscape in Nineteenth-Century America* (Regnery, 2001), Veith examines the Hudson River School of landscape painting (including Thomas Cole, Asher B. Durand, Jasper Cropsey, and Frederic Church) and shows how the faith and theology of these American painters influenced their art.

Literature

Guroian, Vigen.

Tending the Heart of Virtue: How Classic Stories Awaken a Child's Moral Imagination. Oxford University Press, 1998. 198 pp. ISBN 0195117875.

Vigen Guroian, an Eastern Orthodox theology professor and writer, examines classic children's stories like *Pinocchio*, *The Little Mermaid*, and *Bambi* to show that these tales involve characters making difficult choices between right and wrong. For example, she talks about the virtue of love in *The Velveteen Rabbit*; friendship in *The Wind in the Willows* and *Charlotte's Web*; redemption in *The Lion, the Witch and the Wardrobe*; and faith and courage in *The Princess and the Goblin*. Such stories, Guroian says, help form children's understanding of morality.

Subjects: Character, Children's Literature, Parenting

More: *Books That Build Character: A Guide to Teaching Your Child Moral Values Through Stories* by William Kilpatrick (Touchstone, 1994). Also try Walter Wangerin's *Swallowing the Golden Stone* (Augsburg Fortress, 2001), which includes essays on the nature and importance of stories; it also includes some of Wangerin's stories and poems.

Hudson, Robert.

The Christian Writer's Manual of Style. Updated and expanded edition. Zondervan, 2004 (1988). 432 pp. ISBN 0310487714.

Religious writing has its own collection of style issues. This book has an A-to-Z format and covers many topics such as British style, capitalization of biblical and religious terms, guidelines for obtaining Bible permissions, abbreviations, proofreading, computer-related language styles, and much more.

Subjects: Authorship, Editing, Writing

More: *The Little Style Guide to Great Christian Writing and Publishing* by Leonard G. Goss and Carolyn Stanford Goss (B&H Publishing, 2004).

Jenkins, Jerry B.

Writing for the Soul: Instruction and Advice from an Extraordinary Writing Life. Writer's Digest, 2006. ISBN 1582974179.

Jerry Jenkins has written more than 150 books, but he is most famous for writing the best-selling Left Behind series with Tim LaHaye. In this book, Jenkins talks about his life as a writer. An avid sports fan since childhood, Jenkins started writing about sports for local newspapers. One thing led to another, and soon he had the opportunity to write a biography of Hank Aaron. Jenkins gives advice to writers about interviewing and many other parts of the craft: pace, conflict, plot, research, characters, perspective, getting published, etc. He also talks about the Left Behind series—how it got started and what the success has been like.

Subjects: Authorship, Writing

More: Also try best-selling Christian novelist Gilbert Morris's *How to Write and Sell a Christian Novel* (Write Now Publications, 2001). Anne Lamott talks about writing and being a writer in her sometimes-humorous book *Bird by Bird: Some Instructions on Writing and Life* (Anchor, 1995). To hear other Christian authors talk about writing, read Diane Eble's *Behind the Stories: Christian Novelists Reveal the Heart in the Art of Their Writing* (Bethany, 2002). For still more about Christian fiction authors, see *Contemporary Christian Authors: Lives and Works* by Janice DeLong and Rachel Schwedt (Scarecrow Press, 2000).

L'Engle, Madeleine.

Walking on Water: Reflections on Faith and Art. North Point Press, 1995 (Shaw, 1980). 198 pp. ISBN 0865474877.

> In this collection of thoughts and stories from the life of a writer, Madeleine L'Engle gives insight into what it means not only to be creative but also to be human. L'Engle (1918–2007) was an American novelist, essayist, and poet. She is well-known for her Newbery Award-winning novel, *A Wrinkle in Time.*
>
> **Subjects:** Art, Writing
>
> **More:** Readers may also enjoy *The Timeless Moment: Creativity and the Christian Faith* by D. Bruce Lockerbie (Cornerstone, 1980). For other books about the life and thinking of a writer, try *Grace Is Where I Live: The Landscape of Faith & Writing* by John Leax (WordFarm, 2004) and *Bird by Bird: Some Instructions on Writing and Life* by Anne Lamott (Anchor, 1995).

Ryken, Leland, editor.

The Christian Imagination: The Practice of Faith in Literature and Writing. Revised and expanded edition. Shaw, 2002 (Baker, 1981). 465 pp. ISBN 0877881235.

> This rich collection of essays from more than fifty authors such as C. S. Lewis, Wendell Berry, Francis Schaeffer, Annie Dillard, J. R. R. Tolkien, G. K. Chesterton, T. S. Eliot, Flannery O'Connor, and Madeleine L'Engle is organized around themes like Christian philosophy of literature, imagination, poetry, reading, writing, realism, and myth. Leland Ryken is professor of English at Wheaton College.
>
> **Subjects:** Essays, Literature, Writing
>
> **More:** *Reality and the Vision: 18 Contemporary Writers Tell Who They Read and Why* by Philip Yancey, editor (Word, 1990).

Stuart, Sally.

Christian Writers' Market Guide 2007: The Essential Reference Tool for the Christian Writer. WaterBrook, 2007 (1985). 640 pp. ISBN 1400071259.

> Similar to *Writers' Market*, this book gives readers submission guidelines and contact information for hundreds of book publishers, periodicals, poetry markets, contests, agents, writers' conferences, and more. More than twenty annual editions of this book have been published.
>
> **Subjects:** Authorship, Publishing, Writing
>
> **More:** A related book by Stuart is *Sally Stuart's Guide to Getting Published* (Shaw, 2000).

Veith, Jr., Gene Edward.

Reading Between the Lines: A Christian Guide to Literature. Crossway Books, 1990. 254 pp. ISBN 0891075828.

This book discusses nonfiction, fiction, poetry, drama, fantasy, etc., all from a Christian perspective. Gene Edward Veith, Jr., goes through history and talks about the great periods of literature such as the Enlightenment, Romanticism, modernism, postmodernism, etc. This book deals with past and present worldview issues through history and literature. Veith is the director of the Cranach Institute at Concordia Theological Seminary. He is also the culture editor of *World* magazine. He was formerly professor of English and dean of arts and sciences at Concordia University Wisconsin.

Subject: Literature

More: Another study of literature from a Christian perspective is *Literature Through the Eyes of Faith* by Susan V. Gallagher and Roger Lundin (HarperSanFrancisco, 1989). Also try James Sire's *How to Read Slowly* (Shaw, 2000). For an examination of the faith or lack of faith in the writings of those such as Matthew Arnold, Emily Dickinson, Walt Whitman, Ralph Waldo Emerson, Stephen Crane, Mark Twain, Thomas Hardy, William Butler Yeats, James Joyce, F. Scott Fitzgerald, and Ernest Hemingway, try *Dismissing God: Modern Writers' Struggle Against Religion* by D. Bruce Lockerbie (Baker, 1998).

Music

Best, Harold.

Music Through the Eyes of Faith. HarperSanFrancisco, 1993. 225 pp. ISBN 0060608625.

Is there such a thing as sinful music? Harold Best, dean of the conservatory of music at Wheaton College, explains how music is morally neutral by making a distinction between musical content and musical context. In other words, if you associate a certain song or style of music with sinful behavior, you are likely to think that the music is inherently bad. But, as Best points out, there are many church hymns and anthems that are sung to the tune of old drinking songs. Thus, the author challenges readers to reconsider making, listening to, and appreciating music.

Subject: Music

More: Readers may also enjoy *Taking Note of Music* by William Edgar (SPCK Publishing, 1986).

Joseph, Mark.

Faith, God and Rock & Roll: How People of Faith Are Transforming American Popular Music. Baker, 2003. 256 pp. ISBN 0801065003.

Did you know that Van Halen (of all groups) once had a lead singer who is a Christian? Gary Cherone was with Van Halen for two years. The band P.O.D. (Payable on Death) has signed deals with Atlantic records and toured with Ozzfest, but they also play Christian rock festivals. Mark Joseph explains how Christian musicians are influencing modern rock music. These musicians often sign with secular labels, but they are people of faith nonetheless. The book covers many other musicians and bands as well, such as Alice Cooper, Lauryn Hill, Destiny's Child, Jessica Simpson, Mary Mary, MxPx, and Dashboard Confessional.

Subject: Music—Rock and Roll

More: Two other books that explore the spirituality of famous musicians are *Spiritual Journeys: How Faith Has Influenced Twelve Music Icons* (Relevant, 2003) and *Walk On: The Spiritual Journey of U2* by Steve Stockman (Relevant, 2005). Two books that look for truth and spirituality in the world of rock music are *The Rock Cries Out: Finding Eternal Truth in Unlikely Music* by Steve Stockman (Relevant, 2004) and *The Gospel According to the Beatles* by notable music journalist Steve Turner (Westminster John Knox Press, 2006).

Kavanaugh, Patrick.

The Music of Angels: A Listener's Guide to Sacred Music from Chant to Christian Rock. Loyola Press, 1999. 334 pp.

Patrick Kavanaugh, director of the Christian Performing Artists' Fellowship, guides the reader through almost 2,000 years of sacred music from chant and the Renaissance to the hymnwriters and modern classical composers. Kavanaugh also covers modern church choir music, gospel music, and contemporary Christian music. Throughout the book, he provides biographic profiles and listening recommendations while discussing the development of music and the historical contexts and important issues for each style of music.

Subjects: Music, Music—Classical, Music—Contemporary Christian, Music—Gospel

Lane, Deforia, and Rob Wilkins.

Music As Medicine: Deforia Lane's Life of Music, Healing, and Faith. Zondervan, 1994. 216 pp. ISBN 031020660X.

In this moving autobiography by music therapist Deforia Lane, the author describes the power of music in the lives of many patients, from children dying of leukemia to the mentally retarded. She describes how music has allowed the grace and healing of God to flow in many ways to these people. Lane also writes about the many struggles and victories of her life. She serves as director of music therapy at the University Hospitals of Cleveland, Ireland Cancer Center, and Rainbow Babies & Children's Hospital.

Subjects: Biography, Deforia Lane (1948–), Music Therapy

Powell, Mark Allan.

Encyclopedia of Contemporary Christian Music. Hendrickson, 2002. 1,088 pp. ISBN 1565636791.

Covering the time from the beginning of the Jesus Movement in the late 1960s through 2001, this comprehensive one-volume reference work offers a discography and an informative essay for almost 2,000 bands and solo artists. For the more popular artists, Mark Allan Powell lists chart hits and awards. This impressive book is invaluable for libraries and Christian music fans.

Subjects: Collective Biography, Musicians, Reference

More: *CCM Presents: The 100 Greatest Albums in Christian Music* edited by Thom Granger (Harvest House Publishers, 2001). Also, *CCM Magazine Presents 100 Greatest Songs in Christian Music* by Tori Taff and Christa Farris (Integrity Publishers, 2006).

Smithouser, Bob, and Bob Waliszewski.

Chart Watch: More Than 400 Album Reviews, and Practical Ways to Help Families Make Sound Music Choices. Focus on the Family, 1998. 349 pp. ISBN 156179628X.

Designed for parents who want to know what their kids are listening to, this guide reviews more than 400 CDs. Each review briefly describes the band/singer and alerts the reader to objectionable content as well as to positive factors of that particular CD. As the book ages, readers can visit the free Web site for updates and current reviews at http://www.pluggedinonline.com/music.

Subjects: Music—Secular, Music Reviews

More: Readers wanting to learn about the excesses and harms of secular rock music may want to read *Truth About Rock: Shattering the Myth of Harmless Music* by Steve Peters and Mark Littleton (Bethany, 1998).

Thiessen, Donald.

Selah: A Guide to Music in the Bible. 3rd Edition. Cornerstone Press, 2002 (1983). 169 pp. ISBN 0940895471.

Donald Thiessen, academic dean at Steinbach Bible College in Steinbach, Manitoba, Canada, goes through every book of the Bible, listing each scriptural reference to music and offering his comments (New American Standard Version).

Subject: Music in the Bible

More: A similar book is *All the Music of the Bible* by Herbert Lockyer (Hendrickson, 2004).

Warren, Gwendolin Sims.

Ev'ry Time I Feel the Spirit: 101 Best-Loved Psalms, Gospel Hymns, and Spiritual Songs of the African-American Church. Henry Holt, 1999. 370 pp. ISBN 0805044116.

This book collects music from a variety of sources, including Negro spirituals (also known as plantation songs and jubilee songs), Euro-American hymns (by songwriters such as Isaac Watts and Charles Wesley), and contemporary gospel songs (by songwriters like Andre Crouch and Kirk Franklin). Gwendolin Sims Warren provides the words and music to each hymn or song, its history, and a brief biography of the person behind the music.

Subjects: Hymns, Music—Gospel

More: For more on African American spiritual music, try *Touched by God: Black Gospel Greats Share Their Stories of Finding God* by Bobby Jones (Pocket Books, 1998).

Culture

Is there a Christian way to "do" history? How has Christianity shaped civilization? The titles in this section answer these questions and also cover global church history. When perusing the history section, don't forget to consult Chapter One ("Life Stories") because biographies are a wonderful way to approach history.

Books specifically addressing worldview issues are in the philosophy section as well as histories of philosophy from a Christian perspective. There are also titles that explain what it means to "think Christianly." Readers should note that some of the books included in this philosophy section could also have been placed in the apologetics section of Chapter Four (books that answer questions like "Why does God allow suffering?"). See both sections.

The social issues section includes books on politics, race reconciliation, law, crime, AIDS, hunger, Islam, and more. Social issues are of particular interest to those following such biblical commands as Galatians 2:10: "We should continue to remember the poor," and Christ's words in Matthew 25:40: "Whatever you did for one of the least of these brothers of mine, you did for me."

The last subsection here is popular culture, which covers a variety of topics like media, film, and television. I particularly recommend

Ken Myers's *All God's Children and Blue Suede Shoes* and Dick Staub's *The Culturally Savvy Christian*—both of these titles offer penetrating insights into how Christians should think and live in the midst of popular culture.

History

Aikman, David.

Jesus in Beijing: How Christianity Is Transforming China and Changing the Global Balance of Power. Regnery, 2006. 336 pp. ISBN 1596980257.

> David Aikman briefly describes how Christianity came to China, and then spends the majority of his book discussing the history and current situation of the modern Christian church in China. He writes about the brave Chinese patriarchs such as Wang Mingdao, Allen Yuan, Samuel Lamb, Moses Xie, and Li Tianen. These men, and many others like them, have gone through great suffering for Christ. Such persecution, however, did not stop the gospel, and Aikman describes how Christianity has spread and is growing throughout China. He talks about the house church movement and the Back-to-Jerusalem movement (to send out hundreds of thousands of missionaries)—all part of the Chinese underground church. Aikman also writes about the state-sanctioned church known as the Three Self church, the Catholic Church in China, and cults such as Falun Gong and Eastern Lightning. Aikman is an accomplished reporter and the former Beijing bureau chief for *Time* magazine.
>
> **Subjects:** Chinese Church—History, History, Persecution of Christians
>
> **More:** For more on the Back-to-Jerusalem movement, try *Back to Jerusalem: Three Chinese House Church Leaders Share Their Vision to Complete the Great Commission* by Paul Hattaway (Gabriel, 2003). For a recent testimony from a member of the Chinese underground church, try *The Heavenly Man: The Remarkable True Story of Chinese Christian Brother Yun* by Brother Yun and Paul Hattaway (Monarch, 2002).

Cunningham, Mary.

Faith in the Byzantine World. InterVarsity, 2002. 192 pp. ISBN 0830823522.

> This concise history, with many helpful and beautiful color illustrations, covers the history of the Byzantine Church from the year 330 (when Constantine inaugurated Constantinople as the New Rome) to 1453 (when the Ottoman Turks sacked Constantinople).

At the back of the book, there is a helpful chronology, a list of suggestions for further reading, and an index. This book is part of the IVP Histories Series.

Subjects: History—Byzantine Church, 330–1453

Evans, G. R. (Gillian Rosemary).

Faith in the Medieval World. InterVarsity, 2002. 160 pp. ISBN 0830823530.

This concise history, with many helpful and beautiful color illustrations, covers the 1,000-year period from the end of the ancient world (somewhere around the 300s or 400s) to the Reformation and Renaissance (around the 1500s). At the back of the book, you'll find a helpful chronology, a list of suggestions for further reading, and an index. This is another book in the IVP Histories Series.

Subject: History—Middle Age (400–1500)

Gaustad, Edwin S., and Leigh Schmidt.

The Religious History of America: The Heart of the American Story from Colonial Times to Today. Revised edition. HarperSanFrancisco, 2004 (1966). 464 pp. ISBN 0060630566.

This has been a popular text for the study of American religious history since it was first published in 1966. Edwin Gaustad is professor emeritus of history and religious studies at the University of California, Riverside. Leigh Schmidt is a professor of religion at Princeton University.

Subjects: American Religious History, History—United States

More: Lutheran historian and religious scholar (and *Christian Century* columnist) Martin E. Marty also has a book on American religious history called *Pilgrims in Their Own Land: 500 Years of Religion in America* (Penguin reprint, 1985). Noted scholar George Marsden wrote an award-winning history, now in its second edition, called *Fundamentalism and American Culture* (Oxford University Press, 2006). For a collection of primary-source documents relevant to this subject, see the two-volume set edited by Edwin Gaustad and Mark Noll, *A Documentary History of Religion in America to 1877* and *A Documentary History of Religion in America Since 1877* (Eerdmans, 2003).

Keillor, Steven J.

This Rebellious House: American History & the Truth of Christianity. InterVarsity, 1996. 368 pp. ISBN 0830818774.

Using the best scholarship available, Steven Keillor seeks to explain American history from the biblical Christian (evangelical)

worldview. Is it valid to interpret history through the eyes of biblical authority? Keillor says yes. Many social commentators and academics claim that Christianity is disproved by the past behavior of American white males. For instance, Christians participated in the slave trade, therefore Christianity is irrelevant and evil. Keillor offers a corrective view. He argues that the evil behavior of American white males is not a *result* of Christianity, it is a *rebellion against* true Christianity (and thus the title of this book). In Keillor's interpretation, such rebellion against Christian principles accounts for many wrongdoings in our country's past; but God is able to accomplish His purposes despite the behavior of American men and women who claim to be Christian. This approach shows readers what history would be like if, as he says, "the claim 'Jesus Christ is Lord' is not a private value but a public fact." Therefore, Keillor does not shrink from the fact that his is a revisionist scholarship that provides—not just a "Christian" view of history valid only for believers—but a better and "truer" view of the facts of U.S. history.

Subject: History—United States

More: Keillor recently published another book along similar lines titled *God's Judgments: Interpreting History and the Christian Faith* (InterVarsity, 2007). This book looks at certain events in American history, including the burning of Washington in 1814 and the 9/11 attacks.

Marshall, Peter, and David Manuel.

The Light and the Glory. Revell, 1980. 384 pp. ISBN 0800750543.

This popular work gives the story of the founding of America from a Christian perspective. It covers the Colonial period and the American Revolution, showing the hand of God in the lives and events involved in shaping our country. An abridged children's version is available. Peter Marshall is the son of Catherine Marshall, the writer, and Peter Marshall, the Senate chaplain.

Subject: History—United States—1492–1787

More: *From Sea to Shining Sea* is the sequel, which covers the first fifty years of American history (1787–1837) including the Second Great Awakening and slavery (Revell, 1986). A third book, also by Marshall and Manuel, is *Sounding Forth the Trumpet* (Revell, 1997). It covers the events (1837–1860) leading up to Civil War, including the Mexican War, the Gold Rush, Bleeding Kansas, Abraham Lincoln, and John Brown.

Schaeffer, Francis.

How Should We Then Live?: The Rise and Decline of Western Thought and Culture. L'Abri 50th anniversary edition. Crossway, 2005 (Revell, 1976). 288 pp. ISBN 1581345364.

First published in 1976, this book surveys key moments in history that have shaped our current culture and thought. Ancient Rome, the Middle Ages, the Renaissance, the Reformation, the Enlightenment: Schaeffer sweeps through Western history up to the twentieth century. Then he analyzes modern culture including science, philosophy, theology, art, music, literature, and film. This landmark book shows readers how ideas have built up or destroyed individual people, countries, and all of Western civilization. There is a video documentary version of this title available as well.

Subjects: Culture, History—Western Civilization, Philosophy, Worldview

More: A Francis A. Schaeffer Trilogy (Crossway, 1990) includes three more books by Schaeffer that analyze Western thought and culture. Chuck Colson and Nancy Pearcey have picked up where Schaeffer left off in their book *How Now Shall We Live?* (Tyndale, 1999).

Schmidt, Alvin J.

How Christianity Changed the World. Zondervan, 2004 (2001). 448 pp. ISBN 0310264499.

Retired professor of sociology Alvin Schmidt shows how Christianity has shaped the Western world in just about every area of life, including science, labor, economics, education, charity, art, architecture, music, and literature. Christianity has been a major force in securing justice in law, rights for women, the abolition of slavery, the sanctity of human life, and hospitals and health care. From the Roman Empire to the modern world, Schmidt reveals the incredible force Christianity has been for all that is good in Western civilization. This book was previously titled *Under the Influence: How Christianity Transformed Civilization* (Zondervan, 2001).

Subject: History—Western Civilization

More: For a similar book, try *What Has Christianity Ever Done for Us?: How It Shaped the Modern World* by Jonathan Hill (InterVarsity, 2005). Thomas Woods gives a Catholic perspective in *How the Catholic Church Built Western Civilization* (Regnery, 2005). Another book by sociologist Rodney Stark on the influence of Christianity on Western civilization is *The Victory of Reason: How Christianity Led to Freedom, Capitalism, and Western Success* (Random House, 2005).

Shelley, Bruce.

Church History in Plain Language. Updated 2nd edition. Thomas Nelson, 1996 (Word, 1982). 544 pp. ISBN 0849938619.

This is a well-known introduction to church history written in a very readable style. Bruce Shelley, professor of church history at Denver Theological Seminary, divides church history into eight segments, from the Age of Jesus and the Apostles (6 BCE–AD 70) to the Age of Ideologies (1914–1996).

Subject: Church History

Spencer, Robert.

The Politically Incorrect Guide to Islam (and the Crusades). Regnery, 2005. 270 pp. ISBN 0895260131.

American author Robert Spencer is the director of Jihad Watch and its popular Web site (http://jihadwatch.org). In this book (a *New York Times* best seller), Spencer discusses Muhammad, the Qur'an, the Islamic religion, the Crusades in history, and jihad in today's world. Spencer asserts that Muhammad did not teach peace and tolerance, that the Qur'an commands Muslims to wage war on Christians, that Islam oppresses women and stifles science, and that the Crusades were a response to Muslim aggression. Spencer frequently appears on TV, radio, and in print discussing Islam and terrorism issues.

Subjects: Crusades, History—Islam, Islam, Jihad, Muhammad, Qur'an

More: Ergun Mehmet Caner and Emir Caner also have a book on the Crusades called *Christian Jihad: Two Former Muslims Look at the Crusades and Killing in the Name of Christ* (Kregel, 2004). Another *New York Times* best seller by Spencer is *The Truth About Muhammad: Founder of the World's Most Intolerant Religion* (Regnery, 2006).

Stout, Harry S.

Upon the Altar of the Nation: A Moral History of the Civil War. Viking, 2006. 552 pp. ISBN 0670034703.

This is an in-depth look at a pivotal point in American history by noted Yale professor of American religious history Harry Stout. As the subtitle suggests, this is not a history of various battles or military strategy. Instead, Stout examines letters, sermons, newspaper articles, diaries, and other wartime sources to show that both the North and South believed they were fighting a sacred war; each thought God was on their side.

Subjects: American Religious History, Award Winners (CT), History—United States Civil War, 1861–1865, Just-War Doctrine

More: Another book on the topic, also by a noted scholar, is *The Civil War As a Theological Crisis* by Mark A. Noll (University of North Carolina Press, 2006). For other scholarly treatments of American (and British) religious history, try books from the

History of Evangelicalism Series, such as Mark Noll's *The Rise of Evangelicalism: The Age of Edwards, Whitefield, and the Wesleys* (InterVarsity, 2004) and David Bebbington's *The Dominance of Evangelicalism: The Age of Spurgeon and Moody* (InterVarsity, 2005).

Wells, Ronald A.

History Through the Eyes of Faith: Western Civilization and the Kingdom of God. HarperCollins, 1989. 262 pp. ISBN 0060692960.

Part of the Through The Eyes of Faith Series by the Christian College Coalition, this book examines Western civilization from a Christian worldview. Ronald Wells also discusses the various approaches to history that have been debated among historians. Wells is a professor of history at Calvin College in Michigan.

Subject: History

Philosophy

Brown, Colin.

Philosophy and the Christian Faith: A Historical Sketch from the Middle Ages to the Present Day. InterVarsity, 1980. 320 pp. ISBN 0877847126.

From Thomas Aquinas in the Middle Ages to Francis Schaeffer in the twentieth century, Colin Brown surveys the main thinkers and intellectual movements of Western philosophy, noting how they have affected the development Christian thought. Brown covers all the big names like Descartes, Hume, Kant, Hegel, Kierkegaard, Nietzsche, Barth, and hundreds of other thinkers. Colin Brown is professor of systematic theology at Fuller Theological Seminary.

Subjects: Philosophy, Philosophy—History

More: For an explanation of basic philosophical ideas and issues like logic, metaphysics, epistemology, ethics, etc., try *Philosophy Made Slightly Less Difficult* by Garrett J. DeWeese and J. P. Moreland (InterVarsity, 2005). For more on the history of philosophy, Brown also wrote volume one of a two-volume survey of philosophy, *Christianity and Western Thought: A History of Philosophers, Ideas and Movements* (InterVarsity, 1990). The first volume covers the ancient world to the Age of Enlightenment.

Brown, Montague.

Restoration of Reason: The Eclipse and Recovery of Truth, Goodness, and Beauty. Baker Academic, 2006. 272 pp. ISBN 0801031540.

Montague Brown, chair of St. Anselm College's philosophy department, proposes that the scientific method is not the only method of accessing knowledge. For instance, science cannot show us that it is wrong to be greedy. Science cannot prove whether I love my wife or whether love or beauty are real (as opposed to being mere constructs of the mind). Although Brown is not opposed to the scientific method, he believes that it is not enough. Brown seeks to restore a premodern understanding of reason, which allows for the recovery of the true, the good, and the beautiful. Starting with Francis Bacon's misleading idea of scientific method as the only path to knowledge, Brown traces it and later ideas through the writings of thinkers like Descartes, Hobbes, Kant, Hegel, Whitehead, Lonergan, and others. Based on other thinkers like Aristotle, Aquinas, Plato, and Augustine, he shows that reason includes not only truth, but also goodness and beauty.

Subjects: Philosophy, Scientific Method

Lewis, C. S.

The Problem of Pain. HarperOne, 2001 (1940). 192 pp. ISBN 0060652969.

The famous Christian apologist C. S. Lewis skillfully addresses the age-old question of "Why does God allow pain and suffering?" He explains the providence and goodness of God, the wickedness of man, human and animal pain, and even heaven and hell.

Subjects: Apologetics, Classics, Pain, Philosophy, Suffering

More: Two more classic treatments of the problem of pain are *Where Is God When It Hurts?* by Philip Yancey (Zondervan, 2002) and *When God Weeps: Why Our Sufferings Matter to the Almighty* by Joni Eareckson Tada and Steve Estes (Zondervan, 1997).

Moreland, J. P.

Love Your God with All Your Mind: The Role of Reason in the Life of the Soul. NavPress, 1997. 249 pp. ISBN 1576830160.

J. P. Moreland discusses the importance of thinking and the mind for Christians. Chapter Two covers what the Bible has to say about the life of the mind. Moreland shows what a mature Christian mind looks like and how to develop one. He includes useful sections on logic and apologetics. Two bibliographies recommend further resources. Moreland is distinguished professor of philosophy at Talbot School of Theology in La Mirada, California.

Subject: Intellectual Life

More: James Sire has at least two good books on this subject: *Discipleship of the Mind* (InterVarsity, 1990) and *Habits of the Mind: Intellectual Life As a Christian Calling* (InterVarsity, 2000). Three short books on the topic are *The Life of the Mind* by Clifford Williams (Baker, 2002), *A Mind for God* by James Emery White (InterVarsity,

2006), and *Your Mind Matters* by John Stott (InterVarsity reprint, 2007).

Noll, Mark A.

The Scandal of the Evangelical Mind. Eerdmans, 1995. 274 pp. ISBN 0802841805.

"The scandal of the evangelical mind," says noted scholar Mark Noll, "is that there is not much of an evangelical mind." This landmark book laments the lack of thinking among today's evangelicals in America. Noll says that evangelicals have ignored "high culture," including the university and the arts. In the process of examining the current and past American landscape to identify how the current situation occurred, he talks about revivalism, politics, fundamentalism, modern science, and creation science. Noll, professor of history at the University of Notre Dame, was previously a professor at Wheaton College.

Subjects: Award Winners (CT), Evangelicalism, Intellectual Life, Scholarship

More: Os Guinness has also addressed this issue in *Fit Bodies, Fat Minds: Why Evangelicals Don't Think and What to Do About It* (Baker, 1994). Gene Edward Veith has a book that shows Christians how to think and interact in today's intellectual environment: *Loving God with All Your Mind: Thinking As a Christian in the Postmodern World* (Crossway, 2003). Even though Noll partially blames Pentecostalism for the lack of intellectualism, there is now a book for Pentecostals on the subject. It is called *Full Gospel, Fractured Minds?: A Call to Use God's Gift of the Intellect* by Rick Nanez (Zondervan, 2006). Readers in academia will be interested in fellow scholar George Marsden's *The Outrageous Idea of Christian Scholarship* (Oxford University Press reprint, 1998).

Pearcey, Nancy.

Total Truth: Liberating Christianity from Its Cultural Captivity. Study guide edition. Crossway, 2005 (2004). 512 pp. ISBN 1581347464.

Nancy Pearcey describes what it is to have a Christian worldview. She discusses past and present cultural forces that have shaped our thinking and have weakened a biblical understanding of reality. Pearcey explains the "faith versus fact" split in our thinking. This upper story/lower story analogy (first described by Francis Schaeffer in his books) provides insights into how Christian faith has been marginalized by an unbelieving society. Pearcey addresses a variety of issues that are shaping our world: education, feminism, science, politics, etc. Pearcey is the Francis

Schaeffer Scholar at the World Journalism Institute and a senior fellow at the Discovery Institute.

Subjects: Award Winners (ECPA, CT), Intellectual Life, Worldview

More: Harry Blamires (who was tutored by C. S. Lewis at Oxford) writes about how Christians have succumbed to secularization and about what they can do about it in *The Christian Mind* (Vine Books, 1997) and *The Post-Christian Mind* (Regent, 2005).

Schaeffer, Francis.

A Francis A. Schaeffer Trilogy: Three Essential Books in One Volume. Crossway, 1990. 368 pp. ISBN 0891075615.

Francis Schaeffer (1912–1984) was an American evangelical theologian, philosopher, apologist, and Presbyterian pastor who founded the L'Abri community in Switzerland and was one of the most famous Christian thinkers and writers of his time. This book collects Schaeffer's three most important books. *The God Who Is There* traces modern philosophy and its effects upon society as they trickled down from the arena of philosophy to art, music, and finally to general culture. It also shows the impact of these ideas upon theology. *Escape from Reason* traces modern ideas starting with Aquinas and going through the Reformation, early modern science, Kant, Rousseau, Hegel, and Kierkegaard. It discusses the "leap" of existentialism and its influence on the art of Malraux, Picasso, Bernstein, and others. The third book in the trilogy is *He Is There and He Is Not Silent*. In this book, Schaeffer discusses metaphysics, morals, and epistemology, and shows that it makes sense to believe in God and that it is even possible to know God.

Subjects: Apologetics, Art, History, Philosophy, Worldview

More: All of Schaeffer's books are collected in a five-volume set called *The Complete Works of Francis A. Schaeffer: A Christian Worldview* (Crossway Books, 1985).

Walsh, Brian J., and J. Richard Middleton.

The Transforming Vision: Shaping a Christian World View. InterVarsity Press, 1984. 214 pp. ISBN 0877849730.

Brian Walsh and J. Richard Middleton present a Reformational Christian worldview following the biblical model of "creation, fall, and redemption." They discuss dualism (which divides reality into sacred and secular departments) and how Christians should interact with and shape culture. There is an extensive bibliography at the end of the book.

Subjects: Philosophy, Worldview

More: *Creation Regained: Biblical Basics for a Reformational Worldview* by Albert Wolters (Eerdmans, 2005) gives a brief overview of the creation, fall, redemption model of a biblical worldview.

White, Heath.

Postmodernism 101: A First Course for the Curious Christian. Brazos, 2006. 176 pp. ISBN 158743153X.

Philosophy professor Heath White provides readers with a valuable introduction to this sometimes-intimidating subject. He begins by placing postmodernism in its historical context and goes on to briefly describe the premodern mind (summed up in one word, "authority"), which eventually leads to the modern way of thinking (in a word, "reason"). Modernism eventually led to postmodernism, he says, which abandons both authority and reason. White also discusses postmodern perspectives on moral absolutes, the self, language, culture, and history. The last section deals with Christianity and postmodernism.

Subjects: Philosophy, Postmodernism

More: In *Postmodern Times: A Christian Guide to Contemporary Thought and Culture* (Crossway, 1994), Gene Edward Veith, Jr., talks about postmodernism and how it has impacted various areas of culture such as film, religion, art, architecture, and politics.

Social Issues

Adams, Stephen P.

Christian Family Guide Explains the Middle East Conflict. Alpha, 2003. 336 pp. ISBN 1592570909.

With a wealth of information written in an easy-to-understand style, Adams discusses the three major groups of the Middle East by religion (Jews, Christians, and Muslims), their history (ancient and recent), the lands (nation-by-nation profile), the situation (Middle East oil, terrorism, etc.), and more.

Subject: Middle East Conflict

Allegretti, Joseph G.

The Lawyer's Calling: Christian Faith and Legal Practice. Paulist Press, 1996. 141 pp. ISBN 0809136511.

Legal ethics professor Joseph Allegretti writes for and about lawyers who question the spiritual significance of their profession. He describes professional codes of conduct and the concept of a "calling." Suggesting that lawyers should not look at clients as "cases" but as people, he discusses covenant relationships between attorneys and their clients. Lawyers with such relationships can encourage moral reflection in their clients. Allegretti is Catholic and includes a Catholic perspective on work that can be beneficial for all Christians. Allegretti shows that there is much meaning and spiritual significance to be found in the legal profession.

Subjects: Catholics, Lawyers

More: For those desiring "to be Christian lawyers, our faith integrated with our calling," read Michael P. Schutt's *Redeeming Law: Christian Calling and the Legal Profession* (IVP Academic, 2007). Also try *Can a Good Christian Be a Good Lawyer?* edited by Thomas Baker and Timothy Floyd (University of Notre Dame, 1997) and *Christian Perspectives on Legal Thought*, a collection of essays edited by Michael W. McConnell, Robert F. Cochran, Jr., and Angela C. Carmella (Yale University Press, 2001). For non-lawyers who want a Christian perspective on legal matters, read *The Believer's Guide to Legal Issues* by Stephen Bloom, a practicing attorney and adjunct instructor at Messiah College. (Living Ink Books, 2008).

Barton, David.

Original Intent: The Courts, the Constitution, & Religion. 3rd Edition. WallBuilder Press, 2002 (1996). 534 pp. ISBN 1932225269.

This book argues that the U.S. Supreme Court as well as state and local courts have reinterpreted the Constitution and weakened the foundations upon which the Constitution was based. Barton claims that the phrase "separation of church and state" is a recent concept used to justify many harmful court decisions. He gives many examples of such cases and shows how our founding fathers have been misquoted. Barton is founder of WallBuilders, an organization that desires to reclaim the Christian roots of American history.

Subject: Constitutional Law

Boyd, Gregory A.

The Myth of a Christian Nation: How the Quest for Political Power Is Destroying the Church. Zondervan, 2005. 207 pp. ISBN 0310267307.

Pastor Gregory Boyd (a former theology professor) encourages evangelicals to think twice before requiring the Christian church to adhere to a certain political position or party. He reminds readers that the kingdom of God is not the kingdom of this world. Why do so many confuse the two kingdoms? Boyd says many people mistakenly believe that America is a Christian nation—that is why so many Christians are trying to "take America back for

God." Boyd says that is not what the gospel is about, and that Christians should not desire to rule over people spiritually with worldly governmental power. Pointing out that the gospel transforms people's hearts through the cross, he says that government forces people to obey with the "sword."

Subjects: Conservatism, Evangelism, Politics

More: *A Secular Faith: Why Christianity Favors the Separation of Church and State* by Darryl Hart (Ivan R. Dee, 2006).

Budziszewski, J.

Written on the Heart: The Case for Natural Law. InterVarsity, 1997. 252 pp. ISBN 083081891X.

J. Budziszewski, a professor of government and philosophy at the University of Texas, Austin, says that natural law is important to politics and political theory because it applies to both believers and unbelievers. For example, everyone agrees that certain things are wrong (betrayal, selfishness, etc.) and certain things are right (loyalty, honesty, etc.). Budziszewski goes on to say that eternal law is reflected in "the very structure of the created rational mind, directing us to our natural good." Concerning these themes of natural law, politics, and government, he examines the ideas of four thinkers: Aristotle, Aquinas, John Locke, and John Stuart Mill.

Subjects: Award Winners (CT), Law, Natural Law, Philosophy, Politics

More: Budziszewski also wrote *What We Can't Not Know: A Guide* (Spence Publishing, 2004) and *The Revenge of Conscience: Politics and the Fall of Man* (Spence Publishing, 2004).

Caner, Ergun Mehmet, and Emir Fethi Caner.

Unveiling Islam: An Insider's Look at Muslim Life and Beliefs. Kregel, 2002. 251 pp. ISBN 0825424003.

Written by two brothers who were raised as Sunni Muslims and now are Christian theologians and seminary professors, this book discusses Muhammad, the story of Islam, the Qur'an, the five pillars of Islam, the status of women, Muslim salvation, the Islamic calendar/holy days, Islamic sects, terrorism, and jihad. One appendix gives a topical index to the Qur'an. Another gives a comparison of beliefs in Christianity and Islam.

Subjects: Award Winners (ECPA), Islam, Qur'an

More: Another book by a former Muslim is *Inside Islam: Exposing and Reaching the World of Islam* by Reza F. Safa (Charisma House, 1996). Safa, a former radical Shiite Muslim who now leads a Christian ministry called Harvesters World Outreach, focuses more on sharing the gospel with Muslims.

Colson, Charles.

Justice That Restores: Why Our Justice System Doesn't Work and the Only Method of True Reform. Tyndale, 2001. 175 pp. ISBN 0842352457.

>Charles Colson spent seven months in prison for his part in the Watergate scandal. Since his release in 1975, he has worked with prisons and prisoners all over the world. The founder of Prison Fellowship Ministries, the world's largest prison ministry, he has personally visited hundreds of prisons in America as well as 600 prisons in forty different countries. In this book, Colson addresses the Christian basis for a just society, the roots of crime, redemption, and true reform.
>
>**Subjects:** Criminal Justice, Prison Ministry
>
>**More:** Prison Fellowship Ministries' *When Prisoners Return* by Pat Nolan (Xulon, 2004) is designed to help people and churches assist prisoners who are returning to society.

Crespo, Orlando.

Being Latino in Christ: Finding Wholeness in Your Ethnic Identity. InterVarsity, 2003. 167 pp. ISBN 0830823743.

>In this book, Orlando Crespo discusses his Latino ethnic identity, Christianity in the context of ethnic culture, and racial reconciliation. In an appendix, he recommends Latino books, films, and Web sites. Crespo is director of La Fe, the Latino Fellowship of InterVarsity Christian Fellowship.
>
>**Subjects:** Hispanic Americans, Race Relations

Curtis, Barbara.

Reaching the Left from the Right: Talking About Social Issues with People Who Don't Think Like You. Beacon Hill, 2006. 187 pp. ISBN 0834122022.

>Barbara Curtis, a former hippie and political activist, says she was a "certified" member of the "left," that is, a radical feminist, an abortion-rights activist, and more. Then she became a Christian. In this book, Curtis shows readers how to build bridges and to understand and communicate with those that hold radically different views. By sharing her testimony, she helps "conservatives" see the way other people think and live and thereby encourages people to view "liberals" not as enemies but as human beings in need of just as much grace and love as "conservatives."
>
>**Subjects:** Liberals, Social Issues

Dortzbach, Deborah, and W. Meredith Long.

The AIDS Crisis: What We Can Do. InterVarsity, 2006. 157 pp. ISBN 0830833722.

Three million people died of AIDS in 2005. What has caused this problem? What is the solution? How should the church be involved? International experts Deborah Dortzbach and W. Meredith Long answer from a Christian perspective. Along the way, they give statistics and tell stories of real people who are victims of this crisis. Dortzbach is World Relief's international director for HIV/AIDS programs. Long is vice president for planning and integration at World Relief.

Subjects: AIDS, Church Work with the Sick, Health Care

More: Two more titles on the subject are *The Skeptic's Guide to the Global AIDS Crisis* (Authentic, 2004) and *The Hope Factor: Engaging the Church in the HIV/AIDS Crisis* by Tetsunao Yamamori, et al., editors (Authentic, 2004).

Gilbreath, Edward.

Reconciliation Blues: A Black Evangelical's Inside View of White Christianity. InterVarsity, 2006. 207 pp. ISBN 0830833676.

Edward Gilbreath was the first African American staff member at *Christianity Today*, the preeminent American evangelical magazine. Today he is editor at large for *Christianity Today* and editor of *Today's Christian*. In this book, Gilbreath walks readers through a history of racial reconciliation in the evangelical churches of the United States. After discussing individuals who have influenced race issues (such as Jackie Robinson, Dolphus Weary, Tom Skinner, Martin Luther King, Jr., and Jesse Jackson), Gilbreath talks about his personal experiences in white evangelical colleges and churches.

Subjects: Award Winners (CT), Race Relations

Harris, Paula, and Doug Schauppp.

Being White: Finding Our Place in a Multiethnic World. InterVarsity, 2004. 192 pp. ISBN 0830832475.

This book is for white people who are serious about understanding, loving, and sharing their lives with people of different cultures or races. The authors share their struggles, failures, and successes as they discuss cross-cultural friendships, white identity, justice, being color-blind, and displacement.

Subject: Race Relations

More: *Divided by Faith: Evangelical Religion and the Problem of Race in America* by Michael O. Emerson and Christian Smith (Oxford University Press, 2001) is a landmark book that explores how white evangelicals feel about racism and how they often contribute to the problem even as they desire to fix the issue. *Letters Across the Divide: Two Friends Explore Racism, Friendship, and Faith* by David Anderson and Brent Zuercher (Baker, 2001) consists of letters between two friends, an African American pastor and a white accountant, in which they ask and answer honest and sometimes blunt questions (for example, "Why is everything a racial issue with blacks?" and "Why do so many whites refuse to believe that racism is a problem in America?").

Hugen, Beryl, and T. Laine Scales, editors.

Christianity and Social Work: Readings on the Integration of Christian Faith and Social Work Practice. 2nd Edition. North American Association of Christians in Social Work, 2002 (1998). 402 pp. ISBN 0962363499.

The essays in this collection were written by a variety of social workers, professors, and urban ministers. They discuss how faith and a Christian worldview affect social work in such areas as mental illness recovery, end-of-life care, addiction, child welfare practice, social work practice, faith-based initiatives, poverty, and more. They also describe the challenges of being a Christian in the secular profession of social work, drawing upon some historical examples of Christian social work. Beryl Hugen is a professor of social work at Calvin College. T. Laine Scales is assistant professor of social work at Baylor University.

Subject: Social Work

Kassian, Mary.

The Feminist Mistake: The Radical Impact of Feminism on Church and Culture. Crossway Books, 2005. 336 pp. ISBN 1581345704.

In examining the history and development of feminism from the 1960s through the 1990s, Mary Kassian concludes that it has had a detrimental effect on society. Although she agrees that feminism has raised some important and good questions concerning women's issues and rights, she believes that feminists have given devastatingly wrong answers. The title is a play on words based on feminist Betty Friedan's very influential 1963 book *The Feminine Mystique*.

Subjects: Feminism, Sociology, Women

More: Diane Passno writes about the damaging effects of the feminist worldview in her book *Feminism: Mystique or Mistake?: Rediscovering God's Plan for Women* (Tyndale, 2000).

Lupton, Robert D.

Renewing the City: Reflections on Community Development and Urban Renewal. InterVarsity, 2005. 237 pp. ISBN 0830833269.

> Christian community developer Robert Lupton envisions Nehemiah's biblical story of rebuilding Jerusalem in the light of contemporary urban renewal issues. While retelling Nehemiah's story, he discusses vision, leadership, and the difficulties and issues involved with such projects. He also talks about the part of the church in establishing a healthy community in urban areas. Lupton has worked with inner-city ministry for several decades.
>
> **Subjects:** Community Development, Urban Renewal
>
> **More:** Pastor and civil-rights leader John M. Perkins wrote *Beyond Charity: The Call to Christian Community Development* (Baker, 1993). For a book on what the Bible says about cities and urban ministry, try Ray Bakke's *A Theology As Big As the City* (InterVarsity Press, 1997).

Perkins, Spencer, and Chris Rice.

More Than Equals: Racial Healing for the Sake of the Gospel. Revised and expanded edition. InterVarsity, 2000 (1993). 285 pp. ISBN 0830822569.

> Spencer Perkins (1954–1998) and Chris Rice believe that Christians need to admit that race problems exist and that failure in race issues destroys the credibility of the gospel. In this book, they write about various aspects of racial reconciliation and how they struggled with these issues as they forged a friendship in an interracial community in Jackson, Mississippi. Perkins remembers visiting his father (pastor John M. Perkins) in jail when Spencer was sixteen years old. White police officers had beaten his father almost to death for protesting racial injustice. How could Spencer forgive, much less live in community with whites? That is exactly what he did for fourteen years with Rice. Perkins and Rice became friends and worked together in a racial reconciliation ministry called Reconcilers Fellowship.
>
> **Subjects:** Award Winners (CT), Race Relations
>
> **More:** Spencer Perkins's father, John M. Perkins, wrote an autobiography that became a civil-rights classic, *Let Justice Roll Down* (first published in 1976; reprinted by Regal, 2006). Pastor Tony Evans, founder of Urban Alternative, wrote a book on race relations called *Let's Get to Know Each Other: What White and Black Christians Need to Know About Each Other* (Thomas Nelson, 1995).

Sider, Ronald J.

Rich Christians in an Age of Hunger: Moving from Affluence to Generosity. Thomas Nelson, 2005 (1977). 352 pp. ISBN 0849945305.

First published in 1977, this classic work boldly addresses the causes of and solutions to hunger, starvation, and poverty. How should wealthy Christians live in this world of both poverty and abundance? When Ronald J. Sider examines what the Bible has to say about these tough issues, neither conservatives nor liberals escape blame. Sider is a Canadian-born American theologian and founder of Evangelicals for Social Action. He is also professor of theology, holistic ministry, and public policy at Palmer Theological Seminary in Wynnewood, Pennsylvania.

Subjects: Award Winners (CT), Economics, Hunger, Materialism, Wealth

More: For a book that helps churches embrace both evangelism and social ministry, try *Churches That Make a Difference: Reaching Your Community with Good News and Good Works* by Ronald J. Sider, Philip N. Olson, and Heidi Rolland Unruh (Baker, 2002). Sider is also the author of *The Scandal of the Evangelical Conscience: Why Are Christians Living Just Like the Rest of the World?* (Baker, 2005), a scathing indictment of American believers.

Sweetman, Brendan.

Why Politics Needs Religion: The Place of Religious Arguments in the Public Square. InterVarsity, 2006. 256 pp. ISBN 0830828427.

Brendan Sweetman challenges the idea that people should keep their religious ideas to themselves when it comes to public debate. He says that restricting religion from politics is "based on a misunderstanding of basic ideas concerning modern pluralism." Everyone has a worldview. Secularism (founded on the idea that God is made up by people), he says, is a worldview just like Christianity, and both should be allowed in public discussion in a democratic society. Sweetman has a lot to say about worldviews, but he also discusses specific issues such as school prayer, tolerance, John Rawls's political ideas, displays of religious symbols in public places, euthanasia, whether religious beliefs should be a factor in hiring employees, and more.

Subject: Politics

More: Legal scholar, law professor, and *Christianity Today* columnist Stephen L. Carter also talks about religion's place in politics in *God's Name in Vain: The Wrongs and Rights of Religion in Politics* (Basic Books, 2000).

Taylor, Daniel.

Is God Intolerant?: Christian Thinking About the Call for Tolerance. Tyndale House, 2003. 134 pp. ISBN 0842354395.

This small-format book deals masterfully with the issue of tolerance. Daniel Taylor, an English professor at Bethel College, presents a history of the issue of tolerance. He also explains the use and misuse of tolerance in the so-called "culture wars," supplying definitions and distinctions along the way. Taylor also addresses what the Bible says about God and tolerance.

Subject: Tolerance

Twiss, Richard.

One Church, Many Tribes: Following Jesus the Way God Made You. Regal, 2000. 219 pp. ISBN 0830725458.

Richard Twiss presents a redemptive view of native culture and shows the surprisingly biblical worldview of Native Americans. He tells the tragic and heroic story of Chief Spokane Garry and discusses broken treaties and issues of strife and healing. Twiss also describes hurtful mindsets, attitudes, and misconceptions that Americans and American Christians have harbored against Native Americans. There is also a fascinating description of what God is doing among and through indigenous peoples of the world. Twiss is a member of the Rosebud Lakota/Sioux tribe and the cofounder and president of Wiconi International (http://www.wiconi.com).

Subject: Indigenous Peoples, Native Americans, Race Relations

More: Craig Stephen Smith writes about growing up Native American in a white man's world in *Whiteman's Gospel* (Indian Life Ministries, 1998).

Van Ness, Daniel W.

Crime and Its Victims: What We Can Do. InterVarsity, 1986. 240 pp. ISBN 0877845123.

Dan Van Ness addresses the issue of crime and America's criminal justice system from two sides: the victim's and the criminal's. After briefly surveying the world history (including biblical) of criminal justice systems and philosophy, he discusses problems with the system and solutions. Van Ness is executive director of the Centre for Justice and Reconciliation, a program of Prison Fellowship International.

Subjects: Award Winners (ECPA), Criminal Justice

Popular Culture

Barsotti, Catherine M., and Robert K. Johnston.

Finding God in the Movies: 33 Films of Reel Faith. Baker, 2004. 319 pp. ISBN 0801064813.

This is a guide for people who want to understand their culture in light of their faith and for those who wish to host a film night for their families, friends, or a wider audience. It gives a synopsis and theological reflection for each movie, along with discussion questions and relevant scripture quotes. Movie selections are arranged around themes such as humanity, beauty, racial reconciliation, faith, and doubt.

Subject: Film

More: Mark Stibbe and J. John have collaborated on two books that examine themes in popular movies. *The Big Picture: Finding the Spiritual Message in Movies* (Authentic Media, 2003) covers *The Godfather Trilogy*; *Lara Croft*; *Tomb Raider*; *Billy Elliot*; *Saving Private Ryan*; *Titanic*; *Fargo*; *Cast Away*; and *The Matrix*. *The Big Picture 2* (Authentic Media, 2004) covers *Minority Report*, *The Green Mile*, *The Lord of the Rings: The Fellowship of the Ring*, *What Women Want*, *Shrek*, *Unfaithful*, *Simon Birch*, and *Bridget Jones's Diary*. Also try Christian scriptwriter Brian Godawa's *Hollywood Worldviews: Watching Films with Wisdom & Discernment* (InterVarsity, 2002).

Colson, Charles, and Nancy Pearcey.

How Now Shall We Live? Tyndale, 1999. 574 pp. ISBN 084235588X.

Charles Colson and Nancy Pearcey share real accounts of life in today's culture and examine the ideas and philosophies that shape our lives. They discuss everything from science and the evolution debate to Christian involvement with popular culture venues such as television and music. The authors assert that only the biblical, Christian worldview is based in reality and can lead us to truth, peace, justice, and joy.

Subjects: Award Winners (ECPA, CT), Worldview

More: Readers may also enjoy Pearcey's follow-up book, *Total Truth: Liberating Christianity from Its Cultural Captivity* (Crossway, 2004).

Cook, Coleen.

All That Glitters: A Newsperson Explores the World of Television. Moody, 1992. 267 pp. ISBN 0802407366.

Out of print, but worth searching for, this book discusses the inherent limitations and illusions of television. Coleen Cook, a former television news anchor, producer, talk-show host, and reporter, gives an insider's view of the medium that we are influenced by but do not really understand.

Subjects: Mass Media, Television

More: In his book *Christ and the Media* (Regent College Publishing, 2003), British media figure Malcolm Muggeridge shows how the mass media can't help but distort reality.

Fornof, John.

Movie Nights for Kids: 25 Fun Flicks to Inspire, Entertain, and Teach Your Children. Tyndale, 2004. 160 pp. ISBN 1589972147.

Covering twenty-five movies including *Chicken Run*, *Spy Kids*, *Anne of Green Gables*, *Ice Age*, and *Toy Story 2*, this guide offers plot summaries, scripture references, discussion questions, and a caution section that warns readers of bad language, rude behavior, and so on. This is a Focus on the Family book.

Subject: Film—Children

More: Also see *Movie Nights for Teens: 25 More Movies to Spark Spiritual Discussions with Your Teen* by Bob Smithouser (Focus on the Family, 2005). For books on film that can be used in youth/children's ministry, try *Videos That Teach* by Doug Fields and Eddie James (Zondervan, 1999) and *More Than A Movie: 20 Fun Specials for Your Children's Ministry* by Teryl Cartwright and Mikal Keefer, editors (Group Publishing, 2005).

Fraser, Peter, and Vernon Edwin Neal.

ReViewing the Movies: A Christian Response to Contemporary Film. Crossway Books, 2000. 187 pp. ISBN 1581342039.

Fraser, a film and English professor, and Neal, a freelance movie critic, help readers learn the language of film by explaining the different elements of film, including motion, sound, acting, editing, story, shot composition, and photography. The authors explore certain questions like: "Why are certain movies popular at certain times?" and "When are sex and violence appropriate in film?" Answering these questions helps Christian readers navigate their culture and understand and be in touch with various segments of society. The last chapter offers fifteen annotated lists of movies on various subjects such as love and romance, films for young children, movies about dysfunctional families, prison films, etc. This book is part of the Focal Point Series.

Subject: Film

Hipps, Shane.

The Hidden Power of Electronic Culture: How Media Shapes Faith, the Gospel, and Church. Zondervan, 2005. 176 pp. ISBN 0310262747.

In this book, Shane Hipps shows readers how culture, including the church, is influenced by mass media and electronic culture. Hipps, whose media theory is influenced by Marshall McLuhan, talks about various media, including language, alphabets, printed text, radio, and visual media such as photographs and television. He discusses communicating the gospel and accomplishing community in today's electronic world. There are also chapters on leadership and worship in electronic culture. Hipps, who started his career in the advertising industry, is pastor of Trinity Mennonite Church in Glendale, Arizona.

Subjects: Emerging Church Movement, Mass Media, Popular Culture, Technology

Lewerenz, Spencer, and Barbara Nicolosi, editors.

Behind the Screen: Hollywood Insiders on Faith, Film, and Culture. Baker, 2005. 216 pp. ISBN 080106547X.

Should Christians avoid Hollywood? Or should they infiltrate and conquer it? Act One, a nonprofit program consisting of Christians involved with Hollywood, says no to both questions. Instead, their vision is to love those in the film industry and to see Hollywood transformed by Christian artists who work in various levels of the business. Ralph Winter, producer of *X-Men; Fantastic Four; I, Robot;* and other blockbusters, writes an essay called "A Hollywood Survival Guide." Barbara Hall, producer of *Joan of Arcadia, Judging Amy, Chicago Hope, Northern Exposure,* and more, write "An Open Letter to Beginning Screenwriters." Television producer Karen Covell and her husband, musician Jim Covell, writes "The World's Most Influential Mission Field." There are fifteen other essays in this collection that will challenge and educate readers about faith and culture.

Subjects: Actors, Essays, Film, Hollywood, Screenwriting

More: Bob Briner's *Roaring Lambs* (Zondervan, 2000) is a well-known book encouraging Christians to shape culture instead of hiding from it.

Myers, Kenneth A.

All God's Children and Blue Suede Shoes: Christians & Popular Culture. Crossway, 1989. 224 pp. ISBN 0891075380.

In this book on popular culture, Kenneth A. Myers exposes some of the pitfalls of our entertainment-addicted society. After discussing the role Christians should play in culture, he examines different aspects of high culture, folk culture, and popular culture. Myers also addresses specific areas of popular culture such as rock music and television. Myers, a former producer and editor for National Public Radio, is the executive producer of *Mars Hill Audio Journal.* This book is part of the Turning Point Christian Worldview Series.

Subjects: Music, Popular Culture, Television

Niebuhr, H. Richard.

Christ and Culture. 50th Anniversary expanded edition. Harper Perennial, 2001 (1951). 320 pp. ISBN 0061300039.

This classic book addresses the problem of how Christians should respond to culture. Christian ethicist H. Richard Niebuhr examines the following five typical answers to this problem: Christ against culture, the Christ of culture, Christ above culture, Christ and culture in paradox, and Christ as the transformer of culture. Niebuhr (1894–1962) was a professor at Yale Divinity School and the younger brother of theologian Reinhold Niebuhr.

Subjects: Classics, Culture

More: In *Rethinking Christ and Culture: A Post-Christendom Perspective* (Baker, 2006), Craig A. Carter explains and critiques Niebuhr's approach, pointing out that his underlying assumptions are no longer valid. Carter offers an alternative view of how Christians should understand their place in culture and respond to it.

Overstreet, Jeffrey.

Through a Screen Darkly. Regal, 2007. 351 pp. ISBN 0830743154.

Jeffrey Overstreet is a film critic who writes reviews for several publications, including *Christianity Today* and his own Web site, http://lookingcloser.org. In this book, he describes what it is like to be a Christian who reviews Hollywood movies. Overstreet looks for (and shows the reader how to find) and discusses what is artful and true in movies. Throughout the book, he examines films and shows the power that movies have to move us, shape us, and challenge us.

Subject: Film

In *Saint Paul Returns to the Movies* (Eerdmans, 1999), Robert Jewett examines ten major films focusing on the theme of shame. Some of the movies are *Babe, Forrest Gump, Mr. Holland's Opus, Groundhog Day, Unforgiven,* and *The Shawshank Redemption.*

Perkins, Mitali.

Ambassador Families: Equipping Your Kids to Engage Popular Culture. Brazos Press, 2005. 206 pp. ISBN 1587431246.

How should Christians approach life in today's culture? Should they withdraw so as not to be stained by all the sin? Mitali Perkins says Christians should approach popular culture as ambassadors for the kingdom of God. Perkins offers suggestions for how to do this in regards to popular music, public school, the Internet, and other things children and their parents face in today's world. An appendix recommends many helpful resources for further study.

Subjects: Parenting, Popular Culture

Romanowski, William D.

Eyes Wide Open: Looking for God in Popular Culture. Revised and expanded edition. Brazos, 2007 (2001). 272 pp. ISBN 1587432013.

William Romanowski, professor of communication arts and sciences at Calvin College, questions why many Christians have strong opinions about the moral content of today's movies and television shows but do not seem to be interested in a serious Christian analysis of Hollywood productions. Either the movie is good or bad. The song is right or wrong. Romanowski goes deeper than shallow, black-and-white critique. In this book, he analyzes, from a Christian worldview, many well-known movies and television characters. He discusses whether popular culture is art or merely entertainment. He also discusses sex and violence in the media. Christian colleges use this as a textbook for popular-culture classes. A three-part video series based on *Eyes Wide Open* has been produced by the Calvin Media Foundation.

Subjects: Award Winners (ECPA), Popular Culture

More: Another book addressing faith and popular culture is *A Matrix of Meanings: Finding God in Pop Culture* by Craig Detweiler and Barry Taylor (Baker, 2003). Romanowski has a book on the same topic called *Pop Culture Wars: Religion & the Role of Entertainment in American Life* (InterVarsity, 1996).

Sommerville, John C.

How the News Makes Us Dumb: The Death of Wisdom in an Information Society. InterVarsity, 1999. 155 pp. ISBN 0830822038.

In this thought-provoking look at the news media from a different angle, John C. Sommerville does not discuss political agendas or media bias in any way. Instead, he says that the reason the news makes us dumb is because it is published daily. Turning news into a product that must be churned out daily (or even hourly) prevents it from truly informing us. Ironically, we feel that we really are informed if we read a newspaper or even two or three daily papers. But the author asserts that this is an illusion, and he gives some convincing arguments as well as disturbing examples of how our flawed news system influences our government and culture at large. Sommerville is professor of history at the University of Florida in Gainesville, Florida.

Subject: Mass Media

Staub, Dick.

The Culturally Savvy Christian: A Manifesto for Deepening Faith and Enriching Popular Culture in an Age of Christianity-Lite. Jossey-Bass, 2007. 256 pp. ISBN 0787978930.

Author and radio personality Dick Staub confronts superficial American culture and superficial Christian faith. Staub believes that shallow faith produces shallow culture. In this book, which collects a lifetime's worth of reflections on culture and faith, Staub provides both the wisdom to understand and the inspiration to engage culture. He also offers guidance for artists, the creators of culture. Staub challenges Christians to deepen their faith so they will have something substantial to say, for Christianity is not opposed to art. In fact, faith inspires art. In this vein, Staub quotes Swedish filmmaker Ingmar Bergman, who said, "Art lost its basic creative drive the moment it was separated from worship." Staub believes that culturally savvy Christians can be agents for healthy cultural transformation.

Subjects: Art, Culture, Popular Culture

More: Staub also wrote *Too Christian, Too Pagan: How to Love the World Without Falling for It* (Zondervan, 2000), which reminds Christians to view culture as a mission field and to avoid the temptation to insulate themselves from society by retreating "into holy cocoons from the surrounding culture."

Education

What are the legal boundaries for Christian teachers in public schools? Can they use the Bible to teach? Kimberlee Wood Colby's *Teachers & Religion in Public Schools* answers this and many other pressing questions. What about parents who want to participate in their children's education? Cheri Fuller has many suggestions in *School Starts at Home*. Other topics in the general-education section include storytelling, math education, educational philosophy, and issues that college students and academics face—all from a Christian perspective.

There are more and more nonreligious homeschooling families in America (and families from other religions that choose home education). But in large part, the homeschooling phenomenon in America is a Christian movement. Publishing in this area has really taken off in the last ten or twenty years. Public librarians across the land quickly caught on to the fact that homeschoolers love to use the library. There are several guides written just for librarians to serve such patrons. One recent example is *Serving Homeschooled Teens and Their Parents* by Maureen Lerch and Janet Welch (Libraries Unlimited, 2004). Books in this section focus on why and how to homeschool, including various approaches to homeschooling and helpful curriculum-planning guides.

General Education

Colby, Kimberlee Wood, and the Christian Legal Society, Center for Law and Religious Freedom.

Teachers & Religion in Public Schools. 4th Edition. Christian Educators Association International, 2006. 109 pp. ISBN 0966830911.

Can public school students pray at lunchtime? Can they sing songs that mention God? Is it legal for public school teachers to use the Bible in class? Harvard Law School graduate Kimberlee Wood Colby answers these and other common concerns that public school teachers and students have. Readers will also find a brief legal background that deals with specific issues such as religious holiday observances, distribution of religious material, prayer in classrooms and graduation ceremonies, clothing with religious messages, and more. Colby is a staff attorney for the Center for Law and Religious Freedom (Christian Legal Society). This book is sold only by the Christian Educators Association International: http://www.ceai.org.

Subjects: Church and State, Public Schools—Law and Legislation, Public Schools—Religion, Teachers—Public School

More: David French (also a Harvard Law School graduate) wrote a book about legal persecution against Christians in schools, universities, churches, and the workplace entitled *A Season for Justice: Defending the Rights of the Christian Home, Church, and School* (B&H Publishing, 2002).

Doud, Guy Rice.

Molder of Dreams. Focus on the Family, 1999 (1990). 288 pp. ISBN 156179712X.

Guy Doud, National Teacher of the Year in 1986, discusses his experiences and his vision for teaching. Emphasizing the impact that teachers have on the lives of young students, Doud says teachers can build dreams or shatter hopes. This is a classic book for educators about the power of love and encouragement. There is also a video version of this title.

Subjects: Education, Teachers

Fuller, Cheri.

School Starts at Home: Simple Ways to Make Learning Fun. Pinon Press, 2004. 159 pp. ISBN 1576836002.

There are tons of things you can do with your preschool children to unlock their potential. Don't wait for them to be "school aged." This helpful book encourages parents to get involved with their children's education. Cheri Fuller discusses how to raise children who love to read and learn, the importance of the parent-teacher connection, and developing math skills, among other things.

Subjects: Education—Early Childhood, Education—Parent Participation, Parenting

More: For another book by Fuller in the School Savvy Kids Series, try *Raising Motivated Kids* (Pinon, 2004).

Forbes, Cheryl.

Imagination: Embracing a Theology of Wonder. Multnomah, 1986. 199 pp. ISBN 0880701366.

Cheryl Forbes explores the nature of imagination and shows how too many of us have inactive imaginations. She says our imaginations are given to us by God (they are the "image of God" in us), and believes that this interesting faculty, if used properly, can stimulate us to worship and to a proper understanding of God's word. Forbes has an insightful section on television and the imagination.

Subjects: Education, Imagination, Theology

Fuller, Cheri.

Talkers, Watchers, and Doers: Unlocking Your Child's Unique Learning Style. Pinon Press, 2004. 169 pp. ISBN 1576835995.

Are you clashing with your children? Perhaps your child has a different learning style than you. Understanding your child's learning style is important not only for school but also for home. Fuller shows you how to discover the way your kids learn and how learning styles affect reading skills. She discusses how to understand and develop your child's talents and gifts, and tells you what to do at home and in the classroom with your child's weaknesses.

Subjects: Education—Parent Participation, Learning Styles, Parenting

More: Another title by Fuller is *Opening Your Child's Nine Learning Windows* (Zondervan, 2001). Cynthia Ulrich Tobias also has a book on learning styles called *The Way They Learn* (Focus on the Family, 1998).

Hendricks, Howard.

Teaching to Change Lives: Seven Proven Ways to Make Your Teaching Come Alive. Multnomah, 2003 (1987). 160 pp. ISBN 1590521382.

Howard Hendricks, well-known professor at Dallas Theological Seminary, conveys a passion for teaching, communicating, and helping his students. Drawing from a classic book on teaching by

John Milton Gregory, Hendricks expounds on teaching and learning. He shows the reader how to motivate and encourage students. In discussing how to get students involved with learning and with meaningful activity, he says that education is not so much about pouring knowledge and ideas into students but about drawing it out of them. The concepts and principles in this book are useful and inspiring for teachers, mentors, parents, Sunday-school teachers, or anyone with a passion to communicate.

Subjects: Education, Leadership, Teaching

More: One of Henricks's students was Bruce Wilkinson, author of the *New York Times* best sellers *The Prayer of Jabez* and *Secrets of the Vine*. Wilkinson has a book on teaching, inspired by Hendricks, called *The Seven Laws of the Learner: How to Teach Almost Anything to Practically Anyone* (Multnomah, 2005). The classic book that Hendricks drew from in writing his own book is still in print. It was first published in 1884 and was written by John Milton Gregory (1822–1898), a Christian teacher known as the "father of the University of Illinois." The book is titled *The Seven Laws of Teaching* (Baker, 2004).

Kullberg, Kelly Monroe.

Finding God at Harvard: Spiritual Journeys of Thinking Christians. Revised edition. InterVarsity, 2007 (Zondervan, 1996). 374 pp. ISBN 0830834338.

This book presents the testimonies of forty-two people associated with Harvard who are believers and thinkers and are not afraid to face the sometimes-difficult intellectual issues of the day with faith and reason. Those who have contributed essays include William Edgar, Aleksandr Solzhenitsyn, Nicholas Wolterstorff, Charles Thaxton, Owen Gingerich, Mother Teresa, and Charles Malik. This book was first published in 1996.

Subjects: Award Winners (ECPA), Harvard University, Intellectuals, Professors

More: Kelly Monroe Kullberg also wrote *Finding God Beyond Harvard: The Quest for Veritas* (InterVarsity, 2006), which chronicles her own spiritual and intellectual journey as well as the history of the Veritas Forum. The Veritas Forum was started at Harvard in 1992 and has spread to at least fifty other colleges and universities (http://www.veritas.org).

Nickel, James.

Mathematics: Is God Silent? 2nd Edition. Ross House, 2001 (1990). 409 pp. ISBN 187999822X.

No, God is not silent about math. Yes, a Christian worldview does include mathematics. In this book, designed for a general audience, James Nickel shows how worldviews can either further or hinder mathematics. Nickel surveys the whole history of mathematics from a Christian perspective. A section for educators will be useful for teachers, homeschoolers, and parents. The resource section includes a fascinating bibliographic essay on math and Christianity.

Subjects: Education, Mathematics

More: For a collection of essays on the philosophy of mathematics, try *Mathematics in a Postmodern Age: A Christian Perspective* by Russell Howell and W. James Bradley, editors (Eerdmans, 2001).

Nye, Abby.

Fish Out of Water: Surviving and Thriving As a Christian on a Secular Campus. New Leaf Press, 2005. 233 pp. ISBN 0892216212.

Abby Nye, a recent college graduate, relays her eye-opening and faith-challenging experience in school. It started with freshman orientation, which Nye says should be called freshman indoctrination. In her first English class, instead of reading great classics of literature, she read essays explaining why "under God" should be removed from the Pledge of Allegiance. She describes professors who graded her writing poorly because they disagreed with her beliefs (these professors apparently believed it was academic dishonesty to believe that the Bible was true), and shows readers how to deal with the ever-present and often-misused issue of tolerance. Nye also discusses the party scene and its associated sex and alcohol issues that drag down just about all students. An appendix recommends dozens of Web sites, books, and organizations that can help students get through the college experience as Christians.

Subjects: College Students, Worldview

More: Two other books to prepare students for the university experience are: *How to Stay Christian in College* by J. Budziszewski (Th1nk Books, 2004) and *Chris Chrisman Goes to College: And Faces the Challenges of Relativism, Individualism and Pluralism* by James W. Sire (InterVarsity, 1993). Also try *The Fabric of Faithfulness: Weaving Together Belief and Behavior* by Steven Garber (InterVarsity, 2007).

Schultze, Quentin.

An Essential Guide to Public Speaking: Serving Your Audience with Faith, Skill, and Virtue. Baker Academic, 2006. 112 pp. ISBN 0801031516.

Professor Quentin Schultze of Calvin College seeks to reclaim "public speaking as a noble practice for Christians." Although he addresses typical issues like verbal expressiveness and nonverbal gestures, when to use visual aids, logic, storytelling, and other techniques that make for a good speech, this is not merely a technical manual. Schultze believes that speech is a gift from God involving a responsibility toward serving our neighbors. He says that faith, virtue, and skill are elements to be applied to what he calls "servant speaking."

Subjects: Communication—Interpersonal, Education, Public Speaking

More: For a book that focuses more on interpersonal communication, try *Creating Understanding: A Handbook for Christian Communication Across Cultural Landscapes* by Dr. Donald K. Smith (Zondervan, 1992).

Snow, Donald B.

English Teaching As Christian Mission: An Applied Theology. Herald, 2001. 190 pp. ISBN 0836191587.

In this book, Donald Snow discusses English teaching as a profession and a ministry. Many Christians today go overseas to teach English. Should they do it for evangelistic reasons or merely to offer a social service? Donald B. Snow, who has worked with organizations that send Christian English teachers abroad, has been an English teacher in Taiwan, Hong Kong, the Chinese mainland, and the United States.

Subjects: English as a Second Language, Teaching—Language

More: Two English as a second language (ESL) books designed for churches or individuals are *ESL: Creating a Quality English As a Second Language Program: A Guide for Churches* by Susan E. Burke (Faith Alive, 1998) and *Handbook for Teaching Bible-Based ESL* by J. Wesley Eby (Beacon Hill Press, 2003). Also, a book for foreign-language teachers is *The Gift of the Stranger: Faith, Hospitality, and Foreign Language Learning* by David Smith (Eerdmans, 2000).

Walsh, John.

The Art of Storytelling: Easy Steps to Presenting an Unforgettable Story. Moody, 2003. 185 pp. ISBN 0802433065.

John Walsh, president of International Learning Solutions, shares his experience and wisdom for storytelling, and shows how to prepare and present stories for any occasion—for children, Sunday-school classes, preaching, and teaching. He also covers such topics as storytelling and the family, storytelling and the church, storytelling and education, and how to organize a storytelling event. The appendices include a storytelling resource list.

Subjects: Education, Storytelling

More: Award-winning storyteller Steven James has a book that includes fifteen storytelling workshops, reproducible handouts, storytelling techniques, activities, and more than 300 story starters. The title is *Creative Storytelling Guide for Children's Ministry: When All Your Brain Wants to Do Is Fly* (Standard Publishing, 2003).

Wilson, Douglas.

Recovering the Lost Tools of Learning: An Approach to Distinctively Christian Education. Crossway, 1991. 215 pp. ISBN 0891075836.

Douglas Wilson, who helped found the Logos School in Idaho, has experience in applying the methods and principles he proposes. In this book, he discusses the failure of American public education due to the "amoral" and "Godless" public-school environment and unsound teaching methods; he offers practical alternatives, including a return to classical education. This book is part of the Turning Point Christian Worldview Series.

Subjects: Education—Classical

More: Wilson has a follow-up book called *The Case for Classical Christian Education* (Crossway, 2002).

Homeschooling

Andreola, Karen.

A Charlotte Mason Companion: Personal Reflections on the Gentle Art of Learning. Charlotte Mason Research & Supply, 1998. 383 pp. ISBN 1889209023.

This is a practical book based on Charlotte Mason's philosophy of education. Mason (1842–1923), a British educator, published a series of books about home education in 1880. Packed with wisdom and advice for today's homeschoolers wanting to implement a Mason-style homeschool, this guide covers topics such as recognizing a living book; using narration; appreciating art, music, poetry, Shakespeare, and Dickens; keeping a nature notebook; hero admiration (for learning history); and establishing helpful habits. Also gives advice for teaching reading, spelling, and composition.

Subjects: Education, Homeschooling, Living Books, Charlotte Mason

More: Another guide to Charlotte Mason-style homeschooling is *A Charlotte Mason Education* by Catherine Levison (Champion Press, 1999).

Bauer, Susan Wise, and Jessie Wise.

The Well-Trained Mind: A Guide to Classical Education at Home. Revised and updated edition. Norton, 2004 (1999). 810 pp. ISBN 0393059278.

This massive work covers the whole range of classical education. For every stage in a classical education (such as the grammar stage, logic stage, and rhetoric stage), the authors recommend and evaluate textbooks, curricula, and other materials. They discuss every subject at each grade level, introducing and explaining subjects such as math, grammar, logic, history, and languages, giving guidance and tips along the way. They also provide suggestions for planning schedules.

Subjects: Education—Classical, Homeschooling

More: Bauer also has written a book on the same topic designed for adults who want to teach themselves. It is called *The Well-Educated Mind: A Guide to the Classical Education You Never Had* (Norton, 2003).

Berquist, Laura M.

Designing Your Own Classical Curriculum: A Guide to Catholic Home Education. 3rd Edition. Ignatius, 1998 (1994). 265 pp. ISBN 0898706602.

Laura M. Berquist gives a framework for parents to design their own curriculum from kindergarten to twelfth grade. For each grade, books and curricula are recommended for subjects such as religion, math, grammar, composition, spelling, literature (which is correlated with history), poetry, science, history, geography, Latin, art, and music. Each section also provides a sample Monday-through-Friday schedule and a resource list that includes literature and history readings, Latin prayers, saints, and other information. All of this is presented in the context of a classical education. For instance, grades three through six are in the grammar stage. Throughout the book, Berquist offers direction and advice for the homeschooling teacher/planner.

Subjects: Catholics, Curriculum Planning, Education—Classical, Homeschooling

More: For other approaches to homeschooling for Catholics, try *The Catholic Homeschool Companion* by Maureen Wittmann and Rachel Mackson, editors (Sophia Institute Press, 2006).

Caruana, Vicki.

The Organized Homeschooler. Crossway, 2001. 159 pp. ISBN 1581343051.

Practical advice for organizing time, space, supplies, paperwork, and more. Chapter Twelve is "A Homeschool File System." A resource guide at the back of the book points to other books, articles, and Web sites about organizing.

Subjects: Homeschooling, Organization

Davis, Chris, and Ellyn Davis.

I Saw the Angel in the Marble. Elijah Company, 2004. 196 pp. ISBN 188409824X.

In this collection of fifteen years of articles that appeared in the Elijah Company catalogue or newsletter, Chris and Ellyn Davis, homeschoolers with twenty years of experience, talk about why they, and other parents, homeschool their children. Although the Davises give several "whys," they state that the real reason is because of close family relationships. They love their children and wanted to be a part of their lives as they grew up. Included are essays about the "ancient paths," the nature of education, various teaching approaches, learning environments, identity-directed homeschooling, and more. Several of the essays offer wisdom for parenting. Elijah Company was started by Chris and Ellyn Davis as a home-based business. They ran the Elijah Company Bookstore (which eventually closed), and now run Home School Marketplace, a Web site designed to offer resources for homeschooling and home-based businesses (http://www.homeschoolmarketplace.com).

Subjects: Essays, Homeschooling, Parenting

Duffy, Cathy.

100 Top Picks for Homeschool Curriculum: Choosing the Right Curriculum and Approach for Your Child's Learning Style. B&H Publishing, 2005. 314 pp. ISBN 0805431381.

In this book, Cathy Duffy helps parents decide upon the right educational philosophy for their homeschool and suggests curricula that fit. Duffy recommends and reviews curricula, books, and materials that work with the following homeschool styles: traditional, Charlotte Mason, classical education, unit study, independent study, unschooling, eclectic, and umbrella programs.

Subjects: Curriculum Planning, Education, Homeschooling

More: For a more comprehensive guide to curriculum choices and homeschooling in general, try *Mary Pride's Complete Guide to Getting Started in Homeschooling* by Mary Pride (Harvest House, 2004).

Hensley, Sharon C.

Home Schooling Children with Special Needs. Noble Publishing Associates, 1995. 181 pp. ISBN 1568570104.

This book helps readers locate much-needed and often hard-to-find resources for homeschooling children with special needs. After defining various kinds of learning disabilities such as visual disorders, motor-system disorders, auditory-system (language) disorders, and attention-system disorders, Hensley discusses and recommends resources for slow learners, mental retardation, autism, and more. She covers issues like having realistic expectations for homeschooling, feeling inadequate, and dealing with grief, acceptance, anger, discouragement, and behavior problems. The last section, "Planning Your Program," discusses testing, setting goals, and choosing teaching methods and curricula. Hensley has a master's degree in special education. Her oldest daughter is autistic.

Subjects: Autism, Homeschooling, Special Education

Klicka, Christopher J.

Home Schooling: The Right Choice: An Academic, Historical, Practical, and Legal Perspective. B&H Publishing, 2001. 480 pp. ISBN 0805425853.

Christopher Klicka, senior counsel for the Home School Legal Defense Association, says that the U.S. public-school system is "academically and morally bankrupt." In this book, Klicka talks about the failure and dangers of public education as well as the benefits and history of homeschooling. Klicka gives a brief overview of how to get involved with homeschooling. Several chapters are devoted to governmental and legal issues that threaten the rights of people to parent and educate their own children in America.

Subjects: Education, Homeschooling, Homeschooling—Law and Legislation, Law, Schools—Law and Legislation

More: For more legal issues, see Klicka's *The Right to Home School: A Guide to the Law on Parents' Rights in Education* (Carolina Academic Press, 2002). Harvard Law School graduate David French's *A Season for Justice: Defending the Rights of the Christian Home, Church, and School* (B&H Publishing, 2002) gives a startling view of the persecution that is happening in our schools (including universities), churches, and workplaces.

Lerch, Maureen T., and Janet Welch.

Serving Homeschooled Teens and Their Parents. Libraries Unlimited, 2004. 242 pp. ISBN 0313320527.

This book shows public librarians how and why to target services specifically for homeschooled teens. It has program ideas, program planning sheets, and marketing ideas. The authors present background information about the homeschooling movement, write about the developmental and social needs of teens as they relate to public libraries, and give practical advice for collection development. The authors (one a young-adult librarian and the other a mother of a homeschooled teen) also discuss services that homeschoolers frequently request.

Subjects: Homeschooling, Libraries and Homeschooling

Macaulay, Susan Schaeffer.

For the Children's Sake: Foundations of Education for Home and School. Crossway, 1984. 165 pp. ISBN 089107290X.

This book is for anyone interested in the education of their children, whether they go to a public, private, or home school. Susan Schaeffer Macaulay, the daughter of noted writers Francis and Edith Schaeffer, presents foundational principles of what it means to be a person and a parent. Using the philosophy of British educator Charlotte Mason, Macaulay explains the nature of children and of education. These insights will also be useful for public- and private-school teachers.

Subjects: Education, Education—Parent Participation, Homeschooling

More: Elaine Cooper edited a book billed as a follow-up to this book (geared toward classroom teachers) called *When Children Love to Learn: A Practical Application of Charlotte Mason's Philosophy Today* (Crossway, 2004). For more on Charlotte Mason-style homeschool education, try *A Charlotte Mason Companion: Personal Reflections on the Gentle Art of Learning* by Karen Andreola (Charlotte Mason Research & Supply, 1998).

Whelchel, Lisa.

So You're Thinking about Homeschooling: Fifteen Families Show How You Can Do It. 2nd Edition. Multnomah, 2006 (2003). 228 pp. ISBN 1601420331.

This great book shows how different people in different circumstances have found ways to homeschool their children. Here are real people under actual circumstances. You will meet families dealing with ADHD, families where the grandparents are homeschooling, and families where the father is homeschooling (and the mother works full time). You'll read how one family sold their house and bought an RV; they travel across the country due to the husband's job, and they have the nation for their classroom. You will read the story of a single mom who homeschools and works. You will even get the perspective of a teenager when a fifteen-year-old homeschooler describes why he is glad to be homeschooled. The author is known for her role as Blair on the television comedy, *The Facts of Life*. This book is endorsed by Focus on the Family.

Subject: Homeschooling

More: *Educating the Wholehearted Child* by Clay and Sally Clarkson (Whole Heart Ministries, 2001) shows parents why and how to start homeschooling. Their book is full of advice, encouragement, and helpful ideas to educate both a child's mind and heart.

Bibliographies

These annotated bibliographies recommend literature for Christian readers. The titles are not limited to books written by Christian authors but are selected by Christians for Christians and cover children's nonfiction, children's fiction, and classic literature. These bibliographies should be very valuable for both Christian parents seeking "something good" for their children to read and for home educators designing their homeschool curricula.

Bloom, Jan.

Who Should We Then Read?: Authors of Good Books for Children and Young Adults. Revised and expanded edition. Booksbloom, 2001 (1999). 340 pp. ISBN 0970962819.

Jan Bloom does not write annotations for her booklists, but she does provide something that no one else does. For each of the 140-plus authors that she includes, Bloom writes a one-page biography packed with interesting facts and helpful information. For instance, did you know that Caldecott Medal winner Robert McCloskey used red wine to slow down his pet ducks so he could draw them better? Bloom also includes comprehensive lists of more than thirty series of books such as the popular Landmark books or the Childhood of Famous Americans Series. This bibliography will appeal to homeschoolers or to anyone wanting to discover good (and many times out-of-print) books and authors who have become forgotten and lost treasures. In addition to more authors and series, this revised edition includes reading-level suggestions, reading-interest suggestions, and updated series lists and author bibliographies.

Subjects: Best Books, Children's Literature, Homeschooling, Living Books

More: Bloom also has a book on building a home library called *What Should We Then Know: About Constructing, Furnishing, Maintaining, and Enjoying a Home Library* (BooksBloom, 2003).

Cowan, Louise, and Os Guinness, editors.

Invitation to the Classics: A Guide to Books You've Always Wanted to Read. Baker, 2006. 384 pp. ISBN 080106810X.

This is a rich and helpful handbook to classic literature covering everyone from Homer, Sophocles, and Plato to Melville, Dostoyevsky, and Faulkner. For each author, Louise Cowan and Os Guinness discuss major works and give helpful biographical and historical information. There are also sections covering different literary movements like "Spanish Classics," "Modern Poetry in English," and "Early Christian Writers." Beautifully illustrated in full color. Cowan is professor of literature at the University of Dallas and is a founding fellow of the Dallas Institute of Humanities and Culture. Guinness is a noted author and speaker and senior fellow with The Trinity Forum.

Subjects: Award Winners (CT), Books and Reading, Literature—Classic

Hunt, Gladys.

Honey for a Child's Heart: The Imaginative Use of Books in Family Life. 4th Edition. Zondervan, 2002 (1969). 251 pp. ISBN 0310242460.

This classic volume about books, now in its fourth edition, was first published in 1969. The first hundred or so pages are comprised of a collection of bibliographic essays on such topics as parenting and books, poetry, fantasy and realism, the influence of television, and building a child's library. The last half of the book provides annotated book lists arranged by the following age groups: 0–3 (first books), 4–8 (picture books and books for beginning readers), 9–12 (classics, animal stories, historical novels, and fantasy), and 12–14 (young-adult novels). It also includes booklists for poetry, spiritual growth, grief, loss, Christmas stories, Easter stories, and Thanksgiving stories.

Subjects: Best Books, Children's Literature, Parenting

Hunt, Gladys, and Barbara Hampton.

Honey for a Teen's Heart: Using Books to Communicate with Teens. Zondervan, 2002. 301 pp. ISBN 0310242606. **YA**

In Chapter One, Gladys Hunt says, "This book is about books—about using good stories in raising healthy teens." Other chapters include essays on television and computer habits, what makes a good book, censorship and moral values, developing a Christian worldview, fantasy literature, and the Bible. The second part of the book is an annotated list of more than 400 recommended books for teenagers. Each review has a notation indicating whether it is for early teens (middle school), mid teens (early high school), late teens (senior high to college), and all ages (good family read-alouds for all ages). An asterisk notes which books belong in a basic collection for any school library. Booklists fall under these categories: adventure and suspense, contemporary, fantasy, historical, mystery, nonfiction, science fiction, sports, and tried and true.

Subjects: Parenting, Teenagers, Young-Adult Interest, Young-Adult Literature

Kilpatrick, William, Gregory Wolfe, and Suzanne M. Wolfe.

Books That Build Character: A Guide to Teaching Your Child Moral Values Through Stories. Touchstone, 1994. 332 pp. ISBN 0671884239.

This book begins with five essays about the nature of books and moral character. The authors note that books provide much needed "good examples" for children. They say that imagination is one of the keys to virtue, noting that it is not enough to know what is right—one must also desire to do what is right. Imagination can fuel that desire. "This is why books are so important for moral education. They inspire a love of goodness," the authors say. Shying away from the popular "realistic" problem novels, which teach children how to think about and cope with divorce, sex, gender, anorexia, and so on, the authors suggest that this type of literature encourages children to become preoccupied with "self." The books recommended in this book, however "are animated by a sense of moral order" where "evil is punished, virtue is rewarded, things are set straight, effort pays off, and riddles are solved." The book recommends about 300 books arranged by the following topics: picture books, fables/fairy tales, myths/legends/folktales, sacred texts (Jewish and Christian), books for holidays/holy days, historical fiction, contemporary fiction, fantasy/science fiction, and biography. An appendix recommends two children's videos. William Kilpatrick is professor of education at Boston College. Gregory Wolfe is editor and publisher of *Image: A Journal of the Arts & Religion*. Suzanne Wolfe is a writer and editor for *Image*.

Subjects: Best Books, Character, Children's Literature, Parenting

Levison, Catherine.

A Literary Education. Champion Press, 2001. 95 pp. ISBN 1891400231.

This is a brief, annotated bibliography of books recommended for kids from kindergarten to high school and up. It is designed for people pursuing a Charlotte Mason educational style (or for anyone looking for good children's literature). Catherine Levison notes which books were actually used in Charlotte Mason's schools. Her annotations include book descriptions (sometimes noting which edition is best), appropriate reading level, and explanations of how the book can be useful educationally. Levison recommends books on the following topics: literature, history, science/nature, poetry, art, biography, and music.

Subjects: Best Books, Children's Literature, Education, Homeschooling, Living Books, Charlotte Mason

Lindskoog, Kathryn, and Ranelda Mack Hunsicker.

How to Grow a Young Reader: Books from Every Age for Readers of Every Age. Updated and expanded edition. Harold Shaw, 1999 (Cook, 1978). 391 pp. ISBN 0877884080.

This volume recommends more than 1,800 books. Each section features a brief essay followed by an annotated list of books. Kathryn Lindskoog and Ranelda Hunsicker discuss family reading, classics, fantasy/science fiction, realistic fiction, biography, animal stories, adventure stories, mysteries, humor books, series books, and picture books. The authors also include chapters on multimedia resources (like audio books and videos) and spiritual growth (Bible stories, prayer, biography, etc.). Lindskoog (1934–2003) was a writer, teacher, and biographer of C. S. Lewis. Hunsicker is a writer and former teacher.

Subjects: Best Books, Children's Literature, Education

McCallum, Elizabeth, and Jane Scott.

The Book Tree: A Christian Reference for Children's Literature. Canon Press, 2001. 222 pp. ISBN 1885767714.

Elizabeth McCallum and Jane Scott (a mother-daughter team) recommend their favorite children's literature for kids of all ages, from preschool through high school. For each recommended title they include a helpful description/plot summary. The guide covers preschool literature, as well as fiction and biography for elementary, middle school, and high school students. McCallum is a high school/college English teacher. Scott is a writer and editorial consultant.

Subjects: Best Books, Children's Literature, Education

McEwan, Elaine K.

How to Raise a Reader. Baker, 1999. 205 pp. ISBN 0801011841.

Elaine McEwan works as an educational consultant, training teachers and administrators in raising reading achievement in their schools. She has been a teacher, a librarian, and a principal. In this book, she shows parents how to help their children learn to read and how to encourage reluctant readers. She provides annotated lists of book—including poetry, read-aloud novels, folktales, classics, picture books—for children of various ages. In an appendix, McEwan recommends books that repeat phonetic elements. For instance, if a child is learning the short "a" sound, then the parent can read *Angus and the Cat* by Marjorie Flack at home to reinforce what they are learning at school. In another appendix, McEwan recommends books for parents who want to understand language development.

Subjects: Children's Literature, Education, Reading

More: *Survey of Recommended Reading Lists* by the Association of Christian Schools International shows what Christian schoolteachers assign for outside reading from preschool through twelfth grade.

Miller, Christine.

All Through the Ages: History Through Literature Guide. Revised 2nd edition. Nothing New Press, 2004 (1997). 318 pp. ISBN (none).

This book lists more than 5,600 "living books" arranged by historical era and geographic region. For instance, if a sixth-grade student wants a biography of Stonewall Jackson, he can find one for his grade level by going to the index or by going straight to the section on the U.S. Civil War. In that same section, a second-grader could find a biography for her age—as well as a book about culture during that time. A ninth-grade student could also get a biography or a recommendation for historical fiction set in this period. The second section of this book arranges books by geographical region. Historical fiction set in Germany, biographies of Italian artists, books covering specified events in Japan, and overviews of South America can all be found in the geography section—also arranged by grade level. Three other main sections include history of science and math, history of the arts, and great books of Western civilization and the Christian tradition. This book must be ordered through the publishers at http://www.nothingnewpress.com.

Subjects: Children's Literature, Education, History, Homeschooling, Living Books

More: A similar book (and one of the sourcebooks for Miller) is *Let the Authors Speak: A Guide to Worthy Books Based on Historical Setting* by Carolyn Hatcher (Old Pinnacle Publishing, 1995). *A Family Program for Reading Aloud* by Rosalie June Slater (Foundation for American Christian Education F.A.C.E., 1997) is a good resource for homeschoolers using the "principle approach," which focuses on the Christian heritage of America.

Wilson, Elizabeth.

Books Children Love: A Guide to the Best Children's Literature. Revised edition. Crossway, 2002 (1987). 330 pp. ISBN 1581341989.

This book offers a treasure trove of recommendations for both fiction and nonfiction children's literature. The titles, selected with Christian standards in mind, are not limited to Christian authors or publishers. In addition to suggestions for folktales, fairy tales, fantasy fiction, and realistic literature, Wilson also covers topics like art and architecture, Bible/spiritual teaching, biography, crafts, hobbies and domestic arts, dance, drama, geography, history, handicaps, and horticulture. This is the revised edition of this classic work first published in 1987.

Subjects: Best Books, Children's Literature, Education

Chapter 6

Business and Leadership

Introduction

There is a new movement underway involving spirituality and Christians in the marketplace. David Miller calls it the "faith-at-work" movement in his recent book, *God at Work*. This movement has its predecessors stretching back 100 years. Ministries founded and led by businessmen go as far back as 1899, when Gideons International was founded by two traveling salesmen. The Bibles that travelers find in their hotel rooms were placed there by the Gideons, who are still going strong today with more than 200,000 members around the world.

In 1951, successful businessman Demos Shakarian started the non-denominational, Pentecostal ministry for businessmen called the Full Gospel Business Men's Fellowship International. This ministry created one of the largest networks of Christian businessmen in the world with chapters in 160 countries. These people take their business and their faith seriously; they have discovered that Christianity is not just for Sunday morning.

A related interest, personal finance, is also inspiring more book titles as Christians seek to learn how to manage their money and estates with biblical wisdom. Another category of publishing that overlaps somewhat with business is leadership. Some of the most well-known thinkers and writers on leadership are Christians. For instance, leadership expert and best-selling writer John Maxwell (author of *Developing the Leader Within You*) was a Wesleyan pastor for more than twenty years.

Christians in the Marketplace

Today, there is a new wave of "faith-at-work" books being published. Some of them, like *God Is at Work* by Ken Eldred, talk about "kingdom businesses." Eldred shows how Christian businessmen can affect world missions through various business strategies. For more titles about business and missions, check the section on missions in Chapter Four. Other books, like Larry Burkett's *Business by the Book*, show business owners how to run their companies with biblical principles.

Beckett, John D.

Loving Monday: Succeeding in Business Without Selling Your Soul. Expanded edition. InterVarsity, 2006 (1998). 197 pp. ISBN 0830833900.

> MIT graduate and R. W. Beckett Corporation president John Beckett describes his life, his conversion to Christianity, and his business experiences. Beckett explains how he found meaning in life and in business. He also writes on such topics as service, giving back to the community, balancing work and family, and vision and values in business decisions.

Subjects: Business, Work

More: Beckett's most recent book is *Mastering Monday: A Guide to Integrating Faith and Work* (InterVarsity, 2006).

Burkett, Larry.

Business by the Book: The Complete Guide of Biblical Principles for the Workplace. Nelson, 2006 (Christian Financial Concepts, 1984). 304 pp. ISBN 0785287973.

> Larry Burkett (1939–2003), one of the foremost names in Christian financial issues, gives biblical advice on personal and business goals, management problems, hiring and firing decisions, business tithing, whether to incorporate or form a partnership, retirement, and more.

Subject: Business

More: For a biblical discussion of deeper, more basic concepts like ownership, productivity, profit, competition, and other business issues, try *Business for the Glory of God: The Bible's Teaching on the Moral Goodness of Business* by noted Bible and theology professor Wayne Grudem (Crossway, 2003).

Chewning, Richard C., John W. Eby, and Shirley J. Roels.

Business Through the Eyes of Faith. Harper and Row, 1990. 266 pp. ISBN 0060613505.

In association with the Christian College Coalition's Through the Eyes of Faith Series, this book was written for college students studying business. It offers a Christian perspective on business, work, and leadership. Concerning business, the authors ask what God requires of Christians in business, and they discuss the social responsibility of business owners toward the communities in which they live and do business. In regards to leadership, the authors present a Christian concept of leadership by discussing the Christian's use of power; they also explore other related issues such as motivation and communication.

Subjects: Business, Leadership, Work

More: For more on a Christian perspective (and an historical overview) of work and vocation, try *The Fabric of This World: Inquiries Into Calling, Career Choice, and the Design of Human Work* by Lee Hardy (Eerdmans, 1990).

Eldred, Ken.

God Is at Work. Regal, 2005. 336 pp. ISBN 0830738061.

Ken Eldred, CEO of Living Stones Foundation, talks about the "kingdom business" movement in which Christian business leaders find opportunities to impact world missions. Eldred gives the example of one kingdom business called ET, a call-center business in India with 1,000 college-trained employees. In a country where only two out of 100 call themselves Christian, 600 ET employees are self-proclaimed Christians. Eldred suggests these kingdom businesses further the mission of local churches and can help transform nations.

Subject: Business and Missions

More: Eldred coedited with Tetsunao Yamamori *On Kingdom Business: Transforming Missions Through Entrepreneurial Strategies* (Crossway, 2003).

Julian, Larry S.

God Is My CEO: Following God's Principles in a Bottom-Line World. Adams Media, 2002. 320 pp. ISBN 1580627641.

Consultant and leadership-development speaker Larry Julian explores from the Christian perspective business and related issues like meaning, purpose, success, courage, and leadership. As he discusses these issues, he weaves in the stories of twenty Christian business leaders such as S. Truett Cathy (founder of Chick-Fil-A), Bill George (CEO, Medtronic), C. William Pollard (CEO, ServiceMaster), and Tony Dungy (head coach of the Tampa Bay Buccaneers).

Subjects: Business, Chief Executive Officers, Leadership

More: Readers may be interested in a book that Julian refers to called *Halftime: Changing Your Game Plan from Success to Significance* by Bob Buford (Zondervan, 1997). Buford, who was profiled in Julian's book, shows that midlife for businessmen does not need to be a time of crisis. Also profiled is Linda Rios Brook. She has a book titled *Frontline Christians in a Bottom-Line World* (Destiny Image, 2004).

Nash, Laura, and Scotty McLennan.

Church on Sunday, Work on Monday: The Challenge of Fusing Christian Values with Business Life. Jossey-Bass, 2001. 352 pp. ISBN 0787956988.

Laura Nash is a senior research fellow at the Harvard Business School. Scotty McLennan is the dean for religious life at Stanford University. In this book, based on interviews of clergy and businesspeople and a review of the literature, Nash and McLennan examine the tension between clergy and businesspeople and discuss such issues as personal wealth, business ethics, and how to (or whether it is possible to) integrate religion and business.

Subjects: Business, Work

More: This book is a follow up to Nash's previous groundbreaking book called *Believers in Business* (Thomas Nelson, 1994). Readers may also be interested in David Ward Miller's recent history of the faith-at-work movement titled *God at Work: The History and Promise of the Faith at Work Movement* (Oxford University Press, 2007).

Pierce, Gregory F. Augustine.

Spirituality @ Work: 10 Ways to Balance Your Life On-the-Job. Loyola, 2005. 157 pp. ISBN 0829421165.

Gregory F. Augustine Pierce, past president of the National Center for the Laity and a founding member of Business Executives for Economic Justice, offers a workplace spirituality with a Catholic focus that can benefit all Christians. His workplace spirituality involves disciplines to help people deal with others, balance responsibilities, discover meaning in work, choose right and wrong, and more.

Subjects: Catholics, Work

Rundle, Steve, and Tom Steffen.

Great Commission Companies: The Emerging Role of Business in Missions. InterVarsity, 2003. 204 pp. ISBN 0830832270.

Believing that globalization is a part of God's plan to bring the gospel to the world, Steve Rundle and Tom Steffen write about the parallel impact of globalization on missions. In their research, they have spoken to hundreds of people working at for-profit companies that are impacting missions. The authors discuss these "great-commission" companies and profile five of them in the second part of the book. Rundle is an economics professor at Biola University, and Steffen is a former missionary in the Philippines and an intercultural studies professor at Biola.

Subject: Business and Missions

More: An essay by Rundle is included in another interesting book on this subject (which gives more case studies and essays) called *On Kingdom Business: Transforming Missions Through Entrepreneurial Strategies*, edited by Tetsunao Yamamori and Kenneth Eldred (Crossway, 2003).

Schultz, Bob.

Created for Work: Practical Insights for Young Men. Great Expectations, 2006. 181 pp. ISBN 1883934117. **YA**

Packed with man-sized wisdom for young men about work and character, this book has about thirty three- or four-page chapters on topics like confidence, difficulty, holding grudges, initiative, maintenance, greed, discouragement, vision, diligence, and more. All of the stories spring from Bob Schultz's on-the-job experience as a carpenter. The insights he shares are transferable to any job, career, or profession. Schultz desires to see young men who are honest, think creatively, and not scared to get dirty, work hard, and trust in God. He says these are the people who will become tomorrow's fathers, teachers, and leaders.

Subject: Attitude, Character, Work, Young-Adult Interest

More: Schultz has written a similar book (not limited to work-related virtues) called *Boyhood and Beyond: Practical Wisdom for Becoming a Man* (Great Expectations, 2004).

Sherman, Doug.

Your Work Matters to God. Navpress, 1987. 285 pp. ISBN 0891093729.

What does going to work have to do with Christianity? In this book, president of Career Impact Ministries Doug Sherman answers this question by presenting a biblical view of work. Sherman talks about a host of issues related to faith and work, including how to find the right job, how to handle income and leisure, and how to interact with other workers.

Subjects: Work

More: Another great book discussing the meaning of work and vocation (of doing everything for God's glory) is Gene Edward

Veith, Jr.'s, *God at Work: Your Christian Vocation in All of Life* (Crossway, 2002). Readers may also enjoy *Doing God's Business: Meaning and Motivation for the Marketplace* by R. Paul Stevens (Eerdmans, 2006).

Shook, Robert L., and David L. Steward.

Doing Business by the Good Book: 52 Lessons on Success Straight from the Bible. Hyperion, 2004. 288 pp. ISBN 1401300626.

David Steward is the founder and CEO of the nation's largest African American owned company. In this book, he describes how in 1990 he founded World Wide Technology, Inc., on biblical principles. Being an African American in the technology world, Steward faced resentment and adversity in various forms. This book is not so much a scriptural study as it is an examination of life and business, in which Steward discusses teamwork, mentoring, vision, competition, communication, branding, and other topics. He also talks about the importance of having a supportive spouse, as he found in his wife. Steward, cochairman of the St. Louis United Way, shares how he finds joy in giving back to his community by serving and tithing.

Subjects: African American Businessmen, Business, Chief Executive Officers

More: Another CEO writes about his radical approach to leadership and management in *Joy at Work: A Revolutionary Approach to Fun on the Job* by Dennis Bakke (PVB, 2005).

Silvoso, Ed.

Anointed for Business: How Christians Can Use Their Influence in the Marketplace to Change the World. Regal, 2002. 195 pp. ISBN 0830728619.

Christians who work at secular jobs are not second-class believers. Ed Silvoso, founder and president of Harvest Evangelism, says that Christians are called and anointed by God to minister in the marketplace. By "minister" Silvoso doesn't mean to merely talk about Jesus; he means that these people can also transform their jobs and their communities. He offers examples from the Bible that support this approach.

Subject: Business and Ministry

More: A very similar book is Rich Marshall's *God @ Work* (Destiny Image, 2000).

Whelchel, Mary.

The Christian Working Woman: What You Need to Know. 2nd Edition. Revell, 1998 (1986). 188 pp. ISBN 0800755375.

Mary Whelchel writes for women who go to the office every day. She shows the reader how to handle dirty jokes, cursing, and sexual remarks/harassment, and how to deal with stress, ambition, money, self-esteem, job-hunting, and fatigue. Whelchel also discusses handling relationships with fellow workers who are men.

Subjects: Women's Issues, Work

More: Verla Gillmor has a devotional book with fifty-two very short chapters for people in the workplace called *Reality Check: A Survival Manual for Christians in the Workplace* (Horizon, 2001). Gillmor writes about topics such as ambition, burnout, insecurity, waiting, sexual temptation, and conflict.

Whitwer, Glynnis.

Work@home: A Practical Guide for Women Who Want to Work from Home. New Hope, 2007. 237 pp. ISBN 1596690445.

Glynnis Whitwer shows readers how to work at home. She describes the three main types of home-based employment, including home-based businesses, direct-sell businesses, and telecommuting. For each of these three types of employment, Whitwer explains the pros and cons and gives practical advice about legal issues and financing. She also covers Internet issues, setting up a home office, and balancing work and home. Since working at home requires discipline and planning, Whitwer also covers scheduling, organizing, and budgeting.

Subjects: Home-Based Business, Telecommuting, Work

Personal Finance

Because the concept of tithing (giving ten percent of one's income to God) is found in the Bible, and because the Bible speaks against materialism, there is a market for books addressing these and related personal-finance issues for Christians. For many years, Larry Burkett (1939–2003) was the standard "go to" author for Christians. Now he has passed the baton to others, such as Ron Blue (author of *The New Master Your Money*) and Dave Ramsey (author of *The Total Money Makeover*). Ramsey's books on debt reduction have taken the book industry by storm, making them best sellers in both Christian and secular markets.

Alcorn, Randy.

Money, Possessions, and Eternity. Revised and updated edition. Tyndale, 2003 (1989). 503 pp. ISBN 0842353607.

What are Christians in America to do about wealth and materialism? Alcorn says that to gain the right perspective, Christians need to think of money and possessions in the light of eternity. Serious about tithing, he explains the importance of biblical giving to faith. He also offers advice on personal debt, church debt, investing, life insurance, retirement, and other financial issues that people face. Includes a twenty-five-page study guide.

Subjects: Materialism, Personal Finance, Tithing

More: *Rich in Every Way: Everything God Says About Money and Possessions* by Gene A. Getz (Howard Books, 2004). For an "oldie but goodie" on materialism, try *The Golden Cow: Materialism in the Twentieth-Century Church* by John White (InterVarsity, 1979).

Blue, Ron, and Jeremy White.

The New Master Your Money: A Step-by-Step Plan for Gaining and Enjoying Financial Freedom. 4th edition. Moody, 2004 (Thomas Nelson, 1978). 272 pp. ISBN 0802481612.

Ron Blue, financial planner, is a CPA with an MBA. In this book, he gives the reader biblical principles for money management. Building from there, Blue explains the objectives of financial planning and writes about guaranteed financial success, inflation, debt, tax planning, investment planning, and more. Blue provides many graphs, charts, and worksheets to both illustrate his points and help readers design a personal financial plan.

Subjects: Debt, Investments, Personal Finance

More: Howard Dayton, the CEO of Crown Financial Ministries, has a similar guide called *Your Money Map: A Proven 7-Step Guide to True Financial Freedom* (Moody, 2006). Also try *Family Finance Handbook: Discovering the Blessings of Financial Freedom* by Frank Damazio and Rich Brott (City Bible Publishing, 2004). Ron and Judy Blue also have a book to help couples communicate about money issues called *Money Talks and So Can We* (Zondervan, 1999).

Blue, Ron, and Jeremy White.

Splitting Heirs: Giving Your Money and Things to Your Children Without Ruining Their Lives. Northfield, 2004. 224 pp. ISBN 1881273059.

Christian financial planner Ron Blue shows readers how to transfer wealth to the next generation. He talks about financial decisions that need to be dealt with in light of a person's inevitable death: estate planning, taxes, and legal issues. Inheritance money, if not dealt with wisely, he says, can actually harm your children and grandchildren. Blue shows readers how to make decisions concerning in-laws, stepchildren, grandchildren, and others. One of his focuses is on giving money to the kingdom of God by wisely donating to charities.

Subjects: Estate Planning, Personal Finance, Wealth Transfer

More: To help organize your finances, plan your estate, and gather all your important financial information in one place, Crown Financial Ministries has a guide called *Set Your House in Order: A Workbook to Organize Your Finances and Plan Your Estate* (1998). Also see *Your Money After the Big 5-0: Wealth for the Second Half of Life* by Larry Burkett, Ron Blue, and Jeremy White (B&H Publishing, 2007).

Blue, Ron, Judy Blue, and Jeremy White.

Your Kids Can Master Their Money: Fun Ways to Help Them Learn How. Focus On The Family, 2006. 272 pp. ISBN 1589971914.

This book helps parents guide their children in understanding and applying financial concepts and principles. The authors (well-known Christian financial planners) show parents how to explain giving, shopping, planning, goal setting, investment, saving, earning interest, and other concepts. To help do this, the authors recommend games, movies, and books and include sample budget worksheets and charts. They also answer common questions that parents have about certain issues such as allowance.

Subjects: Parenting, Personal Finance—Children

More: *Financial Parenting: Showing Your Kids That Money Matters* by Larry Burkett and Rick Osborne (Moody, 1999).

Burkett, Larry, and Marnie Wooding.

Money Matters for Teens. Revised edition. Moody, 2001 (1997). 158 pp. ISBN 0802446361. **YA**

Founder of Christian Financial Concepts Larry Burkett writes for teens. He explains biblical concepts like stewardship and tithing, financial concepts such as banking, checking accounts, saving, debt, credit, and budgeting, and character issues like contentment, attitude, diligence, and generosity. Burkett also writes about getting a job, career planning, and starting a business.

Subjects: Personal Finance—Children, Personal Finance—Teenagers, Young-Adult Interest

More: Another book written for teenagers is *Discovering God's Way of Handling Money: A Financial Study for Teens* (Crown Financial Ministries, 2004) by Howard Dayton and Bev Dayton. For younger readers (eight- to twelve-year-old girls), try *The Christian Girl's Guide to Money* by Rebecca Park Totilo (Legacy Press, 2005) and Larry Burkett's *Money Matters for Kids* (Moody, 2001).

Burkett, Larry, and Randy Southern.

The World's Easiest Guide to Finances. Northfield, 2001. 409 pp. ISBN 1881273385.

Famous Christian finance expert Larry Burkett discusses personal finances, and shows how to budget money and escape debt. He also covers investments, savings, major purchases like cars, retirement, insurance, wills and trusts, and charitable giving. There are sections that address the needs of single parents, families, and single people. Many worksheets are included to help readers budget for vacations and for Christmas, pay off credit cards, and determine life-insurance needs. The book comes with a CD-ROM that has a budget calculator and debt-eliminator software.

Subjects: Debt, Personal Finance

More: Burkett has also written *Money Matters: Answers to Your Financial Questions* (Thomas Nelson, 2001).

Burkett, Larry, Ron Blue, and Jeremy White.

Your Money After the Big 5-0: Wealth for the Second Half of Life. B&H Publishing, 2007. 228 pp. ISBN 0805444327.

In this book, these popular Christian personal finance writers address money issues for older people. They show readers how to make income last for the rest of their lives. They talk about financial planning, decision-making, Social Security, retirement, insurance, investment, and more from a biblical perspective. There is also a section called "What Women Need to Know Before They Are Widows." First published as *Wealth to Last*.

Subjects: Investments, Personal Finance

More: Blue and White have a related book called *Splitting Heirs: Giving Your Money and Things to Your Children Without Ruining Their Lives* (Northfield, 2004). Also, to help organize finances, plan an estate, and gather all important financial information in one place (in case one spouse dies), Crown Financial Ministries has a guide called *Set Your House in Order: A Workbook to Organize Your Finances and Plan Your Estate* (1998).

Pope, Ethan.

Social Security: What's in It for You? Moody, 2005. 144 pp. ISBN 0802409733.

Certified financial planner Ethan Pope explains the Social Security Trust Fund and discusses the meaning of retirement. Asserting that Social Security is in trouble, he exposes some of the myths about Social Security, presents possible solutions that the government can follow, and shows readers how they can prepare financially for the future.

Subjects: Personal Finance, Social Security

Pope, Ethan.

Identity Theft: Protecting Yourself from an Unprotected World. Moody, 2006. 144 pp. ISBN 0802409741.

> Millions of Americans fall victim to identity theft each year. Certified financial planner Ethan Pope helps readers determine if they are at risk for this crime, and shows how to avoid getting scammed. Pope discusses credit reports, credit card fraud, and how to recover from identity theft. He also lists resources to get help for these and similar issues.
>
> **Subjects:** Identity Theft, Personal Finance

Pryor, Austin.

The Sound Mind Investing Handbook: A Step-by-Step Guide to Managing Your Money from a Biblical Perspective. 4th Edition. Sound Mind Investing, 2004 (Moody, 1993). 368 pp. ISBN 0970595611.

> This book teaches readers all about investing. Pryor explains mutual funds, bonds, stock market basics, and portfolios. He describes different types of risks and strategies and gives advice for retirement planning, including Social Security, work pensions, IRAs, and annuities. A large appendix reprints more than twenty articles from Austin Pryor's *Sound Mind Investing* newsletter on topics such as debt, credit cards, housing, paying for college, interest rates, load funds, and life insurance.
>
> **Subjects:** Investments, Personal Finance
>
> **More:** For another book on investing, try *A Christian's Guide to Investing* by stockbroker Danny Fontana (Revell, 2005). He explains different types of investments and the most common mistakes investors make. He also talks about business cycles, risk, greed, retirement plans, and taxes.

Ramsey, Dave.

The Total Money Makeover: A Proven Plan for Financial Fitness. Revised and updated edition. Nelson, 2007 (2003). 272 pp. ISBN 0785289089.

> Dave Ramsey is a nationally syndicated talk-radio host with a show about life and money. In this book, a *New York Times* best seller, Ramsey shows readers how to get out of debt and get their finances in order. He explains the "debt snowball" which is his strategy for becoming debt free. Ramsey includes the testimonies of many people who have successfully used this strategy as well as answers to common money myths.
>
> **Subjects:** Debt, Personal Finance

More: Three more titles about debt are *Debt-Proof Your Marriage: How to Achieve Financial Harmony* by Mary Hunt (Baker, 2003), *Free and Clear: God's Roadmap to Debt-Free Living* by Howard Dayton (Moody, 2006), and *Debt-Free Living* by Larry Burkett (Moody, 2001).

Leadership

Jesus Christ is generally considered to be one of history's greatest leaders. It is not just Christian ministers who have sought to model Christ's leadership; business leaders have also studied Christ's teachings and methods of leading others. The concept of servant leadership (exemplified by Christ in Mark 10:42–45) has had an interesting influence on corporate culture, as evidenced in the writings of Robert K. Greenleaf, who first pioneered the idea of servant leadership in 1970. Servant leadership has resulted in a host of management/leadership books over the last few decades by authors such as Max De Pree and Ken Blanchard. Here are books not only for managers and business leaders but also for church leaders or any kind of leader who seeks to guide with Christian principles.

Allender, Dan B.

Leading with a Limp: Turning Your Struggles into Strengths. Water-Brook, 2006. 224 pp. ISBN 1578569508.

> Dan Allender, a therapist and the president of Mars Hill Graduate School, shows readers how to be a leader when everything goes wrong. Leaders are not perfect; neither are the people they work with, he says. Addressing issues like failure, stress, ambition, admitting faults, the loneliness and the burden of leading, facing crises, betrayal, and exhaustion, Allender offers guidance and support. He also discusses forming character in others and the importance of community. Some of his examples are drawn from the business world, but most of them come from various church ministries or his experience as one of the founders of Mars Hill Graduate School in Seattle, Washington.
>
> **Subjects:** Failure, Leadership

Bakke, Dennis W.

Joy at Work: A Revolutionary Approach to Fun on the Job. PVB, 2005. 314 pp. ISBN 0976268604.

> Dennis Bakke, cofounder and former CEO (1994–2002) of AES Corporation, describes a kind of leadership that treats employees as people with dignity and allows for an employment situation

where people actually enjoy their work and experience personal growth on the job. Rejecting the idea of dividing people into management and labor, he suggests giving employees the freedom to make important decisions. Having the word "fun" in the title may mislead readers into thinking that this is a trivial book, but the ideas presented here are serious, and Bakke has successfully implemented them all over the world. He offers insights on humility, love, courage, dignity, accountability, and joy—concepts that are too often rare in corporate and workplace environments.

Subjects: Chief Executive Officers, Leadership, Management

Blanchard, Ken.

The Heart of a Leader: Insights on the Art of Influence. Cook Communications, 1999. 160 pp. ISBN 1562924885.

Businessman Ken Blanchard is famous for his management and leadership books, including *The One Minute Manager*. This book is a collection of his favorite sayings along with commentary about each. The quotes have been gleaned from his books and other sources.

Subject: Leadership

Butler, Phill.

Well Connected: Releasing Power and Restoring Hope Through Kingdom Partnerships. Authentic Media, 2005. 332 pp. ISBN 1932805540.

What are the keys to effective kingdom collaboration and ministry partnership? How can God's people work together across organizational lines to achieve a common vision? How can the skills and services of Christian ministries and individuals be harnessed and mobilized effectively to reach a community? Former journalist and head of Intercristo, Phill Butler (now director of Vision Synergy), says we need to be "well connected." He uses this book to show us how, by presenting effective strategies, practical advice, case histories, and stories of others who have failed and succeeded.

Subjects: Leadership, Ministry—Collaboration

De Pree, Max.

Leadership Is an Art. Currency, 2004 (Michigan State University Press, 1987). 176 pp. ISBN 0385512465.

Noted leader and businessman Max De Pree writes about leadership from a human perspective. Understanding that people are made in the image of God affects our beliefs and attitudes toward people and leadership. In this vein, De Pree talks about intimacy, passion, the worth of individuals and their talents, respect, communication, and covenantal relationships.

Subject: Leadership

More: De Pree also wrote *Leading Without Power: Finding Hope in Serving Community* (Jossey-Bass, 2003), which deals with nonprofits—as does his book *Called to Serve: Creating and Nurturing the Effective Volunteer Board* (Eerdmans, 2001).

Ford, Leighton.

Transforming Leadership: Jesus' Way of Creating Vision, Shaping Values, and Empowering Change. InterVarsity, 1991. 308 pp. ISBN 0830816526.

Leighton Ford examines Jesus' ministry as a model for leadership today, and gives many stories from famous contemporaries that address the issue of leadership. Ford, a leader in the Lausanne Committee on World Evangelization, is Billy Graham's brother-in-law.

Subject: Leadership

Greenleaf, Robert K.

Servant Leadership: A Journey into the Nature of Legitimate Power and Greatness. 25th Anniversary edition. Paulist Press, 2002 (1977). 370 pp. ISBN 0809105543.

Robert K. Greenleaf (1904–1990), a famous management consultant and director of management research at AT&T for many years, coined the phrase "servant leadership," which started a remarkable movement in the world of management ideas and publishing. Greenleaf's idea that institutions do not exist to glory in their power but to serve people was a paradigm shift for many. This book, first published in 1977, is a collection of articles in which Greenleaf defines servant leadership, gives biographical profiles, and applies the notion of servant leadership to various situations and fields including trustees, universities, foundations, churches, and businesses.

Subjects: Classics, Leadership, Management

More: Don Frick wrote a biography of Greenleaf (which includes a discussion of his spirituality) called *Robert K. Greenleaf: A Life of Servant Leadership* (Berrett-Koehler, 2004). Larry Spears, president of the Robert K. Greenleaf Center, and Michele Lawrence edited a collection of essays on servant leadership titled *Practicing Servant Leadership: Succeeding Through Trust, Bravery, and Forgiveness* (Jossey-Bass, 2004).

Hewitt, Hugh.

In, but Not Of: A Guide to Christian Ambition and the Desire to Influence the World. Nelson, 2003. 213 pp. ISBN 0785263950.

Hugh Hewitt says that Christians need to seek and acquire influence, explaining that this can be used to change the world. However, influence does not come automatically or by wishful thinking. In this book, Hewitt offers shrewd and practical advice for Christians who are serious about making a mark in the world—Christians such as William Wilberforce, who used his influence in Great Britain's Parliament to end the British slave trade. He specifies good choices to make and bad choices to avoid. He discusses what books to read and what cities to move to (for people really serious about being agents of change). He also gives advice for dealing with personal flaws, being a good conversationalist, success on the job, choosing a church, and many other topics. Several chapters address younger readers who are still making choices about college, personal life, and career. Hewitt is the host of a nationally syndicated radio talk-show (*The Hugh Hewitt Show*) and a law school professor at Chapman University.

Subjects: College, Leadership, Vocational Guidance, Work

Hybels, Bill.

Courageous Leadership. Zondervan, 2002. 253 pp. ISBN 031024823X.

Bill Hybels shares thirty years of wisdom gained from leading Willow Creek Community Church, the famed megachurch located in a Chicago suburb. He discusses burnout, endurance, vision, action, decision-making, finding financial resources, and developing a personal leadership style. In a chapter on self-leadership, Hybels gives pointers on self-management and self-discipline. These pages represent hard-learned lessons that can help not just other pastors, but other leaders who want to use their talents to the fullest degree possible.

Subject: Leadership

More: Hybels refers to one of Catholic writer Garry Wills' books, which gives biographical portraits of sixteen leaders, including Franklin Roosevelt, Harriet Tubman, Napoleon, King David, Socrates, Mary Baker Eddy, and others. The title is *Certain Trumpets: The Nature of Leadership* (Simon and Schuster, 1994).

Jones, Laurie Beth.

Jesus CEO: Using Ancient Wisdom for Visionary Leadership. Hyperion, 1996. 352 pp. ISBN 0786881267.

Laurie Beth Jones, a seminar speaker and consultant, centers her guidance on Jesus' leadership ability. She divides the book into three areas: Jesus' self-mastery, Jesus' strength of action, and Jesus' strength of relationships. Through Jesus' example, Jones shows readers how to empower others with confident leadership.

Subject: Leadership

More: Another book that examines Jesus' example in the Bible is *Leadership Lessons of Jesus* by Bob Briner and Ray Pritchard (B&H Publishing, 1997).

Maxwell, John C.

Developing the Leader Within You. 2nd Revised edition. Thomas Nelson, 2005 (1993). 208 pp. ISBN 0785281126.

In this classic book on leadership (first published in 1993), John Maxwell defines leadership (in a word, leadership is influence) and describes five different levels of leadership. For instance, the first and lowest level is position. At this stage, people follow because they have to. The next level is permission. At this stage, people follow because they want to. The levels go up from there. Maxwell also discusses integrity, creating positive change, attitude, vision, self-discipline, staff development, and more.

Subject: Leadership

More: Maxwell also wrote *Developing the Leaders Around You: How to Help Others Reach Their Full Potential* (Thomas Nelson, 2005) and *The 21 Irrefutable Laws of Leadership* (Thomas Nelson, 1998).

Sanders, J. Oswald.

Spiritual Leadership. Moody, 1994 (1967). 189 pp. ISBN 0802467997.

J. Oswald Sanders (1917–1992), a Christian leader and author of more than forty books, worked as an administrator at the Bible College of New Zealand and as the director of the China Inland Mission (now Overseas Missionary Fellowship). In this classic book (first published in 1967), Sanders defines leadership and contrasts natural and spiritual leadership. He discusses fifteen essential qualities of leaders, including vision, discipline, decisiveness, wisdom, humor, and patience. He describes vital disciplines for leaders, like prayer and reading, and he gives insights from biblical leaders such as Peter, Paul, Nehemiah, and Moses. Toward the end of the book, Sanders talks about the various perils of leadership, including pride, popularity, and depression.

Subjects: Leadership, Ministry

More: Another book on the topic is *Spiritual Leadership: Moving People to God's Agenda* by Henry and Richard Blackaby (B&H Publishing, 2001).

Bibliographies

Hammond, Pete, R. Paul Stevens, and Todd Svanoe.

The Marketplace Annotated Bibliography: A Christian Guide to Books on Work, Business & Vocation. InterVarsity, 2002. 222 pp. ISBN 0830826726.

> This annotated list includes more than 1,200 books on topics of interest to Christians related to business and the workplace. It was compiled by two ministers and a writer/publicist to help people integrate their faith with their careers.
>
> **Subjects:** Best Books, Business, Work—Bibliography

Chapter 7

Science and Nature

Introduction

For Christians, nature is the handiwork of a loving and wise creator. For thousands of years, nature has inspired people to praise God for the luxurious beauty and generous provision that is found around the planet. In Psalm 19, David wrote, "The heavens declare the glory of God; the skies proclaim the work of his hands."

Today, nature is still a source of inspiration—and investigation. The natural world is the sole object of scientific study. People are often surprised to learn that some of the most famous scientists in history were devout Christians. The list includes men such as astronomer Johannes Kepler, mathematician Blaise Pascal, Robert Boyle (the founder of modern chemistry), John Dalton (the father of modern atomic theory), Gregor Mendel (the father of genetics), and James Clerk Maxwell (the father of modern physics).

This chapter collects a wide range of books related to the natural world and science: nature writing, gardening, animals, pets, astronomy, evolution, hunting, the history of science, environmentalism, and other topics—all from a Christian perspective.

Science and Faith

Many people mistakenly believe that Christians cannot be scientists or that science is inherently anti-Christian. This is simply not true. Science is basically gathering knowledge of the natural world through observation and experimentation. Christians refer to the natural world as "creation." For Christians, studying creation goes hand in hand with scriptural mandates like Genesis 1:28: "Be fruitful and increase in number; fill the earth and subdue it. Rule over the fish of the sea and the birds of the air and over every living creature that moves on the ground." The books in this section show where Christianity and science conflict, where they agree, and how they can be reconciled.

Chappell, Dorothy F., and E. David Cook, editors.

Not Just Science: Questions Where Christian Faith and Natural Science Intersect. Zondervan, 2005. 308 pp. ISBN 0310263832.

This book is a collection of essays from more than twenty-five professors from Wheaton, Calvin, and Dordt colleges on a variety of topics and scientific disciplines. For instance, mathematics professor Terence Perciante answers the question, "Whose idea was mathematics"; geology professor Stephen Moshier addresses, "Is God responsible for natural disasters?"; and engineering professor Gayle Ermer asks, "Does engineering contribute to a better future?" There are essays on environmental stewardship, computer science, geology, physics, technology, chemistry, health care, pharmaceuticals, and much more.

Subjects: Chemistry, Computer Science, Engineering, Geology, Mathematics, Natural Disasters, Physics, Science and Faith, Technology

Forster, Roger, and Paul Marston.

Reason, Science and Faith. Wipf and Stock, 2001 (Monarch, 1999). 479 pp. ISBN 1579106617.

This hefty book is packed with a wealth of information on science and faith. The authors discuss the history of science, the historical interpretation of Genesis and in light of modern science, miracles, evolution, young-earth creation science, intelligent design, and more. One section gives a helpful overview of different Christian approaches to science. The authors present a strong case for an old earth. Paul Marston, senior lecturer in the faculty of science at the University of Central Lancashire and a minister with the London-based Ichthus Fellowship, studied theology and mathematics at Cambridge and has won a Templeton prize for one of his courses on science and Christianity. Roger Forster is a Cambridge graduate and the founder of the Ichthus Christian Fellowship in England.

Subjects: Age of Earth, Apologetics, Evolution, Intelligent Design, Philosophy, Science—History, Science and Faith

More: *Science and Christianity: Four Views,* edited by Richard Carlson (InterVarsity, 2000), explores the relationship between science and faith by offering four different approaches.

Gingerich, Owen.

God's Universe. Belknap Press of Harvard University Press, 2006. 139 pp. ISBN 0674023706.

This slim volume, adapted from the 2005 William Belden Noble Lectures given by Harvard professor of astronomy and history of science Owen Gingerich, asks if it is safe for scientists to believe in intelligent design in nature. Although his answer is yes, he does not endorse intelligent design as a movement because it is not true science. Gingerich also discusses the "fine-tuning" of the universe, evolution, and historical figures such as Nicolaus Copernicus, Johannes Kepler, and Galileo Galilei.

Subjects: Anthropic Principle, Science and Faith, Theistic Evolution

More: The following two books are excellent collections of essays which include pieces by Gingerich: *Spiritual Evolution: Scientists Discuss Their Beliefs*, edited by John Marks Templeton and Kenneth Seeman Giniger (Templeton Foundation Press, 1998), and *Is God a Creationist?: The Religious Case Against Creation-Science*, edited by Roland Mushat Frye (Scribner's, 1983).

Hyers, Conrad M.

The Meaning of Creation: Genesis and Modern Science. John Knox Press, 1984. 203 pp. ISBN 0804201250.

Professor of religion Conrad Hyers examines Genesis and concludes that the creation account is not a scientific document. He asserts that reading Genesis in its historical context unburdens the reader from hostility between the Bible and modern science. Still in print after twenty years, this book is still relevant today for its instruction in biblical interpretation and its guidance on religion and science.

Subjects: Biblical Interpretation, Creationism, Evolution, Genesis, Science and Faith

More: Readers may also be interested in an early and influential book on science and faith called *The Christian View of Science and Scripture* by Bernard Ramm (Eerdmans, 1954).

Pearcey, Nancy, and Charles B. Thaxton.

The Soul of Science: Christian Faith and Natural Philosophy. Crossway, 1994. 298 pp. ISBN 0891077669.

In their solid overview of the history of science, Nancy Pearcey and Charles B. Thaxton show how the birth and rise of modern science is indebted to the Christian worldview. Part Two covers the first scientific revolution, which involves Isaac Newton and the field of biology. Part Three has two chapters on mathematics.

Part Four is about the second scientific revolution, which involves Albert Einstein, relativity, quantum physics, and DNA. This book is part of the Turning Point Christian Worldview Series.

Subjects: Mathematics, Science—History, Science and Faith

Polkinghorne, John C.

One World: The Interaction of Science and Theology. Templeton Foundation Press, 2007. 160 pp. ISBN 1599471116.

This was one of the first books on science and faith that Polkinghorne wrote after he gave up his chair as professor of mathematical physics at Cambridge to become an Anglican priest (it was first published in 1986). In it, Polkinghorne makes the point that scientists and theologians are both studying "one world." Science and theology are different aspects of that "one world," he says, but they are complementary, not opposing disciplines.

Subjects: Science and Faith, Theistic Evolution

More: For a more recent title by Polkinghorne, try *Science and the Trinity: The Christian Encounter with Reality* (Yale University Press, 2004). For two other prominent scientist-theologians, try *Creation and the World of Science: The Re-Shaping of Belief* by Arthur Peacocke (Oxford University Press, 2004) and *When Science Meets Religion: Enemies, Strangers, or Partners?* by Ian G. Barbour (HarperSanFrancisco, 2000).

Ratzsch, Del.

Science & Its Limits: The Natural Sciences in Christian Perspective. 2nd Edition. InterVarsity, 2000 (1986). 191 pp. ISBN 0830815805.

Del Ratzsch, professor of philosophy at Calvin College, discusses the nature and scope of science. He describes the traditional conception of science, including such people and ideas as Francis Bacon, Karl Popper, rationality, empirical data, objectivity, positivism, and falsification. Then he moves on to Thomas Kuhn and the postempiricist philosophy of science. Ratzsch explores what science can and cannot tell us. He then examines so-called scientific challenges to religious belief as well as intelligent-design issues. This book was first published with the title *Philosophy of Science: The Natural Sciences in Christian Perspective.*

Subjects: Science—Philosophy, Science and Faith

Ross, Hugh, Kenneth Samples, and Mark Clark.

Lights in the Sky & Little Green Men: A Rational Christian Look at UFOs and Extraterrestrials. NavPress, 2002. 255 pp. ISBN 1576832082.

The authors cover a broad range of issues involving UFOs, including types of UFOs, life on other planets, alien abductions, government cover-ups (including Roswell, Project Blue Book, and Area 51), residual UFOs, and UFO cults. Ultimately, they conclude that, in a few cases, something unusual is happening, and it probably has something to do with the supernatural realm. They then discuss what the Bible has to say about this.

Subject: UFOs

More: For a different perspective (leaving room for the existence of alien life), see *Alone in the Universe?: Aliens, the X-Files & God* by David Wilkinson (InterVarsity, 1997).

Ward, Keith.

Pascal's Fire: Scientific Faith and Religious Understanding. Oneworld Publications, 2006. 270 pp. ISBN 1851684468.

Theologian and philosopher Keith Ward, an ordained priest in the Church of England, is professor of divinity at Gresham College, London, and a proponent of theistic evolution. In this book, Ward examines many facets of the science and religion debate. Concerning cosmology, he writes about the fine-tuning of the universe and the many-worlds theory. He presents different ways to interpret evolution, genetics, how the soul emerged, quantum physics, life after death, and more.

Subjects: Anthropic Principle, Cosmology, Evolution, Quantum Physics, Science and Faith, Theistic Evolution, Theology

More: Ward also wrote *God, Faith, and the New Millennium: Christian Belief in an Age of Science* (Oneworld Publications, 1998). Readers who like Ward will also enjoy *One World: The Interaction of Science and Theology* by J. C. Polkinghorne (Templeton Foundation Press, 2007) and *Creation and the World of Science: The Re-Shaping of Belief* by Arthur Peacocke (Oxford University Press, 2004).

Wilkinson, David.

Alone in the Universe?: Aliens, the X-Files & God. Saltshaker Books, 1998. 156 pp. ISBN 083081938X.

After giving a brief history of UFO alien phenomena, David Wilkinson discusses evidence for life on Mars, whether other planets could sustain life, and efforts to receive/transmit messages to other life forms. He considers the idea that the Bible records alien encounters. Wilkinson is a fellow of the Royal Astronomical Society in England and a Christian, but he does not deny the existence of aliens. This book offers a balanced alternative to typical Christian rejection of alien life.

Subject: UFOs

More: For a different perspective, see *Lights in the Sky & Little Green Men: A Rational Christian Look at UFOs and Extraterrestrials* by Hugh Ross, Kenneth Samples, and Mark Clark (NavPress, 2002).

Wood, Nathan R.

The Trinity in the Universe. Kregel, 1978 (Revell, 1932). 220 pp. ISBN 0825440130.

Formerly titled *The Secret of the Universe*, this unique book shows how the trinity is the pattern for the structure of creation. Nathan R. Wood breaks down all that exists into three categories: space, matter, and time. Each of these also consists of three elements. Space has three dimensions: length, breadth, and height. Matter consists of energy, motion, and phenomena (for example, light, color, sound, etc.). Time is also a trinity: past, present, and future. The science may be dated, and Wood is not a scientist, but this book still holds interest.

Subjects: Cosmology, Science and Faith, Trinity

More: Two other, older books that are valuable for their creative insights into science and humanity are *Science and Faith* by Arthur C. Custance (volume eight of the Doorway Papers, Zondervan, 1978) and *The King of the Earth: The High Calling of Man According to the Bible and Science* by Erich Sauer (Paternoster, 1959).

Nature

People are part of nature, and Philip Yancey's award-winning *Fearfully and Wonderfully Made* artfully describes the glory and fascinating design of the human body. As for the rest of nature, this section includes nature writing by Thomas Merton and Annie Dillard and theological meditations by Mark Futato.

Stewardship of the earth is a growing concern in the Christian community; therefore, books on ecology and environmental protection are included in this chapter. Many Christians feel an obligation to understand and care for the world that we live in and share with the rest of creation. In Genesis 1:28, God tells Adam and Eve: "Be fruitful and increase in number; fill the earth and subdue it. Rule over the fish of the sea and the birds of the air and over every living creature that moves on the ground." To Christians, God's creation is both a gift and a responsibility. Recently, there have been more books by Christian publishers calling believers to care for nature.

The Human Body

Cosgrove, Mark P.

The Amazing Body Human: God's Design for Personhood. Baker, 1987. 202 pp. ISBN 0801025176.

> Mark P. Cosgrove examines the anatomical differences between humans and animals to show that we are designed in God's image, for personhood. Extolling the many wonders of the human body, he discusses the face, the skin, sexuality, childhood, the brain, the foot, and more. This fascinating book is out of print, but it clearly and uniquely shows how the image and purpose of God manifests in the design of our bodies.
>
> **Subjects:** Design in Nature, Human Body, Nature

Swenson, Richard A.

More Than Meets the Eye: Fascinating Glimpses of God's Power and Design. NavPress, 2000. 205 pp. ISBN 1576830691.

> Richard A. Swenson, a physician and former medical school professor, explores the wonders of nature, finding God's artistry and genius everywhere. He starts by examining the human body, including the heart, blood, lungs, the senses, the brain and nervous system, cells and DNA, and the skin. He moves on to discuss more conceptual topics, such as physics, energy, stars, time, space, and light.
>
> **Subjects:** Human Body, Nature

Yancey, Philip, and Paul Brand.

Fearfully and Wonderfully Made. Zondervan, 1997 (1980). 224 pp. ISBN 031035451X.

> An award-winning writer and a world-famous hand surgeon team up to give readers an opportunity to behold the glory of the human body from a biological and biblical perspective. This book is divided into four sections about cells, bones, skin, and motion. Each fact-filled section discusses the wonders of God's design of the human body, and correlates it to the church (the body of Christ).
>
> **Subjects:** Award Winners (ECPA), Human Body, Nature
>
> **More:** Yancey and Brand also collaborated on the sequel to this book called *In His Image* (Zondervan, 1997). Another book by both authors is *The Gift of Pain* (Zondervan, 1997). For a biography of Paul Brand, see *Ten Fingers for God: The Life and Work of Dr. Paul Brand* by Dorothy Clarke Wilson (Paul Brand Publishing, 1996).

Animals

Keller, W. Phillip.

Lessons from a Sheep Dog: A True Story of Transforming Love. W Publishing Group, 2002 (1983). 75 pp. ISBN 0849917654.

W. Phillip Keller's border collie, Lass, helps him on his sheep ranch. Lass's previous owner was cruel, so Keller had to patiently train Lass to do the job she was meant to do. Keller shows how Lass's transformation has spiritual parallels to our lives as Christians.

Subject: Animals

More: Keller is best-known for his classic book, *A Shepherd Looks at Psalm 23* (Zondervan, 2007).

Linzey, Andrew.

Animal Gospel. Westminster John Knox Press, 2000. 171 pp. ISBN 0664221939.

Andrew Linzey, an Anglican priest, theologian, and authority on Christianity and animals, is the director of the Oxford Centre for Animal Ethics. In this book, he discusses how the gospel applies to animals, along with animal rights, animal cruelty in scientific research, and certain issues in biotechnology such as cloning.

Subject: Animal Rights

More: Another book on animal welfare and ethics is Robert N. Wennberg's *God, Humans, and Animals: An Invitation to Enlarge Our Moral Universe* (Eerdmans, 2006). Stephen Webb writes about animals, pets, and theology in *On God and Dogs: A Christian Theology of Compassion for Animals* (Oxford University Press, 2002). For a book on pets, try *All God's Creatures: The Blessing of Animal Companionship* by Debra K. Farrington (Paraclete Press, 2006).

Stott, John.

The Birds Our Teachers: Biblical Lessons from a Lifelong Bird-Watcher. Baker, 2001 (Shaw, 1999). 96 pp. ISBN 0801012384.

Anglican minister John Stott is also a bird-watcher and photographer. In this book, he presents fascinating bird facts and discusses various birding expeditions he has been on. In discussing the natural wonders of birds, he weaves in spiritual truths. Stott includes more than 150 full-color photos in this beautiful book.

Subject: Birds

More: For a wonderful collection of bird encounters, try *Under His Wings: What I Learned from God While Watching Birds* by Joy DeKok and Cristine Bolley (Barbour, 2002). Also try *Conversations with a Barred Owl* by Edith Margaret Clarkson (Zondervan, 1974).

Ecology and Environmental Protection

Hoezee, Scott.

Remember Creation: God's World of Wonder and Delight. Eerdmans, 2006. 132 pp. ISBN 0802844707.

God gave Adam the charge to rule over creation, but does this mean we have the right to trash it? Should Christians resent efforts to preserve the environment? What does our attitude toward ecology reveal about our theology? Scott Hoezee, an ordained pastor in the Christian Reformed Church, answers these questions in this brief, easy-to-read book about enjoying and valuing God's creation.

Subjects: Ecology, Nature

More: In *Living the Good Life on God's Good Earth* by David Koetje, editor (Faith Alive, 2006), Christian scholars write about stewardship of the earth, addressing issues such as the clothes we wear, the food we eat, the energy we use, and work, rest, and play.

Pratney, Winkie.

Healing the Land: A Supernatural View of Ecology. Chosen, 1993. 236 pp. ISBN 0800792106.

Winkie Pratney asserts that people's sin affects the environment—not just due to natural causes, but also because of God's judgment. He explains how famine and pestilence have spiritual causes. Pratney also questions our understanding about the nature of nature, asking questions such as, "Can plants and animals respond to unseen spiritual dimensions?"

Subjects: Ecology, Nature

Schaeffer, Francis, and Udo Middlemann.

Pollution and the Death of Man: The Christian View of Ecology. Crossway, 1992 (Tyndale, 1970). 168 pp. ISBN 0891076867.

In this brief but classic book, Schaeffer illustrates how our worldviews affect our behavior toward nature. He discusses Eastern religion, pantheism, and the Christian view of nature and environmental crisis.

Subjects: Ecology, Nature

More: Readers may also enjoy *The Reenchantment of Nature: The Denial of Religion and the Ecological Crisis* by Alister McGrath (Doubleday, 2003).

Sleeth, J. Matthew.

Serve God, Save the Planet: A Christian Call to Action. Zondervan, 2007. 256 pp. ISBN 0310275342.

> J. Matthew Sleeth, a medical doctor, gave up his materialistic lifestyle to focus on creation care. As a doctor, he saw patients dying from cancer and other ailments that pointed to environmental causes. He concluded that if we clean up our environment and rethink the way we live our lives in industry and in our homes, problems (like health, pollution, overpopulation, etc.) can be fixed and prevented. Sleeth cuts through many of the excuses that Christians have, such as, "I'll be dead before the oceans play out" and "Tree huggers worship nature; I don't want to be involved with them." He shows that living out your faith concerning these issues involves many areas of life, including, work, rest, parenting, health, entertainment, nutrition, and more.

> **Subjects:** Ecology, Environmental Protection

> **More:** *Saving God's Green Earth: Rediscovering the Church's Responsibility to Environmental Stewardship* by Tri Robinson and Jason Chatraw (Ampelon Publishing, 2006).

Van Dyke, Fred, David C. Mahan, Joseph K. Sheldon, and Raymond H. Brand.

Redeeming Creation: The Biblical Basis for Environmental Stewardship. InterVarsity, 1996. 213 pp. ISBN 0830818723.

> The authors, Christian biologists, discuss the value of creation, the place of humanity in God's creation, ecology and the Christian mind, and more. This book includes such issues as acid rain, global warming, population explosion, rain forest destruction, ozone layer depletion, and national parks.

> **Subjects:** Ecology, Environmental Protection, Nature

> **More:** Try *Earth-Wise: A Biblical Response to Environmental Issues* by Calvin B. Dewitt (Faith Alive, 1994). Steven Bouma-Prediger presents a theological case for creation care in his book *For the Beauty of the Earth: A Christian Vision for Creation Care* (Baker Academic, 2001).

General Nature

Becknell, Thomas, compiler.

Of Earth and Sky: Spiritual Lessons from Nature. Augsburg, 2001. 156 pp. ISBN 0806642602.

Thomas Becknell has collected poems and short essays about nature by classic and contemporary writers. Wendell Berry, Kathleen Norris, Henry David Thoreau, Thomas Merton, Rainer Maria Rilke, and others write about faith, hope, living, and the natural world.

Subjects: Essays, Nature

More: Another collection of nature writtings by famous writers is *A Spiritual Field Guide: Meditations for the Outdoors* by Bernard Brady and Mark Neuzil, editors (Brazos, 2005). For some brief essays/meditations about nature and the outdoors, try Ernest Herndon's *Nature Trails and Gospel Tales: Stories of Grace from the Wilds of Mississippi* (InterVarsity, 2004).

Cruise, Jason.

The Heart of the Sportsman: Strategies, Tips and Thoughts for Going Beyond the Chase. B&H Publishing, 2004. 127 pp. ISBN 0805430946.

Jason Cruise gives both hunting tips and spiritual advice in this brief, colorfully illustrated book. Topics covered include camouflage, calling, scent control, fishing, and deer hunting. Cruise, a pastor and a hunter, is involved with the outdoors-ministry movement and directs the Tennessee Outdoor Network.

Subjects: Hunting, Nature

More: A similar book by outdoorsman, musician, and motivational speaker Joey Hancock is *Success Afield: Stories of a Sportman's Life* (B&H Publishing, 2006). Cruise has also cowritten, with Jimmy Sites, *Into the High Country: Spiritual Outdoor Adventures* (B&H Publishing, 2006).

Dillard, Annie.

Pilgrim at Tinker Creek. Harper Perennial Modern Classics, 2007 (1974). 304 pp. ISBN 0061233323.

Annie Dillard (1945–) is an American poet, novelist, essayist, and diarist. Through her personal nonfiction narrative (Dillard notes on her Web site that this book is not a collection of essays), the reader views the world of nature as found in Tinker Creek, located in a valley of Virginia's Blue Ridge Mountains. From small frogs to giant water bugs, Dillard captures the mystery, terror, and wonder of the world. This book won the Pulitzer Prize for general nonfiction in 1975.

Subjects: Creative Nonfiction, Nature Writing

More: Dillard has authored many other books, including more nature writing in her "one and only collection of essays" called

Teaching a Stone to Talk: Expeditions and Encounters (Harper and Row, 1982). Fans of Dillard may also enjoy Kathleen Norris's *Dakota: A Spiritual Geography* (Houghton Mifflin, 1993).

Futato, Mark D.

Creation: A Witness to the Wonder of God. P&R Publishing, 2000. 121 pp. ISBN 0875522033.

Mark D. Futato, professor of Old Testament at Reformed Theological Seminary in Orlando, explains how "the heavens declare the glory of God" as stated in Psalm 19. He describes how God's attributes—glory, power, wisdom, love, justice, and faithfulness—are revealed through the natural world.

Subjects: Attributes of God, Nature

Kehler, Laurie Ostby.

Gardening Mercies: Finding God in Your Garden. Bethany, 2001. 202 pp. ISBN 0764223933.

Reflecting on her past and present gardening endeavors, Laurie Ostby Kehler relates them to spiritual issues. Demonstrating her love of gardening, she covers topics from weeding and composting to pruning, noting similarities in the ways in which God works in our lives. Kehler is the daughter and granddaughter of award-winning gardeners.

Subject: Gardening

More: Niki Anderson gives fifty short meditations/essays on plants and gardening in *What I Learned from God While Gardening* (Promise Press, 2000). Also try *A Gardener Looks at the Fruits of the Spirit* by W. Phillip Keller (W Publishing, 1987). For more life lessons through gardening, try *The Garden of the Soul: Cultivating Your Spiritual Life* by Keri Wyatt Kent (InterVarsity, 2002).

Merton, Thomas.

When the Trees Say Nothing: Writings on Nature. Sorin, 2003. 192 pp. ISBN 1893732606.

Thomas Merton was a famous Catholic author and a Trappist monk. This book, edited by Kathleen Deignan and illustrated by John Giuliani, collects hundreds of snippets and paragraphs of Merton's writings on nature. Deignan arranges them by themes such as winter, spring, fire, water, sky and clouds, sun and moon, animals, rain, mountains, and so on. Some of the writings focus on ecological and environmental issues.

Subjects: Animals, Catholics, Ecology, Nature

More: For another collection of nature writing, this time by various authors, try *Canticles of the Earth: Celebrating the Presence of God in Nature* by Lynne Bachleda, editor (Loyola, 2004). Also try *The View from Goose Ridge: Watching Nature, Seeing Life* by Women-of-Faith.com columnist Cheryl Bostrom (Thomas Nelson, 2001) and *Ask the Animals: Spiritual Wisdom from All God's Creatures* by Elizabeth J. Canham (Morehouse, 2006).

Creationism and Evolution

In the scientific community, Darwinian evolution is by far the most reliable explanation for the origin and development of life on earth. Many Christians disagree. Some Christian schools of thought depart radically from this common scientific understanding, and some agree almost totally with the scientific community. Thus, there is diversity within the Christian community, and a continuum of ideas that begins with young-earth creationists. There are four main Christian schools of thought: young-earth creation science, old-earth creation science, intelligent design, and theistic evolution.

Young-earth creationists are the most widely known group and the most critical of current science. They hold to a narrow (or literal) interpretation of the Bible, especially of the Book of Genesis, saying the earth is only six to ten thousand years old, and that the universe is also relatively young. Modern geology and astronomy are therefore in error. They also believe that humans do not share ancestry with any other creatures, thus refuting modern biology and paleontology. Some of the major young-earth creationists include Henry Morris, Duane Gish, Ken Ham, and Carl Wieland.

Next on the continuum is old-earth creationism. Old-earth creationists, sometimes called progressive creationists, agree more with current scientific thought. They affirm modern geology and astronomy by accepting the standard scientific age of the universe and of the earth. However, like the young-earth creationists, they reject Darwinian evolution and the premise that humans evolved from other creatures. The main proponent of old-earth creationism is Hugh Ross.

Intelligent design (ID) is the next school of thought on the continuum. ID takes yet another step closer to current scientific thought. ID accepts an old universe and an old earth. Also, some ID proponents may embrace evolution on various levels. ID affirms science while refuting naturalism, materialism, and the idea that the supernatural world (including God) does not exist. ID proponents (and others) embrace the notion of the anthropic principle (as do old-earth creationists), which considers the fine-tuning of the universe as evidence for design. Some of the main figures in the ID movement include Philip Johnson, William Dembski, and Michael Behe.

The fourth and last major category of Christian thought on the origins issue is theistic evolution (some prefer the name "evolutionary creationism"). This school is the most "scientific" in the sense that it agrees with current science. Theistic evolutionists believe that science and the theory of evolution do not conflict with the Bible at all. For quite some time, this has been the least-publicized view, but recently more books are being published about the topic. Advocates include Kenneth R. Miller, Denis Lamoureux, Darrel Falk, and Arthur Peacocke.

Although these are the major movements, variations within these schools exist, and there are other movements as well. The boundaries are not always rigid and well-defined. Some ID proponents might consider themselves theistic creationists; young-earth and old-earth creationists borrow from ID. These groups are also sometimes critical of one another. Their common denominator is belief in basic Christian tenets. They all agree that God created the universe, that Jesus Christ is God, and that the Bible is God's word.

Young-Earth Creation Science

Custer, Stewart.

The Stars Speak: Astronomy in the Bible. 2nd Edition. Bob Jones University Press, 2002 (1977). 212 pp. ISBN 1579248187.
>   Stewart Custer describes the constellations to be found during spring, summer, autumn, and winter and where to locate them. He gives interesting facts about the sun, the moon, the planets, and our galaxy, the Milky Way. All along, he explains various biblical references to these heavenly bodies. When he accounts for stars that are millions of light years away, his position as a young-earth creationist becomes apparent.
>
>   **Subjects:** Astrology, Astronomy, Creationism—Young Earth, Stars
>
>   **More:** D. Russell Humphreys dealt with the problem of distant stars in *Starlight and Time: Solving the Puzzle of Distant Starlight in a Young Universe* (Master Books, 1994). Another young-earth view of astronomy is *Taking Back Astronomy: The Heavens Declare Creation* by Jason Lisle (Master Books, 2006). For more about astronomy (this time from an old-earth perspective), see Hugh Ross's *The Creator and the Cosmos: How the Greatest Scientific Discoveries of the Century Reveal God* (NavPress, 2001).

Gitt, Werner.

If Animals Could Talk: Creation Speaks for Itself. Master Books, 2006. 144 pp. ISBN 0890514607.

Werner Gitt (1937–) retired as director at the German Federal Institute of Physics and Technology in Braunschweig, Germany (his degrees are in engineering). A young-earth creation scientist (working with Answers in Genesis in America), he believes that information theory refutes evolution. In this book, Gitt lets the animals tell their own story. The creatures "narrate" from a first-person perspective, extolling the amazing design of animals such as the field sparrow, the whale, the platypus, the glowworm, and others. After presenting fascinating facts (baby blue whales grow seven pounds an hour while nursing) about each animal, Gitt uses this data to refute evolution.

Subjects: Animals, Creationism—Young Earth, Design in Nature, Evolution

More: Gitt also has written *In the Beginning Was Information: A Scientist Explains the Incredible Design in Nature* (Master Books, 2006).

Ham, Ken, editor.

The New Answers Book: 25 Top Questions on Creation/Evolution and the Bible. Master Books, 2006. 378 pp. ISBN 0890515093.

Ken Ham of Answers in Genesis ministry edits this book in which noted Christians respond to questions about the age of the earth, human evolution, Noah's ark and the flood, Cain's wife, dinosaurs, radiometric dating, the Ice Age, UFOs, distant starlight, and more. A good overall handbook for understanding the young-earth creationism perspective.

Subjects: Age of Earth, Creationism—Young Earth, Evolution

More: For more on radioisotope dating and the age of the earth from a young-earth perspective, try *Thousands Not Billions: Challenging an Icon of Evolution, Questioning the Age of the Earth* by Donald Deyoung (Master Books, 2005).

Lubenow, Marvin L.

Bones of Contention: A Creationist Assessment of Human Fossils. Revised and updated edition. Baker Books, 2004 (1992). 400 pp. ISBN 0801065232.

Bible professor Marvin Lubenow has studied the "human fossil issue" for thirty-five years and thinks someone has been deceitfully monkeying around with human fossils in order to support the theory of evolution. In this book, he discusses a variety of human fossils, such as those from the *Homo Erectus* species (for example, Java Man and Wadjak Man). An entire section is devoted to a discussion of Neanderthals. Lubenow assumes that all evolutionists are atheists and believes that evolution is used to justify genocide, racism, and abortion.

Subjects: Creationism—Young Earth, Evolution—Human, Fossils

More: *Evolution: The Fossils Still Say No!* by Duane Gish (Institute for Creation Research, 1995). Also try *Buried Alive: The Startling Truth About Neanderthal Man* by Jack Cuozzo (Master Books, 1998).

Patterson, Roger.

Evolution Exposed: Your Answer Book for the Classroom. Answers in Genesis, 2006. 301 pp. ISBN 1600920160.

Roger Patterson, a former schoolteacher, examines popular secular school textbooks to expose and refute evolutionary concepts. Including charts with concept lists and page references for each major textbook (Glencoe, Prentice Hall, and Holt), Patterson covers many issues in biology and other sciences including DNA, genetics, mutation, fossils, natural selection, and more. Written from a young-earth perspective, this book is designed to help students challenge evolutionary ideas in the classroom.

Subjects: Creationism—Young Earth, Evolution, Science Textbooks

More: Intelligent design proponent Jonathan Wells's book also deals with science textbooks: *Icons of Evolution: Science or Myth?: Why Much of What We Teach About Evolution Is Wrong* (Regnery, 2000).

Petersen, Dennis R.

Unlocking the Mysteries of Creation: The Explorer's Guide to the Awesome Works of God. 2nd Edition. Creation Resource Publications, 2002 (1986). 239 pp. ISBN 0967271304.

This full-color book is packed with illustrations and short two-page chapters on a variety of topics that reconcile a literal six-day interpretation of creation with modern science. It provides readers with an informed introduction to young-earth creation science. Dennis R. Peterson is the founder of the Creation Resource Foundation in California.

Subjects: Creationism—Young Earth, Evolution

Whitcomb, John C., and Henry M. Morris.

The Genesis Flood: The Biblical Record and Its Scientific Implications. P&R Publishing, 1961. 518 pp. ISBN 0875523382.

Still in print, though it begs to be updated, this book is a landmark for young-earth creationism. John C.Whitcomb (1924–), a Bible professor, and Henry M. Morris (1918–2006), an engineer and the founder of the Institute of Creation Research who is often called the father of young-earth creation science, treat the Book of Genesis as though it gives technically and scientifically accurate information about the origins of man and of the earth. The book covers many aspects of flood geology, discussing strata, fossils, radiocarbon dating, oil deposits, and much more.

Subjects: Creationism—Young Earth, Evolution, Flood of Noah, Geology

More: Morris also wrote *Biblical Creationism: What Each Book of the Bible Teaches About Creation and the Flood* (Master Books, 2000).

Old-Earth Creation Science

Rana, Fazale, and Hugh Ross.

Who Was Adam?: A Creation Model Approach to the Origin of Man. NavPress, 2005. 299 pp. ISBN 1576835774.

Biochemist Fuz Rana and astronomer Hugh Ross examine fossil and DNA evidence for the origin of man. Concluding that evolution comes up short, they present their own model of creation. They discuss bipedalism, brain size, Neanderthals, "junk" DNA, and more. Both authors work with Reasons to Believe, a creationist organization that accepts scientific evidence for an old earth and universe.

Subjects: Creationism—Old Earth, Evolution—Human, Science and Faith

More: Rana and Ross also discuss abiogenesis and "primordial soup" related issues in *Origins of Life: Biblical and Evolutionary Models Face Off* (NavPress, 2004).

Ross, Hugh.

Creation As Science: A Testable Model Approach to End the Creation/Evolution Wars. NavPress, 2006. 291 pp. ISBN 1576835782.

Hugh Ross presents a biblical creation model that accounts for such things as the earth's unique and ideal location for viewing the cosmos, the Cambrian explosion, the timing of Earth's petroleum production and storage peak, the emergence of "soulish" behavior expressed in higher animals, apparent "bad design" in complex organisms, and much more. The idea behind the discussion is that the earth, the solar system, and the universe was designed by a wise and loving creator to set the stage for human life.

Subjects: Anthropic Principle, Cosmogony, Cosmology, Creationism—Old Earth, Evolution

Ross, Hugh.

A Matter of Days: Resolving a Creation Controversy. NavPress, 2004. 301 pp. ISBN 1576833755.

Hugh Ross shows how it is biblical and scientific to believe that both the earth and universe are old. He argues that the six days of creation in Genesis were not twenty-four-hour days, but instead epochs or ages. Without being contentious, Ross traces the history of the young-earth view and points out many of the biblical and scientific weaknesses of young-earth creationism, answering many questions that Christians may have about an old-earth interpretation of scripture and nature.

Subjects: Age of Earth, Creationism—Old Earth

More: Ross wrote an earlier book on this subject called *Creation and Time: A Biblical and Scientific Perspective on the Creation-Date Controversy* (NavPress, 1994). Also see Mark Whorton's *Peril in Paradise: Theology, Science, and the Age of the Earth* (Authentic Media, 2005).

Ross, Hugh.

The Creator and the Cosmos: How the Greatest Scientific Discoveries of the Century Reveal God. 3rd Expanded edition. NavPress, 2001 (1993). 266 pp. ISBN 1576832880.

Astronomer Hugh Ross explains what the Big Bang and many other recent astronomical discoveries say about God. He discusses the fine-tuning of our planet, galaxy, and the universe. Ross also looks at Stephen Hawking's book, *A Brief History of Time.*

Subject: Anthropic Principle, Cosmology, Creationism—Old Earth

More: Also see Ross' first book which is a little more technical: *The Fingerprint of God: Recent Scientific Discoveries Reveal the Unmistakable Identity of the Creator* (Whitaker, 2000). For more on the anthropic principle, try *Privileged Planet* by Guillermo Gonzalez and Jay W. Richards (Regnery, 2004).

Ross, Hugh.

The Genesis Question: Scientific Advances and the Accuracy of Genesis. 2nd Edition. NavPress, 2001 (1998). 239 pp. ISBN 1576832309.

Ross examines the first eleven chapters of Genesis and addresses issues such as the six days of creation, the flood of Noah, long life spans, the Nephilim, and more. After explaining what happened on each creation day from an old-earth perspective, he discusses why he believes the flood at Noah's time was a local flood, not global.

Subjects: Age of Earth, Creationism—Old Earth, Flood of Noah, Genesis

Snoke, David.

A Biblical Case for an Old Earth. Baker Books, 2006. 223 pp. ISBN 0801066190.

Physics professor David Snoke says that studying science has led him to believe the earth is not young. In this book, he shows that an ancient earth is compatible with both scientific evidence and a conservative, orthodox view of the Bible. Snoke examines assumptions about biblical interpretation and lays out the proof for an old earth, asserting that each creation "day" was really an "age." He also explores the issue of animal death before Adam and questions whether the flood was global or local. In covering these topics, Snoke offers his interpretation of Genesis 1 and 2 and offers his own translation of Genesis 1:1–12:7.

Subjects: Age of Earth, Creationism—Old Earth, Science and Faith

More: For a discussion of various interpretations of Genesis, try *The Genesis Debate: Three Views on the Days of Creation* by David Hagopian, editor (Crux Press, 2001). The three views are 1) the twenty-four-hour view, 2) the day-age view, and 3) the framework view.

Intelligent Design

Behe, Michael.

Darwin's Black Box: The Biochemical Challenge to Evolution. Free Press, 2006 (1996). 352 pp. ISBN 0743290313.

In this landmark book for the ID movement, Michael Behe, a professor of biochemistry at Lehigh University, discusses the concept of irreducible complexity. In this book, Behe first puts forth his famous example of the bacterial flagellum, the tiny (microscopic) but complex motor that propels certain bacteria, which seems to be irreducibly complex (take away any part and the motor does not work). Behe asserts that this concept reveals a weakness of the theory of evolution at the microbiological level.

Subjects: Award Winners (CT), Biology, Evolution, Intelligent Design, Irreducible Complexity, Microbiology

More: Behe edited and contributed to *Science and Evidence for Design in the Universe* (Ignatius Press, 2000). Behe's latest book is *The Edge of Evolution: The Search for the Limits of Darwinism* (Free Press, 2007).

Dembski, William A., and James M. Kushiner, editors.

Signs of Intelligence: Understanding Intelligent Design. Brazos, 2001. 224 pp. ISBN 1587430045.

> Here are fourteen essays by the major players in the ID movement, including Phillip Johnson, Michael Behe, William Dembski, Nancy Pearcey, Jonathan Wells, and Stephen Meyer. Topics include irreducible complexity, natural selection, the Cambrian explosion, the fine-tuning of the universe, and apologetics.
>
> **Subjects:** Evolution, Intelligent Design
>
> **More:** Dembski has written or edited other important books on ID: *Intelligent Design: The Bridge Between Science and Theology* (InterVarsity, 1999) and *The Design Revolution: Answering the Toughest Questions About Intelligent Design* (InterVarsity, 2004). On the more technical side, Dembski wrote *The Design Inference: Eliminating Chance Through Small Probabilities* (Cambridge University Press, 2006) and *No Free Lunch: Why Specified Complexity Cannot Be Purchased Without Intelligence* (Rowman & Littlefield, 2001).

Gonzalez, Guillermo, and Jay W. Richards.

The Privileged Planet: How Our Place in the Cosmos Is Designed for Discovery. Regnery, 2004. 444 pp. ISBN 0895260654.

> How is it that our planet is situated in just the right place in our galaxy to allow for life and for scientific discovery? Astronomy and physics professor Guillermo Gonzalez and Discovery Institute fellow Jay W. Richards argue that the laws that govern our universe are so fine-tuned that they affirm ID. The authors reveal surprising facts about eclipses, the harmony of the earth and moon, and how the size of Jupiter and Saturn affects our planet. They also discuss implications of these ideas to the Copernican principle and SETI (Search for Extra-Terrestrial Intelligence).
>
> **Subjects:** Anthropic Principle, Cosmology, Intelligent Design
>
> **More:** *The Creator and the Cosmos: How the Greatest Scientific Discoveries of the Century Reveal God* by Hugh Ross (NavPress, 2001). Also, there is a chapter discussing the anthropic principle in *A Meaningful World: How the Arts and Sciences Reveal the Genius of Nature* by Benjamin Wiker and Jonathan Witt (InterVarsity, 2006).

Johnson, Phillip E.

Darwin on Trial. InterVarsity Press, 1993 (Regnery, 1991). 220 pp. ISBN 0830813241.

> Retired law professor Phillip Johnson (1940–) is one of the most prominent detractors of Darwinism. Johnson is also one of the leaders in the ID movement of which this book is a landmark

work. In it, he makes a distinction between microevolution and macroevolution, exposing weaknesses in the fossil evidence for the evolution of human life. Much of the book deals with the philosophic problems of atheistic Darwinism.

Subjects: Award Winners (CT), Evolution, Intelligent Design

More: Johnson expands on those philosophic issues and their societal influences in *Reason in the Balance: The Case Against Naturalism in Science, Law & Education* (InterVarsity, 1995.) Also see Johnson's *The Wedge of Truth: Splitting the Foundations of Naturalism* (InterVarsity, 2000).

Strobel, Lee.

The Case for a Creator: A Journalist Investigates Scientific Evidence That Points toward God. Zondervan, 2004. 341 pp. ISBN 0310259134.

In the same investigative journalistic style of his earlier works, Lee Strobel interviews a variety of scientists and philosophers to ask them about the scientific proof for God. Strobel talks to the main proponents of ID, including Jonathan Wells, Stephen C. Meyer, Guillermo Gonzalez, and Michael Behe, as well as to philosophers William Lane Craig and J. P. Moreland on topics ranging from cosmology, physics, and astronomy to evolution, biochemistry, and consciousness. Strobel's easy-to-read style makes this a great overview of ID arguments.

Subjects: Apologetics, Award Winners (ECPA, CT), Creationism, Evolution, Intelligent Design, Science

Wells, Jonathan.

Icons of Evolution: Science or Myth?: Why Much of What We Teach About Evolution Is Wrong. Regnery, 2000. 338 pp. ISBN 0895262002.

Jonathan Wells exposes flaws in information about evolution commonly found in textbooks. Topics include Haeckel's embryos, the archaeopteryx, peppered moths, Darwin's finches, and mutant fruit flies. An appendix evaluates ten textbooks in reference to the aforementioned misleading data. Wells is notable among ID proponets because he is a member of the Unification Church, founded by Sun Myung Moon.

Subjects: Creationism, Evolution, Intelligent Design, Science Textbooks

More: Wells also wrote *The Politically Incorrect Guide to Darwinism and Intelligent Design* (Regnery, 2006).

Woodward, Thomas.

Doubts About Darwin: A History of Intelligent Design. Baker Books, 2003. 303 pp. ISBN 0801065216.

Woodward, a professor at Trinity College of Florida, discusses the origin and development of the ID movement, focusing on Michael Denton (author of *Evolution: A Theory in Crisis*), Michael Behe (author of *Darwin's Black Box*), Philip Johnson (author of *Darwin on Trial*), and William Dembski (author of *The Design Inference*). This book is a reworking of the author's 2001 doctoral thesis for the University of South Florida.

Subjects: Award Winners (CT), Evolution, Intelligent Design, Intelligent Design—History

Theistic Evolution

Collins, Francis S.

The Language of God: A Scientist Presents Evidence for Belief. Free Press, 2006. 294 pp. ISBN 0743286391.

Physician-geneticist and Human Genome Project head Francis Collins begins his book by describing his journey from atheism to Christianity. He also discusses the origins of the universe and life on earth as well as his specialty, the human genome. He presents four different ways to approach science, including atheism/agnosticism, creationism, intelligent design, and his own approach, called BioLogos, an alternate name for theistic evolution. An appendix includes a helpful section on bioethics, including stem cell research, cloning, and more.

Subjects: Apologetics, Award Winners (CT), Creationism, Evolution, Genetics, Theistic Evolution

Falk, Darrel R.

Coming to Peace with Science: Bridging the Worlds Between Faith and Biology. InterVarsity Press, 2004. 235 pp. ISBN 0830827420.

Darrel Falk, a Christian and a veteran professor of biology, presents clear evidence that the earth is old and that life evolved gradually. Falk writes about the fossil record (including the evolution of elephants, whales, and turtles) and clearly explains that transitional forms do not present a problem to evolution like creation scientists suppose. This author is never haughty or divisive. On the contrary, his calm, evenhanded style is refreshing. He presents genetic evidence for evolution informatively and persuasively. Falk's discussion of biblical interpretation—especially of the book of Genesis—may be very helpful for those trying to come to peace with science.

Subjects: Age of Earth, Creationism, Evolution, Fossils, Theistic Evolution

Johnson, Phillip E., and Denis O. Lamoureux.

Darwinism Defeated? The Johnson-Lamoureux Debate on Biological Origins. Regent College, 1999. 174 pp. ISBN 1573831336.

This book is a result of a debate between evolutionary creationist Denis Lamoureux, a biologist and theologian, and ID advocate Phillip Johnson, a retired law professor. After the text of their debate, nine additional essays respond to the issues. Some of the contributors are key figures in their camps: Howard J. Van Til, Stephen C. Meyer, Michael Behe, Keith B. Miller, Jonathan Wells, and Michael J. Denton.

Subjects: Creationism, Evolution, Intelligent Design, Theistic Evolution

Miller, Keith B., editor.

Perspectives on an Evolving Creation. Eerdmans, 2003. 528 pp. ISBN 0802805124.

This collection of essays by Christians who support theistic evolution represents a variety of disciplines: biochemistry, anthropology, geology, astronomy, philosphy, theology, and others. The authors advocate science as a Christian vocation and argue that evolution (not materialism) is a worthy science. In fact, many of the essays utilize scientific research that many in the evangelical community may not know.

Subjects: Creationism, Evolution, Theistic Evolution

Miller, Kenneth R.

Finding Darwin's God: A Scientist's Search for Common Ground Between God and Evolution. Harper Perennial, 2007 (1999). 368 pp. ISBN 0061233501.

Kenneth R. Miller, a cell biologist and distinguished professor of biology at Brown University, argues that evolution is real and that it does not detract from spirituality, the Bible, or Christianity. Several chapters are devoted to a discussion of Michael Behe's irreducible complexity and other challenges to evolution. Miller also refutes materialism, and has some interesting views on quantum physics.

Subjects: Biology, Evolution, Theistic Evolution

More: Biology professor David Wilcox wrote *God and Evolution: A Faith-Based Understanding* (Judson Press, 2004).

Peacocke, Arthur.

Evolution: The Disguised Friend of Faith?: Selected Essays. Templeton Foundation Press, 2004. 287 pp. ISBN 1932031723.

In this collection of essays on the theme of reconciling evolution with Christian belief, Arthur Peacocke claims that truths discovered in the natural world cannot falsify those about human relationships with God; however, such scientific knowledge can enhance the understanding of creation, man, and God. Peacocke (1924–2006) was a biochemist who became an Anglican priest and a theologian.

Subjects: Evolution, Theistic Evolution

More: For another book by Peacocke, try *Theology for a Scientific Age: Being and Becoming—Natural, Divine, and Human* (Augsburg Fortress, 1993). For another book on science and faith by a scientist-turned-Anglican priest, John Polkinghorne, see *Science & Theology: An Introduction* (Augsburg Fortress, 1998).

Chapter 8

Bible and Theology

Introduction

The Bible is the single most important nonfiction book for Christians. It is actually a collection of sixty-six books (or more if you count the apocryphal books that are often included). This collection includes many "genres" of literature: poetry (the Psalms), wise sayings (the Proverbs), history (First and Second Kings), genealogy (Numbers), prophecy (Isaiah), apocalypse (Daniel and Revelation), letters (First and Second Corinthians) and parables (Luke).

The Bible was originally written in Hebrew and Greek, with some Aramaic, so English-speaking Christians must rely upon translations to read it. There are three main styles of translation: 1) literal, 2) dynamic equivalence, and 3) paraphrase. A literal translation of the Bible attempts to translate "word for word" the meaning of the Hebrew and Greek into English. Three examples of a literal translation of the scriptures are the well-known King James Version, the New American Standard Version, and the English Standard Version.

The dynamic equivalence style attempts to translate "thought for thought" the meaning of the Hebrew and Greek. It focuses less on precisely translating each word and more on capturing the meaning of the text in the English language. The New International Version is one of the most popular and well-respected examples of this "middle-of-the-road" style.

When a dynamic equivalence translation gets really loose, it moves into the third style—the paraphrase. The purpose of this style is to focus totally on getting the scriptures to make sense to today's readers by using everyday language. *The Message* is an actual translation from the Hebrew and Greek done in a very loose "paraphrase" style. *The Living Bible* is a paraphrase done by Kenneth Taylor. Taylor did not translate from the original languages; he based his paraphrase on an earlier English translation.

The Bible is the sourcebook for Christian theology. Theology is a vast area of study as its focus is the creator of the universe and because there are thousands of years of writing on the topic. This chapter collects and annotates only some titles on subjects like heaven, hell, sin, and the attributes of God. It includes some ancient classics such as Augustine's *City of God* and some recent classics like J. I. Packer's *Knowing God*. To find more books related to the Bible and theology, refer to the bibliography at the end of this chapter.

Bible

This section annotates four popular English translations of the Bible, including a Catholic version. Most of them are study Bibles, which means that notes have been added to the bottom of the text to explain words, places, or concepts that may be unfamiliar or hard to understand. These four translations, and those in the "More" section, comprise a core collection for libraries.

Because the Bible was written thousands of years ago in foreign languages by ancient cultures, other tools are needed for successful Bible study. The small number of bible reference books annotated here (handbooks, concordances, and word-study tools) represent the basics of what libraries should have for this purpose—for both patron and reference use. At the very minimum, libraries will want to acquire a few good Bible dictionaries, concordances, and Bible handbooks.

"Other Books about the Bible" includes works on biblical archaeology and titles that discuss biblical authority (How reliable is the Bible?) and biblical interpretation.

This section offers a very brief sample of the many books available. For more study tools, refer to the bibliography section at the end of the chapter that lists some very helpful bibliographies that recommend hundreds of books concerning Bible study—for new students as well as advanced students of the Bible.

Bible—English Translations

Barker, Kenneth L., editor.

NIV Study Bible. Zondervan, 2002 (1985). 2198 pp. ISBN 0310923069.

The New International Version (NIV) Study Bible is probably the most popular study bible today, using the most trusted English Bible translation. The NIV translation, done by an international committee of Bible scholars, took ten years to complete (finished in 1978). This 2002 edition includes 20,000-plus recently revised study notes, which help clarify meaning and offer insight concerning biblical background information and history, linguistics, and archaeology. This study Bible also has sixteen pages of full-color maps as well as timelines, charts, and diagrams. The words of Christ are presented in red letters. A concordance (which is a key word index) is included, along with an index to subjects and study notes.

Subjects: Award Winners (ECPA), Bible in English, Study Bibles

More: The Today's New International Version (TNIV) (Zondervan, 2002) is a revision of the NIV done by the same group of scholars who translated the NIV. The TNIV was completed in 2002. Among other revisions, the TNIV makes use of some gender-inclusive language, but it does not change masculine references to God (for example, "father," "son," etc). Also try the *New Living Translation* (Tyndale, 2004), which is a bit freer in its translation.

Beers, Ronald A.

Life Application Study Bible, NASB. Zondervan, 2000. 2,560 pp. ISBN 0310900956.

This is a study Bible edition of the New American Standard translation of the Bible (NASB). The NASB was first published in 1971 by the Lockman Foundation. Updated in 1995, the NASB, intended to replace the popular King James, or Authorized Version of the Bible, which was translated in 1611, is billed as the most literal translation of the English Bible in common use today. This study Bible edition includes a dictionary/concordance, book introductions, maps, timelines, overviews, outlines, and more than 10,000 application notes.

Subjects: Bible in English, Study Bibles

More: Another well-respected translation designed to update the King James translation is the New Revised Standard Version. Try the *New Oxford Annotated Bible with the Apocrypha, Third Edition, New Revised Standard Version*, edited by Michael D. Coogan, et al. (Oxford University Press, 2001). Of course, many people will not accept anything other than the King James Version of the Bible, for which there are a plethora of editions. For the popular New King James Version, try the *Open Bible* (Thomas Nelson, 2006), which is a study Bible edition of the New King James Version. The New King James Version removes the "thees and thous" so common in the older King James Version.

Hiesberger, Jean Marie, editor.

The Catholic Bible, Personal Study Edition. 2nd Edition. Oxford University Press, 2007 (1995). 2400 pp. ISBN 0195289269.

This study edition of the New American Bible was originally translated by a group of American Catholic scholars. It features extensive reading guides, essays, maps, and a concordance, as well as the complete Sunday and weekday lectionary readings for all three liturgical years of the church. As a Catholic Bible, it includes the deuterocanonical (apocrypha) books, which are not included in Protestant Bibles.

Subjects: Bible in English, Catholics, Study Bibles

More: Another popular and well-respected Catholic translation is the *New Jerusalem Bible*, edited by Henry Wansbrough (Doubleday, 1999). An English translation of the original Hebrew, Aramaic, and Greek languages, it was completed in 1985 and relates to the earlier *Jerusalem Bible*. The earlier *Jerusalem Bible* was an English translation from the French *Bible de Jerusalem* (1966).

Peterson, Eugene, editor and translator.

The Message: The Bible in Contemporary Language. NavPress, 2005 (2002). 1,723 pp. ISBN 1576836738.

This popular paraphrased translation of the Bible was completed by Eugene Peterson, a Presbyterian pastor, scholar, and author. Peterson did his paraphrasing/translating from the original biblical languages (Hebrew, Aramaic, and Greek). Peterson's translation of Genesis 1:1–3 is: "First this: God created the Heavens and Earth— all you see, all you don't see. Earth was a soup of nothingness, a bottomless emptiness, an inky blackness. God's Spirit brooded like a bird above the watery abyss. God spoke: 'Light!' And light appeared." *The Message* paraphrase was completed in 2002.

Subjects: Award Winners (ECPA, CT), Bible in English

More: Another paraphrase of the Bible by Kenneth Taylor is the *Living Bible* (Tyndale, 1976). Taylor did not translate from the original languages; he just paraphrased an English translation. *The Word on the Street* by Rob Lacey (Zondervan, 2004) is a recent paraphrase done in a very informal style. For instance, here is a selection from Genesis 1:1–2: "God says the word and WHAP! Stuff everywhere!"

Bible Study Tools

Baker, Warren, Tim Rake, and David Kemp, editors.

The Complete Word Study Old Testament. AMG Publishers, 1998. 2,608 pp. ISBN 0899576656.

This book contains the entire King James Version of the Old Testament. Above the English text are 1) letters that refer to explanations of Hebrew and Aramaic grammar and 2) numbers that refer the reader to Strong's *Hebrew Dictionary*, which is included at the back of the book. At the bottom of the page are many study and commentary notes. Besides Strong's dictionary, other "lexical aids" are included, compiled from other Hebrew dictionaries, which offer a more detailed definition than Strong's does.

Subjects: Bible in English, Bible Study Tools, Concordances, Hebrew Word Studies

More: For a more in-depth and up-to-date Hebrew dictionary, try *Mounce's Complete Expository Dictionary of Old and New Testament Words* by William D. Mounce (Zondervan, 2006).

Fee, Gordon D., and Douglas Stuart.

How to Read the Bible for All Its Worth. 3rd Edition. Zondervan, 2003 (1981). 288 pp. ISBN 0310246040.

This book is designed to help both beginners and more experienced readers understand the Christian Bible. In addition to explaining the different types of translations available, Gordon D. Fee and Douglas Stuart discuss the different types of biblical literature and how to read each type. One does not read apocalyptic writing (like Revelation) the same as poetry (Psalms) or as an epistle, which is a letter (Galatians). The authors include a helpful appendix that discusses the use of commentaries and recommends titles for each book of the Bible.

Subject: Bible Commentaries

More: Fee and Stuart have a companion volume to this book called *How to Read the Bible Book by Book: A Guided Tour* (Zondervan, 2002).

Freedman, David Noel, Allen C. Myers, and Astrid B. Beck, editors.

Eerdmans Dictionary of the Bible. Eerdmans, 2000. 1,425 pages. ISBN 0802824005.

This one-volume dictionary of the Christian Bible is useful for people wanting more information about people, places, events, and terms found in the Bible. There are nearly 5,000 articles, signed by the (almost) 600 Bible scholars who contributed to this work.

Subjects: Award Winners (CT, ECPA), Bible Dictionaries, Bible Study Tools

More: For two more well-known one-volume Bible dictionaries, try the *New International Bible Dictionary* edited by J. D. Douglas and Merrill C. Tenney (Zondervan, 1999) and *The New Unger's Bible Dictionary* by Merrill Unger (Moody, 2006). For a multivolume dictionary, try the four-volume *International Standard Bible Encyclopedia (ISBE)*, edited by Geoffrey W. Bromiley (Eerdmans, 1988). ISBE is based on the *Revised Standard Version*.

Halley, Henry H.

Halley's Bible Handbook. 25th Edition. Zondervan, 2000. 1,136 pp. ISBN 0310224799.

Henry H. Halley's handbook goes chapter by chapter through the Bible offering brief commentary. Filled with background information pertaining to the cultural, religious, and geographic settings of Bible stories, it offers a wealth of archaeological information, and it is packed with interesting maps, photographs, and illustrations. This edition uses the New International Version (earlier editions used the King James Version). In his day, Halley (1874–1965) was famous for memorizing whole books of the Bible.

Subjects: Bible Commentaries, Bible Handbooks, Bible Study Tools, Classics

More: Nick Page's *The MAP: Making the Bible Meaningful, Accessible, Practical* (Zondervan, 2004) is a standout handbook to the Bible because of its clear and concise explanations and helpful maps, charts, and timelines. Henrietta Mears also has a well-known guide to the Bible called *What the Bible Is All About* (Regal, 2007).

Kohlenberger, John R., and James A. Swanson.

The Hebrew-English Concordance to the Old Testament. Zondervan, 1998. 2,208 pp. ISBN 0310208394.

This book lists all occurrences of a given Hebrew (or Aramaic) word, using the Goodrick/Kohlenberger numbering system (cross-referenced to Strong's numbers). There is a complete NIV-to-Hebrew index so readers don't have to know Hebrew to do a word study. For instance, if you want to do a word study on the concept of "the fear of the Lord," you can look up the English word "fear" in the NIV-to-Hebrew index. You will see that there are several different Hebrew words that are translated into English as "fear." One of the main Hebrew words is "yare." You can now look up "yare" in the concordance where each use of this word in the Old Testament is listed book by book. Here you will see that "yare" is translated into many different English words: sometimes as "afraid," sometimes as "awesome," and sometimes as "revere." You can also see where "yare" appears in the phrases "fear of the Lord," "fear the Lord," "fear him," and so forth. To facilitate advanced study, this book is keyed to the *Brown-Driver,- Briggs' Hebrew and English Lexicon* by Francis Brown, S. Driver, and C. Briggs; *The Hebrew and Aramaic Lexicon of the Old Testament* by Ludwig Koehler and Walter Baumgartner; and *A Concise Hebrew and Aramaic Lexicon of the Old Testament* by William Lee Holladay.

Subjects: Bible Study Tools, Hebrew Concordances, Hebrew Word Studies, Reference

More: The equivalent for the New Testament is *The Greek-English Concordance to the New Testament*, edited by John R. Kohlenberger III, Edward W. Goodrick, and James A. Swanson (Zondervan, 1997).

Mounce, William D.

Mounce's Complete Expository Dictionary of Old and New Testament Words. Zondervan, 2006. 1316 pp. ISBN 0310248787.

For many years, Vine's *Expository Dictionary* has been a standard word-study tool for the Bible, but it is about sixty years old and fairly out of date. This book does what Vine's *Expository Dictionary* does, only (so the publisher claims) better. William Mounce's dictionary claims to be more current, more accurate, and "based on the best of modern evangelical scholarship." Readers do not need to know Greek or Hebrew to use this book. A fourteen-page section called "How to Do Word Studies" is included. Here is how the book works: Look up an English word, like "holy," that is found in the Bible. Mounce gives both the Hebrew (Old Testament) words that are translated as "holy" and the Greek (New Testament) words that are translated into the English word "holy." He defines the words, notes how many times they are found in the Bible, and supplies the Strong's reference number and the Goodrick-Kohlenberger (GK) number (which refers to another language-study tool). Mounce also discusses each word in its biblical context and tries to provide something unique about it that provides for a good illustration.

Subjects: Bible Dictionaries, Bible Study Tools, Greek Word Studies, Hebrew Word Studies, Reference, Word Studies

More: Readers may want to also consult the old standard, *Vine's Expository Dictionary of Old and New Testament Words* (Thomas Nelson, 1996); Vine's first Greek dictionary was published in 1939. For another word-study tool by Mounce, try *Interlinear for the Rest of Us: The Reverse Interlinear for New Testament Word Studies* (Zondervan, 2006). For Greek-language material by Mounce, try *Greek for the Rest of Us: Mastering Bible Study Without Mastering Biblical Languages* (Zondervan, 2003).

Strong, James.

Strong's Exhaustive Concordance of the Bible. Hendrickson, 2007 (1890). 1,685 pp. ISBN 1565633598.

A concordance is a reference book that indexes every word in a book. An "exhaustive" concordance even lists words normally skipped, such as "a," "the," "or," etc. James Strong's concordance has been a standard Bible reference book since it was first published in 1890. The two main reasons people refer to this book is 1) to find a scripture that they know is in the Bible but can't remember where and 2) to do word studies on the Bible. For his concordance (using the King James Version of the Bible), Strong numbered every Hebrew and Greek root word and included a glossary defining these terms in the back of the concordance. This numbering system is still used today by other lexicons and reference books. This current edition of Strong's concordance also includes a CD-ROM with Strong's text, along with other Bible study tools such as commentaries and Bible dictionaries.

Subjects: Bible Study Tools, Classics, Concordances, Reference, Word Studies

More: Owing to the extreme popularity of the New International Version (NIV) of the Bible, another must-have concordance is *The Strongest NIV Exhaustive Concordance* by Edward W. Goodrick and John R. Kohlenberger III (Zondervan, 2004).

Wright, Tom.

Matthew for Everyone: Chapters 1–15. John Knox Press, 2004. 224 pp. ISBN 0664227864.

This is the first volume of the fourteen-volume New Testament for Everyone Series, which is a set of commentaries by Anglican Bishop and Bible scholar N. T. "Tom" Wright. Wright goes through the New Testament passage by passage, giving background information and commentary in an easy, conversational style. His goal is to make the Bible relevant to the thought and life of today's reader. Wright uses his own translation of the New Testament. This affordable set of commentaries is free from all academic jargon, making it suitable for a broad audience.

Subject: Bible Commentaries

More: For more advanced (but still accessible for the layperson) New Testament study, try the *Tyndale New Testament Commentary*, twenty volumes, edited by Leon Morris (InterVarsity, 2007). For the Old Testament, try *The Expositor's Bible Commentary*, seven volumes, edited by Frank E. Gaebelein (Zondervan, 1992).

Zodhiates, Spiros.

The Complete Word Study New Testament with Greek Parallel. AMG Publishers, 1992. 1,296 pp. ISBN 0899576524.

This book contains the entire King James Version of the New Testament with the original Greek text in a column on the side.

Above the English text are 1) letters that explain Greek grammar and 2) numbers that refer the reader to Strong's *Greek Dictionary*, which is included at the back of the book. Besides Strong's dictionary, other "lexical aids" are included. This section of "lexical aids" is basically another Greek dictionary compiled by Spiros Zodhiates from sources like Vine's *Expository Dictionary of New Testament Words*, *A Greek-English Lexicon to the New Testament* by John Parkhurst, and two other sources. Also included is a Greek concordance, which lists the scripture references for each use of a certain Greek word. For instance, the concordance shows that the Greek word "abba" (father) is used three times in the New Testament: Mark 14:36, Romans 8:15, and Galatians 4:6.

Subjects: Award Winners (ECPA), Bible in English, Bible Study Tools, Greek Concordances, Greek Dictionaries, Greek Word Studies

More: A similar New Testament is *Word Study Greek-English New Testament* by Paul McReynolds (Tyndale, 1999). McReynolds' work has the complete text of the Greek New Testament with an interlinear translation and the New Revised Standard Version translation in the side column. A Greek concordance is included (keyed to Strong's). For a more in-depth and up-to-date Greek dictionary, try *Mounce's Complete Expository Dictionary of Old and New Testament Words* by William D. Mounce (Zondervan, 2006). For a more in-depth concordance, try *The Greek-English Concordance to the New Testament*, edited by John R. Kohlenberger III, Edward W. Goodrick, and James A. Swanson (Zondervan, 1997); this book is geared toward the NIV translation.

Other Books About the Bible

Bruce, F. F.

The New Testament Documents: Are They Reliable? 6th Edition. Eerdmans, 2003 (1943). 135 pp. ISBN 0802822193.

Famous Bible scholar F. F. Bruce (1910–1990) shows the reliability of New Testament documents. In this classic introduction, Bruce discusses the date and attestation of the New Testament documents, the canon of the New Testament, the Gospels, Paul's evidence, Luke's writings, archaeological evidence, early Jewish writings, early gentile writings, and more. The first edition of this book was published in 1943.

Subjects: Biblical Authority, New Testament

More: For a longer book collecting essays on the authority, inspiration, and translation of the Bible, try *The Origin of the Bible* (Tyndale, 2004), edited by Philip Comfort.

Enns, Peter.

Inspiration and Incarnation: Evangelicals and the Problem of the Old Testament. Baker Academic, 2005. 208 pp. ISBN 0801027306.

Evangelical Bible professor Peter Enns deals with three major, thorny issues that question the authority of the Bible: 1) What should we think about other ancient creation myths and other stories that are similar to the Bible and predate the Bible? 2)What should we think about the fact that the Old Testament offers different points of view on the same topics? 3) What should we think about the fact that New Testament authors seemingly "misused" Old Testament quotes. Written for the layperson, the book shows that "the messiness of the Old Testament, a source of embarrassment for some, is actually a positive." The word "incarnation" in the title refers to the fact that "Christ is the ultimate example of how God enters the messiness of history to save his people." Scripture, says Enns, is like Christ in this regard—indeed, Christ is the embodied word—therefore, Christians need not fear these thorny issues, but should embrace them.

Subjects: Biblical Authority, Biblical Interpretation

Hoerth, Alfred J.

Archaeology and the Old Testament. Baker Academic, 1998. 448 pp. ISBN 0801011299.

Easy to read yet scholarly in its research, this guide goes chronologically through the Old Testament (following the biblical narrative), pointing out the cultural and historical settings. It is a layperson's guide that presents an evangelical view (that the Bible is reliable). Alfred Hoerth taught at Wheaton College for almost thirty years and was its director of archaeology.

Subjects: Archaeology, Bible, Bible Atlases, Bible Study Tools

More: The companion volume for the New Testament is called *Archaeology and the New Testament* by John McRay (Baker Academic, 1991). For a brief introduction to the history, vocabulary, and methods of Palestinian archaeology, see *Doing Archaeology in the Land of the Bible: A Basic Guide* by John D. Currid (Baker Academic, 1999). For two good Bible atlases, try *The IVP Atlas of Bible History* by Paul Lawrence (InterVarsity, 2006) and the *Zondervan NIV Atlas of the Bible* by Carl G. Rasmussen (Zondervan, 1999).

Peterson, Eugene H.

Eat This Book: A Conversation in the Art of Spiritual Reading. Eerdmans, 2006. 186 pp. ISBN 0802829481.

Eugene Peterson is the author of *The Message*, a translation of the whole Bible into American English vernacular. In this book,

Peterson discusses words, communication, and reading the Bible. *Lectio Divina*, or spiritual reading, refers to the ancient practice of reading, meditating, praying, and living the Bible. In the last section of the book, Peterson addresses the issue of translating the Bible.

Subjects: Award Winners (CT), Bible Reading, Spiritual Growth

Smith, Charles Merrill, and James W. Bennett.

How the Bible Was Built. Eerdmans, 2005. 97 pp. ISBN 0802829430. YA

Minister and author Charles Merrill Smith wrote this book to answer questions that his teenage daughter had about the Bible. At least, he started to write it. Smith died, and James Bennett finished the manuscript and prepared it for publication. Written in a conversational style, this book explains how the Bible as we know it came to be. With no denominational axes to grind, Merrill discusses the Old Testament, the Apocrypha, the New Testament, the Canon (which explains how certain writings became "official"), and various Bible translators and translations. An easy-to-understand explanation for teens and adults.

Subjects: Bible—History, Young-Adult Interest

More: For another brief treatment, try *How We Got the Bible* by Neil R. Lightfoot (Baker Books, 2003). For a fuller, scholarly treatment, try F. F. Bruce's *The Canon of Scripture* (InterVarsity Press, 1988), which won the Gold Medallion Award. Another scholarly book on the subject is Bruce Metzger's *The Canon of the New Testament: Its Origin, Development, and Significance* (Oxford, 1997).

Wright, N. T.

The Last Word: Beyond the Bible Wars to a New Understanding of the Authority of Scripture. HarperSanFrancisco, 2005. 146 pp. ISBN 0060816090.

N. T. "Tom" Wright (1948–), Bishop of Durham in the Church of England, is a leading (and sometimes controversial) Bible scholar. In this book, he discusses the place and authority of the Bible for today's Christian believers. Describing the continuity of the Old and New Testaments, he says that the key to understanding the Bible is to know how the New Testament writers viewed the Old Testament. Wright asserts that they recognized that some parts of the Old Testament were no longer relevant for their lives because those parts had reached their climax (not because they were less inspired). Wright also addresses common misreadings of the Bible from both conservative and liberal camps.

Subjects: Award Winners (CT), Biblical Interpretation

Yamauchi, Edwin M.

Africa and the Bible. Baker Academic, 2004. 297 pp. ISBN 0801026865.

Trusted Bible scholar Edwin Yamauchi, former professor of history at Miami University, Ohio, gives a balanced and well-researched view of Africa and the Bible, avoiding and correcting extremes in both Eurocentric and Afrocentric interpretations of the Bible. Yamauchi writes about the curse of Ham, Moses' Cushite wife, Solomon, the Ethiopian eunuch, Simon of Cyrene, and more.

Subjects: Award Winners (CT), Biblical Interpretation, Blacks in the Bible

Theology

This section recommends books on various topics related to the Bible, including heaven, hell, the attributes of God, women in ministry, angels, and eschatology. Eschatology refers to Christ's return to earth and the "end times," or the end of the world. The best-selling <u>Left Behind</u> series by Tim LaHaye and Jerry B. Jenkins explores, through fiction, what the end of the world will look like according to LaHaye's interpretation of scripture. LaHaye lays out his eschatology in nonfiction, graphical format in *Charting the End Times: A Visual Guide to Understanding Bible Prophecy.*

To understand typical evangelical theology, see Wayne Grudem's *Christian Beliefs: Twenty Basics Every Christian Should Know.* To understand basic Catholic theology, try Peter Kreeft's *Catholic Christianity: A Complete Catechism of Catholic Beliefs Based on the Catechism of the Catholic Church.* To learn about the Eastern Orthodox branch of Christianity, read *Facing East: A Pilgrim's Journey into the Mysteries of Orthodoxy* by Frederica Mathewes-Green.

This small section does not even begin to represent the vast body of theological literature. There are whole bibliographies on this subject, and three are included at the end of this chapter.

Alcorn, Randy.

Heaven. Tyndale, 2004. 516 pp. ISBN 0842379428.

For those looking for real answers about heaven, Randy Alcorn, who has taught this material in seminaries, shows that heaven is not a boring place where we will float on clouds for eternity. This book raises and answers just about every conceivable question one could ask on the subject. For instance, "Will there be oceans in heaven?," "Will we drink coffee in heaven?," and, "Will there be marriage and family in heaven?" This book may change the way you look at life, death, the Bible, heaven, and God. Alcorn is known mainly for his pro-life writing and speaking and his fiction novels.

Subject: Heaven

More: For personal accounts of those who claim to have been to heaven, try *To Heaven and Back* by Rita Bennett (Zondervan, 1997), which includes the stories of people who purportedly encountered heaven through near-death experiences. For the account of a man who experienced heaven in a vision, try *Heaven: Close Encounters of the God Kind* by Jesse Duplantis (Harrison House, 1996). Also try *We Saw Heaven: True Stories of What Awaits Us on the Other Side* by Roberts Liardon (Destiny Image, 2006), which includes four accounts—some visions and some near-death experiences.

Augustine, Saint, Bishop of Hippo.

The City of God. Modern Library, 1994. 912 pp. ISBN 0679600876.

In this classic work of theology which was written in Latin during the beginning of the fifth century (just after Rome was sacked in 410 AD), Augustine compares and contrasts the city of God (the Kingdom of Heaven) with the city of man. It shows the empty and wicked nature of humanity and worldly (Roman/pagan) culture and the glory of God's city. This Modern Library edition features an introduction by Thomas Merton.

Subjects: Classics, Philosophy, Theology

More: For another classic work on theology, try Peter Kreeft's *A Summa of the Summa* (Ignatius, 1990), which is a shortened and annotated version of Saint Thomas Aquinas' 4,000-page masterpiece called the *Summa Theologica*.

Boyd, Gregory A.

God of the Possible: A Biblical Introduction to the Open View of God. Baker, 2000. 176 pp. ISBN 080106290X.

In this simple, clear introduction to the "open view of God," also known as open theism, Gregory Boyd offers a brief overview of the classical view of divine foreknowledge (that the future is totally settled, that is, "set in stone") and then offers his alternative view of divine foreknowledge (that the future is partially open and partially settled). Boyd, a theologian, author, and senior pastor of Woodland Hills Church of St. Paul, Minnesota, eloquently addresses the hard issues related to this difficult subject.

Subjects: Open Theism, Providence and Government of God, Theology

More: Another pro-open theism book is *The God Who Risks: A Theology of Providence* by John Sanders (InterVarsity, 1998). For a book that presents the opposing viewpoint, try *God's Lesser Glory: The Diminished God of Open Theism* by Bruce A. Ware (Crossway, 2000). For a book that gives alternate viewpoints, try *Divine Foreknowledge: Four Views*, edited by James K. Beilby and Paul R. Eddy (InterVarsity, 2001).

Crockett, William.

Four Views on Hell. Zondervan, 1997. 192 pp. ISBN 0310212685.

In this book, four theologians present different interpretations of what the Bible says about hell. John Walvoord (former president of Dallas Theological Seminary) says that hell is literal and eternal. William Crockett (professor of the New Testament at Alliance Theological Seminary) argues that hell is metaphorical, that it is not a physical place but a place of eternal conscious punishment. Clark Pinnock (professor emeritus of systematic theology at McMaster Divinity College) believes that hell is conditional, that is, souls in hell will eventually be destroyed (also known as the annihilationist view). Zachary J. Hayes (retired teacher of theology at the Catholic Theological Union) writes about purgatory.

Subjects: Biblical Interpretation, Hell, Purgatory, Theology

More: For more theological essays on hell, try *Hell Under Fire: Modern Scholarship Reinvents Eternal Punishment*, edited by Christopher Morgan and Robert Peterson (Zondervan, 2004).

Cunningham, Loren, David Joel Hamilton, and Janice Rogers.

Why Not Women: A Biblical Study of Women in Missions, Ministry, and Leadership. YWAM, 2000. 288 pp. ISBN 1576581837.

The idea that women must not be in public ministry is entrenched in many societies. Many people are taught that women are more easily deceived than men. Yet another idea is that women are inferior to men or even subhuman. These authors clearly demonstrate that these beliefs are not biblical, and explain that many of these ideas came from the misguided philosophy of the ancient world. They go on to say that such beliefs hinder the growth of the church and the worldwide spread of the gospel. Most of the book is devoted to a scriptural study of women in ministry.

Subjects: Women in Church Work, Women in the Bible

Forster, Roger, and Paul Marston.

God's Strategy in Human History. Expanded edition. Wipf & Stock, 2001 (Tyndale, 1974). 386 pp. ISBN 1579102735.

Examining the biblical history of the conflict among God, man, and the devil, Roger Forster and Paul Marston describe how God can be sovereign at the same time that man is free to make historic choices—even to reject the plan of God. They look at different cases from the Bible, including Job, Daniel, and the story of God hardening the pharaoh's heart. Included are word studies on the following: chosen and elect, righteousness, harden, and foreknowledge.

Subjects: History, Providence and Government of God, Theology

More: For a book that shows how God moves in modern history, try *God's Judgments: Interpreting History and the Christian Faith* by Steven J. Keillor (InterVarsity, 2007).

Graham, Billy.

Angels: God's Secret Agents. Thomas Nelson, 2000 (Doubleday, 1975). 208 pp. ISBN 0849942144.

Famous evangelist Billy Graham writes about angels, discussing how they are different from people, how angels are organized, and the personal ministry of angels. He describes good angels in the Bible and angels who have rebelled against God, like Lucifer and the demons. He also shares stories about people who have encountered angels in today's world and during Bible times.

Subjects: Angels, Demons

More: Also try *Angelic Encounters: Engaging Help from Heaven* by James W. Goll and Michal Ann Goll (Charisma House, 2007), which gives personal testimonies of angelic encounters and biblical teaching on the subject. For another testimony of a man who had personal encounters with angels, try *Angels on Assignment* by Roland Buck (Whitaker House, 2005).

Grudem, Wayne.

Christian Beliefs: Twenty Basics Every Christian Should Know. Zondervan, 2005. 159 pp. ISBN 0310255996.

Wayne Grudem, professor of biblical and systematic theology at Trinity Evangelical Divinity School in Deerfield, Illinois, discusses basic Christian doctrines by answering questions like, "What is the Bible," "What is sin?," "What is the atonement?," "What are justification and adoption?," and "What is the final judgment?" Historic confessions of faith are listed in an appendix.

Subjects: Doctrine, Systematic Theology, Theology

More: *Christian Beliefs* is a condensed version of an earlier work by Grudem. For the full treatment, try Grudem's *Systematic Theology: An Introduction to Biblical Doctrine* (Zondervan, 1995). For those readers wanting to dive in to the depths of theology, try

Norman L. Geisler's four-volume *Systematic Theology* (Bethany House, 2002–2004).

Kreeft, Peter.

Catholic Christianity: A Complete Catechism of Catholic Beliefs Based on the Catechism of the Catholic Church. Ignatius Press, 2001. 426 pp. ISBN 0898707986.

This book, based on the official *Catechism of the Catholic Church*, answers just about all the questions one could have about Catholic belief and life. It discusses faith, God, creation, Jesus Christ, forgiveness of sins, the resurrection of the body, and more. In regards to how Catholics live (morality), Peter Kreeft examines virtues, vices, and the Ten Commandments. Concerning Catholic worship, he discusses Catholic liturgy including the sacraments of baptism, confirmation, the Eucharist, penance, matrimony, etc. Kreeft, who writes lucidly and articulately, is professor of philosophy at Boston College.

Subjects: Catholic Church, Theology

More: Kreeft and Ronald K. Tacelli also wrote *Handbook of Christian Apologetics: Hundreds of Answers to Crucial Questions* (InterVarsity, 1994).

LaHaye, Tim, and Thomas Ice.

Charting the End Times: A Visual Guide to Understanding Bible Prophecy. Harvest House, 2001. 143 pp. ISBN 0736901388.

Tim LaHaye, coauthor of the best-selling Left Behind Series of novels, presents the popular evangelical view of what's going to happen on earth during the "last days." With scores of full-color charts, diagrams, time lines and maps, LaHaye and Thomas Ice present a clear overview of their dispensationalist end times theology. This book may be used as a theological handbook to LaHaye's Left Behind series.

Subjects: End of the World, Eschatology

More: For a theologically similar approach, try David Reagan's *God's Plan for the Ages: The Blueprint of Bible Prophecy* (Lamb & Lion Ministries, 2005). For two books that explain alternative views of the book of Revelation (and end-times topics), try *Revelation: Four Views: A Parallel Commentary* by Steve Gregg (Thomas Nelson, 1997) and *Four Views on the Book of Revelation* by C. Marvin Pate, editor (Zondervan, 1998).

Lewis, C. S.

The Great Divorce. HarperOne, 2001 (MacMillan, 1946). 160 pp. ISBN 0060652950.

This book is about heaven and hell. As the story opens, people in hell are waiting in a bus line to take a field trip to heaven. It turns out that those from hell don't enjoy heaven, and most decide to return to hell despite invitations and pleadings for them to stay. Issues like universalism, salvation, selfishness, and liberalism are addressed throughout the story. Although this book is a work of fiction, it is included here because it usually has a nonfiction call number in libraries and is shelved with nonfiction at bookstores.

Subjects: Classics, Heaven, Hell, Theology

More: Readers may also enjoy Lewis's *The Screwtape Letters* (HarperOne, 2001), which also uses fiction to convey spiritual truths. Also try books by Dorothy Sayers, a fellow British writer and thinker who was friends with Lewis. She wrote about the trinity and the nature of creativity in *The Mind of the Maker* (Continuum, 2004).

McDermott, Gerald R.

God's Rivals: Why Has God Allowed Different Religions? InterVarsity, 2007. 181 pp. ISBN 0830825649.

What are the "gods" that the Old Testament talks about? What are the "powers" found in the New Testament? What should Christians think about the fact that goodness and truth are found in different religions? How is it that the Bible acknowledges faith and truth in the actions and words of pagan people? In this groundbreaking book, Gerald McDermott, professor of religion at Roanoke College in Salem, Virginia, examines the Bible and the early church fathers to find some surprising answers. These could change the way people think about other religions and about who God's rivals really are.

Subjects: Comparative Religion, World Religions

More: McDermott wrote another book on world religions called *Can Evangelicals Learn from World Religions?* (InterVarsity, 2000).

McLaren, Brian D.

A Generous Orthodoxy. Youth Specialties Books (Zondervan), 2004. 297 pp. ISBN 0310257476.

Brian McLaren, a prominent leader in the Emerging Church Movement, attempts to answer the cries of a postmodernist generation with the good news of Jesus Christ. Not afraid to say that the kingdom of God and Christianity do not always line up, McLaren suggests that because the church too often asks the wrong questions, it too often offers answers that are not relevant to contemporary searchers for truth. This book attempts to correct that problem by presenting a "generous orthodoxy." The ideas in this volume are insightful and challenging (and some would say controversial).

Subjects: Emerging Church Movement, Theology

More: For a book critical of the Emerging Church Movement, try *Becoming Conversant with the Emerging Church: Understanding a Movement and Its Implications* by D. A. Carson (Zondervan, 2005).

Mathewes-Green, Frederica.

Facing East: A Pilgrim's Journey into the Mysteries of Orthodoxy. HarperSanFrancisco, 2006. 245 pp. ISBN 0060850000.

Frederica Mathewes-Green was the wife of an Episcopal priest; now she is the wife of an Orthodox priest. She didn't switch husbands; her husband converted to the Orthodox Church. This book describes her journey into Orthodoxy. Throughout one year of the Orthodox calendar, starting with Lent, Mathewes-Green describes, in her light and witty tone, the rituals and customs of Orthodoxy, weaving in personal stories from her life past and present. Mathewes-Green has written seven books and has been a commentator for National Public Radio.

Subjects: Autobiography, Conversion Stories, Frederica Mathewes-Green (1952–), Orthodox Eastern Church

More: For another book by Frederica Mathewes-Green, try *The Illumined Heart: Capture the Vibrant Faith of Ancient Christians* (Paraclete Press, 2007). Also try Timothy Ware's landmark introduction, *The Orthodox Church* (Penguin, 1997). *Becoming Orthodox: A Journey to the Ancient Christian Faith* (Conciliar Press, 2002) by Peter E. Gillquist is a well-known book describing Gillquist's conversion from evangelical Christianity to the Orthodox Church.

McGrath, Alister.

The Twilight of Atheism: The Rise and Fall of Disbelief in the Modern World. Galilee Trade, 2006. 320 pp. ISBN 0385500629.

Oxford professor of historic theology Alister McGrath was once an atheist who is now a leading Christian scholar. In this book, he presents a fascinating history of atheism. McGrath writes about Ludwig Feuerbach, Karl Marx, Sigmund Freud, the French Revolution, the Death of God Movement, and the battle between science and faith. He also discusses the Reformation's sacred/secular split, postmodernism, the growth of religion, and the failure of atheism.

Subject: Atheism—History

More: Apologist Ravi Zacharias writes about the hopelessness and despair that atheism brings in his book *The Real Face of Atheism* (Baker, 2004).

Metaxas, Eric.

Everything You Always Wanted to Know About God (but Were Afraid to Ask). WaterBrook, 2005. 226 pp. ISBN 1400071011.

>This book uses a question-and-answer format to discuss such issues as the existence of God, hell, prayer, miracles, Jesus Christ, religion, Adam and Eve, suffering, angels and demons, UFOs, homosexuality, and more. Eric Metaxas, a humor writer (not a theologian), keeps the tone light. This might be viewed as a weakness in this book, but it is also a strong point because Metaxas tackles complex theological and philosophical issues in accessible language.
>
>**Subjects:** Apologetics, Theology

Packer, J. I.

Knowing God. 20th Anniversary edition. InterVarsity, 1993 (1973). 316 pp. ISBN 0830816518.

>This classic study of God and His attributes was first published more than thirty-five years ago. J. I. Packer discusses the unchanging nature of God as well as God's majesty, wisdom, love, grace, wrath, goodness, jealousy, and more. Packer (1926–) is professor of theology at Regent College in Vancouver, British Columbia.
>
>**Subject:** Attributes of God
>
>**More:** Another study (this one brief) of the attributes of God from a Calvinistic tradition is Arthur W. Pink's *Attributes of God* (Baker reprint, 2006). Also try *God As He Longs for You to See Him* by Chip Ingram (Baker, 2004).

Pratney, Winkie.

The Nature and Character of God. Bethany, 1988. 462 pp. ISBN 1556610416.

>This thick work is part devotional study, part reference book. For each topic, like the glory of God for instance, Winkie Pratney lists pertinent scriptures and then presents a biblical word study on key Hebrew and/or Greek words (for example, "kabed"—a Hebrew word for glory—means to be heavy). This is followed by a question-and-answer section and then an analysis-and-discussion section. Finally, there is a historical discussion section including quotes and excerpts from great thinkers and writers of the past who have something to say about the topic at hand. Besides the glory of God, Pratney discusses God's love, action in history, holiness, and His triune and infinite nature. This is the first in an anticipated trilogy of books (yet to be written); the other two will deal with the character of God in His creation and in the reconciliation of His creation.

Subject: Attributes of God

More: For a shorter but well-loved devotional study of God's attributes, try *The Knowledge of the Holy* by A. W. Tozer (Harper-Collins, 1992). In the unique devotional study called *Jesus: Man of Joy* (Harvest House, 1999), Sherwood Eliot Wirt talks about the "forgotten attribute of God." For more by Winkie Pratney, try *Ultimate CORE: Church on the Radical Edge* (Bethany, 2004), *Revival: Principles to Change the World* (Christian Life Books, 2002), and *The Thomas Factor: The Key to Believing When You Cannot Find an Answer* (Chosen, 1989).

Taylor, Barbara Brown.

Speaking of Sin: The Lost Language of Salvation. Cowley, 2000. 105 pp. ISBN 1561011894.

In this slim book, gifted author and speaker Barbara Brown Taylor, a former Episcopal priest and a professor at Piedmont College in Georgia, writes about various conflicting ideas of sin. Is sin merely a medical condition that needs to be treated with drugs? Taylor says that sin may actually be our only hope, since those who admit they are broken can get help. She also talks about repentance, which, she says, "begins with the decision to return to relationship: to accept our God-given place in community." Along with repentance, Taylor writes about penance, which has to do with repairing the damage done by sin.

Subjects: Salvation, Sin, Spiritual Growth

More: Taylor writes about ending her fifteen-year ministry as a priest in the memoir *Leaving Church: A Memoir of Faith* (HarperSanFrancisco, 2006). For a collection of Taylor's well-loved sermons, try *Home by Another Way* (Cowley, 1999). A collection of sermons by another celebrated writer (and Presbyterian minister) is *Secrets in the Dark: A Life in Sermons* by Frederick Buechner (HarperOne, 2007). Readers who enjoy Barbara Brown Taylor may also like Dorothy C. Bass. Try *Receiving the Day: Christian Practices for Opening the Gift of Time* (Jossey-Bass, 2001).

Reference and Bibliographies

Allison, Joe.

Swords & Whetstones: A Guide to Christian Bible Study Resources. 3rd Edition. Jordan Publishing, 1999 (Thomas Nelson, 1982). 217 pp. ISBN 1891314017.

This guide is geared toward people who want to study the Bible but do not have an advanced education. Joe Allison recommends commentaries, Bible translations, topical bibles, concordances, dictionaries, Bible atlases, and other tools to help readers study the Bible. Allison explains what each of the tools is used for and how they work, making this a good tool for both new and experienced students.

Subjects: Bible Commentaries, Bible Study Tools

Barrett, David B., George T. Kurian, and Todd M. Johnson.

World Christian Encyclopedia: A Comparative Survey of Churches and Religions in the Modern World. 2nd Edition. Oxford University Press, 2001 (1982). 2 Volumes. 1,699 pp. ISBN 0195079639.

Volume one of this landmark reference work contains a country-by-country overview of statistics and data on global Christianity, describing each nation's religions, Christian churches, human-rights status, and basic geographic information (population, flag, languages, life expectancy, etc.) Volume two provides more in-depth data for 270 of the largest distinct religions in the world, 12,600 racial and ethnic cultures, 13,500 language profiles, 7,000 city profiles, and more. Barrett's data is used as source material for the *World Almanac* and the *Encyclopedia Britannica Book of the Year*. It is also used by mission organizations and many other researchers worldwide.

Subjects: Geography—Christianity, Missions, Statistics—Christianity

More: The *World Christian Encyclopedia* has been incorporated into the World Christian Database, a fee-based online service, at http://worldchristiandatabase.org. *Religious Congregations & Membership in the United States 2000*, edited by Dale E. Jones, et al. (Glenmary Research Center, 2002), covers 149 religious groups in America. This book allows readers to find out how many churches and members there are in a particular county or state for various Christian denominations.

Bauer, David R.

An Annotated Guide to Biblical Resources for Ministry. Hendrickson, 2003. 327 pp. ISBN 1565637232.

In this well-organized guide, designed to be used by ministers, seminary students, or anyone interested in study of the Bible or Christianity, David Bauer recommends commentaries for each book of the Bible; he also suggests resources for those studying the history of the Canon, the history of interpretation, Judaism and Jewish culture, the Apocrypha and Pseudepigrapha, the Dead Sea Scrolls, Old and New Testament theology and ethics, exegetical methods, hermeneutics, and biblical archaeology. In addition, Bauer annotates and describes tools like Bible atlases, concordances, dictionaries, and Hebrew and Greek grammars and lexicons. Bauer is

Ralph W. Beeson Professor of inductive biblical studies at Asbury Theological Seminary in Wilmore, Kentucky.

Subjects: Bible Commentaries, Bible Study Tools

More: Another book with a similar purpose is *Commentary and Reference Survey: A Comprehensive Guide to Biblical and Theological Resources* by John Glynn (Kregel, 2003).

Danker, Frederick W.

Multipurpose Tools for Bible Study. 4th Edition, with CD-ROM. Augsburg Fortress, 2003 (Concordia, 1960). 330 pp. ISBN 0800635957.

For seminary students or serious Bible students in general, professor Frederick Danker discusses resources that aid in the study of the Hebrew Old Testament and the Greek Old and New Testaments. He also discusses concordances, Hebrew and Greek grammars and lexicons, Bible dictionaries, Bible versions/translations, Judaica, archaeology, the Dead Sea Scrolls, and commentaries. This book has been around for more than forty years. This fourth edition has an accompanying CD-ROM powered by the Libronix Digital Library System (from the makers of the Logos Library System).

Subjects: Bible Commentaries, Bible Study Tools

Melton, J. Gordon

Encyclopedia of American Religions. 7th Edition. Gale Group, 2003 (McGrath, 1978). 1,408 pp. ISBN 0787663840.

This impressive reference book covers every religion or cult in the United States. With excellent coverage of Christian denominations, each of the more than 2,600 entries includes the name and address of the denomination/group, membership statistics, educational facilities, periodicals, and an informative discussion of the history, structure, and beliefs of the group. The groups are organized into "families." For instance, the Assemblies of God denomination is listed under the "Pentecostal Family." The Amish and Quakers are listed under the "European Free-Church Family." In addition to traditional Christian groups, this book also includes cults, Mormons, New Age groups, witchcraft groups, and other religions such as Judaism, Islam, Hinduism, etc.

Subjects: Churches—Directories, Comparative Religion, Cults, Denominations, Reference, Religions

More: If Melton's work is out of your price range (it is more than $300), try *Handbook of Denominations in the United States*, 12th edition, by Frank S. Mead, Samuel S. Hill, and Craig D. Atwood (Abingdon, 2005). It is very similar in scope and content to Melton. For a book that covers only Christian denominations, try *The Complete Guide to Christian Denominations: Understanding the History, Beliefs, and Differences* by Ron Rhodes (Harvest House, 2005).

Appendix A

Christian Nonfiction Book Awards

There are two main book awards that include Christian nonfiction categories: the Evangelical Christian Publishers Association (ECPA) Christian Book Awards and the *Christianity Today* (CT) Book Awards.

The **ECPA Christian Book Awards**, formerly called the Gold Medallion Awards, started in 1978. Awards are given in each of six categories: 1) Bibles, 2) Fiction, 3) Children and Youth, 4) Inspiration and Gift, 5) Bible Reference and Study, and 6) Christian Life.

Winners are announced every summer at the CBA and ECPA Awards Celebration held in conjunction with the Christian Retail Show. Award information, including current and past winners, is available online at http://www.ecpa.org/christianbookawards.

The *Christianity Today* **(CT) Book Awards** started in 1990. For this award, books are nominated by publishers and selected by CT editors. Ten panels of judges (one panel per category) then vote to choose the winners. The winners are titles that "bring understanding to people, events, and ideas that shape evangelical life, thought, and mission."

The ten categories are 1) Apologetics/Evangelism, 2) Biblical Studies, 3) Christianity and Culture, 4) Christian Living, 5) The Church/Pastoral Leadership, 6) Fiction, 7) History/Biography, 8) Missions/Global Affairs, 9) Spirituality, and 10) Theology/Ethics.

For each category there are two titles selected: the award winner and the runner up, which is called the Award of Merit.

The winners are announced in the annual Book Issue (usually in June) of *Christianity Today* magazine.

Appendix B

Review Sources

This appendix shows librarians where they can find book reviews and other selection tools for Christian nonfiction.

Trade Journals

Booklist (ISSN 0006–7385) is published twice monthly by the American Library Association. Its nonfiction adult books review area has a section for religion. Occasionally, it has a "Spotlight on Religion," which includes reviews, top-ten lists, and core-collection lists.

Catholic Library World (ISSN 0008–820X) is published quarterly by the Catholic Library Association. It has review sections entitled Theology/Spirituality, Pastoral, Church History, and other subjects that include, among other things, Christian nonfiction.

Library Journal (ISSN 0363–0277) publishes twenty-two issues each year. Its "Arts and Humanities" review area includes a section on religion. Also, there are sometimes special review articles (like a 2007 article called "Spiritual Living"), including Christian nonfiction.

Publishers Weekly (ISSN 0000–0019) is the preeminent magazine for the book trade. Its nonfiction review area has a section titled "Religion." It also publishes news articles on Christian nonfiction publishing as well as hardcover and paperback best-seller lists for religion.

Consumer Journals

America (ISSN 0002–7049) is a national weekly Catholic magazine published by the Jesuits of the United States and covers religious, political, and social issues. It includes book reviews for Christian nonfiction (as well as secular and fiction titles) in almost every issue. It also has "Spring Books" and "Fall Books" issues every year.

Books and Culture (ISSN 1082–8931) is published six times a year by Christianity Today International. It is a Christian (evangelical) review journal that reviews Christian nonfiction books as well as secular titles and the occasional fiction title.

The Christian Century (ISSN 0009–5281) is published biweekly from a liberal mainline Protestant perspective. It publishes book reviews, including special issues like the "Fall Books" issue, which has best-seller lists and large review sections (dozens of short reviews and half a dozen or more longer reviews) that focus on Christian nonfiction.

Christianity Today (ISSN 0009–5753) is a conservative evangelical monthly Protestant magazine covering theology, politics, and social issues. Every issue has a book review section that reviews eight to ten titles and sometimes includes interviews with authors. It also has an annual books issue that includes the winners of the *Christianity Today* Book Awards, which is one of the two main book awards for Christian nonfiction. (See appendix A for more on book awards.)

Commonweal (ISSN 0010–3330) is published biweekly twenty-two times a year. It is a Catholic review of arts, literature, politics, religion, and social issues by Catholic laypeople. It regularly publishes book reviews, including "Spring Books" and "Fall Books" issues that review Christian nonfiction titles. These issues also include bibliographic essays.

Internet Resources

Christian Book Summaries (**http://www.christianbooksummaries.com**) is an independent not-for-profit corporation and Web site that offers free book summaries of what the group considers to be "the best" of evangelical Christian nonfiction. These are not book reviews, but summaries. The site describes a summary as "a 5,000-word encapsulation of the book's core content—designed to give the reader the key points and the gist of the book." It also offers a free notification service alerting subscribers when new summaries are posted.

Hearts & Minds (**http://www.heartsandmindsbooks.com**) is a bookstore and Web site run by Byron Borger in Dallastown, Pennsylvania. The site allows mail-order access to a huge inventory of new and hard-to-find Christian titles (fiction and nonfiction). Readers and librarians will also be interested in some of the useful features of the Web site, including scores of book reviews. It offers a monthly book-review column, a "Booknotes" blog, and an annotated list of books arranged by subjects like history, economics, literature, popular culture, etc.

Christianbook.com (**http://www.christianbook.com**) is a book distributor for Christian products—fiction, nonfiction, music, videos, and gifts. It is the online affiliate of Christian Book Distributors, Inc. The company claims to be the world's largest distributor of Christian products. Located in Peabody, Massachusetts, it has run a "direct-to-consumer" catalogue-order company since 1978. Its prices frequently beat Amazon.com, and, like Amazon.com, the company Web site allows users to view product details such as the table of contents, excerpts, and front/back covers.

Appendix C

Christian Nonfiction Publishers

Here are the top fifty publishers that librarians selecting Christian nonfiction should know. Mailing and e-mail addresses are supplied so librarians can request catalogs. The "top fifty" were chosen based on a number of factors, including the number of titles on best-seller lists and the total number of titles published.

Abingdon Press
201 8th Ave. S.
PO Box 801
Nashville, TN 37202
http://www.abingdonpress.com

Baker Publishing Group
PO Box 6287
Grand Rapids, MI 49516-6287
http://www.bakerbooks.com

Barbour Publishing, Inc.
1810 Barbour Dr.
PO Box 719
Uhrichsville, OH 44683
http://www.barbourbooks.com

Bethany House Publishers
http://www.bethanyhouse.com

Bridge-Logos
17750 NW 115th Ave.
Bldg. 200, Ste. 220
Alachua, FL 32615
http://www.bridgelogos.com

B & H Publishing Group
127 9th Ave. N.
Nashville, TN 37234-0115
http://www.broadmanholman.com

CLC Publications
PO Box 1449
Fort Washington, PA 19034
http://www.clcpublications.com

Concordia Publishing House
3558 S. Jefferson Ave.
St. Louis, MO 63118-3968
http://www.cph.org

Continuum International Publishing
80 Maiden Lane, Ste. 704
New York, NY 10038-4814
http://www.continuumbooks.com

Cook Communications Ministries
4050 Lee Vance View
Colorado Springs, CO 80918
http://www.cookministries.com

Crossway Books and Bibles
1300 Crescent St.
Wheaton, IL 60187
http://www.crosswaybooks.com

Destiny Image Publishers
PO Box 310
Shippensburg, PA 17257
http://www.destinyimage.com

Doubleday Religion
1745 Broadway
New York, NY 10019
http://www.randomhouse.com

Eerdmans Publishing Company
2140 Oak Industrial Dr. NE
Grand Rapids, MI 49505
http://www.eerdmans.com

FaithWords (formerly Warner Faith)
10 Cadillac Dr., Ste. 220
Brentwood, TN 37027
http://www.hachettebookgroupusa.com/christian

FamilyLife Publishing
PO Box 711
Little Rock, AR 72223
http://www.familylife.com

Focus on the Family Book Publishing
8605 Explorer Dr.
Colorado Springs, CO 80920-1051
http://www.family.org

Fortress Press
PO Box 1209
Minneapolis, MN 55440-1209
http://www.fortresspress.com

Group Publishing Inc.
1515 Cascade Ave.
Loveland, CO 80539-0481
http://www.group.com

HarperSanFransisco
353 Sacramento St., #500
San Francisco, CA 94111-3653
http://www.harpercollins.com

Harrison House Publishers
PO Box 35035
Tulsa, OK 74153
http://www.harrisonhouse.com

Harvest House Publishers
990 Owen Loop N.
Eugene, OR 97402
http://www.harvesthousepublishers.com

Hendrickson Publishers
140 Summit St.
PO Box 3473
Peabody, MA 01961
http://www.hendrickson.com

Howard Books
3117 N. 7th St.
West Monroe, LA 71291
http://www.howardpublishing.com

Ignatius Press
PO Box 1339
Fort Collins, CO 80522
http://www.ignatius.com

InterVarsity Press
PO Box 1400
Downers Grove, IL 60515-1426
http://www.ivpress.com

Jossey-Bass (a Wiley imprint)
989 Market St., 5th Fl.
San Francisco, CA 94103-1741
http://www.jossey-bass.com

Judson Press
PO Box 851
Valley Forge, PA 19482-0851
http://www.judsonpress.com

Kregel Publications
PO Box 2607
Grand Rapids, MI 49501-2607
http://www.kregelpublications.com

Liguori Publications
One Liguori Dr.
Liguori, MO 63057-9999
http://www.liguori.org

Liturgical Press
St. John's Abbey
PO Box 7500
Collegeville, MN 56321-7500
http://www.litpress.org

Loyola Press
3441 N. Ashland Ave.
Chicago, IL 60657
http://www.loyolapress.org

Moody Publishers
820 N. LaSalle Blvd.
Chicago, IL 60610
http://www.moodypublishers.org

Morehouse Publishing Co.
4775 Linglestown Rd.
Harrisburg, PA 17112
http://www.morehousepublishing.com

NavPress
Box 35002
Colorado Springs, CO 80935
http://www.navpress.com

New Leaf Publishing Group
PO Box 726
Green Forest, AR 72638-0726
http://www.newleafpress.net

P & R Publishing Co.
PO Box 817
Phillipsburg, NJ 08865
http://www.prpbooks.com

Paulist Press
997 Macarthur Blvd.
Mahwah, NJ 07430
http://www.paulistpress.com

Pilgrim Press
700 Prospect Ave.
Cleveland, OH 44115-1100
http://www.thepilgrimpress.com

Regal Publishing Group
1957 Eastman Ave.
Ventura, CA 93003
http://www.regalbooks.com

Regnery Publishing
One Massachusetts Ave. NW
Washington, D.C. 20001
http://www.regnery.com

Relevant Books
100 S. Lake Destiny Dr., Ste. 200
Orlando, FL 32810
http://www.relevantbooks.com

Standard Publishing
8121 Hamilton Ave.
Cincinnati, OH 45231
http://www.standardpub.com

Strang Book Group
600 Rinehart Rd.
Lake Mary, FL 32746
http://www.strangbookgroup.com

Thomas Nelson Publishers
PO Box 141000
Nashville, TN 37214-1000
http://www.thomasnelson.com

Tyndale House Publishers
351 Executive Dr.
Carol Stream, IL 60188
http://www.tyndale.com

WaterBrook Press
12265 Oracle Blvd., Ste. 200
Colorado Springs, CO 80921
http://www.waterbrookpress.com

Whitaker House
1030 Hunt Valley Cir.
New Kensington, PA 15068
http://www.whitakerhouse.com

YWAM Publishing
PO Box 55787
Seattle, WA 98155
http://www.ywampublishing.com

Zondervan
5300 Patterson SE
Grand Rapids, MI 49530-0002
http://www.zondervan.com

Author/Title Index

100 Top Picks for Homeschool Curriculum, **223**
101 Hymn Stories, **72**
101 Ways to Reach Your Community, 173
20th Century Apostle, A, **27**
21 Irrefutable Laws of Leadership, The, 248
6 Rules Every Man Must Break, 114
90 Minutes in Heaven, 6
Abiding in Christ, **76**
About My Father's Business, 171–172
Abraham, Ken, **7**, **11**, **35–36**
Absolute Surrender, 76
Act of Marriage, The, 120–121
Adams, Jay E., 145
Adams, Stephen P., **201**
Addison, Doug, 172–173
Adventures in Darkness, 9
Africa and the Bible, **286**
After God's Own Heart, 87
After the Locusts, **151**
Aftershock, 152
Against All Odds, **34–35**
Against All Odds: My Story, **11**
Against the Tide, 28
Age of Opportunity, 138
Age of Spurgeon and Moody, The, 196–197
Ahn, Che, 83, **165–166**
AIDS Crisis, The, **205**
Aikman, David, **15**, **192**
Aimee Semple McPherson, 28

Air I Breathe, The, 73
Akiane, **8**
Alcorn, Randy, 90, 97, 119, **239–240**, **286–287**
Aldrich, Joe, 171
Aldrich, Sandra P., **150–151**
Alexander, Shaun, 40
All God's Children and Blue Suede Shoes, **212**
All God's Creatures, 258
All in Good Time, 112
All My Road Before Me, 43
All of Grace, 19
All That Glitters, **210**
All the Men in the Bible, 59
All the Messianic Prophecies of the Bible, 59
All the Music of the Bible, 191
All the Parables of the Bible, 59
All the Prayers of the Bible, **59**
All the Promises of the Bible, 59
All Things Possible, **39–40**
All Through the Ages, 230
Allegretti, Joseph G., **201–202**
Allen, Scott, 178
Allender, Dan B., **143**, **244**
Allison, Joe, **294–295**
Alone in the Universe?, **255**
Alternative Medicine, **107–108**
Alves, Elizabeth, **65**
Always Enough, **174–175**
Amazing Body Human, The, **257**

Amazing Grace, 24
Ambassador Families, **213**
Anchored in Love, 38
And the Bride Wore White, **119**
And Then I Had Kids, 131
Andersen, Robert S., 104
Anderson, Abbe, 35, 177
Anderson, David, 206
Anderson, Ken, 28
Anderson, Leith, **18**
Anderson, Neil T., 68–69, 108, **143**
Anderson, Niki, 262
Anderson, Paul, 13
Andreola, Karen, **221**, 225
Andrew, Brother, **29**
Angel Unaware, 11
Angelic Encounters, 289
Angels: God's Secret Agents, **289**
Angels on Assignment, 289
Animal Gospel, **258**
Annotated Guide to Biblical Resources for Ministry, An, **295–296**
Anointed for Business, 177, **238**
Anonymous, **88**
Another Sort of Learning, 99
Answering the Eight Cries of the Spirited Child, **129**
Answers to Prayer, 24, 53
Apologia Pro Vita Sua, 19
Apostle: A Life of Paul, The, 18
Aquinas, Thomas, 287
Archaeology and the New Testament, 284
Archaeology and the Old Testament, **284**
Arnold, Ruthie, 117
Aroney-Sine, Christine, 13
Arp, Claudia, **129**
Arp, David, **129**
Arrington, Candy, 152
Arroyo, Raymond, 33
Art and Soul, **182**
Art and the Bible, **183–184**
Art and the Christian Mind, **183**
Art for God's Sake, 184
Art in Action, 184
Art of Forgiving, The, 148
Art of Storytelling, The, **220–221**
Art of Worship, The, **74–73**
Arterburn, Steve, **117–118**, 123, **143–144**
Ask the Animals, 263
Assault on Eden, 42

Association of Christian Schools International, 230
Attributes of God, 293
Atwood, Craig D., 296
Augustine, Saint, Bishop of Hippo, **287**, **30**
Authentic Faith, 96
Authority in Prayer, **63**
Autobiography of G. K. Chesterton, The, 157
Autobiography of George Müller, The, **23–24**, 175
Autobiography of Jeanne Guyon, The, 57
Autobiography of Peter Cartwright, 21

Bachleda, Lynne, 263
Back to Jerusalem, 29, 192
Backus, William, 110, 146–147
Bahnsen, Greg L., 164
Bainton, Roland H., **18**
Bait of Satan, The, **86–87**, 148
Baker, H. A., **5**, 175
Baker, Heidi, 84, **174–175**
Baker, Rolland, 84, **174–175**
Baker, Thomas, 202
Baker, Tim, 162
Baker, Warren, **278–279**
Bakke, Dennis W., 238, **244–245**
Bakke, Ray, 207
Baldwin, Stephen, **10**
Barbour, Ian G., 254
Barker, Kenneth L., **276–277**
Barnes, Emilie, 112
Barnes, Robert G., **129–130**
Barrett, David B., 58, **295**
Barrs, Jerram, **166**
Barsotti, Catherine M., **209–210**
Barton, David, **202**
Basic Christianity, 20, 159
Basic Discipleship, 81, 92
BASIC Steps to Godly Fitness, **109**
Bass, Dorothy C., 294
Battlefield of the Mind, 60, **93**
Battling Unbelief, 94
Bauer, David R., **295–296**
Bauer, Susan Wise, **221–222**
Baumann, Dan, 177
Baxter, Richard, 77
Beamer, Lisa, **7**

Bearing Fresh Olive Leaves, **184**
Beausay, Bill, **130**, 131–132
Beausay, Katherine, 131–132
Beautiful Girlhood, 136–137
Beautiful Places and Spiritual Spaces, 111
Beautiful Side of Evil, The, **4**
Beauty of Aging, The, 103
Beauty of Spiritual Language, The, 85
Bebbington, David, 196–197
Beck, Astrid B., **279–280**
Beckett, John D., **234**
Becknell, Thomas, **260–261**
Beckwith, Francis, 161–162
Becoming a Contagious Christian, 170
Becoming a Prayer Warrior, **65**
Becoming Conversant with the Emerging Church, 292
Becoming Orthodox, 292
Becoming the Parent God Wants You to Be, 134
Beers, Ronald A., **277**
Before Their Time, **106**
Before You Say I Do, 127
Begbie, Jeremy, 185
Behe, Michael, **269**
Behind the Screen, **212**
Behind the Stories, **41**, 186
Beholding the Glory, 185
Beilby, James K., 288
Being Latino in Christ, **204**
Being White, **205–206**
Believer's Guide to Legal Issues, The, 202
Believers in Business, 236
Believing God, **93–94**
Bell, Kathy, **121**
Bell, Rob, **86**
Beloved Disciple, The, 23, 95
Benedict XVI, Pope, **18–19**
Bennett, Arthur, 54
Bennett, Dennis J., **81–82**, 85
Bennett, James W., 285
Bennett, Rita, **6**, **81–82**, 287
Berquist, Laura M., 222
Best, Harold, **188**
Bethge, Eberhard, **19**, 79
Betrayed!, **4–5**
Between: A Girl's Guide to Life, 113
Between Heaven and Hell, 158
Bevere, John, **86–87**, 89, 148
Bevere, Lisa, 115

Bevington, G. C., **52–53**
Beyond Charity, 207
Beyond the Veil, **63–64**
Bible de Jerusalem, 278
Bible Jesus Read, The, 97
Biblical Case for an Old Earth, A, **269**
Biblical Creationism, 267
Biblical Guide to Alternative Medicine, The, 108
Bickle, Mike, **87**
Biebel, David B., **144**
Big Picture 2, The, 210
Big Picture: Finding the Spiritual Message in Movies, The, 210
Big Picture: Getting Perspective on What's Really Important in Life, The, 12
Billheimer, Paul E., **53**
Billy Graham Story, The, 21
Bird by Bird, 186–187
Birds Our Teachers, The, **258–259**
Birth Control for Christians, **104–105**
Blackaby, Henry, 93–94, 248
Blackaby, Richard, 248
Blamires, Harry, 200
Blanchard, Ken, **245**
Blessing, The, **141**
Blood of Christ, The, 76
Bloom, Jan, **226**
Bloom, Stephen, 202
Blue Like Jazz, 42
Blue, Judy, 240, **241**
Blue, Ken, 144
Blue, Ron, 240, **240–241**, **242**
Blumhofer, Edith L., 28
Boa, Kenneth D., **156**
Boehi, David, **138–139**
Bold as a Lamb, 28
Bolley, Cristine, 111, 258–259
Bonar, Andrew, 19
Bondage Breaker, The, 68–69, **143**
Bones of Contention, **265–266**
Bonhoeffer, Dietrich, 19, **78–79**
Bonnke, Reinhard, **166–167**
Book Lover's Guide to Great Reading, **98**
Book of Common Prayer, The, **49**
Book of Moonlight, The, 41
Book That Transforms Nations, The, 79, 180
Book Tree, The, **229**
Books Children Love, **230–231**
Books That Build Character, 186, **228**

Booth-Tucker, Frederick St. George de Lautour, 28
Bordenkircher, Susan, 109
Born Again, **2–3**
Born Fundamentalist, Born Again Catholic, 3
Bostrom, Cheryl, 263
Botkin, Anna Sophia, 136–137
Botkin, Elizabeth, 136–137
Bouma-Prediger, Steven, 260
Boundaries Face-to-Face, 148
Boundaries in Dating, **122–123**
Boundaries with Kids, 131
Bounds, E. M., 53
Bowman, Lee, **148**
Bowman, Robert M., Jr., **156**
Boy Meets Girl, 123
Boyd, Edward K., 157
Boyd, Gregory A., 79, 146, 157, **202–203**, **287–288**
Boyhood and Beyond, 136, **139–141**, 237
Boys!, 132
Brady, Bernard, 261
Brand, Hilary, **182**
Brand, Paul, 15, **257**
Brand, Raymond H., **260**
Braund, Ron, 129
Breaking Free, 68–69
Breaking Intimidation, 87
Breast Cancer Care Book, The, **110**
Bright, Bill, 51, 170
Briner, Bob, 212, 248
Bringing Up Boys, **132**
Broer, Sharon, 106
Broer, Ted, 105, **106**
Bromiley, Geoffrey W., 279–280
Brook, Linda Rios, 236
Brother Yun, 192
Brott, Rich, 240
Brown, Colin, **197**
Brown, Montague, **197–198**
Bruce, F. F., **283**, 285
Bruchko, 33
Bruchko and the Motilone Miracle, **33**
Bryson City Seasons, 14
Bryson City Secrets, 14
Bryson City Tales, **13–14**
Buchanan, Mark, **87**
Buck, Roland, 289
Buckingham, Jamie, **3**

Bucknam, Robert, 140–141
Budziszewski, J., **203**, 219
Buechner, Frederick, **40**, 294
Buford, Bob, 236
Bulletproof, 17
Bunyan, John, **54**
Buried Alive, 266
Burke, Susan E., 220
Burkett, Larry, **234**, **241–242**, 244
Business by the Book, **234**
Business for the Glory of God, 234
Business Through the Eyes of Faith, **234–235**
Bustard, Ned, **182–183**
Butler, Phill, **245**

C. S. Lewis: A Biography, 44
C. T. Studd: Cricketer and Pioneer, 22, **32–33**
Caesar, Shirley, 37
Call, The, **89–90**
Call of Duty, 16
Call to Prayer, A, 58
Called: "Hello, My Name Is Mrs. Jefferson, I Understand Your Plane Is Being Hijacked–", 7
Called to Care, 103
Called to Serve, 246
Cameron, Barbara, **10–11**
Cameron, Kirk, 11, **168**
Cameron, Nigel, 105–106
Campbell, Darrel, **39**
Campbell, Regi, 171–172
Can a Good Christian Be a Good Lawyer?, 202
Can Do It!, 12
Can Evangelicals Learn from World Religions?, 291
Can Homosexuality Be Healed?, **121**
Can Man Live without God?, 29, 165
Cancer, **109**
Caner, Emir Fethi, 4, 32, 196, **203**
Caner, Ergun Mehmet, 4, 196, **203**
Canham, Elizabeth J., 263
Canon of Scripture, The, 285
Canon of the New Testament, The, 285
Canticles of the Earth, 263
Carey, William, 35
Caring for Sexually Abused Children, 143
Caring for Your Aging Parents, 103

Carlson, Betty, **37–38**
Carlson, Richard, 252
Carmella, Angela C., 202
Carmichael, Amy, 31
Carpenter, Humphrey, **40–41**
Carre, E. G., 22, **54**
Carson, Ben, **12**
Carson, D. A., **167**, 292
Carter, Carrie, **102**
Carter, Craig A., 213
Carter, Gary, 39
Carter, Stephen L., 208
Cartwright, Peter, 21
Cartwright, Teryl, 211
Caruana, Vicki, **222**
Case for a Creator, The, 163, **271**
Case for Christ, The, **163**
Case for Classical Christian Education, The, 221
Case for Faith, The, 163
Cash, Carey, 17
Cash, John Carter, 38
Cathedrals, The, 36
Catholic Bible, **278**
Catholic Christianity, **290**
Catholic Homeschool Companion, The, 222
Catholic Lifetime Reading Plan, The, **98–99**
Cavins, Jeff, 3
CCM Magazine Presents 100 Greatest Albums in Christian Music, 190
CCM Magazine Presents 100 Greatest Songs in Christian Music, 190
Celebration of Discipline, **79–80**
Century of the Holy Spirit, 57
Certain Trumpets, 247
Chadwick, Harold J., **32**
Chambers, Oswald, 23, **48**
Chance to Die, A, 24, **31**
Chapian, Marie, 146–147
Chaplin, Adrienne, **182**
Chapman, Gary, **124–125**
Chappell, Dorothy F., **252**
Charismatic Century, The, **57**
Charles Colson: A Story of Power, Corruption, and Redemption, 3
Charlotte Mason Companion, A, **221**, 225
Charlotte Mason Education, A, 221
Chart Watch, **190**
Charting the End Times, **290**

Chatraw, Jason, 260
Chavda, Mahesh, **50–51**, 85
Chesterton, G. K., **30**, **157**
Chewning, Richard C., **234–235**
Chicken's Guide to Talking Turkey with Your Kids About Sex, A, **121**
Child Sexual Abuse, 143
Chole, Alicia Britt, **88**
Choosing Forgiveness, 92, **148**
Choosing God's Best, 123
Chosen Vessels, **116**
Chris Chrisman Goes to College, 219
Christ and Culture, **212–213**
Christ Centered Therapy, 143
Christian Apologetics, **164**
Christian Beliefs, **289–290**
Christian Coaching, 145
Christian Counseling Casebook, 145
Christian Counseling, **144–145**
Christian Counselor's Manual, The, 145
Christian Critique of Art and Literature, A, 184
Christian Family Guide Explains the Middle East Conflict, **201**
Christian Family Guide to Surviving Divorce, **128**
Christian Girl's Guide to Money, The, 241
Christian Imagination, The, **187**
Christian Jihad, 196
Christian Legal Society, **216**
Christian Men of Science, 13
Christian Mind, The, 200
Christian Perspectives on Legal Thought, 202
Christian View of Science and Scripture, The, 253
Christian Working Woman, The, **238–239**
Christian Writer's Manual of Style, The, **186**
Christian Writers' Market Guide 2007, **187**
Christianity and Social Work, **206**
Christianity and Western Thought, 197
Christianity for Modern Pagans, 161
Christian's Guide to Investing, A, 243
Chrnalogar, Mary Alice, 144
Chronicles of Wasted Time, 90
Church Boy, 37
Church History in Plain Language, **195–196**

Church on Sunday, Work on Monday, **236**
Churches That Make a Difference, 208
Churches That Pray, 60
City of God, The, **287**
Civil War As a Theological Crisis, The, 196–197
Clark, Chap, 120
Clark, Mark, **254–255**, 256
Clark, Stephen R., 128
Clarkson, Clay, **130**, 226
Clarkson, Edith Margaret, 258–259
Clarkson, Sally, **130–131**, 226
Clement, Kim, 82
Cloister Walk, The, 44
Cloud, Henry, **122–123**, **131**, 148
Cloud of Unknowing, The, 75
Cochran, Robert F., 202
Coffeehouse Gospel, The, **173**
Colbert, Don, 52, **106–107**, 108
Colby, Kimberlee Wood, **216**
Cole, Edwin Louis, 116
Coleman, Jan, **151**
Coleman, Robert E., 27, **167–168**
Collected Letters of C. S. Lewis, The, **43**
Collier, Richard, 28
Collins, Ace, 72
Collins, David, 14
Collins, Francis S., 272
Collins, Gary R., **144–145**
Colson, Charles W. "Chuck", **2–3**, 105–106, 195, **204**, **210**
Comeback, **39**
Comfort, Philip, 283
Comfort, Ray, 11, **168**
Coming to Peace with Science, **272**
Comiskey, Andrew, **118**
Commentary and Reference Survey, 296
Common Mistakes Singles Make, **124**
Companjen, Anneke, **30**
Complete Book of Christian Parenting & Child Care, The, **140**
Complete Book of Christian Wedding Vows, The, **128–129**
Complete Guide to Christian Denominations, The, 296
Complete Guide to Family Health, Nutrition & Fitness, 104
Complete Word Study New Testament with Greek Parallel, The, **282–283**
Complete Word Study Old Testament, The, **278–279**
Complete Works of E. M. Bounds on Prayer, The, 53
Complete Works of Francis A. Schaeffer, The, 163, 200
Complete Works of Oswald Chambers, The, 23, 48
Complete Worship Leader, The, 72
Complete Worship Service, The, 72
Condi, 15
Confessions, The, **30**
Confident Woman, The, 113–114
Conquering Fear, 146
Conspiracy of Kindness, **173**
Contemporary Christian Authors, 41, 186
Control Freak, The, **147**
Conversations with a Barred Owl, 258–259
Coogan, Michael D., 277
Cook, Coleen, **210**
Cook, E. David, **252**
Cooke, Graham, 61, **82**
Cooper, Elaine, 225
Cooper, Kenneth H., **108–109**
Copan, Paul, **157**
Cornelius Van Til: An Analysis of His Thought, 164
Cornwall, Judson, 151
Cosgrove, Mark P., **257**
Cost of Discipleship, The, 19, **78–79**
Costly Call, The, 32
Coughlin, Paul, 114
Courageous Leadership, **247**
Courtney, Vicki, **113**, **131–132**
Cowan, Louise, **226–227**
Cowan, Steven, 156
Cowman, L. B., **48–49**
Cox, David, 152
Cox, Melissa, 140
Crabb, Larry, **55**, **88**, 145
Crafted Prayer, 61
Crane, Christopher, 171–172
Created for Work, 140, **237**
Creating the Moms Group You've Been Looking For, **139**
Creating Understanding, 220
Creation and the World of Science, 254–255
Creation and Time, 268

Creation: A Witness to the Wonder of God, **262**
Creation As Science, **267–268**
Creation Regained, 201
Creative Correction, 12
Creative Gift, The, 183
Creative Storytelling Guide for Children's Ministry, 221
Creator and the Cosmos, The, 264, **268**, 270
Crespo, Orlando, **204**
Crime and Its Victims, **209**
Crist, Terry, 166
Crockett, William, **288**
Cross and the Switchblade, The, 3
Cross of Christ, The, 20
Cruise, Jason, **261**
Cruz, Nicky, **3**
Culturally Savvy Christian, The, **214–215**
Cunningham, Loren, **31**, **79**, 180, **288**
Cunningham, Mary, **192–193**
Cuozzo, Jack, 266
Currid, John D., 284
Currie, David B., 3
Curtis, Barbara, **204**
Custance, Arthur C., 256
Custer, Stewart, **264**
Cymbala, Jim, 3

D'Souza, Dinesh, **158**
Dad's Everything Book for Daughters, 135
Dad's Everything Book for Sons, 136
Dakota: A Spiritual Geography, 262
Dale Evans Rogers: Rainbows on a Hard Trail, **11**
Dallas, Joe, 118, 122
Dallimore, Arnold A., **19**, 23–24
Damazio, Frank, 240
Damsels in Distress, 126
Dance with a Purpose, 74
Dance!, 74
Dancing for Joy, 74
Dancing into the Anointing, 74
Danger of Raising Nice Kids, The, **141**
Danker, Frederick W., **296**
Danner, Ruth McHaney, 111
Daring to Live on the Edge, 31, 79
Dark Night of the Soul, **75**
Darwin on Trial, **270–271**
Darwinism Defeated?, **273**

Darwin's Black Box, **269**
Daughters of Hope, 30
David: A Man of Passion & Destiny, **94–95**
David Martyn Lloyd-Jones, 20
Davis, Chris, **223**
Davis, Ellyn, **223**
Davis, Jeffry, 99
Davis, Marietta, 6
Davis, Paul, 38
Davis, Robert, 103
Dawson, John, **65–66**, 69
Dawson, Joy, 66, 81, **82–83**, **88–89**
Day, Dorothy, **20**, 42
Day I Died, The, **6**
Dayton, Bev, 241
Dayton, Howard, 240, 241, 244
de Caussade, Jean-Pierre, 76
De Pree, Max, **245–246**
de S. Cameron, Nigel M., **105–106**
de Vinck, Christopher, **41**
Deane, Barbara, 103
Debt-Free Living, 244
Debt-Proof Your Marriage, 244
Deep Wounds, Deep Healing, 85–86, 110, **146**
Deepening Your Conversation with God, 64
Deeper Experiences of Famous Christians, **22**
Deere, Jack, **83**, 85
Defeating Dark Angels, **66–67**
Defense of the Faith, The, 164
DeKok, Joy, 258–259
Deliver Us from Evil, 4, **165**
Deliverance from Evil Spirits, 67
Delivering the Captives, **70–71**
DeLong, Janice, 41, 186
Dembski, William A., **270**
DeMoss, Nancy Leigh, **113–114**
Dennis, Lane T., 25
Derek Prince: A Biography, **27**
Design Inference, The, 270
Design Revolution, The, 270
Designing Your Own Classical Curriculum, **222**
Desire, **89**
Desires in Conflict, 118
Desiring God, **94**
Destined for the Throne, **53**

Detweiler, Craig, 214
Developing the Leader Within You, **248**
Developing the Leaders Around You, 248
Developing Your Prophetic Gifting, **82**
Devotional Classics, 77–78
DeVries, Robert, 151
DeWeese, Garrett J., 197
Dewitched, 162
Dewitt, Calvin B., 260
Deyoung, Donald, 265
Dickerson, Matthew, 37
Dickson, John, **72–73**
Dietrich Bonhoeffer: A Biography, **19**, 79
Dillard, Annie, **261–262**
Dillow, Linda, 120–121
Dirty Little Secret, The, **119–120**
Discipleship of the Mind, 198–199
Disciplines of a Godly Man, 116
Discipling Nations, **178**
Discovering God's Way of Handling Money, 241
Discovering the Mind of a Woman, 127
Dismissing God, 188
Divided by Faith, 206
Divine Conspiracy, The, 81
Divine Foreknowledge: Four Views, 288
Divine Hours, **49–50**
Divorce and Remarriage, **125**
Dobson, Danae, 113
Dobson, James, **114**, 129, **132**
Doctors Who Followed Christ, **12**
Doctrine of Repentance, The, 77
Documentary History of Religion in America Since 1877, A, 193
Documentary History of Religion in America to 1877, A, 193
Does God Need Our Help?, 105–106
Doing Archaeology in the Land of the Bible, 284
Doing Business by the Good Book, **238**
Doing God's Business, 237–238
Dominance of Evangelicalism, The, 196–197
Don't Let the Goats Eat the Loquat Trees, 13
Doornbos, Mary Molewyk, **102–103**
Dormon, Sara, 133
Dorsett, Lyle W., 43, 53, **168–169**
Dortzbach, Deborah, **205**
Doubts About Darwin, **271–272**

Doud, Guy Rice, **216**
Douglas Gresham, 44
Douglas, J. D., 279–280
Dravecky, Dave, **39**
Dravecky, Jan, 39
Drawing Near, 87
Dream Language, 84
Dreaming with God, 91
Dreams and Visions, **84**
Driven by Eternity, 87
Dudley-Smith, Timothy, **20**
Dueck, Murray, **83–84**
Duffy, Cathy, **223**
Duncan, Michael, 102
Duplantis, Jesse, 5, 287
Dying with Grace, 151

E. M. Bounds, Man of Prayer, 53
Earth-Wise, 260
Eastman, Dick, **55**
Eat This Book, **284–285**
Eble, Diane, **41**, 186
Eby, J. Wesley, 220
Eby, John W., **234–235**
Eddy, Paul R., 288
Eden, Dawn, **118–119**
Edgar, William, **164**, 188
Edge of Evolution, The, 269
Educating the Wholehearted Child, 226
Edwards, David, **97–98**
Edwards, Gene, **89**, 144
Edwards, Jonathan, 22
Eerdmans Dictionary of the Bible, **279–280**
Effective Biblical Counseling, 145
Egan, Hope, **107**
Eggerichs, Emerson, 125
Ehman, Karen, 111–112, **114**, 136
Eims, LeRoy, 168
Eldred, Kenneth, **235**, 237
Eldredge, John, **89**
Elie, Paul, **41–42**
Elijah Task, The, 82
Eller, T. Suzanne, 7, 131
Elliot, Elisabeth, 24, **31–32**, 113–114, 123, 126, **175**
Ellsberg, Robert, 42
Embodied Prayer, 74
Emerson, Michael O., 206
Emily Dickinson and the Art of Belief, 44

Emotional Phases of a Woman's Life, 113–114
Encyclopedia of American Religions, **296**
Encyclopedia of Contemporary Christian Music, **190**
End of the Spear, 32
English Teaching As Christian Mission, **220**
Enjoying Intimacy with God, 87
Enns, Peter, **284**
Episcopal Church, **49**
Eric Liddell: Pure Gold, 33
Eros Defiled, **122**
ESL: Creating a Quality English As a Second Language Program, 220
Essential Guide to Public Speaking, An, **219–220**
Estes, Steve, 198
Eternity in Their Hearts, 34, **178–179**
Ethridge, Shannon, 118, **119**
Evangelism and a Lifestyle, 172
Evangelism by Fire, 167
Evangelism for Our Generation, 172
Evangelism in the Early Church, 169
Evans, Dale, 11
Evans, Gillian R., **193**
Evans, Tony, 207
Ever Increasing Faith, 28
Everlasting Man, The, 157
Everson, Eva Marie, 120
Everson, Jessica, 120
Every Heart Restored, 117
Every Man's Battle, **117**
Every Woman's Battle, **119**
Every Young Woman's Battle, 119
Everything You Always Wanted to Know About God (but Were Afraid to Ask), 159, **293**
Evidence Bible, The, 168
Evolution Exposed, **266**
Evolution: The Disguised Friend of Faith?, **273–274**
Evolution: The Fossils Still Say No!, 266
Ev'ry Time I Feel the Spirit, 37, **191**
Excellent Wife, The, **126**
Executive Influence, 171–172
Expecting Miracles, 84
Experiencing God, 93–94
Experiencing the Depths of Jesus Christ, **56–57**, 76

Exploring Worship, 73–74
Expositor's Bible Commentary, The, 282
Eyes of the Heart, The, **40**
Eyes Wide Open, **214**
Eynikel, Hilde, 33
Ezzo, Gary, 140–141

Fabric of Faith, 111
Fabric of Faithfulness, The, 219
Fabric of This World, The, 235
Facedown, 73
Facing East, **292**
Facts of Life, The, **11–12**
Faith, God and Rock & Roll, **188–189**
Faith Has Its Reasons, **156**
Faith in the Byzantine World, **192–193**
Faith in the Medieval World, **193**
Faith Under Fire, **17**
Faith-Based Fitness, **108–109**
Falk, Darrel R., **272**
Falling to Heaven, 6
Families Where Grace Is in Place, **142**
Family Finance Handbook, 240
Family Program for Reading Aloud, A, 230
Fanestil, John, **151**
Fann, Anne-Geri, **175–176**
Farrar, Steve, 136
Farrington, Debra K., 258
Farris, Christa, 190
Farris, Michael, 135
Fasting for Spiritual Breakthrough, **51**
Fasting Made Easy, 52
Fatal Attractions, 122
Father Forgive Us, 66
Father Heart of God, The, **91–92**
Fear of the Lord, The, 89
Fearfully and Wonderfully Made, 15, **257**
Fearless, **145–146**
Feathers from My Nest, **23**
Fee, Gordon D., **279**
Feinberg, Margaret, **97–98**
Feldhahn, Shaunti, **115**
Felix, Antonia, 15
Felton, Jack, **143–144**
Felton, Sandra, 112
Feminine Appeal, 113–114
Feminism: Mystique or Mistake?, 206
Feminist Mistake, The, **206**
Fields, Doug, 211

Fife, Dale, 87
Financial Parenting, 241
Finding a Lasting Love, 123
Finding Darwin's God, **273**
Finding God at Harvard, **218**
Finding God Beyond Harvard, 218
Finding God in the Movies, **209–210**
Finding Mr. Right, 123
Fingerprint of God, 268
Finney, Charles G., **20–21**, **55–56**, 62
Finney's Systematic Theology, 21
Fintel, William A., **109**
Fire Evangelism, **165–166**
Fire of God, The, 89
Fish Out of Water, **219**
Fit Bodies, Fat Minds, 199
Fit Kids!, 109
Fitzgerald, Sally, 42
Fitzpatrick, Elyse, **145**
Five Love Languages for Singles, The, 125
Five Love Languages of Children, The, 125
Five Love Languages, The, **124–125**
Five Views on Apologetics, 156
Flannery O'Connor: Spiritual Writings, 42
Flew, Antony, 158
Floyd, Timothy, 202
Flynt, Sherri, **104**
Focus on the Family Complete Book of Baby and Child Care, The, 140
Focus on the Family Complete Guide to Caring for Aging Loved Ones, **103**
Focus on the Family Physicians Resource Council, **103**
Fontana, Danny, 243
For Kirk and Covenant, 18
For the Audience of One, 71
For the Beauty of the Earth, 260
For the Children's Sake, **225**
For Women Only, **115**
Forbes, Cheryl, **217**
Ford, Leighton, **246**
Ford, Marcia, **98**
Forest in the Seed, The, 178
Forever and Ever, Amen, 38
Forgive and Forget, 8, 148
Forgiving the Dead Man Walking, 8
Fornof, John, **211**
Forster, Roger, **252**, **288–289**
Forsyth, P. T., 54

Foster, Richard J., **56**, 77–78, **79–80**
Fountain, Daniel E., **110**
Four Views on Hell, **288**
Four Views on the Book of Revelation, 290
Foxe, John, **32**
Frame, John, 164
Francis A. Schaeffer Trilogy, A, 25, 163, 195, **200**
Francis of Assisi and His World, **30**
Franklin, Kirk, 37
Fraser, Peter, **211**
Free and Clear, 244
Freedman, David Noel, **279–280**
Freedom of Simplicity, 80
Freeman, Becky, 117, 131–132, **132**
French, David, 216, 224
Fresh Wind, Fresh Fire, 3
Frick, Don, 246
Friendship Factor, The, **147**
From Jerusalem to Irian Jaya, **179–180**
From Sea to Shining Sea, 194
Frontline Christians in a Bottom-Line World, 236
Frye, Roger, 146
Frye, Roland Mushat, 253
Fugate, Virginia, 126
Fulfilled Journey, **14–15**
Full Gospel, Fractured Minds?, 199
Full House of Growing Pains, A, **10–11**
Fuller, Cheri, 61–62, **145–146**, **216–217**
Fundamentalism and American Culture, 193
Futato, Mark D., **262**
Future War of the Church, The, 73

Gaebelein, Frank E., 282
Gaither, Bill, **35–36**
Gaither, Gloria, 36
Gallagher, Susan V., 188
Galli, Mark, 30
Gamer, The, 39
Garber, Steven, 219
Garden of the Soul, The, 262
Gardener Looks at the Fruits of the Spirit, A, 262
Gardening Mercies, **262**
Garlock, Ruthanne, 65
Garrett, Ginger, **132–133**
Gasque, Laurel, **183**
Gaustad, Edwin S., **193**

Geisler, Norman L., 157, 289–290
General Next to God, The, 28
Generous Orthodoxy, A, **291–292**
Genesee Diary, The, 93
Genesis Debate, The, 269
Genesis Flood, The, **266–267**
Genesis Question, The, **268–269**
George Müller of Bristol, 24
George Washington Carver: Man's Slave Becomes God's Scientist, 14
George Whitefield: The Life and Times of the Great Evangelist of the Eighteenth-Century Revival, 23
George Whitefield's Journals, 27, 75
George, Elizabeth, 113
Get Out of That Pit, 68–69, 93–94
Getz, Gene A., 116, 240
Gibson, Tim, 176
Gift of Grandparenting, The, **142**
Gift of Music The, **37–38**
Gift of Pain, The, 257
Gift of the Stranger, The, 220
Gifted Hands, **12**
Gifts and Ministries of the Holy Spirit, 82
Gifts of the Spirit, The, 82
Giglio, Louie, 73
Gilbert, Lela Gilbert, **92**
Gilbreath, Edward, **205**
Gillham, Anabel, 113–114
Gillmor, Verla, 239
Gillquist, Peter E., 292
Gingerich, Owen, **253**
Giniger, Kenneth Seeman, 253
Girl Meets God, **45**
Girls, 131–132
Gish, Duane, 266
Gitt, Werner, **265**
Givler, Amy, 109
Gladys Aylward: The Little Woman, 35
Glahn, Sandra L., **103**
Glaspey, Terry, **98**
Glorious Pursuit, The, 96
Glynn, John, 296
GO Manual, **180**
Goble, Kathleen, 129
Goble and Shea's Complete Wedding Planner, 129
God @ Work, 238
God and Evolution, 273
God and the Oval Office, 15

God As He Longs for You to See Him, 293
God at Work, 236, 237–238
God Between the Covers, **98**
God Chasers, The, 78
God, Faith, and the New Millennium, 255
God Gave the Song, 36
God, Humans, and Animals, 258
God I Love, The, **26**
God in the Dock, 76
God in the Pits, **8–9**
God Is at Work, **235**
God Is Closer Than You Think, 80
God Is My CEO, **235–236**
God, Medicine, and Miracles, **110**
God of the Possible, **287–288**
God on Mute, 63
God Through the Looking Glass, **184–185**
God Who Risks, The, 288
God's Call, 29
God's Chosen Fast, **51–52**
God's Design for Sex series, 121
God's Design for the Highly Healthy Child, 104
God's Design for the Highly Healthy Person, **104**
God's Design for the Highly Healthy Teen, 104
God's Generals, 28
God's Judgments, 194, 289
God's Lesser Glory, 288
God's Name in Vain, 208
God's Plan for the Ages, 290
God's Rivals, **291**
God's Smuggler, 29
God's Strategy in Human History, **288–289**
God's Universe, **253**
Godawa, Brian, 210
Going Public with Your Faith, **171–172**
Golden Cow, The, 240
Goll, James W., 66, 82, 84, 289
Goll, Michal Ann, 84, 289
Gonzalez, Guillermo, 268, **270**
Good News for the Chemically Dependent and Those Who Love Them, **150**
Goodrick, Edward W., 281–283
Gordon, Ernest, **16**
Gospel According to the Beatles, The, 189
Goss, Carolyn Stanford, 186
Goss, Leonard G., 186

Gowler, Kathy, 131–132
Goyer, Tricia, **133**
Grace and Truth Paradox, The, 97
Grace Awakening, The, 95
Grace Disguised, A, **153**
Grace Is Where I Live, 187
Grace-Based Parenting, 142
Graham, Billy, **21**, **169**, **289**
Graham, Michelle, **115**
Graham, Ruth, 133
Grandparenthood, 142
Granger, Thom, 190
Grant, Janet Kobobel, **110**
Graves, Dan, **12–13**
Gray, Alice, 17
Great Commission Companies, 177, **236–237**
Great Divorce, 76, **290–291**
Great Omission, The, 81
Great Physician's Rx for Health and Wellness, The, **108**
Great Revival in Wales, The, 62
Greek for the Rest of Us, 281
Greek-English Concordance to the New Testament, The, 281, 283
Green, Melody, **36**
Green, Michael, **169**
Green, Roger Lancelyn, 44
Greenleaf, Robert K., **246**
Gregg, Steve, 290
Gregory, John Milton, 218
Greig, Pete, **56**, 63
Gresh, Dannah, **115**, **119**
Grief Observed, A, 43, 45, **152**
Grier, Rosey, 40
Grieving a Suicide, **152**
Griggs, Janella, **97–98**
Gross, Craig, **119–120**
Grubb, Norman, **21–22**, **32–33**, 54
Grudem, Wayne, 234, **289–290**
Guide to the Law on Parents' Rights in Education, A, 224
Guinness, Os, 29, **89–90**, 199, **226–227**
Guroian, Vigen, **185–186**
Guthrie, Stan, **178**
Guyon, Jeanne, **56–57**, 76

Habit of Being, 42
Habits of the Mind, 198–199
Hagopian, David, 269

Hahn, Kimberly, **3**
Hahn, Scott, **3**
Hale, Mabel, 136–137
Hale, Thomas, **13**
Halftime, 236
Hall, Ron, **7–8**, 9
Halley, Henry H., **280**
Halley's Bible Handbook, **280**
Halliday Steve, **104**
Ham, Ken, **265**
Hamel, Mike, 171–172
Hamiltion, David Joel, **288**
Hamlin, Catherine, **13**
Hammers and Nails, 37
Hammond, Pete, **249**
Hammond, Wayne, 41
Hamon, Bill, 82
Hamon, Jane, **84**
Hampton, Barbara, **227–228**
Hanby-Robie, Sharon, **111**
Hancock, Joey, 261
Hancock, Maxine, 143
Handbook for Spiritual Warfare, The, 70
Handbook for Teaching Bible-Based ESL, 220
Handbook of Christian Apologetics, 157, 290
Handbook of Denominations in the United States, 296
Hans Rookmaaker: A Biography, 183
Happy Trails, 11
Hardon, John A., **98–99**
Hardy, Lee, 235
Harris, Joshua, 119, **123**
Harris, Paula, **205–206**
Hart, Darryl, 203
Hatcher, Carolyn, 230
Hattaway, Paul, **28–29**, 192
Having a Mary Heart in a Martha World, **96–97**
Having a Mary Spirit, 97
Hawthorne, Steven C., 176
Hayford, Jack W., **57**, 58, 122, **151–152**
Hazard, David, 31, **36**
He Cares for You, 95
He Chose the Nails, **91**
He Is There and He Is Not Silent, **162–163**
He Knows My Name, 73

He-Motions, 116
Healing, **67**, 85–86
Healing America's Wounds, 66
Healing Power of a Christian Mind, The, 110
Healing Reawakening, The, 67
Healing Spiritual Abuse, 144
Healing the Land, **259**
Healing Victims of Sexual Abuse, 143
Healthy Country Cooking, 106
Hearing God, 81
Heart Like His, A, 23, 95
Heart of a Leader, The, **245**
Heart of Anger, The, **137–138**
Heart of Evangelism, The, **166**
Heart of the Sportsman, The, **261**
Heartfelt Discipline, **130**
Heaven, 26, **286–287**
Heaven: Close Encounters of the God Kind, 5, 287
Heaven Is a Place on Earth, 92
Heaven Is Not My Home, **92**
Heavenly Man, **28–29**, 192
Heavilin, Marilyn Willett, 151
Hebrew-English Concordance to the Old Testament, The, **280–281**
Heitritter, Lynn, 143
Hell Under Fire, 288
Help! I'm Turning into My Mother … With a Few Quirks of My Own, 117
Helping Victims of Sexual Abuse, 143
Helping Your Struggling Teenager, 138
Hendricks, Howard, **217–218**
Hendrickson, Laura, **145**
Hensley, Sharon C., **223–224**
Her Choice to Heal, 152
Here for You, 131–132
Here I Am to Worship, **71**
Here I Stand, **18**
Heretics, 157
Herman, Doug, **120**
Herndon, Ernest, 261
Hersh, Sharon A., **133**
Hewitt, Hugh, **246–247**
Hicks, Cynthia, 115
Hidden in Plain Sight, 87
Hidden Keys of a Loving, Lasting Marriage, **127**
Hidden Power of Electronic Culture, The, **211–212**

Hidden Power of Prayer and Fasting, The, **50–51**
Hidden Power of Speaking in Tongues, The, 85
Hidden Smile of God, The, 25
Hiding Place, The, 16, **26**, 95
Hiebert, Paul G., **176**
Hiesberger, Jean Marie, **278**
Hill, Jonathan, 195
Hill, Samuel S., 296
Hipps, Shane, **211–212**
History of Evangelicalism Series, 196–197
History Through the Eyes of Faith, **197**
Hoekstra, Ronald, **106**
Hoerth, Alfred J., **284**
Hoezee, Scott, **259**
Hoffeditz, David, 124
Hollywood Worldviews, 210
Holton, Chuck, 17
Holy Cow!, **107**
Holy Spirit and You, The, **81–82**
Holy Wild, The, **87**
Homan, Daniel, 112
Home by Another Way, 294
Home by Choice, 134
Home Court Advantage, 134
Home Schooling, **224**
Home Schooling Children with Special Needs, **223–224**
Homecoming, 36
Homestead, **42**
Honey for a Child's Heart, 227
Honey for a Teen's Heart, **227–228**
Honey for a Woman's Heart, **99**
Hooper, Walter, **43**, 44
Hope Factor, The, 205
Hope in the Face of Cancer, 109
Hospital by the River, The, **13**
Hour That Changes the World, The, 55
House, H. Wayne, **125**
How Christianity Changed the World, **195**
How Now Shall We Live?, 3, 195, **210**
How Should We Then Live?, **194–195**
How the Bible Was Built, **285**
How the Catholic Church Built Western Civilization, 195
How the News Makes Us Dumb, **214**
How to Be a Christian in a Brave New World, **105–106**

How to Be Your Own Selfish Pig, **159**
How to Cast Out Demons, 68, 146
How to Fast Successfully, 51
How to Get a Date Worth Keeping, 123
How to Get Ready for Short-Term Missions, **175–176**
How to Give Away Your Faith, **170**
How to Grow a Young Reader, **229**
How to Hear from God, 60, 93–94
How to Minister Freedom, 68
How to Pray, 56
How to Pray for Healing, 83, 166
How to Pray for Lost Loved Ones, 63
How to Pray for the Release of the Holy Spirit, 85
How to Raise a Reader, **229–230**
How to Read a Christian Book, **100**
How to Read Slowly, 188
How to Read the Bible Book by Book, 279
How to Read the Bible for All Its Worth, **279**
How to Share Your Faith, 172
How to Stay Christian in College, 219
How to Write and Sell a Christian Novel, 186
How We Got the Bible, 285
Hsu, Albert Y., **90, 123–124, 152**
Hudson, Robert, **186**
Hudson Taylor's Spiritual Secret, 32, **35**
Huff, Nancy, 58
Hugen, Beryl, **206**
Hughes, R. Kent, 116
Hughes, Tim, **71**
Human Dignity in the Biotech Century, 105–106
Humility, 76
Humphreys, D. Russell, 264
Hunger for God, A, **51**
Hunger for Significance, The, **149**
Hunsicker, Ranelda Mack, **229**
Hunt, Gladys, **99**, **227–228**
Hunt, Mary, 244
Hunter, Brenda, 134
Hunter, Christine, 35
Hurt: Inside the World of Today's Teenagers, 120
Husbands and Fathers, 116, **137**
Hybels, Bill, **57–58, 170, 247**
Hyers, Conrad M., **253**

I Dared to Call Him Father, **4**, 34, 178
I Give You Authority, 67, 70
I Kissed Dating Goodbye, 119, **123**
I Love Mormons, **161–162**
I Saw the Angel in the Marble, **223**
I Saw the Welsh Revival, 22
Ice, Thomas, **290**
Icons of Evolution, 266, **271**
I'd Like to Believe, But ... Answers for Spiritual Seekers, 169
Identity Theft, **243**
If Animals Could Talk, **265**
If Jesus Were Mayor, 178
If Mama Ain't Happy, Ain't Nobody Happy!, 117
If This Were a Dream, What Would It Mean?, **83–84**
If You Want to Walk on Water, You've Got to Get Out of the Boat, 80
Illumined Heart, The, 292
I'll Hold You in Heaven, **151–152**
I'm Pregnant—Now What?, 133
Imagination, **217**
Imagine: A Vision for Christians in the Arts, 182
Imitation of Christ, The, 30, **77–78**
Impact of God, The, 75
Imprisoned in Iran, 177
Improving Your Serve, 95
In, but Not Of, **246–247**
In His Image, 15, 257
In His Presence, 49
In My Father's House, 26
In Pursuit of God: The Life of A. W. Tozer, **25–26**
In Pursuit of Peace, 93
In the Beginning Was Information, 265
In the Grip of Grace, 91
Indelible Ink, **99**
Infertility Companion, The, **103**
Informed Intercession, **69**
Ingram, Chip, 293
Inklings, The, 40
Inside Islam, 203
Inspiration and Incarnation, **284**
Instruments in the Redeemer's Hands, **149**
Intelligent Design: The Bridge Between Science and Theology, 270
Intended for Pleasure, 120–121
Intercession, Thrilling and Fulfilling, 66

Author/Title Index   321

Intercessory Prayer, 63
Interior Castle, 75
Interlinear for the Rest of Us, 281
International Adventures Series, 177
International Standard Bible Encyclopedia, 279–280
Intimate Friendship with God, 81, **88–89**
Intimate Issues, 120–121
Into the High Country, 261
Intra Muros, 6
Invading the Impossible, 58
Invitation to the Classics, **226–227**
Irresistible Evangelism, 173
Is God a Creationist?, 253
Is God Intolerant?, **208–209**
Is That Really You, God?, **31**, 79, 180
It Was Good, **182–183**
It's More Than the Music, **35–36**
It's Not About Me, 88
It's Not About You—It's About God, 116
IVP Atlas of Bible History, 284
Izard, Susan S., **111**

J. R. R. Tolkien: Artist and Illustrator, 41
Jack: A Life of C. S. Lewis, **44**
Jack's Life, 44
Jackson, John Paul, **66**
Jacobs, Alan, 44
Jacobs, Cindy, 4, 22, **66**, **84–85**
Jacobson, Michael, 108
Jakes, T. D., 116, 147
James, Eddie, 211
James, Steven, 221
Jamison-Peterson, Vicki, 6
Jane Kenyon: A Literary Life, **44**
Janssen, Al, 29
Jarrell, Jane, 112
Jefferson, Lisa, **7**
Jenkins, Jerry B., 36, **186**
Jerusalem Bible, 278
Jesus: An Intimate Portrait of the Man, His Land, and His People, **18**
Jesus CEO, **247–248**
Jesus I Never Knew, The, 97
Jesus in Beijing, **192**
Jesus, Man of Joy, 294
Jesus, the Model, 89
Jesus, the One and Only, 18
Jewett, Robert, 213
Joel, **9**

John of the Cross, Saint, **75**
John Stott, A Global Ministry, 20
John Stott, The Making of a Leader, **20**
John, J., 210
Johnson, Barbara, 117
Johnson, Bill, 84, **90–91**
Johnson, David, 144
Johnson, Greg, 136
Johnson, Jeff, **153**
Johnson, Lissa Halls, **10–11**
Johnson, Phillip E., **270–271**, 273
Johnson, Rick, 132
Johnson, Todd M., 58, **295**
Johnston, Robert K., **209–210**
Johnstone, Jill, 58
Johnstone, Patrick, **58**
Joly, Reona Peterson, 177
Jonathan Edwards: A Life, **22–23**
Jones, Bobby, **36–37**, 191
Jones, Brenna, 121
Jones, Dale E., 295
Jones, Laurie Beth, **247–248**
Jones, Stan, 121
Joni, 26
Jordan, Peter, **176**
Jorgensen, Susan S., **111**
Joseph, Mark, **188–189**
Journal of John Wesley, The, **27**
Journey, The, 21
Journey of Desire, The, 114
Joy at Work, 238, **244–245**
Joy I'd Never Known, A, 39
Judah, Stephen M., **125**
Julian, Larry S., **235–236**
Just As I Am, **21**, 169
Just Don't Marry One, **124**
Just Hand Over the Chocolate and No One Will Get Hurt, 117
Just Like Jesus, 91
Just Walk Across the Room, **170**
Justice That Restores, **204**

Kassian, Mary, **206**
Kavanaugh, Patrick, 38, **189**
Keaggy, Bernadette, 152
Kearney, R. Timothy, 143
Keefer, Mikal, 211
Kehler, Laurie Ostby, **262**
Keillor, Steven J., **193–194**, 289
Keller, W. Phillip, **91**, **258**, 262

Kemp, David, **278–279**
Kennedy, Nancy, **125–126**
Kent, Keri Wyatt, 262
Key to Your Child's Heart, The, 131
Kilner, John F., 105–106
Kilpatrick, William, 186, **228**
Kimmel, Darcy, 142
Kimmel, Tim, **133–134**, 142
King James Version, 277
King Me, 136
King of the Earth, The, 256
King, Claude, 93–94
Kingdom of the Cults, The, **160**
Kinnear, Angus, 28
Kirkpatrick, Jane, **42**
Klicka, Christopher J., **224**
Kneeling Christian, The, 55
Knitting into the Mystery, **111**
Know Why You Believe, 170
Knowing God, **293**
Knowledge of the Holy, The, 26, 74, 78, 294
Knox, Sally M., **110**
Koenig, Harold G., **144**
Koetje, David, 258–259
Kohlenberger, John R., **280–281**, 283
Koop, C. Everett, 105–106
Kovacs, Aimee, 74
Kraeuter, Tom, 73–74
Kraft, Charles H., **66–67**, 70, 85–86, 110, **146**
Kramarik, Akiane, **8**
Kramarik, Foreli, **8**
Kreeft, Peter, **58–59**, 157, **158**, 161, 287, **290**
Kroeger, Catherine Clark, **147**
Krummrich, Carter, **119–120**
Kullberg, Kelly Monroe, **218**
Kurian, George T., 58, **295**
Kushiner, James M., **270**

L'Abri, **25**
L'Engle, Madeleine, **187**
Lacey, Rob, 278
Lady, The Melody, and the Word, The, 37
LaHaye, Beverly, 120–121
LaHaye, Tim, 120–121, **290**
Lai, Patrick, **176–177**
Lamott, Anne, **42**, 186–187
Lamoureux, Denis O., **273**

Lancaster, D. Thomas, **107**
Lane, Deforia, **189–190**
Language of God, The, **272**
Larimore, Walt, **13–14**, **104–105**, **107–108**, **171–172**
Larmoyeux, Mary, **134**
Larsen, Scott, **99**
Last Word, The, **285**
Laurie, Greg, 172
Law, William, **75**
Lawrence, Brother, 57, **75–76**
Lawrence, Michele, 246
Lawrence, Paul, 284
Lawson, James Gilchrist, **22**
Lawyer's Calling, The, **201–202**
Leachman, Richard, 102
Leadership Is an Art, **245–246**
Leadership Lessons of Jesus, 248
Leading with a Limp, **244**
Leading Without Power, 246
Learning the Language of Babylon, 166
Leaving Church, 294
Leax, John, 187
Lectures on Revivals of Religion, 21, 62
Lee-Thorp, Karen, 115
Leman, Kevin, **120–121**, 130, 133, **134–135**
Lenten Lands, 44
Lerch, Maureen T., **224–225**
Lessons from a Sheep Dog, 91, **258**
Let Justice Roll Down, 207
Let Me Be a Woman, 113–114, 126
Let the Authors Speak, 230
Let Us Pray, **61**
Let's Get to Know Each Other, 207
Let's Roll!, 7
Let's Talk!, 113
Letters Across the Divide, 206
Letters and Papers from Prison, 19, 79
Letters from a Skeptic, 157
Letters of C. S. Lewis, 43
Letters of Francis A. Schaeffer, 25
Letters of J. R. R. Tolkien, The, 40
Letters to a Devastated Christian, 89, 144
Letters to Children, 43
Letters to Malcolm, **59**
Levison, Catherine, 221, **228–229**
Lewerenz, Spencer, **212**
Lewis, C. S., **42–43**, 45, **59**, 76, 152, **158–159**, 198, **290–291**

Lewis, Gregg, **8**, **9**
Lewis, Robert, **135–136**
Lewis, W. H., 43
Liardon, Roberts, 6, 28, 287
Lies Women Believe and the Truth That Sets Them Free, **113–114**
Life and Diary of David Brainerd, The, 22
Life Application Study Bible, **277**
Life Interrupted, **133**
Life of Abraham, The, 95
Life of God in the Soul of Man, The, **77**
Life of John Calvin, A, 18
Life of Moses, The, 95
Life of the Mind, The, 198–199
Life on the Edge, 114
Life That Says Welcome, A, 111–112
Life Together, 19, 79
Life You Save May Be Your Own, The, **41–42**
Life You've Always Wanted, The, **80**
Lifestyle Evangelism, 171
Light and the Glory, The, **194**
Light Force, 29
Lightfoot, Neil R., 285
Lights in the Sky & Little Green Men, **254–255**, 256
Like a Mighty Wind, 175
Linamen, Karen Scalf, 117
Lindskoog, Kathryn, **229**
Link Between A.D.D. And Addiction, The, 105
Linzey, Andrew, **258**
Lisle, Jason, 264
Literary Education, A, **228–229**
Literature Through the Eyes of Faith, 188
Little Primer on Humble Apologetics, A, 163
Little Style Guide to Great Christian Writing and Publishing, The, 186
Little, John, **13**
Little, Paul E., **170**
Littleton, Mark, 190
Livin It: Testimonies, 10
Livin It: What It Is, 10
Living Bible, 278
Living in a Step-family Without Getting Stepped On, 130
Living on the Devil's Doorstep, 35, **177**
Living Proof, 172
Living Stones of the Himalayas, **13**

Living the Good Life on God's Good Earth, 258–259
Loaves and Fishes, 20
Lockerbie, D. Bruce, 187–188
Lockyer, Herbert, **59**, 191
Long, W. Meredith, **205**
Long Distance Grandma, 142
Long Journey Home, 90
Long Loneliness, The, **20**, 42
Lord, Teach Us to Pray, 54
Lords of the Earth, 34, 179
Losing You Too Soon, 152
Lost Art of Disciple Making, The, 168
Lotus and the Cross, The, 164
Love & Respect, 125
Love Talk, 125
Love Your God with All Your Mind, **198–199**
Loving God with All Your Mind, 199
Loving Homosexuals As Jesus Would, **121–122**
Loving Monday, **234**
Loving Your Spouse Through Prayer, 61–62
Lubenow, Marvin L., **265–266**
Lucado, Max, 88, **91**
Lundin, Roger, 44, 188
Lupton, Robert D., **207**
Lush, Jean, 113–114

Macaulay, Susan Schaeffer, **159**, **225**
Maccaro, Janet, 102
Mackson, Rachel, 222
MacMurray, John, 114
MacNutt, Francis, **67**, 85–86, **121**, **137**
MacNutt, Judith, **137**
Madrid, Patrick, 3
Mahan, David C., **260**
Mahaney, Carolyn, 113–114
Maier, Bill, **127–128**
Mains, Karen, **111–112**
Mains, Karen Burton, 143
Maker's Diet, The, 108
Making Children Mind Without Losing Yours, **134**
Making It Real, 7
Making Jesus Lord, 31, **79**
Making Peace with Your Mom, 139
Making Room, 112
Mallouhi, Christine A., **177–178**

Malon, Gracie, 142
Malone, Henry, **68**, 70
Man Called Cash, The, **38**
Man Called Peter, A, 15
Man in the Mirror, The, **116**
Man of Faith, A, **15**
Man with the Bird on His Head, The, 35, 177
Managing Your Emotions, 93
Mandryk, Jason, **58**
Manners of the Heart, 139
Manning, Brennan, 97
Mansfield, Stephen, 14, **16**, 27
Manuel, David, **194**
MAP: Making the Bible Meaningful, Accessible, Practical, 280
Maravich, Pete, **39**
Maria, 38
Marketplace Annotated Bibliography, The, **249**
Marriage on Trial, **127–128**
Married for Good, 127
Marsden, George M., **22–23**, 193, 199
Marshall, Catherine, 15
Marshall, Paul A., **92**
Marshall, Peter, **194**
Marshall, Rich, 238
Marshall, Sharon, **153**
Marston, Paul, **252**, **288–289**
Martin, James, 20
Martin, Linette, 183
Martin, Thomas, 99
Martin, Walter, **160**
Marty, Martin E., 193
Martyrs Mirror, **35**
Mary Pride's Complete Guide to Getting Started in Homeschooling, 223
Masonic Rites and Wrongs, 160
Massee, Sydna, 152
Master: A Life of Jesus, The, 18
Master Plan of Evangelism, **167–168**
Mastering Monday, 234
Mathematics: Is God Silent?, **219**
Mathewes-Green, Frederica, **292**
Mathews, David, 22
Matrix of Meanings, A, 214
Matter of Days, A, **268**
Matthew, Iain, 75
Matthew for Everyone, **282**
Maximized Manhood, 116

Maximum Energy, **106**
Maximum Energy Cookbook, The, 106
Maximum Solutions for ADD, Learning Disabilities and Autism, 105
Maxwell, John C., **59–60**, 248
McCallum, Elizabeth, **229**
McCasland, David, 18, **23**, 33, 48
McClung, Floyd, 35, 81, **91–92**, 177
McCollister, John, 15
McConnell, Michael W., 202
McDermott, Gerald R., **109**, **291**
McDonald, Stacy, **136–137**
McDowell, Josh, **159–160**
McEwan, Elaine K., **229–230**
McGee, Robert S., **146–147**
McGinnis, Alan Loy, **147**
McGrath, Alister, 18, 259, **292**
McKenna, David, **100**
McKenzie, Sabrina, 74
McKnight, Scot, 50
McLaren, Brian D., 86, **291–292**
McLennan, Scotty, **236**
McRay, John, 284
McReynolds, Paul, 283
Mead, Frank S., 296
Mead, Marjorie Lamp, 43
Meaning of Creation, The, **253**
Meaningful World, A, 270
Mears, Henrietta, 280
Measure of a Man, The, 116
Meeker, Meg, 135
Melton, J. Gordon, **296**
Memoir and Remains of the Rev. Robert Murray McCheyne, 19
Mere Christianity, **158–159**
Merrill, Dean, **17–18**
Merton, Thomas, 42, **43–44**, **92–93**, **262–263**
Message, The, **278**
Messianic Judaism Is Not Christianity, 5
Messies Manual, The, 112
Metaxas, Eric, 24, 159, **293**
Metzger, Bruce, 285
Metzger, Will, **170–171**
Meyer, F. B., 95
Meyer, Joyce, **60**, **93**, 94
Michaelsen, Johanna, **4**
Michell, C. Ben, 105–106
Middlebrooks, Felicia, 7
Middlemann, Udo, **259**

Middleton, J. Richard, **200–201**
Milestones, **18–19**
Miller, Basil, 35
Miller, Christine, **230**
Miller, Darrow L., **178**
Miller, David Ward, 236
Miller, Donald, 42, 114
Miller, Keith B., **273**
Miller, Kenneth R., **273**
Milligan, Ira, 84
Mind for God, A, 198–199
Mind of the Maker, The, 291
Miniskirts, Mothers & Muslims, **177–178**
Ministry of Intercession, The, 22, 61
Minority Report, The, 210
Miracles, 76
Mission of Motherhood, The, **130–131**
Mittelberg, Mark, 170
Modern Art and the Death of a Culture, **183**
Moffitt, Bob, 178
Molder of Dreams, **216**
Molokai, 33
Mom, Dad ... I'm Pregnant, 133
Mom, Everyone Else Does!, **133**
Mom Factor, The, 139
Mom, I Feel Fat!, 133
Mom I Want to Be, The, 131
Mom's Everything Book for Daughters, 131–132
Mom's Everything Book for Sons, **132**
Moms Make a Difference, **24**
Money Matters for Kids, 241
Money Matters for Teens, **241**
Money Matters, 242
Money, Possessions, and Eternity, 90, **239–240**
Money Talks and So Can We, 240
Montgomery, Leslie, 24
Moody, D.L., 169
Moore, Beth, 18, **23**, **68–69**, **93–94**, 95
Moore, Denver, **7–8**, 9
Moore, S. David, **57**
Moral Darwinism, 158
More Than a Carpenter, 160
More Than A Movie, 211
More Than Equals, **207**
More Than Meets the Eye, **257**
Moreland, J. P., 197, **198–199**
Morgan, Christopher, 288

Morgan, Robert, 72
Morley, Patrick, **116**
Morning and Evening, 49
Morris, Debbie, **8**
Morris, Gilbert, 186
Morris, Henry M., **266–267**
Morris, Leon, 282
Mosser, Carl, 161–162
Mother Angelica: The Remarkable Story of a Nun, Her Nerve, and a Network of Miracles, 33
Mounce, William D., 279, **281**, 283
Mounce's Complete Expository Dictionary of Old and New Testament Words, 279, **281**, 283
Movie Nights for Kids, **211**
Movie Nights for Teens, 211
Mrs. Hunter's Happy Death, **151**
Mudhouse Sabbath, 45
Mueller, Walt, 120
Muggeridge, Kitty, 76
Muggeridge, Malcolm, **33**, 90
Mulfinger, George, 13
Müller, George, **23–24**, 53, 175
Mullins, Traci, **104**
Multipurpose Tools for Bible Study, **296**
Murphey, Cecil, 6, **12**
Murphy, Ed, 70
Murray, Andrew, 22, **60–61**, 76
Murray, Iain H., 20
Music As Medicine, **189–190**
Music of Angels, The, **189**
Music Through the Eyes of Faith, **188**
Musk, Bill, 178
Muslims Next Door, 4, 178
My Dream of Heaven, 6
My God and I, **25**
My Journey into Alzheimer's Disease, 103
My Life on the Rock: A Rebel Returns to the Catholic Faith, 3
My Life with the Saints, 20
My Second Chapter, 36
My Utmost for His Highest, 23, **48**
Myers, Allen C., **279–280**
Myers, Kenneth A., **212**
Myth of a Christian Nation, The, **202–203**

Nair, Ken, 127
Nanez, Rick, 199

Narnian: The Life and Imagination of C. S. Lewis, The, 44
Nash, Laura, **236**
Nason-Clark, Nancy, **147**
Nature and Character of God, The, **293–294**
Nature Trails and Gospel Tales, 261
Navarro, Kevin, 72
Neal, Vernon Edwin, **211**
Nee, Watchman, **61**, 89, **94**
Needless Casualties of War, **66**
Neuzil, Mark, 261
Never Give In, **16**
New Answers Book, The, **265**
New Birth Order Book, The, **135**
New Encyclopedia of Christian Martyrs, The, 35
New Evidence That Demands a Verdict, The, **159–160**
New Foxe's Book of Martyrs, The, **32**
New International Bible Dictionary, 279–280
New Jerusalem Bible, 278
New Kind of Christian, A, 86
New Light on Depression, **144**
New Living Translation, 277
New Master Your Money, The, **240**
New Mormon Challenge, The, 161–162
New Oxford Annotated Bible with the Apocrypha, 277
New Revised Standard Version, 277
New Seeds of Contemplation, 93
New Strong-willed Child, The, 129
New Testament Documents, The, **283**
New Unger's Bible Dictionary, The, 279–280
Newman, Elizabeth, 112
Newman, John Henry Cardinal, 19
Newman, Randy, **171**
Nickel, James, **219**
Nicolosi, Barbara, **212**
Niebuhr, H. Richard, **212–213**
Night Offices, The, 50
Nine Days in Heaven, 6
Nine O'Clock in the Morning, 85
NIV Study Bible, **276–277**
No Compromise, **36**
No Easy Road, **55**
No Free Lunch, 270
No Man Is an Island, 44, **92–93**
No More Christian Nice Guy, 114
No Place for Abuse, 147
No-Gimmick Guide to Raising Fit Kids, The, 104
Nolan, Pat, 204
Noll, Mark A., 193, 196–197, **199**
Normal Christian Life, The, 94
Norris, Chuck, **11**
Norris, Kathleen, 44, 262
Not Ashamed, 5
Not Good If Detached, **95**
Not I, but Christ, 26, 95
Not Just Science, **252**
Nothing to Do but to Save Souls, 27, 168
Nouwen, Henri, 93
Nye, Abby, **219**
Nygren, Bruce, **138**
Nystrom, Carolyn, 54

Objects of Grace, 183
O'Connor, Karen, 103
O'Connor, Lindsey, **24**, 117
Of Earth and Sky, **260–261**
Off My Rocker, 142
O'Leary, Jeff, 17
Olson, Bruce, **33**
Olson, Philip N., 208
Omartian, Stormie, **61–62**
O'Mathuna, Donal, **107–108**
On a Positive Note, 37
On Becoming Baby Wise, 140
On Becoming Preteen Wise, 141
On God and Dogs, 258
On Kingdom Business, 235, 237
On the Far Side of Liglig Mountain, 13
On the Other Side of the Garden, 126
One Church, Many Tribes, **209**
One World, **254**, 255
One-Minute Home Organizer, The, 112
Only the Heart Knows How to Find Them, 41
Open Bible, The, 277
Open Heart, Open Home, **111–112**
Opening Your Child's Nine Learning Windows, 217
Operation World, **58**
Organized Homeschooler, The, **222**
Organizing Magic, 112
Origin of the Bible, The, 283
Original Intent, **202**

Author/Title Index   327

Original Memoirs of Charles G. Finney, The, **20–21**
Origins of Life: Biblical and Evolutionary Models Face Off, 267
Ortberg, John, **80**
Orthodox Church, The, 292
Orthodoxy, **157**
Osaigbovo, Rebecca Florence, **116**
Osbeck, Kenneth, **72**
Osborne, Rick, 241
Osteen, Joel, 96
Oswald Chambers: Abandoned to God, 18, **23**, 48
Other Woman in Your Marriage, The, 139
Otis, George, Jr., **69**
Out of the Comfort Zone, 11
Out of the Saltshaker and into the World, **172**
Outrageous Idea of Christian Scholarship, The, 199
Overstreet, Jeffrey, **213**
Overstreet, Paul, 38
Owen, Paul, 161–162
Owens, Virginia Stem, 42

Packer, J. I., 54, **293**
Page, Nick, 280
Painters of Faith, 185
PAPA Prayer, The, **55**, 88
Parenting a Grieving Child, 153
Parenting Today's Adolescent, **138**
Parents' Guide to the Spiritual Mentoring of Teens, The, 138
Paris, Jenell Williams, **104–105**
Park, Andy, **72**
Parkhurst, Louis Gifford, **55–56**
Parrott, Les, 125, **126**, 127, 138, **147**
Parrott, Leslie, 125, **126**, 127
Partners in Prayer, **59–60**
Pascal, Blaise, **161**
Pascal's Fire, **255**
Passion and Purity, 123
Passion for Jesus, **87**
Passion for Souls, A, **168–169**
Passion for the Impossible, A, **34**
Passno, Diane, **105**, 206
Pat Boone: The Authorized Biography, 38
Pate, C. Marvin, 290
Patterson, Ben, 64
Patterson, Roger, **266**

Payne Stewart: The Authorized Biography, 39
Payne, Bill, **70**
Payne, Glen, 36
Peace, Martha, **126**
Peace Child, **34**, 179
Peace with God, **169**
Peacemaker, The, **148**
Peacocke, Arthur, 254, 255, **273–274**
Pearcey, Nancy, 3, 90, 195, **199–200**, **210**, **253–254**
Peel, William Carr, **171–172**
Pegues, Beverly, 58
Pensees, **161**
Peril in Paradise, 268
Perkins, Bill, 114
Perkins, John M., **207**
Perkins, Mitali, **213**
Perkins, Spencer, **207**
Permission Evangelism, 171
Perry, John, 3, **14**, **16–17**
Perspectives on an Evolving Creation, **273**
Pete Maravich: Magician of the Hardwood, 39
Peters, Steve, 190
Petersen, Dennis R., **266**
Peterson, Eugene H., **100**, **284–285**, **278**
Peterson, Jim, 172
Peterson, Robert, 288
Phillips, Joan, 152
Philosophy and the Christian Faith, **197**
Philosophy Made Slightly Less Difficult, 197
Pierce, Cal, 174
Pierce, Chonda, 117
Pierce, Chuck D., 4, 63, **69–70**, **72–73**, 84
Pierce, Gregory F. Augustine, **236**
Pierson, Arthur T., 24
Pilavachi, Mike, 71
Pilgrim at Tinker Creek, **261–262**
Pilgrims in Their Own Land, 193
Ping, Dave, 173
Pink, Arthur W., 293
Pintus, Lorraine, 120–121
Piper, Don, 6
Piper, John, **24–25**, **51**, **94**
Pippert, Rebecca Manley, **172**
Pistol Pete: Heir to a Dream, **39**

Plain Account of Christian Perfection, A, 75
Plan B, 42
Please Don't Say You Need Me, **149**
Pohl, Christine, 112
Politically Incorrect Guide to Darwinism and Intelligent Design, The, 271
Politically Incorrect Guide to Islam (and the Crusades), The, **196**
Polkinghorne, John C., **254**, 255, 274
Pollack, Doug, 173
Pollock, John, 18, 21
Pollution and the Death of Man, **259**
Pop Culture Wars, 214
Pope, Ethan, **134**, **242–243**
Portals to Cleansing, 70
Porter, Kathryn, **112**
Possessing the Gates of the Enemy, 22, **66**
Post-Christian Mind, The, 200
Postmodern Times, 167, 201
Postmodernism 101, 167, **201**
Poust, Mary DeTurris, 153
Powell, Mark Allan, **190**
Power Evangelism, **173–174**
Power Healing, **85–86**
Power of a Praying Husband, The, **61–62**
Power of a Praying Wife, The, 61–62
Power of Simple Prayer, The, **60**
Power of the Powerless, The, **41**
Power Through Prayer, 53
Practice of the Presence of God, The, 57, **75–76**
Practicing Servant Leadership, 246
Pratney, Winkie, 36, **62**, **80–81**, **259**, **293–294**
Pratt, Loni Collins, 112
Prayer, **54**
Prayer: Does It Make Any Difference?, **64**
Prayer Evangelism, 166
Prayer: Finding the Heart's True Home, **56**, 80
Prayer of Jabez, The, 96, 218
Prayer Saturated Church, The, 60
Prayer Shield, 60
Prayer That Heals, The, 67, 137
Prayer: The Great Conversation, **58–59**
Praying: Finding Our Way Through Duty to Delight, 54
Praying for Your Unborn Child, **137**
Praying God's Word, **68–69**
Praying Hyde, 22, **54**
Praying with Authority, 63
Praying with the Church, 50
Preparing for Adolescence, **114**
Preparing the Way, 174
Preparing Your Daughter for Every Woman's Battle, 118
Preparing Your Son for Every Man's Battle, **117–118**
Pressure's Off, The, 55, **88**
Pride, Mary, 223
Prince, Derek, 51, 71, 82, 116, **137**
Principles of Prayer, **55–56**
Priolo, Lou, **137–138**
Pritchard, Ray, 248
Privileged Planet, 268, **270**
Problem of Pain, The, **198**
Professors Who Believe, 13
Prophecy, Dreams, and Evangelism, 172–173
Prophetic Evangelism, **172–173**
Prophets and Personal Prophecy, 82
Protect Your Home and Family from Spiritual Pollution, 70
Protecting Your Home from Spiritual Darkness, 4, **69–70**
Protecting Your Teen from Today's Witchcraft, 4
Pruitt, H. Edward, 32
Pryor, Austin, **243**
Pure Joy, 88
Purity Principle, The, 119
Purnell, Dick, 123
Purpose-Driven Life, The, **96**
Pursuing Sexual Wholeness, 118
Pursuit of God, The, 26, 74, 78

Queen Esther's Secrets of Womanhood, **132–133**
Questioning Evangelism, **171**

Rabey, Steve, **17**
Radical Hospitality, 112
Ragamuffin Gospel, The, 97
Rainbows for the Fallen World, 184
Rainey, Barbara, 114, **126–127**, 138
Rainey, Dennis, 114, **126–127**, **138–139**
Rainey, Rebecca, 114
Rainey, Samuel, 114
Raising a Modern-Day Knight, **135–136**
Raising Great Kids, **131**

Raising Maidens of Virtue, **136–137**
Raising Motivated Kids, 217
Raising Respectful Children in a Disrespectful World, **139**
Rake, Tim, **278–279**
Ramm, Bernard, 253
Ramsey, Dave, **243–244**
Rana, Fazale, **267**
Rasmussen, Carl, G., 284
Ratzsch, Del, **254**
Raunikar, Don, 123
Ravenhill, Leonard, 36, **62**
Re-Entry, **176**
Reaching Out, 93
Reaching the Left from the Right, **204**
Reading Between the Lines, **188**
Reading for Life, 99
Reagan, David, 290
Real Face of Atheism, The, 29, 165, 292
Real Sex, 119
Real Teens, Real Stories, Real Life, **7**
Reality and the Vision, 187
Reality Check, 239
Reason in the Balance, 271
Reason, Science and Faith, **252**
Reasons of the Heart, 164
Receiving the Day, 294
Reconciliation Blues, **205**
Recovering the Lost Tools of Learning, **221**
Red Moon Rising, **56**
Redeeming Creation, **260**
Redeeming Law, 202
Redman, Matt, **73**
Reenchantment of Nature, The, 259
Rees Howells, Intercessor, **21–22**, 54
Refuge from Abuse, **147**
Reisser, Paul C., 104, 140
Release of the Spirit, The, 61, **94**
Releasing the Prophetic Destiny of a Nation, 63
Religious Congregations & Membership in the United States 2000, 295
Religious History of America, The, **193**
Remarkable Miracles, **52–53**
Remedios, David, **108**
Remember Creation, **259**
Renewing the City, **207**
Repenting of Religion, 79
Rest of God, The, 87
Restoration of Reason, **197–198**

Restoring the Dance, **74**
Restoring Your Digestive Health, 108
Rethinking Christ and Culture, 213
Revelation: Four Views, 290
Revenge of Conscience, The, 203
ReViewing the Movies, **211**
Revival Praying, 62
Revival: Principles to Change the World, **62**, 81, 294
Rhodes, Ron, 296
Rice, Chris, **207**
Rich Christians in an Age of Hunger, **207–208**
Rich in Every Way, 240
Rich Mullins: An Arrow Pointing to Heaven, 36, **37**
Richards, Jay W., 268, **270**
Richardson, Don, **34**, **178–179**
Richardson, Wendy, 105, 150
Rickett, Michele, 30
Rigby, Jill, **139**
Right to Home School, The, 224
Rinck, Meg J., 123
Rinehart, Paula, 119
Rische, Jill Martin, **160**
Rische, Kevin, **160**
Rise of Evangelicalism, The, 196–197
Ritchie, Mark Andrew, **8–9**, **179**
Road to Unafraid, The, **17–18**
Roaring Lambs, 212
Robert K. Greenleaf: A Life of Servant Leadership, 246
Roberts, Dave, **56**
Roberts, Wes, 127
Robinson, Mickey, 6
Robinson, Tri, 260
Rock Cries Out, The, 189
Rockness, Miriam Huffman, **34**
Roels, Shirley J., **234–235**
Rogers, Dale Evans, **11**
Rogers, Janice, **31**, **288**
Rogers, Roy, 11
Rohrer, Norman B., **11**
Romaine, James, 183
Romanowski, William D., **214**
Rome Sweet Home: Our Journey to Catholicism, **3**
Rookmaaker, H. R.
Root of the Righteous, The, 78
Roots of Endurance, The, **24–25**

Roses in December, 151
Ross, Hugh, **254–255**, 256, 264, **267–269**, 270
Rowe, David L., **161–162**
Rubin, Jordan, **108**
Ruis, David, 71
Run, Baby, Run, 3
Rundle, Steve, 177, **236–237**
Running the Rapid, 130
Rush, John, 35, 177
Rushford, Patricia, 113–114
Russell, Eric, 20
Russell, Rex, 107
Russo, Steve, 4, 162
Ryken, Leland, 99, **187**
Ryken, Philip Graham, 184

Sacks, Cheryl, 60
Sacrament of the Present Moment, The, 76
Sacred Influence, 126
Sacred Journey, The, 40
Sacred Marriage, **128**
Sacred Parenting, 128
Sacred Pathways, **95–96**
Sacred Romance, The, 89
Safa, Reza F., 203
Saint, Steve, 32
Saint Paul Returns to the Movies, 213
Saint Thomas Aquinas: The Dumb Ox, 30
Saints' Everlasting Rest, The, 77
Sally Stuart's Guide to Getting Published, 187
Same Kind of Different as Me, **7–8**, 9
Samples, Kenneth, **254–255**, 256
Sande, Ken, **148**
Sanders, Catherine Edwards, **162**
Sanders, J. Oswald, 87, **248**
Sanders, John, 288
Sandford, John Loren, 67, 82, 92, 146, **148**
Sandford, Paula, 67, 82, 92, 143, 146, **148**
Sauer, Erich, 256
Savage, Jill, **139**
Savage, My Kinsman, The, 175
Saving God's Green Earth, 260
Saving Your Marriage Before It Starts, 127
Saving Your Second Marriage Before It Starts, **126**

Sawyer, R. S., **29**
Sayer, George, **44**
Sayers, Dorothy, 291
Scales, T. Laine, **206**
Scandal of the Evangelical Conscience, The, 208
Scandal of the Evangelical Mind, The, **199**
Scenes Beyond the Grave, 6
Schaeffer, Edith, **25**
Schaeffer, Francis, 25, 90, 105–106, **162–163**, **183–184**, **194–195**, **200**, **259**
Schall, James, 99
Schauppp, Doug, **205–206**
Scheer, Greg, **73–74**
Schmidt, Alvin J., **195**
Schmidt, Leigh, **193**
Schneider, Richard H., **4**, 178
School of Biblical Evangelism, The, 168
<u>School Savvy Kids Series</u>, 217
School Starts at Home, **216–217**
Schooler, Jayne, 133
Schroeder, Celeste Snowber, 74
Schultz, Bob, **139–140**, 141, **237**
Schultze, Quentin, **219–220**
Schutt, Michael P., 202
Schwedt, Rachel, 41, 186
Science & Its Limits, **254**
Science & Theology, 274
Science and Christianity, 252
Science and Evidence for Design in the Universe, 269
Science and Faith, 256
Science and the Trinity, 254
Scientists of Faith, **12–13**
Scott, Jane, **229**
Scougal, Henry, **77**
Screwtape Letters, The, 159, 291
Scull, Christina, 41
Search for Significance, The, **146–147**
Sears, Martha, **140**
Sears, William, **140**
Season for Justice, A, 216, 224
Second Row Piano Side, 117
Secret Keeper Girls Kit, 115
Secret Keeper, **115**
Secret Place, The, 87
Secret Power, 169
Secrets in the Dark, 294
Secrets of the Prophetic, 82
Secrets of the Vine, 218

Secular Faith, A, 203
Sedler, Michael D., **148–149**
Seeing Is Believing, 146
Seer, The, 82
Seerveld, Calvin, **184**
Selah: A Guide to Music in the Bible, **190–191**
Serious Call to a Devout and Holy Life, A, 75
Servant Leadership, **246**
Serve God, Save the Planet, **260**
Serving Homeschooled Teens and Their Parents, **224–225**
Set Your House in Order, 241–242
Seven Keys to a Healthy Blended Family, 130
Seven Laws of Teaching, The, 218
Seven Laws of the Learner, The, 218
Seven Pillars of Health, The, 107
Seven Storey Mountain, The, 42, **43–44**
Severe Mercy, A, **44–45**, 152
Sex and the Soul of a Woman, 119
Sex, Lies, and the Media, 120
Sgt. York: His Life, Legend, and Legacy, **16–17**
Shadow Boxing, **68**
Shadow of the Almighty, 32, **175**
Shaping History Through Prayer and Fasting, 51
Sharing Your Faith with a Buddhist, **164**
Sharing Your Faith with a Hindu, 164
Sharing Your Faith with Friends and Family, **169**
Shaw, R. Daniel, **176**
Shaw, Solomon Benjamin, 62
She Calls Me Daddy, 135
She Who Laughs, Lasts!, **116–117**
Shea, Cecily, 129
Sheet Music, **120–121**
Sheets, Dutch, **63**
Sheikh, Bilquis, **4**, 34, 178
Sheldon, Joseph K., **260**
Shellenberger, Susie, 131–132
Shelley, Bruce, **195–196**
Shelly, Judith, 103
Shepherd Looks at Psalm 23, A, **91**, 258
Shepherding Your Child's Heart, **141**
Sherman, Dean, **70**
Sherman, Doug, **237–238**
Sherrer, Quin, 65

Sherrill, Elizabeth, **26**, **29**
Sherrill, John L., **26**, **29**, 85
Ships of Mercy, 13
Shook, Robert L., **238**
Short Life of Catherine Booth, the Mother of the Salvation Army, The, 28
Sider, Ronald J., **207–208**
Signs of Intelligence, **270**
Silberling, Murray, 74
Silver, Michael, **39–40**
Silvious, Jan, **149**
Silvoso, Ed, 166, 177, **238**
Simple Home, The, **111**
Simple Hospitality, 112
Simpson, Michael, 171
Singing Through the Night, **30**
Single Parenting That Works, 133, **135**
Singles at the Crossroads, **123–124**
Sire, James W., **163**, 188, 198–199, 219
Sit, Walk, Stand, 94
Sites, Jimmy, 261
Sitting in God's Sunshine ... Resting in His Love, 88
Sittser, Jerry, **63**, **153**
Six Hours One Friday, 91
Sjogren, Steve, **6**, **173**
Skeptic's Guide to the Global AIDS Crisis, The, 205
Slater, Rosalie June, 230
Sleeth, J. Matthew, **260**
Smalley, Gary, **127**, 131, **141**
Smedes, Lewis B., 8, **25**, 148
Smith, Alice, **63–64**, **70–71**
Smith, Charles Merrill, **285**
Smith, Christian, 206
Smith, Craig Stephen, 209
Smith, David, 220
Smith, Donald K., 220
Smith, Eddie, 70
Smith, Gerald B., **74**
Smith, James Bryan, 36, **37**, 77–78
Smith, Jane Stuart, **37–38**
Smith, Timothy, **141**
Smithouser, Bob, **190**, 211
Smoke, Jim, 130
Snoke, David, **269**
Snow, Donald B., **220**
Snyder, James L., **25–26**
So Much More, 136–137
So You Want to Be a Teenager?, 114

So You're Thinking About Homeschooling, 12, **225–226**
Social Security, **242–243**
Socrates Meets Jesus, **158**
Some of the Ways of God in Healing, **82–83**
Something Beautiful for God, 33
Sommerville, John C., **214**
Sonnenberg, Joel, **9**
Sorge, Bob, 73–74
Soul of Prayer, The, 54
Soul of Science, The, **253–254**
Sound Mind Investing Handbook, The, **243**
Sounding Forth the Trumpet, 194
Southern, Randy, **241–242**
Spangler, Ann, **116–117**
Speaking of Sin, **294**
Spears, Dana, 129
Spears, Larry, 246
Spencer, Aida Besancon, **184–185**
Spencer, Nick, 169
Spencer, Robert, **196**
Spencer, William David, **184–185**
Spirit of the Disciplines, The, 80–81
Spirit of the Rainforest, 9, **179**
Spiritual Authority, 89
Spiritual Authority Within the Church, 144
Spiritual Care, 103
Spiritual Classics, 77–78
Spiritual Evolution, 253
Spiritual Field Guide, A, 261
Spiritual Journeys, 189
Spiritual Leadership, **248**
Spiritual Lives of the Great Composers, 38
Spiritual Warfare for Every Christian, **70**
Spirituality @ Work, **236**
Splashes of Joy in the Cesspools of Life, 117
Splitting Heirs, **240–241**, 242
Spraggett, Daphne, 58
Springer, Kevin, **85–86, 173–174**
Springer, Rebecca, 6
Sproul, R. C., **149**
Spurgeon, Charles, **19**, 49
Spurgeon: A New Biography, 19
St. Francis of Assisi, 30
Stafford, Tim, **39**
Stanton, Glenn T., **127–128**

Stark, Rodney, 195
Starlight and Time, 264
Stars Speak, The, **264**
Starting Your Marriage Right, **126–127**
State of the Arts, **185**
Staub, Dick, **214–215**
Staying Close, 127
Staying Together When an Affair Pulls You Apart, **125**
Steffen, Tom, 177, **236–237**
Stephens, Don, 13
Stepping Out, 176
Stevens, R. Paul, 127, **237–238, 249**
Stevenson, Ann, **74**
Steward, David L., **238**
Stewart, Tracey, 39
Stibbe, Mark, **172–173**, 210
Stier, Jim, **34–35**
Stockman, Steve, 189
Stoeker, Brenda, 117
Stoeker, Fred, **117–118**
Stop the Runaway Conversation, **148–149**
Stories Behind the Best-Loved Songs of Christmas, 72
Stories from a Soldier's Heart, 17
Story of the Trapp Family Singers, The, **38**
Stott, John, 20, 159, 198–199, **258–259**
Stout, Harry S., **196–197**
Streams in the Desert, **48–49**
Strength in Weakness, 118
Stress Less, 107
Strobel, Lee, **163, 271**
Strom, Kay Marshall, 30
Strong, James, **281–282**
Strong Fathers, Strong Daughters, 135
Strongest NIV Exhaustive Concordance, The, 282
Strong's Exhaustive Concordance of the Bible, **281–282**
Strong-willed Child or Dreamer?, 129
Strubel, Deb, 111
Struecker, Jeff, **17–18**
Stuart, Douglas, **279**
Stuart, Sally, **187**
Subtle Power of Spiritual Abuse, 144
Suburban Christian, The, **90**
Success Afield, 261
Sullivan, Tom, 9
Summa of the Summa, A, 287
Summa Theologica, 287

Sumrall, Lester, 82
Supernatural Life, The, **84–85**
Supernatural Power of a Transformed Mind, The, 91
SuperSized Kids, **104**
Surprised by Joy, **42–43**
Surprised by the Power of the Spirit, 83
Surprised by the Voice of God, 83, 85
Surprised by Truth, 3
Survey of Recommended Reading Lists, 230
Susanna Wesley: The Mother of John and Charles Wesley, 24
Sussman, Lesley, **36–37**
Svanoe, Todd, **249**
Swallowing the Golden Stone, 186
Swanberg, Dennis, , **105**
Swanson, James A., **280–281**, 283
Sweetman, Brendan, **208**
Swenson, Richard A., **257**
Swindoll, Charles R., **94–95**
Swords & Whetstones, **294–295**
Synan, Vinson, 57
Systema, Rebecca Wagner, **69–70**, 73, 84
Systematic Theology, 289–290
Systematic Theology: An Introduction to Biblical Doctrine, 289–290

Tabb, Mark, **10**
Taber, Shirin, 4, 178
Table in the Presence, A, 17
Tacelli, Ronald K., 157
Tada, Joni Eareckson, **26**, **105–106**, 198
Taff, Tori, 190
Take and Read, **100**
Take My Hand, **153**
Taking Back Astronomy, 264
Taking Note of Music, 188
Taking Our Cities for God, **65–66**, 69
Taking the High Ground, 17
Tale of Three Kings, A, **89**
Tales of a Seasick Doctor, 13
Talkers, Watchers, and Doers, **217**
Tapestry: The Life and Times of Francis and Edith Schaeffer, 25
Tari, Mel, 175
Taylor, Barbara Brown, **294**
Taylor, Barry, 214
Taylor, Daniel, **106**, **208–209**

Taylor, Geraldine, 32, **35**
Taylor, Greg, **175–176**
Taylor, Howard, 32, **35**
Taylor, Kenneth, 278
Teach Me to Pray, 61
Teachers & Religion in Public Schools, **216**
Teaching a Stone to Talk, 262
Teaching to Change Lives, **217–218**
Teenage Boys!, **130**
TeenVirtue, **113**
Teitsort, Janet Colsher, 142
Telchin, Stan, **4–5**
Tell the Truth, **170–171**
Telling the Truth, **167**
Telling Yourself the Truth, 110, 146–147
Templeton, John Marks, 253
ten Boom, Corrie, 16, **26**, **95**
Ten Fingers for God, 12, **15**, 257
Tending the Heart of Virtue, **185–186**
Tenney, Merrill C., **279–280**
Tenney, Tommy, 78
Tentmaking, **176–177**
Teresa of Avila, Saint, 75
Tesch, Karla, 178
That Man of Granite with the Heart of a Child, 20
That's Just Your Interpretation, **157**
That's My Son, 132
Thaxton, Charles B., **253–254**
Then Darkness Fled, 14
Then Sings My Soul, 72
Theology As Big As the City, A, 207
Theology for a Scientific Age, 274
There Is a God, 158
There's No Place Like Home, **134**
They Shall Expel Demons, 71
They Speak with Other Tongues, **85**
They Were Single Too, 124
Thiessen, Donald, **190–191**
Things Pondered, 23
Thirumalai, Madasamy, **164**
This Rebellious House, **193–194**
Thomas Factor, The, 294
Thomas, à Kempis, 30, **77–78**
Thomas, Gary L., **95–96**, 126, **128**
Thompson, Chad W., **121–122**
Thompson, Steve, **27**
Thousands Not Billions, 265
Thrill of the Chaste, The, **118–119**

Through a Screen Darkly, 213
Through Gates of Splendor, **31–32**, 175
Through the Eyes of Faith Series, **188, 197, 234–235**
Tickle, Phyllis, **49–50**
Tienou, Tite, **176**
Time for a Pure Revolution, **120**
Time for Truth, 29
Time Is Running Out, **166–167**
Timeless Moment, The, 187
Timmerman, John H., **44**
To End All Wars, **16**
To Heaven and Back, **6**, 287
To Know You More, **72**
To Live Is Christ, 93–94
To Own a Dragon, 114
Tobias, Cynthia Ulrich, 129, 217
Today's New International Version, 277
Tolkien: A Biography, **40–41**
Tomorrow You Die, 177
Too Busy Not to Pray, **57–58**
Too Christian, Too Pagan, 215
Too Much Stuff, **112**
Torrey, R. A., 56
Tortured for Christ, 32
Total Heart Health for Women, 102
Total Money Makeover, The, **243–244**
Total Truth, 90, **199–200**, 210
Totilo, Rebecca Park, 241
Touchdown Alexander, 40
Touched by God, **36–37**, 191
Towle, Mike, 39
Towns, Elmer L., 51
Townsend, John, **122–123, 131**, 148
Toxic Faith, **143–144**
Toxic Relief, 107–108
Tozer, A. W., 26, **74, 78**, 294
Train Up Your Children in the Way They Should Eat, 106
Tramp for the Lord, 26
Transforming Care, **102–103**
Transforming Leadership, **246**
Transforming Power of Fasting and Prayer, The, 51
Transforming the Inner Man, 67, 92, 146
Transforming Vision, The, **200–201**
Trapp, Maria Augusta, **38**
Traveling Light, 88
Traveling Mercies, **42**
Traveling Through Grief, 151

Trent, John, 135–136, **141**
Tribute and the Promise, The, **138–139**
Trinity in the Universe, The, **256**
Tripp, Paul David, 138, **149**
Tripp, Tedd, **141**
True Spirituality, 90
Truth About Muhammad, The, 196
Truth About Rock, 190
Truth and Community Transformation, 178
Tsoukalas, Steven, 160
Tucker, Ruth A., 5, **179–180**
Turner, Matthew Paul, **97–98**, 173
Turner, Steve, **38**, 182, 189
Turning Point Christian Worldview Series, **185, 212, 221, 253–254**
Twenty Things You Should Read, **97–98**
Twilight Labyrinth, The, 69
Twilight of Atheism, The, **292**
Twiss, Richard, **209**
Twisted Scriptures, 144
Tyndale New Testament Commentary, 282

Ultimate CORE, 36, **80–81**, 294
Under Cover, 89
Under His Wings, 258–259
Under the Overpass, **8, 9**
Understanding Folk Religion, **176**
Understanding the Dreams You Dream, 84
Unger, Merrill, 279–280
Universe Next Door, The, **163**
Unlocking the Mysteries of Creation, **266**
Unquenchable Worshipper, The, **73**
Unruh, Heidi Rolland, 208
Unseen Face of Islam, The, 178
Unshakable Faith, **14**
Untamed Hospitality, 112
Unusual Suspect, The, **10**
Unveiling Islam, 4, **203**
Upon the Altar of the Nation, **196–197**

Valley of Vision, The, 54
Van Braght, Thieleman J., **35**
Van Dyke, Fred, **260**
Van Ness, Daniel W., **209**
Van Til, Cornelius, **164**
Van Til's Apologetic, 164
Vanauken, Sheldon, **44–45**, 152
VanVonderen, Jeff, **142, 144, 150**

Veith, Gene Edward, 167, **185**, **188**, 199, 201, 237–238
Velvet Elvis, **86**
Victory of Reason, The, 195
Victory over the Darkness, 143
Videos That Teach, 211
View from Goose Ridge, The, 263
Vincent, Lynn, **7–8**
Vine's Expository Dictionary of Old and New Testament Words, 281
Visions Beyond the Veil, **5**, 175
Voice of God, The, 85
Vought, Jeanette, 143

Wagner, C. Peter, 60, 82
Wagner, Doris M., 68, 146
Waking the Dead, 89
Waliszewski, Bob, **190**
Walk On, 189
Walker, Tommy, 73
Walking from East to West, **29**
Walking on Water, **187**
Wallis, Arthur, **51–52**
Walsh, Brian J., **200–201**
Walsh, John, **220–221**
Wangerin, Walter, 186
Wansbrough, Henry, 278
Wanting to Be Her, **115**
Ward, Keith, **255**
Ward, Matthew, 36
Ware, Bruce A., 288
Ware, Timothy, 292
Warner, Kurt, **39–40**
Warren, Gwendolin Sims, 37, **191**
Warren, Rick, **96**
Waters, Mark, 35
Watson, Thomas, 77
Way of the Master, The, 11, **168**
Way They Learn, The, 217
We Saw Heaven, 6, 287
Weaver, Joanna, **96–97**
Webb, Stephen, 258
Wedge of Truth, The, 271
Weidmann, Jim, 138
Weigel, George, 19
Weight of Glory, The, **76**
Weintraub, Pamela, **128**
Weir, Al B., 109
Welch, Janet, **224–225**
Well Connected, **245**

Well-Educated Mind, The, 222
Well-Trained Mind, The, **221–222**
Wells, Jonathan, 266, **271**
Wells, Ronald A., **197**
Wennberg, Robert N., 258
Wentroble, Barbara, 63
Were It Not for Grace, 24
Wesley, John, **27**, 75
What a Daughter Needs from Her Dad, 135
What a Difference a Daddy Makes, **134–135**
What Has Christianity Ever Done for Us?, 195
What I Learned from God While Gardening, 262
What I Learned from God While Quilting, 111
What Jesus Demands from the World, 94
What Should We Then Know, 226
What the Bible Is All About, 280
What the Bible Says About Healthy Living, 107
What We Can't Not Know, 203
What Would Jesus Eat?, **106–107**
What Would Jesus Eat Cookbook, The, 107
Whatever Happened to the Human Race?, 105–106
Whatever Happened to Worship?, **74**
What's So Amazing About Grace?, 8, **97**
What's So Great About America?, 158
What's So Great About Christianity?, **158**
What's the Big Deal?, 121
What's the Deal with Wicca?, 162
Wheat, Ed, 120–121
Wheat, Gaye, 120–121
Whelchel, Lisa, **11–12**, **225–226**
Whelchel, Mary S., **124**, **238–239**
When Children Love to Learn, 225
When God Doesn't Answer Your Prayer, 63
When God Speaks, 84
When God Weeps, 26, 198
When God Whispers Your Name, 91
When He Doesn't Believe, **125–126**
When Heaven Invades Earth, 84, **90–91**
When Homosexuality Hits Home, 122
When Prisoners Return, 204
When Science Meets Religion, 254
When the Trees Say Nothing, **262–263**

When to Speak Up and When to Shut Up, 149
When Too Much Isn't Enough, 150
When You Can't Come Back, 39
When Your Doctor Has Bad News, 109
Where Is God When It Hurts?, 97, 198
Whitcomb, John C., **266–267**
White, Heath, 167, **201**
White, James Emery, 198–199
White, Jeremy, **240–241**, **242**
White, Joe, 138
White, John, **122**, 240
Whitefield, George, 27, 75
Whiteman's Gospel, 209
Whitwer, Glynnis, **239**
Who Is This Jesus?, 169
Who Made God?, 157
Who Should We Then Read?, **226**
Who Was Adam?, **267**
Whorton, Mark, 268
Why A.D.H.D. Doesn't Mean Disaster, **105**
Why Beauty Matters, 115
Why Christian Kids Rebel, **133–134**
Why Good Arguments Often Fail, 163
Why Not Women, **288**
Why Politics Needs Religion, **208**
Why Revival Tarries, 36, **62**
Why Should Anyone Believe Anything at All?, 163
Whyte, Alexander, 54
Wicca's Charm, **162**
Wiggin, Eric, **142**
Wigglesworth: The Complete Story, **27–28**
Wiker, Benjamin, 158, 270
Wilcox, David, 273
Wild at Heart, **114**
Wilder-Smith, Arthur Ernest, **14–15**
Wilder-Smith, Beate, **14–15**
Wilkerson, David, 3
Wilkins, J. Steven, 16
Wilkins, Rob, **189–190**
Wilkinson, Bruce, 96, 218
Wilkinson, David, **255**
Will I Ever Be Whole Again?, **150–151**
Will Medicine Stop the Pain?, **145**
Willard, Dallas, 80, **81**
William and Catherine, **28**
Williams, Clifford, 198–199
Williams, Debbie, 112

Willis, Laurette, **109**
Wills, Garry, 247
Wilson, Dorothy Clarke, 12, **15**, 257
Wilson, Douglas, 18, **221**
Wilson, Elizabeth, **230–231**
Wilson, Julian, **27–28**
Wimber, John, **85–86**, **173–174**
Winans, CeCe, 37
Window on the World, 58
Winner, Lauren F., **45**, 119
Winning, 40
Winning the Heart of Your Stepchild, **129–130**
Winston, Kimberly, 111
Wirt, Sherwood Eliot, 294
Wisdom of the Desert, 93
Wise, Jessie, **221–222**
With Christ in the School of Prayer, **60–61**
Witness to Hope, 19
Witnessing without Fear, 170
Witt, Jonathan, 270
Wittmann, Maureen, 222
Wittmer, Michael E., 92
Wolfe, Gregory, **228**
Wolfe, Suzanne M., **228**
Wolgemuth, Robert, 135
Wolters, Albert, 201
Wolterstorff, Nicholas, 184
Woman, Thou Art Loosed!, 147
Woman's Body Balanced by Nature, A, 102
Woman's Guide to Good Health, A, **102**
Woman's Guide to Spiritual Warfare, A, 65
Wood, Nathan R., **256**
Wooding, Marnie, **241**
Woods, Thomas, 195
Woodward, Thomas, **271–272**
Word on the Street, The, 278
Word Study Greek-English New Testament, 283
Work@home, **239**
World as I Remember It, The, 37
World Christian Database, 295
World Christian Encyclopedia, 58, **295**
World's Easiest Guide to Finances, The, **241–242**
Worship God Is Seeking, The, 71
Worship Leader's Handbook, The, 73–74
<u>Worship Series</u>, 73

Worship Warrior, The, **72–73**
Wounded Heart, The, **143**
Wright, H. Norman, 127, **128–129**, 139
Wright, N. T. "Tom", **282**, **285**
Wright, Vinita Hampton, 140
Writing for the Soul, **186**
Written on the Heart, **203**
Wubbels, Lance, 49
Wurmbrand, Richard, 32

Yamamori, Tetsunao, 205, 235, 237
Yamauchi, Edwin M., **286**
Yancey, George A., **124**
Yancey, Philip, 8, 15, **64**, **97**, **187**, **198**, 257
Yancey, Sherelyn Whittum, **124**
Yankoski, Mike, 8, **9**
Yates, Susan Alexander, 131
Yaxley, Trevor, **28**
Yesterday Today and Forever, 38
Yoga for Christians, 109
Yorkey, Mike, **117–118**
You Are My Hiding Place, 31
You Are Not What You Weigh, 115
You Can't Make Me, 129
You Have What It Takes, 136
Younce, George, 36

Young, Ed, 102
Young, Jo Beth, 102
Young Woman After God's Own Heart, A, 113
Your Best Life Now, 96
Your Boy, 132
Your Girl, **131–132**
Your Kids Can Master Their Money, **241**
Your Mind Matters, 198–199
Your Money After the Big 5–0, 241, **242**
Your Money Map, 240
Your Spiritual Gifts Can Help Your Church Grow, 82
Your Work Matters to God, **237–238**
Youth Culture 101, 120
Youth With A Mission, **180**
Yun, Brother, **28–29**

Zacharias, Ravi, **29**, 157, **160**, 164, **165**, 292
Zodhiates, Spiros, **282–283**
Zondervan Guide to Cults & Religious Movements Series, 160
Zondervan NIV Atlas of the Bible, 284
Zonnebelt-Smeenge, Susan, 151
Zuehlke, Julianne, 143
Zuehlke, Terry, 143
Zuercher, Brent, 206

Subject Index

Abolitionists
  The Roots of Endurance, 24–25
Abortion
  I'll Hold You in Heaven, 151–52
Abstinence. *See* Sexual Abstinence
Abuse
  Deep Wounds, Deep Healing, 146
  The Wounded Heart, 143
Abuse – Spiritual
  Toxic Faith, 143–44
Abuse – Women and Wives
  Refuge from Abuse, 147
Actors
  Against All Odds, 11
  Behind the Screen, 212
  Dale Evans Rogers, 11
  The Facts of Life, 11–12
  A Full House of Growing Pains, 10–11
  The Unusual Suspect, 10
Addiction
  Good News for the Chemically Dependent and Those Who Love Them, 150
Addiction to Sex
  The Dirty Little Secret, 119–20
Adolescence. *See Also* Teenagers
  Parenting Today's Adolescent, 138
Adoption – Interracial
  Just Don't Marry One, 124
Adult Children
  The Tribute and the Promise, 138–39

Adultery
  Staying Together When an Affair Pulls You Apart, 125
Adventure
  Against All Odds, 11
  Bruchko, 33
  C.T. Studd, 32–33
  God's Smuggler, 29
  Hudson Taylor's Spiritual Secret, 35
  Is That Really You, God?, 31
  Living on the Devil's Doorstep, 177
  Living Stones of the Himalayas, 34
Africa
  C.T. Studd, 32–33
African American Agriculturists
  Unshakable Faith, 14
African American Businessmen
  Doing Business by the Good Book, 238
African American Educators
  Unshakable Faith, 14
African American Musicians
  Touched by God, 36–37
African American Surgeons
  Gifted Hands, 12
African American Women
  Chosen Vessels, 116
Age of Earth
  A Biblical Case for An Old Earth, 269
  Coming to Peace with Science, 272
  The Genesis Question, 268–69

Age of Earth (*continued*)
   A Matter of Days, 268
   The New Answers Book, 265
   Reason, Science and Faith, 252
Aging. *See* Healthcare – Older People
AIDS
   The AIDS Crisis, 205
Alcohol Abuse. *See* Addiction
Algeria
   A Passion for the Impossible, 34
Aliens. *See* UFOs
Alternative Medicine
   Alternative Medicine, 107–8
American Religious History
   The Religious History of America, 193–94
   Upon the Altar of the Nation, 196–97
Anabaptists
   Martyrs Mirror, 35
Andrew, Brother, 1928–
   God's Smuggler, 29
Angels
   Angels, 289
   Visions Beyond the Veil, 5
Anger in Children
   The Heart of Anger, 137–38
Anglicans
   John Stott, The Making of a Leader, 20
   Prophetic Evangelism, 172–73
   A Severe Mercy, 44–45
   Sharing Your Faith with Friends and Family, 169
Animal Rights
   Animal Gospel, 258
Animals
   If Animals Could Talk, 265
   Lessons from a Sheep Dog, 258
   When the Trees Say Nothing, 262–63
Anthropic Principle
   Creation as Science, 267–68
   The Creator and the Cosmos, 268
   God's Universe, 253
   Pascal's Fire, 255
   The Privileged Planet, 270
Anthropology
   Bruchko, 33
   Eternity in Their Hearts, 178–79
   Spirit of the Rainforest, 179
Anxiety. *See* Fear
Apologetics
   The Case for a Creator, 271

   The Case for Christ, 163
   Christian Apologetics, 164
   Deliver Us from Evil, 165
   Everything You Always Wanted to Know About God (But Were Afraid to Ask), 293
   Faith Has Its Reasons, 156
   A Francis A. Schaeffer Trilogy, 200
   He Is There and He Is Not Silent, 162–63
   How to Be Your Own Selfish Pig, 159
   How to Give Away Your Faith, 170
   The Kingdom of the Cults, 160
   The Language of God, 272
   Mere Christianity, 158–59
   The New Evidence That Demands a Verdict, 159–60
   Orthodoxy, 157
   Pensees, 161
   The Problem of Pain, 198
   Reason, Science and Faith, 252
   Sharing Your Faith With a Buddhist, 164
   Socrates Meets Jesus, 158
   "That's Just Your Interpretation", 157
   The Universe Next Door: A Basic Worldview Catalog, 163
   What's So Great About Christianity?, 158
   Wicca's Charm, 162
Apologists
   L'Abri, 25
   Walking from East to West, 29
Apostles
   A 20th Century Apostle, 27
Archaeology
   Archaeology and the Old Testament, 284
   The New Evidence That Demands a Verdict, 159–60
Army Rangers. *See* Military
Army. *See* Military
Art
   Art and Soul, 182
   Art and the Bible, 183–184
   Art and the Christian Mind, 183
   Bearing Fresh Olive Leaves, 184
   The Culturally Savvy Christian, 214–15
   A Francis A. Schaeffer Trilogy, 200
   God Through the Looking Glass, 184–85

It Was Good, 182–83
Walking on Water, 187
Art – History
  God Through the Looking Glass, 184–85
  State of the Arts, 185
Art – Modern
  Modern Art and the Death of a Culture, 183
  State of the Arts, 185
Artists
  Akiane, 8
Astrology
  The Stars Speak, 264
Astronomy
  The Stars Speak, 264
Atheism
  What's So Great About Christianity?, 158
Atheism – History
  The Twilight of Atheism, 292
Attention-Deficit Hyperactivity Disorder
  Why A.D.H.D. Doesn't Mean Disaster, 105
Attitude
  Created for Work, 237
Attorneys. *See* Lawyers
Attributes of God
  Creation, 262
  Knowing God, 293
  The Holy Wild, 87
  The Nature and Character of God, 293–94
Augustine, Saint, Bishop of Hippo, 354–430
  The Confessions, 30
Authority
  A Tale of Three Kings, 89
Authorship
  The Christian Writer's Manual of Style, 186
  Christian Writers' Market Guide 2007, 187
  Writing for the Soul, 186
Autism
  Home Schooling Children with Special Needs, 223–24
Autobiography. *See also* Biography; Correspondence; Journals and Diaries
  Against All Odds, 34–35

Against All Odds: My Story, 11
All Things Possible, 39–40
Always Enough, 174–175
The Autobiography of George Müller, 23–24
The Beautiful Side of Evil, 4
Betrayed!, 4–5
Born Again, 2–3
Bruchko, 33
Bryson City Tales, 13–14
Comeback, 39
The Confessions, 30
Dale Evans Rogers, 11
The Day I Died, 6
Eerdmans Dictionary of the Bible, 279–80
The Eyes of the Heart, 40
Facing East, 292
The Facts of Life, 11–12
Feathers from My Nest, 23
Forgiving the Dead Man Walking, 8
Fulfilled Journey, 14–15
A Full House of Growing Pains, 10–11
Gifted Hands, 12
Girl Meets God, 45
The God I Love, 26
God in the Pits, 8–9
God's Smuggler, 29
The Hiding Place, 26
Homestead, 42
The Hospital by the River, 13
I Dared to Call Him Father, 4
Is That Really You, God?, 31
It's More than the Music, 35–36
Joel, 9
Just As I Am, 21
Let's Roll!, 7
Living on the Devil's Doorstep, 177
Living Stones of the Himalayas, 13
The Long Loneliness, 20
Milestones, 18–19
My God and I, 25
The Original Memoirs of Charles G. Finney, 20–21
Orthodoxy, 157
Peace Child, 34
Pistol Pete, 39
The Power of the Powerless, 41
Remarkable Miracles, 52–53
The Road to Unafraid, 17–18

Autobiography (*continued*)
  Rome Sweet Home, 3
  Run, Baby, Run, 3
  Same Kind of Different as Me, 7–8
  The Seven Storey Mountain, 43–44
  A Severe Mercy, 44–45
  Surprised by Joy, 42–43
  To End All Wars, 16
  Traveling Mercies, 42
  Under the Overpass, 9
  The Unusual Suspect, 10
  Walking from East to West, 29
Award Winners (CT)
  Africa and the Bible, 286
  The Call, 89–90
  The Case for a Creator, 271
  Comeback, 39
  Darwin on Trial, 270–71
  Darwin's Black Box, 269
  The Divine Conspiracy, 81
  Doubts About Darwin, 271–72
  Eat This Book, 284–85
  Eerdmans Dictionary of the Bible, 279–80
  Faith Has Its Reasons, 156
  My God and I, 25
  Going Public with Your Faith, 171–72
  How Now Shall We Live?, 210
  In Pursuit of God, 25–26
  Invitation to the Classics, 226–27
  Jonathan Edwards, 22–23
  Just As I Am, 21
  The Language of God, 272
  The Last Word, 285
  The Message, 278
  More Than Equals, 207
  The Original Memoirs of Charles G. Finney, 20–21
  Prayer: Does It Make Any Difference?, 64
  Prayer: Finding the Heart's True Home, 56
  Reconciliation Blues, 205
  Rich Christians in an Age of Hunger, 207–8
  The Scandal of the Evangelical Mind, 199
  Total Truth, 199–200
  The Universe Next Door, 163
  Upon the Altar of the Nation, 196–97
  What's So Amazing About Grace?, 97
  Written on the Heart, 203
Award Winners (ECPA)
  The Blessing, 141
  Bringing Up Boys, 132
  The Case for Christ, 163
  The Case for a Creator, 271
  Comeback, 39
  The Complete Word Study New Testament With Greek Parallel, 282–83
  Crime and Its Victims, 209
  Eyes Wide Open, 214
  Faith Has Its Reasons, 156
  Fearfully and Wonderfully Made, 257
  Finding God at Harvard, 218
  From Jerusalem to Irian Jaya, 179–80
  He Chose The Nails, 91
  How Now Shall We Live?, 210
  Just As I Am, 21
  Let's Roll!, 7
  The Man in the Mirror, 116
  The Message, 278
  New Light on Depression, 144
  NIV Study Bible, 276–77
  Operation World, 58
  Oswald Chambers, 23
  Pistol Pete, 39
  The Power of a Praying Husband, 61–62
  Prayer: Finding the Heart's True Home, 17
  Preparing Your Son for Every Man's Battle, 117–18
  The Purpose Driven Life, 96
  A Severe Mercy, 44–45
  TeenVirtue, 113
  Total Truth, 199–200
  Unveiling Islam, 203
  What's So Amazing About Grace?, 97
  When God Doesn't Answer Your Prayer, 63
  Wild at Heart, 114

Baker, Heidi, 1960–
  Always Enough, 174–75
Baker, Rolland, 1947–
  Always Enough, 174–75
Baldwin, Stephen, 1966–
  The Unusual Suspect, 10

Subject Index 343

Baptism of the Holy Spirit. *See* Speaking in Tongues
Baptists
   The Road to Unafraid, 17–18
   Spurgeon, 19
Baseball Players
   Comeback, 39
Basketball Players
   Pistol Pete, 39
Beamer, Lisa, 1969–
   Let's Roll!, 7
Beamer, Todd Morgan, 1968–2001
   Let's Roll!, 7
Beauty
   Wanting to Be Her, 115
Benedict XVI, Pope, 1927–
   Milestones, 18–19
Bereavement. *See* Grief
Best Books
   Book Lover's Guide to Great Reading, 98
   The Book Tree, 229
   Books Children Love, 230–31
   Books that Build Character, 228
   The Catholic Lifetime Reading Plan, 98–99
   God Between the Covers, 98
   Honey for a Child's Heart, 227
   Honey for a Woman's Heart, 99
   How to Grow a Young Reader, 229
   How to Read a Christian Book, 100
   Indelible Ink, 99
   A Literary Education, 228–29
   The Marketplace Annotated Bibliography, 249
   Take and Read, 100
   Twenty Things You Should Read, 97–98
   Who Should We Then Read?, 226
Bevington, G. C. (Guy Carlton), 1849–1938
   Remarkable Miracles, 52–53
Bible
   All the Prayers of the Bible, 59
   Archaeology and the Old Testament, 284
   Praying God's Word, 68–69
Bible – History
   How the Bible Was Built, 285
Bible Atlases. *See also* Bible Study Tools
   Archaeology and the Old Testament, 284
Bible Commentaries
   An Annotated Guide to Biblical Resources for Ministry, 295–96
   Halley's Bible Handbook, 280
   How to Read the Bible for All It's Worth, 279
   Matthew for Everyone, 282
   Multipurpose Tools for Bible Study, 296
   Swords & Whetstones, 294–95
Bible Dictionaries. *See also* Bible Study Tools
   Eerdmans Dictionary of the Bible, 279–80
   Mounce's Complete Expository Dictionary of Old and New Testament Words, 281
Bible Handbooks. *See also* Bible Study Tools
   Halley's Bible Handbook, 280
Bible in English
   The Catholic Bible, Personal Study Edition, 278
   The Complete Word Study New Testament With Greek Parallel, 282–83
   The Complete Word Study Old Testament, 278–79
   Life Application Study Bible, NASB, 277
   The Message, 278
   NIV Study Bible, 276–77
Bible Reading
   Eat This Book, 284–85
Bible Study Tools
   An Annotated Guide to Biblical Resources for Ministry, 295–96
   Archaeology and the Old Testament, 284
   The Complete Word Study New Testament With Greek Parallel, 282–83
   The Complete Word Study Old Testament, 278–79
   Eerdmans Dictionary of the Bible, 279–80
   Halley's Bible Handbook, 280
   The Hebrew-English Concordance to the Old Testament, 280–81
   Mounce's Complete Expository Dictionary of Old and New Testament Words, 281
   Multipurpose Tools for Bible Study, 296

Bible Study Tools (*continued*)
    Strong's Exhaustive Concordance of the Bible, 281–82
    Swords & Whetstones, 294–95
Biblical Authority
    Inspiration and Incarnation, 284
    The New Testament Documents, 283
Biblical Interpretation
    Africa and the Bible, 286
    Four Views on Hell, 288
    Inspiration and Incarnation, 284
    The Last Word, 285
    The Meaning of Creation, 253
Bibliography. *See* Best Books
Bioethics. *See* Medical Ethics
Biography. *See also* Autobiography; Correspondence; Journals and Diaries
    A 20th Century Apostle, 27
    Akiane, 8
    Art and the Christian Mind, 183
    A Chance to Die, 31
    C.T. Studd: Cricketer and Pioneer, 32–33
    David, 94–95
    Dietrich Bonhoeffer, 19
    Fulfilled Journey, 14–15
    A Full House of Growing Pains, 10–11
    The Heavenly Man, 28–29
    Here I Stand, 18
    Hudson Taylor's Spiritual Secret, 35
    In Pursuit of God, 25–26
    Jack, 44
    Jane Kenyon, 44
    Jesus, 18
    John Stott, The Making of a Leader, 20
    Jonathan Edwards, 22–23
    L'Abri, 25
    Let's Roll!, 7
    The Man Called Cash, 38
    A Man of Faith, 15
    Music as Medicine, 189–90
    Never Give In, 16
    No Compromise, 36
    Oswald Chambers, 23
    A Passion for the Impossible, 34
    A Passion for Souls, 168–69
    Praying Hyde, 54
    Rees Howells, Intercessor, 21–22
    Rich Mullins, 37
    Sgt. York, 16–17
    Shadow of the Almighty, 175
    Something Beautiful for God, 33
    Spurgeon, 19
    St. Francis of Assisi, 30
    Ten Fingers for God, 15
    Tolkien, 40–41
    Unshakable Faith, 14
    Wigglesworth, 27–28
    William and Catherine, 28
Biology
    Darwin's Black Box, 269
    Finding Darwin's God, 273
Biotechnology. *See* Medical Ethics
Birds
    The Birds Our Teachers, 258–59
Birth Control
    Birth Control for Christians, 104–5
Birth Order
    The New Birth Order Book, 135
Blacks in the Bible
    Africa and the Bible, 286
Blended Families. *See* Stepfamilies
Body Image
    Wanting to Be Her, 115
Bondage. *See* Deliverance
Bonhoeffer, Dietrich, 1906–1945
    Dietrich Bonhoeffer, 19
Books and Reading. *See also* Literature. *See also* Best Books
    How to Read a Christian Book, 100
    Invitation to the Classics, 226–27
Booth, Catherine, 1829–1890
    William and Catherine, 28
Booth, William, 1829–1912
    William and Catherine, 28
Boys. *See also* Parenting – Boys
    Boyhood and Beyond, 139–40
Brand, Paul, 1914–2003
    Ten Fingers for God, 15
Brazil
    Against All Odds, 34–35
Brokers
    God in the Pits, 8–9
Buddhism
    Sharing Your Faith With a Buddhist, 164
Budgeting. *See* Personal Finance
Buechner, Frederick, 1926–
    The Eyes of the Heart, 40

Subject Index 345

Bush, George Walker, 1946–
  A Man of Faith, 15
Business
  Business By The Book, 234
  Business Through the Eyes of Faith, 234–35
  Church on Sunday, Work on Monday, 236
  Doing Business by the Good Book, 238
  God Is My CEO, 235–36
  Loving Monday, 234
  The Marketplace Annotated Bibliography, 249
Business and Ministry
  Anointed for Business, 238
Business and Missions
  God is at Work, 235
  Great Commission Companies, 236–37
  Tentmaking, 176–77
Business Ethics
  God in the Pits, 8–9

Cameron, Barbara, 1950–
  A Full House of Growing Pains, 10–11
Cameron, Candace, 1976–
  A Full House of Growing Pains, 10–11
Cameron, Kirk, 1970–
  A Full House of Growing Pains, 10–11
Cancer
  Cancer, 109
  Comeback, 39
  Same Kind of Different as Me, 7–8
Cancer – Breast Cancer
  The Breast Cancer Care Book, 110–11
Career. *See* Work
Caregivers
  Focus on the Family Complete Guide to Caring for Aging Loved Ones, 103
  Transforming Care, 102–3
Carmichael, Amy, 1867–1951
  A Chance to Die, 31
Carson, Ben, 1951–
  Gifted Hands, 12
Carver, George Washington, 1864–1943
  Unshakable Faith, 14
Cash, Johnny, 1932–2003
  The Man Called Cash, 38
Catholic Church
  Catholic Christianity, 290

Catholics
  The Catholic Bible, Personal Study Edition, 278
  The Catholic Lifetime Reading Plan, 98–99
  The Confessions, 30
  Dark Night of the Soul, 75
  Designing Your Own Classical Curriculum, 222
  Experiencing the Depths of Jesus Christ, 56–57
  The Imitation of Christ, 77–78
  The Lawyer's Calling, 201–2
  The Life You Save May Be Your Own, 41–42
  The Long Loneliness, 20
  Milestones, 18–19
  No Man Is an Island, 92–93
  Pensees, 161
  The Power of the Powerless, 41
  Prayer, 58–59
  Rome Sweet Home, 3
  The Seven Storey Mountain, 43–44
  Something Beautiful for God, 33
  Spirituality @ Work, 236
  St. Francis of Assisi, 30
  Tolkien, 40–41
  When the Trees Say Nothing, 262–63
Celebrities. *See* Actors
Chambers, Oswald, 1874–1917
  Oswald Chambers, 23
Character. *See Also* Virtue
  Books that Build Character, 228
  Boyhood and Beyond, 139–40
  Created for Work, 237
  Tending the Heart of Virtue, 185–86
Charismatic Movement
  The Holy Spirit and You, 81–82
Charismatic Renewal
  The Charismatic Century, 57
Charlotte Mason
  A Charlotte Mason Companion, 221
  For the Children's Sake, 225
  A Literary Education, 228–29
Chastity
  The Thrill of the Chaste, 118–19
  Time for a Pure Revolution, 120
Chemistry
  Not Just Science, 252

Chesterton, G. K. (Gilbert Keith), 1874–1936
   Orthodoxy, 157
Chief Executive Officers
   Doing Business by the Good Book, 238
   God Is My CEO, 235–36
   Joy at Work, 244–45
Child Care
   The Complete Book of Christian Parenting & Child Care, 140
Child Development
   The Complete Book of Christian Parenting & Child Care, 140
Child Sexual Abuse
   The Wounded Heart, 143
Childbirth
   Praying for Your Unborn Child, 137
   The Complete Book of Christian Parenting & Child Care, 140
Children's Literature
   All Through the Ages, 230
   The Book Tree, 229
   Books Children Love, 230–31
   Books that Build Character, 228
   God Between the Covers, 98
   Honey for a Child's Heart, 227
   How to Grow a Young Reader, 229
   How to Raise a Reader, 229–30
   The Librarian's Guide to Developing Christian Fiction Collections for Children
   A Literary Education, 228–29
   Tending the Heart of Virtue, 185–86
   Who Should We Then Read?, 226
China
   C.T. Studd: Cricketer and Pioneer, 32–33
   Hudson Taylor's Spiritual Secret, 35
   Visions Beyond the Veil, 5
Chinese Church
   The Heavenly Man, 28–29
Chinese Church – History
   Jesus in Beijing, 192
Christian and Missionary Alliance
   In Pursuit of God, 25–26
Christian Fiction Authors
   Behind the Stories, 41
Christianity
   What's So Great About Christianity?, 158

Church and State
   Teachers & Religion in Public Schools, 216
Church History
   The Charismatic Century, 57
   Church History in Plain Language, 195–96
   Revival, 62
Church of England
   John Stott, The Making of a Leader, 20
Church Work with the Sick
   The AIDS Crisis, 205
Churches – Directories
   Encyclopedia of American Religions, 296
Churchill, Winston, Sir, (Leonard Spencer), 1874–1965
   Never Give In, 16
Civil War. *See* History – Civil War
Classic Literature. *See* Literature – Classic
Classical Music. *See* Music Classical
Classics
   Abiding in Christ, 76
   The Autobiography of George Müller, 23–24
   The Book of Common Prayer, 49
   Christ and Culture, 212–13
   The City of God, 287
   The Confessions, 30
   The Cost of Discipleship, 78–79
   Dark Night of the Soul, 75
   Experiencing the Depths of Jesus Christ, 56–57
   The Great Divorce, 290–91
   A Grief Observed, 152
   Halley's Bible Handbook, 280
   The Hiding Place, 26
   Hudson Taylor's Spiritual Secret, 35
   The Imitation of Christ, 77–78
   In Pursuit of God, 25–26
   The Journal of John Wesley, 27
   The Life of God in the Soul of Man, 77
   The Long Loneliness, 20
   Mere Christianity, 158–59
   My Utmost for His Highest, 48
   The New Foxe's Book of Martyrs, 32
   The Original Memoirs of Charles G. Finney, 20–21
   Orthodoxy, 157

Subject Index 347

Pensees, 161
Power Through Prayer, 53
The Practice of the Presence of God, 75–76
Prayer, 54
Praying Hyde, 54
Principles of Prayer, 55–56
The Problem of Pain, 198
The Pursuit of God, 78
The Release of the Spirit, 94
A Serious Call to a Devout and Holy Life, 75
Servant Leadership, 246
Something Beautiful for God, 33
St. Francis of Assisi, 30
Streams in the Desert, 48–49
Strong's Exhaustive Concordance of the Bible, 281–82
Surprised by Joy, 42–43
The Weight of Glory, 76
Why Revival Tarries, 62
With Christ in the School of Prayer, 60–61
Cloning. *See* Medical Ethics
Clutter
  Too Much Stuff, 112
Codependency
  Please Don't Say You Need Me, 149
Cognitive Styles in Children. *See* Learning Styles
Collective Biography
  101 Hymn Stories, 72
  Behind the Stories, 41
  Deeper Experiences of Famous Christians, 22
  Doctors Who Followed Christ, 12
  Encyclopedia of Contemporary Christian Music, 190
  Faith Under Fire, 17
  The Gift of Music, 37–38
  The Life You Save May Be Your Own, 41–42
  Martyrs Mirror, 35
  Moms Make a Difference, 24
  The New Foxe's Book of Martyrs, 32
  Real Teens, Real Stories, Real Life, 7
  The Roots of Endurance, 24–25
  Scientists of Faith, 12–13
  Singing Through the Night, 30
  Through Gates of Splendor, 31–32

  Touched by God, 36–37
  Unshakable Faith, 14
College
  In, But Not Of, 246–47
College Students
  Fish Out of Water, 219
Colson, Charles W., 1931–
  Born Again, 2–3
Commentaries. *See* Bible Commentaries
Communication – Interpersonal
  An Essential Guide to Public Speaking, 219–20
Community Development
  Renewing the City, 207
Community Transformation
  Informed Intercession, 69
  Taking Our Cities for God, 65–66
Comparative Religion
  Encyclopedia of American Religions, 296
  God's Rivals, 291
  The Universe Next Door, 163
Composers
  The Gift of Music, 37–38
Computer Science
  Not Just Science, 252
Concentration Camps
  The Hiding Place, 26
Concordances. *See also* Greek Concordances; Hebrew Concordances
  The Complete Word Study Old Testament, 278–79
  Strong's Exhaustive Concordance of the Bible, 281–82
Conflict. *See* Forgiveness
Conflict Management
  The Peacemaker, 148
Congregationalists
  Jonathan Edwards, 22–23
Conservatism
  The Myth of a Christian Nation, 202–3
Constellations. *See* Astronomy
Constitutional Law
  Original Intent, 202
Contemporary Christian Music. *See* Music – Contemporary Christian
Control (Psychology)
  The Control Freak, 147

Conversion Stories
  The Beautiful Side of Evil, 4
  Betrayed!, 4–5
  Born Again, 2–3
  The Confessions, 30
  Facing East, 292
  Girl Meets God, 45
  I Dared to Call Him Father, 4
  No Compromise, 36
  The Original Memoirs of Charles G. Finney, 20–21
  Real Teens, Real Stories, Real Life, 7
  Rome Sweet Home, 3
  Run, Baby, Run, 3
  The Seven Storey Mountain, 43–44
  A Severe Mercy, 44–45
  Surprised by Joy, 42–43
  to End All Wars, 16
  Traveling Mercies, 42
  The Unusual Suspect, 10
Correspondence
  The Collected Letters of C.S. Lewis, Volume 1, 43
Cosmogony
  Creation as Science, 267–68
Cosmology
  Creation as Science, 267–68
  The Creator and the Cosmos, 268
  Pascal's Fire, 255
  The Privileged Planet, 270
  The Trinity in the Universe, 256
Counseling
  The Bondage Breaker, 143
  Christian Counseling, 144–45
  Instruments in the Redeemer's Hands, 149
Country Music. *See* Music – Country
Courtship. *See* Dating
Creation Scientists
  Fulfilled Journey, 14–15
Creationism. *See also* Age of Earth; Intelligent Design; Theistic Evolution
  The Case for a Creator, 271
  Coming to Peace with Science, 272
  Darwinism Defeated?, 273
  Icons of Evolution: Science or Myth?, 271
  The Language of God, 272
  The Meaning of Creation, 253
  Perspectives on an Evolving Creation, 273
Creationism – Old Earth
  A Biblical Case for An Old Earth, 269
  Creation as Science, 267–68
  The Creator and the Cosmos, 268
  The Genesis Question, 268–69
  A Matter of Days, 268
  Who Was Adam?, 267
Creationism – Young Earth
  Bones of Contention, 265–66
  Evolution Exposed, 266
  The Genesis Flood, 266–67
  If Animals Could Talk, 265
  The New Answers Book, 265
  The Stars Speak, 264
  Unlocking the Mysteries of Creation, 266
Creative Nonfiction
  Bryson City Tales, 13–14
  Pilgrim at Tinker Creek, 261–62
Cricket
  C.T. Studd, 32–33
Crime
  Born Again, 2–3
  Forgiving the Dead Man Walking, 8
  Run, Baby, Run, 3
Criminal Justice
  Crime and Its Victims, 209
  Justice That Restores, 204
Criticism
  Stop the Runaway Conversation, 148–49
Crucifixion
  He Chose The Nails, 91
Crusades
  The Politically Incorrect Guide to Islam (and the Crusades), 196
Cruz, Nicky, 1938–
  Run, Baby, Run, 3
Cults
  Encyclopedia of American Religions, 296
  The Kingdom of the Cults, 160
Culture. *See also* Popular Culture
  Christ and Culture, 212–13
  The Culturally Savvy Christian, 214–15
  How Should We Then Live?, 194–95
Cunningham, Loren, 1936–
  Is That Really You, God?, 31

Subject Index

Curriculum Planning
  100 Top Picks for Homeschool Curriculum, 223
  Designing Your Own Classical Curriculum, 222

Daily Devotionals
  Abiding in Christ, 76
  The Divine Hours, 49–50
  My Utmost for His Highest, 48
  Not Good If Detached, 95
  Principles of Prayer, 55–56
  The Purpose Driven Life, 96
  Streams in the Desert, 48–49
  With Christ in the School of Prayer, 60–61
Dance
  God Through the Looking Glass, 184–85
  Restoring the Dance, 74
Dating
  Boundaries in Dating, 122–23
  Common Mistakes Singles Make, 124
  I Kissed Dating Goodbye, 123
Dating – Interracial
  Just Don't Marry One, 124
David (King of Israel)
  David, 94–95
Day, Dorothy, 1897–1980
  The Life You Save May Be Your Own, 41–42
  The Long Loneliness, 20
De Vinck, Christopher, 1951–
  The Power of the Powerless, 41
Death and Dying
  The Day I Died, 6
  A Grief Observed, 152
  Grieving a Suicide, 152
  I'll Hold You in Heaven, 151–52
  Mrs. Hunter's Happy Death, 151
  Same Kind of Different as Me, 7–8
  Take My Hand, 153
  To Heaven and Back, 6
  Will I Ever Be Whole Again?, 150–51
Debt. *See also* Personal Finance
  The New Master Your Money, 240
  The Total Money Makeover, 243–44
  The World's Easiest Guide to Finances, 241–42

Deliverance
  The Bondage Breaker, 143
  Can Homosexuality Be Healed?, 121
  Deep Wounds, Deep Healing, 146
  Defeating Dark Angels, 66–67
  Delivering the Captives, 70–71
  Healing, 67
  Power Healing, 85–86
  Praying God's Word, 68–69
  Protecting Your Home from Spiritual Darkness, 69–70
  Shadow Boxing, 68
  Spirit of the Rainforest, 179
Deluge. *See* Flood of Noah
Demographics. *See* Geography
Demons
  Angels, 289
Denominations
  Encyclopedia of American Religions, 296
Depression
  Deep Wounds, Deep Healing, 146
  New Light on Depression, 144
  Will Medicine Stop The Pain?, 145
Design in Nature. *See also* Intelligent Design
  The Amazing Body Human, 257
  If Animals Could Talk, 265
Diaries. *See* Journals and Diaries
Dignity
  The Hunger for Significance, 149
Disabilities
  The Day I Died, 6
  The God I Love, 26
  Joel, 9
Disability
  The Power of the Powerless, 41
Discipleship
  The Cost of Discipleship, 78–79
  The Divine Conspiracy, 81
  Making Jesus Lord, 79
  Master Plan of Evangelism, 167–68
  Ultimate CORE, 80–81
Discipline of Children
  Heartfelt Discipline, 130
  Making Children Mind Without Losing Yours, 134
Divine Foreknowledge. *See* Providence and Government of God
Divine Healing. *See* Healing

Divorce. *See Also* Remarriage
  Christian Family Guide to Surviving Divorce, 128
  Divorce and Remarriage, 125
  Staying Together When an Affair Pulls You Apart, 125
Doctors
  Bryson City Tales, 13–14
  Doctors Who Followed Christ, 12
  Gifted Hands, 12
  The Hospital by the River, 13
  Living Stones of the Himalayas, 13
  Ten Fingers for God, 15
Doctrine
  Christian Beliefs, 289–90
Dogs. *See* Animals
Drama
  God Through the Looking Glass, 184–85
Dravecky, Dave, 1956–
  Comeback, 39
Dream Interpretation
  Dreams and Visions, 84
  If This Were a Dream, What Would it Mean?, 83–84
Drug Abuse. *See also* Addiction
  Good News for the Chemically Dependent and Those Who Love Them, 150
  Mom, Everyone Else Does!, 133
  Run, Baby, Run, 3

Ecology
  Healing the Land, 259
  Pollution and the Death of Man, 259
  Redeeming Creation, 260
  Remember Creation, 259
  Serve God, Save the Planet, 260
  When the Trees Say Nothing, 262–63
Economic Development
  Discipling Nations, 178
Economics
  Rich Christians in an Age of Hunger, 207–8
Editing
  The Christian Writer's Manual of Style, 186
Education. *See Also* Special Education
  100 Top Picks for Homeschool Curriculum, 223
  All Through the Ages, 230
  The Art of Storytelling, 220–21
  The Book Tree, 229
  Books Children Love, 230–31
  A Charlotte Mason Companion, 221
  An Essential Guide to Public Speaking, 219–20
  For the Children's Sake, 225
  Home Schooling, 224
  How to Grow a Young Reader, 229
  How to Raise a Reader, 229–30
  Imagination, 217
  A Literary Education, 228–29
  Mathematics, 218–19
  Molder of Dreams, 216
  Teaching to Change Lives, 217–18
Education – Classical
  Designing Your Own Classical Curriculum, 222
  Recovering the Lost Tools of Learning, 221
  The Well-Trained Mind, 221–22
Education – Early Childhood
  School Starts at Home, 216–17
Education – Parent Participation
  For the Children's Sake, 225
  School Starts at Home, 216–17
  Talkers, Watchers, and Doers, 217
Edwards, Jonathan, 1703–1758
  Jonathan Edwards, 22–23
Elderly. *See* Healthcare – Older People
Elliot, Jim, 1927–1956
  Shadow of the Almighty, 175
  Through Gates of Splendor, 31–32
Emerging Church Movement
  A Generous Orthodoxy, 291–92
  The Hidden Power of Electronic Culture, 211–12
  Velvet Elvis, 86
End of the World
  Charting the End Times, 290
Engineering
  Not Just Science, 252
English as a Second Language
  English Teaching as Christian Mission, 220
Environmental Protection. *See also* Ecology
  Redeeming Creation, 260
  Serve God, Save the Planet, 260
Episcopal Church
  The Book of Common Prayer, 49

Epistemology
  He Is There and He Is Not Silent,
    162–63
Eschatology
  Charting the End Times, 290
Essays
  Behind the Screen, 212
  The Christian Imagination, 187
  God Through the Looking Glass, 184–85
  I Saw the Angel in the Marble, 223
  Indelible Ink, 99
  It Was Good, 182–83
  No Man Is an Island, 92–93
  Of Earth And Sky, 260–61
  The Weight of Glory, 76
Estate Planning
  Splitting Heirs, 240–41
Euthanasia. See Medical Ethics
Evangelicalism
  The Myth of a Christian Nation, 202–3
  The Scandal of the Evangelical Mind,
    199
Evangelism
  The Coffeehouse Gospel, 173
  Conspiracy of Kindness, 173
  Fire Evangelism, 165–66
  Going Public with Your Faith, 171–72
  The Heart of Evangelism, 166
  How to Give Away Your Faith, 170
  I Love Mormons, 161–62
  Just Walk Across the Room, 170
  The Kingdom of the Cults, 160
  Master Plan of Evangelism, 167–68
  Out of the Saltshaker and Into the
    World, 172
  A Passion for Souls, 168–69
  Peace with God, 169
  Power Evangelism, 173–74
  Prophetic Evangelism, 172–73
  Questioning Evangelism, 171
  Sharing Your Faith with Friends and
    Family, 169
  Tell the Truth, 170–71
  Telling the Truth, 167
  Time Is Running Out, 166–67
  The Way of the Master, 168
Evangelists
  A 20th Century Apostle, 27
  The Autobiography of George Müller,
    23–24

The Journal of John Wesley, 27
Just As I Am, 21
A Passion for Souls, 168–69
Run, Baby, Run, 3
Walking from East to West, 29
Wigglesworth, 27–28
William and Catherine, 28
Evolution. See also Creationism;
    Intelligent Design; Theistic
    Evolution
  The Case for a Creator, 271
  Coming to Peace with Science, 272
  Creation as Science, 267–68
  Darwin on Trial, 270–71
  Darwinism Defeated?, 273
  Darwin's Black Box, 269
  Doubts About Darwin, 271–72
  Evolution, 273–74
  Evolution Exposed, 266
  Finding Darwin's God, 273
  The Genesis Flood, 266–67
  Icons of Evolution, 271
  If Animals Could Talk, 265
  The Language of God, 272
  The Meaning of Creation, 253
  The New Answers Book, 265
  Pascal's Fire, 255
  Perspectives on an Evolving Creation,
    273
  Reason, Science and Faith, 252
  Signs of Intelligence, 270
  What's So Great About Christianity?,
    158
  Unlocking the Mysteries of Creation,
    266
Evolution – Human
  Bones of Contention, 265–66
  Who Was Adam?, 267
Evolutionary Creationism. See Theistic
    Evolution
Exercise. See Fitness
Extraterrestrial Life. See UFOs

Failure
  Leading with a Limp, 244
Faith
  The Autobiography of George Müller,
    23–24
  When Heaven Invades Earth, 90–91
  Wigglesworth, 27–28

Fasting
    Fasting for Spiritual Breakthrough, 51
    God's Chosen Fast, 51–52
    The Hidden Power of Prayer and Fasting, 50–51
    A Hunger for God, 51
Fatherhood
    Husbands and Fathers, 137
Fathers and Daughters
    What a Difference a Daddy Makes, 134–35
Fathers and Sons
    Preparing Your Son for Every Man's Battle, 117–18
    Raising a Modern-Day Knight, 135–36
Fear
    The Control Freak, 147
    Fearless, 145–46
    The Road to Unafraid, 17–18
    Will Medicine Stop The Pain?, 145
Fear of the Lord
    Intimate Friendship with God, 88–89
Femininity
    Raising Maidens of Virtue, 136–37
Feminism
    The Feminist Mistake, 206
Fiction. *See* Best Books
Fiction – Children. *See* Children's Literature
Fiction – Christian. *See* Christian Fiction
Fiction – Young Adult. *See* Young Adult Literature
Film
    Behind the Screen, 212
    Finding God in the Movies, 209–10
    God Through the Looking Glass, 184–85
    ReViewing the Movies, 211
    Through a Screen Darkly, 213
Film – Children
    Movie Nights for Kids, 211
Finney, Charles Grandison, 1792–1875
    The Original Memoirs of Charles G. Finney, 20–21
Fitness
    BASIC Steps to Godly Fitness, 108–9
Fleming, Pete, 1928–1956
    Through Gates of Splendor, 31–32
Flood of Noah
    The Genesis Flood, 266–67
    The Genesis Question, 268–69

Folk Religion
    Understanding Folk Religion, 176
Football Players
    All Things Possible, 39–40
Forgiveness
    The Bait of Satan, 86–87
    Choosing Forgiveness, 148
    Forgiving the Dead Man Walking, 8
    What's So Amazing About Grace?, 97
Fossils
    Bones of Contention, 265–66
    Coming to Peace with Science, 272
Francis, of Assisi, Saint, 1182–1226
    St. Francis of Assisi, 30
Friendship
    The Friendship Factor, 147
    The Man in the Mirror, 116

Gaither, William J., 1936–
    It's More than the Music, 35–36
Gangs. *See* Crime
Gardening
    Gardening Mercies, 262
Garr, Alfred G., 1874–1944
    A 20th Century Apostle, 27
Genesis
    The Genesis Question, 268–69
    The Meaning of Creation, 253
Genetic Engineering. *See* Medical Ethics
Genetics
    The Language of God, 272
Geography – Christianity
    Operation World, 58
    World Christian Encyclopedia, 295
Geology
    The Genesis Flood, 266–67
    Not Just Science, 252
Gifts of the Spirit. *See* Spiritual Gifts
Goddess Worship. *See* Wicca
Gordon, Ernest Gordon, 1917–2002
    To End All Wars, 16
Gospel
    Peace with God, 169
Gospel Musicians. *See* Music – Southern Gospel
Gossip
    Stop the Runaway Conversation, 148–49
Grace
    What's So Amazing About Grace?, 97

Graham, Billy, 1918–
  Just As I Am, 21
Grandparenting
  The Gift of Grandparenting, 142
Great Britain
  Never Give In, 16
Greek Concordances
  The Complete Word Study New Testament With Greek Parallel, 282–83
Greek Dictionaries
  The Complete Word Study New Testament With Greek Parallel, 282–83
Greek Word Studies
  The Complete Word Study New Testament With Greek Parallel, 282–83
  Mounce's Complete Expository Dictionary of Old and New Testament Words, 281
Green, Keith, 1953–1982
  No Compromise, 36
Grief
  After the Locusts, 151
  Dale Evans Rogers, 11
  A Grace Disguised, 153
  A Grief Observed, 152
  Grieving a Suicide, 152
  I'll Hold You in Heaven, 151–52
  Same Kind of Different as Me, 7–8
  A Severe Mercy, 44–45
  To Heaven and Back, 6
  When God Doesn't Answer Your Prayer, 63
  Will I Ever Be Whole Again?, 150–51
Grief in Children
  Take My Hand, 153

Hahn, Kimberly, 1957–
  Rome Sweet Home, 3
Hahn, Scott, 1957–
  Rome Sweet Home, 3
Hale, Thomas, 1937–
  Living Stones of the Himalayas, 13
Hall, Ron, 1945–
  Same Kind of Different as Me, 7–8
Hamlin, Catherine, 1924–
  The Hospital by the River, 13
Handicapped. *See* Disability
Harvard University
  Finding God at Harvard, 218

Healing
  A 20th Century Apostle, 27
  Fire Evangelism, 165–66
  God, Medicine, and Miracles, 110
  Healing, 67
  Power Evangelism, 173–74
  Power Healing, 85–86
  Remarkable Miracles, 52–53
  Some of the Ways of God in Healing, 82–83
  Surprised by the Power of the Spirit, 83
  Wigglesworth, 27–28
Healthcare
  The AIDS Crisis, 205
  Cancer, 109
  God, Medicine, and Miracles, 110
  God's Design for the Highly Healthy Person, 104
  Transforming Care, 102–3
  A Woman's Guide to Good Health, 102
Healthcare – Children
  Before Their Time, 106
  The Complete Book of Christian Parenting & Child Care, 140
  Super Sized Kids, 104
Healthcare – Older People
  Focus on the Family Complete Guide to Caring for Aging Loved Ones, 103
Healthcare – Women
  The Breast Cancer Care Book, 110–11
Heaven
  The Great Divorce, 290–91
  Heaven, 286–287
  To Heaven and Back, 6
  Visions Beyond the Veil, 5
Hebrew Concordances
  The Hebrew-English Concordance to the Old Testament, 280–81
Hebrew Word Studies
  The Complete Word Study Old Testament, 278–79
  The Hebrew-English Concordance to the Old Testament, 280–81
  Mounce's Complete Expository Dictionary of Old and New Testament Words, 281
Hell
  Four Views on Hell, 288
  The Great Divorce, 290–91
Herbal Remedies. *See* Nutrition

Hinduism
  Sharing Your Faith With a Buddhist, 164
Hispanic Americans
  Being Latino in Christ, 204
History. See also American Religious History; Church History
  All Through the Ages, 230
  A Francis A. Schaeffer Trilogy, 200
  God's Strategy in Human History, 288–89
  History Through the Eyes of Faith, 197
  Jesus in Beijing, 192
History – Byzantine Church, 330–1453
  Faith in the Byzantine World, 192–93
History – Islam
  The Politically Incorrect Guide to Islam (and the Crusades), 196
History – Middle Ages, 400–1500
  Faith in the Medieval World, 193
History – United States
  The Religious History of America, 193
  This Rebellious House, 193–94
History – United States - 1492–1787
  The Light and the Glory, 194
History – United States Civil War, 1861–1865
  Upon the Altar of the Nation, 196–97
History – Western Civilization
  How Christianity Changed the World, 195
  How Should We Then Live?, 194–95
History of Science. See Science – History
Holistic Medicine. See Alternative Medicine
Hollywood
  Behind the Screen, 212
Home Decorating
  The Simple Home, 111
Home-Based Business
  Work@home, 239
Homeless
  The Long Loneliness, 20
  Same Kind of Different as Me, 7–8
  Under the Overpass, 9
Homeschooling
  100 Top Picks for Homeschool Curriculum, 223
  All Through the Ages, 230
  A Charlotte Mason Companion, 221
  Designing Your Own Classical Curriculum, 222
  The Facts of Life, 11–12
  For the Children's Sake, 225
  Home Schooling Children with Special Needs, 223–24
  Home Schooling, 224
  I Saw the Angel in the Marble, 223
  A Literary Education, 228–29
  The Organized Homeschooler, 222
  Serving Homeschooled Teens and Their Parents, 224–25
  So You're Thinking about Homeschooling, 225–26
  The Well-Trained Mind, 221–22
  Who Should We Then Read?, 226
Homeschooling – Law and Legislation
  Home Schooling, 224
Homesteading
  Homestead, 42
Homosexuality
  Can Homosexuality Be Healed?, 121
  Loving Homosexuals as Jesus Would, 121–22
  Pursuing Sexual Wholeness, 118
Hospitality
  Open Heart, Open Home, 111–12
Housekeeping
  Too Much Stuff, 112
Houses – Prayer
  Protecting Your Home from Spiritual Darkness, 69–70
Housewives
  There's No Place Like Home, 134
Howells, Rees, 1879–1950
  Rees Howells, Intercessor, 21–22
Human Body
  The Amazing Body Human, 257
  Fearfully and Wonderfully Made, 257
  More Than Meets the Eye, 257
Humor
  She Who Laughs, Lasts!, 116–17
Hunger
  Rich Christians in an Age of Hunger, 207–8
Hunting
  The Heart of the Sportsman, 261
Hyde, John, 1865–1912
  Praying Hyde, 54

Hymns
  101 Hymn Stories, 72
  Ev'ry Time I Feel the Spirit, 191

Identity Theft
  Identity Theft, 243
Imagination
  Imagination, 217
India
  A Chance to Die, 31
  C.T. Studd, 32–33
  Praying Hyde, 54
  Ten Fingers for God, 15
  Walking from East to West, 29
Indigenous Peoples
  One Church, Many Tribes, 209
Infant Care
  The Complete Book of Christian Parenting & Child Care, 140
Infertility
  The Infertility Companion, 103
Infidelity. *See* Adultery
Inner Healing
  Can Homosexuality Be Healed?, 121
  Deep Wounds, Deep Healing, 146
  Defeating Dark Angels, 66–67
  The Father Heart of God, 91–92
  Praying for Your Unborn Child, 137
Insurance. *See* Personal Finance
Intellectual Life
  Love Your God with All Your Mind, 198–99
  The Scandal of the Evangelical Mind, 199
  Total Truth, 199–200
Intellectuals
  Finding God at Harvard, 218
Intelligent Design. *See also* Anthropic Principle
  The Case for a Creator, 271
  Darwin on Trial, 270–71
  Darwinism Defeated?, 273
  Darwin's Black Box, 269
  Doubts About Darwin, 271–72
  Fulfilled Journey, 14–15
  Icons of Evolution, 271
  The Privileged Planet, 270
  Reason, Science and Faith, 252
  Signs of Intelligence, 270
Intelligent Design – History
  Doubts About Darwin, 271–72

Intercessors
  Rees Howells, Intercessor, 21–22
Intercessory Prayer
  Becoming a Prayer Warrior, 65
  Beyond the Veil, 63–64
  Informed Intercession, 69
  Possessing the Gates of the Enemy, 66
  Praying Hyde, 54
  Rees Howells, Intercessor, 21–22
Interior Decoration. *See* Home Decorating
Interpersonal Relations
  The Peacemaker, 148
Intimacy
  Sheet Music, 120–21
Intimacy with God
  Intimate Friendship with God, 88–89
  Passion for Jesus, 87
Investments. *See also* Personal Finance
  The New Master Your Money, 240
  The Sound Mind Investing Handbook, 243
  Your Money After the Big 5-0, 242
Irian Jaya. *See* New Guinea
Irreducible Complexity
  Darwin's Black Box, 269
Islam
  The Politically Incorrect Guide to Islam (and the Crusades), 196
  Unveiling Islam, 203
Islamic Culture
  Miniskirts, Mothers & Muslims, 177–78

Jesus Christ
  The Case for Christ, 163
  He Chose The Nails, 91
  Jesus, 18
  Master Plan of Evangelism, 167–68
Jews and Judaism
  Betrayed!, 4–5
Jihad
  The Politically Incorrect Guide to Islam (and the Crusades), 196
Journals and Diaries. *See also* Autobiography; Biography; Correspondence
  The Journal of John Wesley, 27
Just War Doctrine
  Upon the Altar of the Nation, 196–97

Kenyon, Jane, 1947–1995
Jane Kenyon, 44
Kingdom of God
When Heaven Invades Earth, 90–91
Kirkpatrick, Jane, 1946–
Homestead, 42
Knitting
Knitting Into the Mystery, 111
Koran. *See* Qur'an
Kramarik, Akiane, 1994–
Akiane, 8

L'Abri (Organization)
L'Abri, 25
Lamott, Anne, 1954–
Traveling Mercies, 42
Lane, Deforia, 1948–
Music as Medicine, 189–90
Larimore, Walter L., 1952–
Bryson City Tales, 13–14
Latinos. *See* Hispanic Americans
Law
Home Schooling, 224
Written on the Heart, 203
Lawyers
The Lawyer's Calling, 201–2
Leadership
Business Through the Eyes of Faith, 234–35
Courageous Leadership, 247
Developing the Leader Within You, 248
God Is My CEO, 235–236
The Heart of a Leader, Insights on the Art of Influence, 245
In, But Not Of, 246–47
Jesus CEO, 247–48
Joy at Work, 20
Leadership is an Art, 245–46
Leading with a Limp, 244
Never Give In, 16
Servant Leadership, 246
Spiritual Leadership, 248
Teaching to Change Lives, 217–18
Transforming Leadership, 246
Well Connected, 245
Learning Styles
Talkers, Watchers, and Doers, 217
Leprosy
Ten Fingers for God, 15
Letters. *See* Correspondence

Lewis, C. S. (Clive Staples), 1898–1963
The Collected Letters of C.S. Lewis, Volume 1, 43
Jack, 44
Surprised by Joy, 42–43
Liberals
Reaching the Left from the Right, 204
Libraries and Homeschooling
Serving Homeschooled Teens and Their Parents, 224–25
Literature
The Christian Imagination, 187
God Between the Covers, 98
God Through the Looking Glass, 184–85
Honey for a Woman's Heart, 99
Jane Kenyon, 44
The Life You Save May Be Your Own, 41–42
Reading Between the Lines, 188
Literature – Classic
Book Lover's Guide to Great Reading, 98
Invitation to the Classics, 226–27
Liturgical Dance
Restoring the Dance, 74
Liturgy
The Book of Common Prayer, 49
Living Books
All Through the Ages, 230
A Charlotte Mason Companion, 221
A Literary Education, 228–29
Who Should We Then Read?, 226
Loss. *See* Grief
Low Birth Weight. *See* Premature Infants
Luther, Martin, 1483–1546
Here I Stand, 18

Management
Joy at Work, 244–45
Servant Leadership, 246
Manners
Raising Respectful Children in a Disrespectful World, 139
Man-Woman Relationships
For Women Only, 115
Maravich, Pete, 1947–1988
Pistol Pete, 39
Marketplace. *See* Business; Work

Marriage
- *The Complete Book of Christian Wedding Vows*, 128–129
- *Divorce and Remarriage*, 125
- *The Excellent Wife*, 126
- *Families Where Grace is in Place*, 142
- *The Five Love Languages*, 124–25
- *Hidden Keys of a Loving, Lasting Marriage*, 127
- *Husbands and Fathers*, 137
- *Lies Women Believe and the Truth That Sets Them Free*, 113–14
- *The Man in the Mirror*, 116
- *Marriage on Trial*, 127–28
- *Sacred Marriage*, 128
- *Saving Your Second Marriage Before It Starts*, 126
- *Sheet Music*, 120–21
- *Starting Your Marriage Right*, 126–27
- *Staying Together When an Affair Pulls You Apart*, 125
- *When He Doesn't Believe*, 125–26

Marriage – Humor. *See* Humor

Marriage – Interracial
- *Just Don't Marry One*, 124

Marriage – Prayer
- *The Power of a Praying Husband*, 61–62

Martial Arts
- *Against All Odds*, 11

Martyrs
- *Dietrich Bonhoeffer*, 19
- *Martyrs Mirror*, 35
- *The New Foxe's Book of Martyrs*, 32
- *Shadow of the Almighty*, 175
- *Singing Through the Night*, 30
- *Through Gates of Splendor*, 31–32

Martyrs – Wives
- *Singing Through the Night*, 30

Mass Media. *See Also* Television
- *All that Glitters*, 210
- *The Hidden Power of Electronic Culture*, 211–12
- *How the News Makes Us Dumb*, 214

Materialism
- *Money Possessions and Eternity*, 239–40
- *Rich Christians in an Age of Hunger*, 207–8
- *The Suburban Christian*, 90
- *Too Much Stuff*, 112

Mathematics
- *Mathematics*, 218–19
- *Not Just Science*, 252
- *The Soul of Science*, 253–54

Mathewes-Green, Frederica, 1952–
- *Facing East*, 292

McClung, Floyd, 1945–
- *Living on the Devil's Doorstep*, 177

McCully, Ed, 1927–1956
- *Through Gates of Splendor*, 31–32

Media. *See* Mass Media

Medical Doctors. *See* Doctors

Medical Ethics
- *How to Be a Christian in a Brave New World*, 105–6

Medical Missions. *See* Missions – Medical

Medicine. *See* Healthcare

Memoirs. *See* Autobiography

Men's Issues
- *Everyman's Battle*, 117
- *The Man in the Mirror*, 116
- *Wild at Heart*, 114

Mercy Killing. *See* Medical Ethics

Merton, Thomas, 1915–1968
- *The Life You Save May Be Your Own*, 41–42
- *The Seven Storey Mountain*, 43–44

Methodists
- *The Journal of John Wesley*, 27

Michaelsen, Johanna, 1949–
- *The Beautiful Side of Evil*, 4

Microbiology
- *Darwin's Black Box*, 269

Middle East Conflict
- *Christian Family Guide Explains the Middle East Conflict*, 201

Military
- *Faith Under Fire*, 17
- *The Road to Unafraid*, 17–18
- *Sgt. York*, 16–17
- *To End All Wars*, 16

Ministers
- *The Autobiography of George Müller*, 23–24
- *Deeper Experiences of Famous Christians*, 22
- *Dietrich Bonhoeffer*, 19
- *The Eyes of the Heart*, 40
- *The God I Love*, 26

Ministers (continued)
  The Hiding Place, 26
  In Pursuit of God, 25–26
  John Stott, The Making of a Leader, 20
  Jonathan Edwards, 22–23
  The Journal of John Wesley, 27
  Just As I Am, 21
  L'Abri, 25
  The Original Memoirs of Charles G. Finney, 20–21
  Oswald Chambers, 23
  The Road to Unafraid, 17–18
  The Roots of Endurance, 24–25
  Spurgeon, 19
  Walking from East to West, 29
  William and Catherine, 28
Ministry
  Spiritual Leadership, 248
Ministry – Collaboration
  Well Connected, 245
Miracles
  Fire Evangelism, 165–66
  Surprised by the Power of the Spirit, 83
  When Heaven Invades Earth, 90–91
Miscarriage
  I'll Hold You in Heaven, 151–52
Missionaries. See also Missions
  Against All Odds, 34–35
  Bruchko, 33
  C.T. Studd, 32–33
  A Chance to Die, 31
  God's Smuggler, 29
  Hudson Taylor's Spiritual Secret, 35
  Is That Really You, God?, 31
  Living on the Devil's Doorstep, 177
  A Passion for the Impossible, 34
  Peace Child, 34
  Praying Hyde, 54
  Shadow of the Almighty, 175
  Something Beautiful for God, 33
  Through Gates of Splendor, 31–32
Missionaries – Reverse Culture Shock
  Re-Entry, 176
Missions. See also Business and Missions; Missionaries
  Always Enough, 174–75
  Discipling Nations, 178
  Eternity in Their Hearts, 178–79
  How to Get Ready for Short-Term Missions, 175–76

Miniskirts, Mothers & Muslims, 177–78
Operation World, 58
Sharing Your Faith With a Buddhist, 164
Spirit of the Rainforest, 179
Understanding Folk Religion, 176
Visions Beyond the Veil, 5
World Christian Encyclopedia, 295
Missions – Directories
  GO Manual, 180
Missions – History
  From Jerusalem to Irian Jaya, 179–80
Missions – Medical
  The Hospital by the River, 13
  Living Stones of the Himalayas, 13
  Ten Fingers for God, 15
Modesty
  Secret Keeper: The Delicate Power of Modesty, 115
Money. See Personal Finance
Monks
  St. Francis of Assisi, 30
  The Seven Storey Mountain, 43–44
Moody, D. L. (Dwight Lyman), 1837–1899
  A Passion for Souls, 168–69
Moore, Beth, 1957–
  Feathers from My Nest, 23
Moore, Denver, 1937–
  Same Kind of Different as Me, 7–8
Moral Law
  Mere Christianity, 158–59
Moral Training. See Character
Morality
  What's So Great About Christianity?, 158
Mormons
  I Love Mormons, 161–62
Morris, Debbie, 1964–
  Forgiving the Dead Man Walking, 8
Mothers
  The Facts of Life, 11–12
  Feathers from My Nest, 23
  A Full House of Growing Pains, 10–11
  The Mission of Motherhood, 130–31
  Moms Make a Difference, 24
  There's No Place Like Home, 134
Mothers – Humor. See Humor

Mothers – Support Groups
  Creating the Moms Group You've Been Looking for, 139
Mothers and Daughters
  Feathers from My Nest, 23
  Mom, Everyone Else Does!, 133
  Queen Esther's Secrets of Womanhood, 132–33
  Raising Maidens of Virtue, 136–37
  Your Girl, 131–32
Mothers and Sons
  Mom's Everything Book for Sons, 132
Motilone Indians
  Bruchko, 33
Motion Pictures. *See* Film
Movies. *See* Film
Mozambique
  Always Enough, 174–75
Muhammad
  The Politically Incorrect Guide to Islam (and the Crusades), 196
Müller, George, 1805–1898
  The Autobiography of George Müller, 23–24
Mullins, Rich, 1955–1997
  Rich Mullins, 37
Music. *See also* Hymns
  101 Hymn Stories, 72
  All God's Children and Blue Suede Shoes, 212
  The Art of Worship, 73–74
  The Music of Angels, 189
  Music Through the Eyes of Faith, 188
  The Story of the Trapp Family Singers, 38
Music – Classical
  The Gift of Music, 37–38
  The Music of Angels, 189
Music – Contemporary Christian
  The Music of Angels, 189
  No Compromise, 36
  Rich Mullins, 37
Music – Country
  The Man Called Cash, 38
Music – Gospel
  Ev'ry Time I Feel the Spirit, 191
  The Music of Angels, 189
  Touched by God, 36–37
Music – Rock and Roll
  Faith, God and Rock & Roll, 188–89
  The Man Called Cash, 38

Music – Secular
  Chart Watch, 190
Music – Southern Gospel
  It's More than the Music, 35–36
Music in the Bible
  Selah, 190–91
Music Reviews
  Chart Watch, 190
Music Therapy
  Music as Medicine, 189–90
Musicians
  Encyclopedia of Contemporary Christian Music, 190
  It's More than the Music, 35–36
  No Compromise, 36
  Rich Mullins, 37
  Touched by God, 36–37
Muslims. *See also* Islam
  I Dared to Call Him Father, 4
  A Passion for the Impossible, 34
Mystics
  Dark Night of the Soul, 75
  Experiencing the Depths of Jesus Christ, 56–57
  The Imitation of Christ, 77–78
  The Practice of the Presence of God, 75–76
  In Pursuit of God, 25–26
  The Pursuit of God, 78
  No Man Is an Island, 92–93
  Pensees, 161
  The Release of the Spirit, 94
  St. Francis of Assisi, 30
  The Seven Storey Mountain, 43–44

Native Americans
  One Church, Many Tribes, 209
Natural Disasters
  Not Just Science, 252
Natural Law
  Written on the Heart, 203
Nature
  The Amazing Body Human, 257
  Creation, 262
  Fearfully and Wonderfully Made, 257
  Healing the Land, 259
  The Heart of the Sportsman, 261
  More Than Meets the Eye, 257
  Of Earth And Sky, 260–61
  Pollution and the Death of Man, 259

Nature (*continued*)
  Redeeming Creation, 260
  Remember Creation, 259
  When the Trees Say Nothing, 262–63
Nature Writing
  Pilgrim at Tinker Creek, 261–62
Near Death Experiences
  The Day I Died, 6
  to Heaven and Back, 6
Neonatology. *See* Premature Infants
Neopaganism. *See* Paganism
Nepal
  Living Stones of the Himalayas, 13
New Guinea
  Peace Child, 34
New Testament
  The New Testament Documents, 283
Newlywed Couples
  Starting Your Marriage Right, 126–27
News. *See* Mass Media
Newton, John, 1725–1807
  The Roots of Endurance, 24–25
Noah's Flood. *See* Flood of Noah
Nonfiction – Children's Literature. *See*
  Children's Literature
Norris, Chuck (Carlos Ray), 1940–
  Against All Odds, 11
North Carolina
  Bryson City Tales, 13–14
Nuns
  Something Beautiful for God, 33
Nursing
  Transforming Care, 102–3
Nutrition
  Alternative Medicine, 107–8
  BASIC Steps to Godly Fitness, 109
  God's Design for the Highly Healthy
    Person, 104
  The Great Physician's Rx for Health
    and Wellness, 108
  Holy Cow!, 107
  Maximum Energy, 106
  What Would Jesus Eat?, 106–7
Nutrition – Children
  Super Sized Kids, 104

Obesity in Children. *See* Healthcare –
  Children
Occultism
  The Beautiful Side of Evil, 4

O'Connor, Flannery, 1925–1964
  The Life You Save May Be Your Own,
    41–42
Offense. *See* Forgiveness
Olson, Bruce, 1941–
  Bruchko, 33
Open Theism
  God of the Possible, 287–88
Organization
  The Organized Homeschooler, 222
  The Simple Home, 111
  Too Much Stuff, 112
Orphans
  The Autobiography of George Müller,
    23–24
Orthodox Eastern Church
  Facing East, 292

Paganism. *See also* Occultism
  Wicca's Charm, 162
Pain
  The Problem of Pain, 198
Painting. *See* Art
Parapsychology. *See* Psychic
  Phenomena
Parenting. *See also* Grandparenting;
    Single Mothers; Teenage
    Mothers
  Ambassador Families, 213
  Answering the Eight Cries of the Spir-
    ited Child, 129
  Before Their Time, 106
  The Blessing, 141
  Books that Build Character, 228
  Boyhood and Beyond, 139–40
  A Chicken's Guide to Talking Turkey
    With Your Kids About Sex, 121
  The Complete Book of Christian Parent-
    ing & Child Care, 140
  The Danger of Raising Nice Kids,
    141
  Families Where Grace is in Place,
    142
  The Heart of Anger, 137–38
  Heartfelt Discipline, 130
  Honey for a Child's Heart, 227
  Honey for a Teen's Heart, 227–28
  Husbands and Fathers, 137
  I Saw the Angel in the Marble, 223
  Just Don't Marry One, 124

Subject Index   361

Lies Women Believe and the Truth That Sets Them Free, 113–14
Life Interrupted, 133
Making Children Mind Without Losing Yours, 134
The Man in the Mirror, 116
The Mission of Motherhood, 130–31
The New Birth Order Book, 135
Parenting Today's Adolescent, 138
Praying for Your Unborn Child, 137
Preparing Your Son for Every Man's Battle, 117–18
Raising a Modern-Day Knight, 135–36
Raising Great Kids, 131
Raising Maidens of Virtue, 136–37
Raising Respectful Children in a Disrespectful World, 139
School Starts at Home, 216–17
Shepherding Your Child's Heart, 141
Single Parenting That Works, 135
Talkers, Watchers, and Doers, 217
Tending the Heart of Virtue, 185–86
There's No Place Like Home, 134
Why A.D.H.D. Doesn't Mean Disaster, 105
Why Christian Kids Rebel, 133–134
Winning the Heart of Your Stepchild, 129–30
Your Kids Can Master Their Money, 241
Parenting – Boys
  Bringing Up Boys, 132
  Mom's Everything Book for Sons, 132
Parenting – Daughters
  Queen Esther's Secrets of Womanhood, 132–33
  What a Difference a Daddy Makes, 134–35
  Your Girl, 131–32
Parenting – Teenage Boys
  Teenage Boys!, 130
Parenting – Teenage Girls
  Mom, Everyone Else Does!, 133
Parent and Adult Child
  The Tribute and the Promise, 138–39
Peer Pressure
  Mom, Everyone Else Does!, 133
Pentecostalism
  The Charismatic Century, 57
Pentecostals
  A 20th Century Apostle, 27
  Wigglesworth: The Complete Story, 27–28
Percy, Walker, 1916–1990
  The Life You Save May Be Your Own, 41–42
Persecution of Christians. *See also* Martyrs
  The Heavenly Man, 28–29
  Jesus in Beijing, 192
  The New Foxe's Book of Martyrs, 32
  Singing Through the Night, 30
Personal Finance
  Identity Theft, 243
  Money Possessions and Eternity, 239–40
  The New Master Your Money, 240
  Social Security, 242
  The Sound Mind Investing Handbook, 243
  Splitting Heirs, 240–41
  The Total Money Makeover, 243–44
  The World's Easiest Guide to Finances, 241–42
  Your Money After the Big 5–0, 242
Personal Finance – Children
  Your Kids Can Master Their Money, 241
  Money Matters for Teens, 241
Personal Finance – Teenagers
  Money Matters for Teens, 241
Philosophy
  Christian Apologetics, 164
  The City of God, 287
  A Francis A. Schaeffer Trilogy, 200
  He Is There and He Is Not Silent, 162–63
  How Should We Then Live?, 194–95
  How to Be Your Own Selfish Pig, 159
  Philosophy and the Christian Faith, 197
  Postmodernism 101, 201
  The Problem of Pain, 198
  Reason, Science and Faith, 252
  Restoration of Reason, 197–98
  Socrates Meets Jesus, 158
  The Transforming Vision, 200–1
  The Universe Next Door, 163
  Written on the Heart, 203
Philosophy – History
  Philosophy and the Christian Faith, 197

Physicians. *See* Doctors
Physics
   Not Just Science, 252
Picture Books. *See* Children's Literature
Playgroups
   Creating the Moms Group You've Been Looking for, 139
Poets
   Akiane, 8
   Jane Kenyon, 44
Politicians
   A Man of Faith, 15
   Never Give In, 16
   The Roots of Endurance, 24–25
Politics
   Born Again, 2–3
   The Myth of a Christian Nation, 202–3
   Why Politics Needs Religion, 208
   Written on the Heart, 203
Pope. *See* Benedict XVI, Pope, 1927–
Popular Culture
   All God's Children and Blue Suede Shoes, 212
   Ambassador Families, 213
   The Culturally Savvy Christian, 214–15
   Eyes Wide Open, 214
   The Hidden Power of Electronic Culture, 211–12
Pornography
   The Dirty Little Secret, 119–20
   Everyman's Battle, 117
Pornography Industry
   The Dirty Little Secret, 119–20
Postmodernism
   Postmodernism 101, 201
   Telling the Truth, 167
Poverty
   Always Enough, 174–75
   Discipling Nations, 178
POWs. *See also* Military
   To End All Wars, 16
Prayer. *See also* Intercessory Prayer; Spiritual Warfare
   All the Prayers of the Bible, 59
   Authority in Prayer, 63
   Becoming a Prayer Warrior, 65
   Beyond the Veil, 63–64
   Destined for the Throne, 53
   Experiencing the Depths of Jesus Christ, 56–57
   Fasting for Spiritual Breakthrough, 51
   God's Chosen Fast, 51–52
   The Hidden Power of Prayer and Fasting, 50–51
   A Hunger for God, 51
   Let Us Pray, 61
   Letters to Malcolm, 59
   No Easy Road, 55
   Operation World, 58
   The PAPA Prayer, 55
   Possessing the Gates of the Enemy, 66
   The Power of a Praying Husband, 61–62
   The Power of Simple Prayer, 60
   Power Through Prayer, 53
   Prayer, 54
   Prayer: Does It Make Any Difference?, 64
   Prayer: Finding the Heart's True Home, 56
   Prayer: The Great Conversation: Straight Answers to Tough Questions About Prayer, 58–59
   Praying for Your Unborn Child, 137
   Praying God's Word, 68–69
   Praying Hyde, 54
   Principles of Prayer, 55–56
   Red Moon Rising, 56
   Rees Howells, Intercessor, 21–22
   Remarkable Miracles, 52–53
   Too Busy Not to Pray, 57–58
   When God Doesn't Answer Your Prayer, 63
   Why Revival Tarries, 62
   With Christ in the School of Prayer, 60–61
Prayer Books
   The Book of Common Prayer, 49
   The Divine Hours, 49–50
Prayer Teams
   Partners In Prayer, 59–60
Pregnancy
   The Complete Book of Christian Parenting & Child Care, 140
   Praying for Your Unborn Child, 137
Premarital Counseling
   Starting Your Marriage Right, 126–27
Premature Infants
   Before Their Time, 106
Presidents
   A Man of Faith, 15

Preteens
  Parenting Today's Adolescent, 138
  Preparing for Adolescence, 114
Prison Ministry
  Justice That Restores, 204
Problem Children. *See* Strong-Willed Children
Prodigies
  Akiane, 8
Professors
  The Collected Letters of C.S. Lewis, Volume 1, 43
  Finding God at Harvard, 218
  Jack, 44
  My God and I, 25
  Scientists of Faith, 12–13
  Surprised by Joy, 42–43
  Tolkien, 40–41
Prophecy
  Developing Your Prophetic Gifting, 82
  Prophetic Evangelism, 172–73
Providence and Government of God
  God of the Possible, 287–88
  God's Strategy in Human History, 288–89
Psalm 23
  A Shepherd Looks at Psalm 23, 91
Psychiatry
  Will Medicine Stop The Pain?, 145
Psychic Phenomena
  The Beautiful Side of Evil, 4
Psychology
  The Control Freak, 147
  The New Birth Order Book, 135
  The Search for Significance, 146–47
Puberty
  Preparing Your Son for Every Man's Battle, 117–18
  A Chicken's Guide to Talking Turkey With Your Kids About Sex, 121
Public Schools – Law and Legislation
  Teachers & Religion in Public Schools, 216
Public Schools – Religion
  Teachers & Religion in Public Schools, 216
Public Speaking
  An Essential Guide to Public Speaking, 219–20
Publishing
  Christian Writers' Market Guide 2007, 187
Purgatory
  Four Views on Hell, 288
Purity
  And the Bride Wore White, 119
  Every Woman's Battle, 119
  Secret Keeper, 115

Quantum Physics
  Pascal's Fire, 255
Quilting
  Knitting Into the Mystery, 111
Qur'an
  The Politically Incorrect Guide to Islam (and the Crusades), 196
  Unveiling Islam, 203

Race Relations
  Being Latino in Christ, 204
  Being White, 205–6
  More Than Equals, 207
  One Church, Many Tribes, 209
  Reconciliation Blues, 205
Rape
  Forgiving the Dead Man Walking, 8
Reading
  How to Raise a Reader, 229–30
Rebellion in Children
  Why Christian Kids Rebel, 133–34
Reconciliation
  The Peacemaker, 148
Reference
  Encyclopedia of American Religions, 296
  Encyclopedia of Contemporary Christian Music, 190
  The Hebrew-English Concordance to the Old Testament, 280–81
  Mounce's Complete Expository Dictionary of Old and New Testament Words, 281
  Strong's Exhaustive Concordance of the Bible, 281–82
Reformers of the Church
  Here I Stand, 18
Relationship Addiction
  Please Don't Say You Need Me, 149

Relief
   Discipling Nations, 178
Religions
   Encyclopedia of American Religions, 296
Remarriage
   The Complete Book of Christian Wedding Vows, 128–29
   Divorce and Remarriage, 125
   Saving Your Second Marriage Before It Starts, 126
   Winning the Heart of Your Stepchild, 129–30
Respect in Children
   Raising Respectful Children in a Disrespectful World, 139
Retirement. *See* Personal Finance
Revival
   The Charismatic Century, 57
   The Original Memoirs of Charles G. Finney, 20–21
   Praying Hyde, 54
   Rees Howells, Intercessor, 21–22
   Revival, 62
   Visions Beyond the Veil, 5
   Why Revival Tarries, 62
Rhetoric. *See* Public Speaking
Richardson, Don, 1935–
   Peace Child, 34
Ritchie, Mark Andrew, 1948–
   God in the Pits, 8–9
Rock and Roll Music. *See* Music – Rock and Roll
Rogers, Dale Evans, 1912–2001
   Dale Evans Rogers, 11
Rookmaaker, H. R. (Hendrik "Hans" Roelof), 1922–1977
   Art and the Christian Mind, 183

Saint, Nate, 1923–1956
   Through Gates of Splendor, 31–32
Saints
   The Confessions, 30
   St. Francis of Assisi, 30
Salvation
   Peace with God, 169
   Speaking of Sin, 294
Salvation Army
   William and Catherine, 28
Same-Sex Marriage
   Marriage on Trial, 127–28

Sawi (Indonesian People)
   Peace Child, 34
Schaeffer, Edith, 1914–
   L'Abri, 25
Schaeffer, Francis A. (August), 1912–1984
   L'Abri, 25
Scholarship
   The Scandal of the Evangelical Mind, 199
Schools. *See* Public Schools
Schools – Law and Legislation
   Home Schooling, 224
Science
   The Case for a Creator, 271
   What's So Great About Christianity?, 158
Science – History
   Reason, Science and Faith, 252
   The Soul of Science, 253–54
Science – Philosophy
   Science and Its Limits, 254
Science and Faith
   A Biblical Case for An Old Earth, 269
   God's Universe, 253
   The Meaning of Creation, 253
   Not Just Science, 252
   One World, 254
   Pascal's Fire, 255
   Reason, Science and Faith, 252
   Science and Its Limits, 254
   The Soul of Science, 253–54
   The Trinity in the Universe, 256
   Who Was Adam?, 267
Science Textbooks
   Evolution Exposed, 266
   Icons of Evolution, 271
Scientific Method
   Restoration of Reason, 197–98
Scientists
   Fulfilled Journey, 14–15
   Scientists of Faith, 12–13
Screenwriting
   Behind the Screen, 212
Second Great Awakening. *See also* Revival
   The Original Memoirs of Charles G. Finney, 20–21
Self-Esteem
   The Search for Significance, 146–47

Subject Index

September 11 Terrorist Attacks
   Let's Roll!, 7
Seventh-Day Adventists
   Gifted Hands, 12
Sex Education
   Preparing Your Son for Every Man's Battle, 117–18
   A Chicken's Guide to Talking Turkey With Your Kids About Sex, 121
Sex in Marriage
   Sheet Music, 120–21
Sexual Abstinence
   And the Bride Wore White, 119
   A Chicken's Guide to Talking Turkey With Your Kids About Sex, 121
   Preparing Your Son for Every Man's Battle, 117–18
   The Thrill of the Chaste, 118–19
   Time for a Pure Revolution, 120
Sexual Abuse. *See also* Abuse
   The Wounded Heart, 143
Sexual Addiction
   Pursuing Sexual Wholeness, 118
Sexual Sin
   The Dirty Little Secret, 119–20
   Eros Defiled, 122
   Every Woman's Battle, 119
   Everyman's Battle, 117
   The Thrill of the Chaste, 118–19
Sexuality
   Every Woman's Battle, 119
Sexually Transmitted Diseases
   Time for a Pure Revolution, 120
Shamans
   Spirit of the Rainforest, 179
Sheikh, Bilquis, 1912–1997
   I Dared to Call Him Father, 4
Short-Term Missions
   How to Get Ready for Short-Term Missions, 175–76
Signs (Miraculous)
   If This Were a Dream, What Would it Mean?, 83–84
Simeon, Charles, 1759–1836
   The Roots of Endurance, 24–25
Sin
   Speaking of Sin, 294
Single Mothers
   Life Interrupted, 133
   Single Parenting That Works, 135

Single People
   Boundaries in Dating, 122–23
   Common Mistakes Singles Make, 124
   Singles at the Crossroads, 123–24
Single Women
   The Thrill of the Chaste, 118–19
Sjogren, Steve, 1955–
   The Day I Died, 6
Skepticism
   "That's Just Your Interpretation", 157
Smedes, Lewis B. (Benedictus), 1921–2002
   My God and I, 25
Social Issues
   How to Be Your Own Selfish Pig, 159
   Reaching the Left from the Right, 204
Social Justice
   The Long Loneliness, 20
Social Security
   Social Security, 242
Social Work
   Christianity and Social Work, 206
Sociology
   The Feminist Mistake, 206
Soldiers. *See* Military
Sonnenberg, Joel, 1977–
   Joel, 9
South America
   Bruchko, 33
Southern Gospel Music. *See* Music – Southern Gospel
Spanking. *See* Discipline of Children
Speaking in Tongues. *See also* Spiritual Gifts
   The Holy Spirit and You, 81–82
   They Speak with Other Tongues, 85
Special Education
   Home Schooling Children with Special Needs, 223–24
Speech Communications. *See* Public Speaking
Spiritual Authority
   A Tale of Three Kings, 89
Spiritual Authority – Abuse
   Toxic Faith, 143–44
Spiritual Disciplines
   Celebration of Discipline, 79–80
   The Life You've Always Wanted, 80
Spiritual Gifts
   Deep Wounds, Deep Healing, 146

Spiritual Gifts (*continued*)
   The Holy Spirit and You, 81–82
   Prophetic Evangelism, 172–73
   The Supernatural Life, 84–85
   Surprised by the Power of the Spirit, 83
   They Speak with Other Tongues, 85
   Wigglesworth, 27–28
Spiritual Growth
   Abiding in Christ, 76
   Anonymous, 88
   Battlefield of the Mind, 93
   Believing God, 93–94
   Book Lover's Guide to Great Reading, 98
   The Call, 89–90
   The Catholic Lifetime Reading Plan, 98–99
   Celebration of Discipline, 79–80
   The Cost of Discipleship, 78–79
   Dark Night of the Soul, 75
   David, 94–95
   Desire, 89
   Desiring God, 94
   The Divine Conspiracy, 81
   Eat This Book, 284–85
   The Father Heart of God, 91–92
   Having a Mary Heart in a Martha World, 96–97
   He Chose The Nails, 91
   The Holy Wild, 87
   Honey for a Woman's Heart, 99
   The Imitation of Christ, 77–78
   Intimate Friendship with God, 88–89
   The Life of God in the Soul of Man, 77
   The Life You've Always Wanted, 80
   Making Jesus Lord, 79
   No Man Is an Island, 92–93
   Not Good If Detached, 95
   Passion for Jesus: Cultivating Extravagant Love for God, 87
   The Practice of the Presence of God, 75–76
   The Pressure's Off, 88
   The Purpose Driven Life, 96
   The Pursuit of God, 78
   The Release of the Spirit, 94
   Sacred Marriage, 128
   Sacred Pathways, 95–96
   A Serious Call to a Devout and Holy Life, 75
   A Shepherd Looks at Psalm 23, 91
   Speaking of Sin, 294
   Take and Read, 100
   A Tale of Three Kings, 89
   Twenty Things You Should Read, 97–98
   Ultimate CORE, 80–81
   Velvet Elvis: Repainting the Christian Faith, 86
   What's So Amazing About Grace?, 97
Spiritual Mapping
   Informed Intercession, 69
Spiritual Warfare
   Authority in Prayer, 63
   Becoming a Prayer Warrior, 65
   Delivering the Captives, 70–71
   Informed Intercession, 69
   Needless Casualties of War, 66
   Possessing the Gates of the Enemy, 66
   Praying God's Word, 68–69
   Protecting Your Home from Spiritual Darkness, 69–70
   Shadow Boxing, 68
   Spiritual Warfare for Every Christian, 70
   Taking Our Cities for God, 65–66
   The Worship Warrior, 52
Sports
   All Things Possible, 39–40
   C.T. Studd, 32–33
   Comeback, 39
   Pistol Pete, 39
Spurgeon, Charles Haddon, 1834–1892
   Spurgeon, 19
Stars
   The Stars Speak, 264
Statesmen. *See* Politicians
Statistics – Christianity
   Operation World, 58
   World Christian Encyclopedia, 295
Stem-Cell Research. *See* Medical Ethics
Stepfamilies
   Winning the Heart of Your Stepchild, 129–30
Stier, Jim, 1950–
   Against All Odds, 34–35
Stillbirth
   I'll Hold You in Heaven, 151–52
Storytelling
   The Art of Storytelling, 220–21

Stott, John R. W. (Robert Walmsley), 1921–
  John Stott, The Making of a Leader, 20
Stress
  A Woman's Guide to Good Health, 102
Strong-Willed Children
  Answering the Eight Cries of the Spirited Child, 129
Struecker, Jeff, 1969–
  The Road to Unafraid, 17–18
Studd, C. T. (Charles Thomas), 1860–1931
  C.T. Studd, 32–33
Study Bibles
  The Catholic Bible, Personal Study Edition, 278
  Life Application Study Bible, NASB, 277
  NIV Study Bible, 276–77
Substance Abuse. *See* Addiction
Suburban Life
  The Suburban Christian, 90
Suffering
  A Grace Disguised, 153
  The Problem of Pain, 198
Suicide
  Grieving a Suicide, 152
Surgeons. *See* Doctors
Systematic Theology
  Christian Beliefs, 289–90

Tada, Joni Eareckson, 1949–
  The God I Love, 26
Taylor, James Hudson, 1832–1905
  Hudson Taylor's Spiritual Secret, 35
Teachers – Public School
  Teachers & Religion in Public Schools, 216
Teachers
  Molder of Dreams, 216
Teaching
  Teaching to Change Lives, 217–18
Teaching – Language
  English Teaching as Christian Mission, 220
Technology
  The Hidden Power of Electronic Culture, 211–12
  Not Just Science, 252
Teenage Girls
  And the Bride Wore White, 119
  Every Woman's Battle, 119
  Raising Maidens of Virtue, 136–37
  Secret Keeper, 115
  TeenVirtue, 113
Teenage Mothers
  Life Interrupted, 133
Teenage Pregnancy
  Life Interrupted, 133
Teenagers
  Honey for a Teen's Heart, 227–28
  Parenting Today's Adolescent, 138
  Preparing for Adolescence, 114
  Real Teens, Real Stories, Real Life, 7
  Time for a Pure Revolution, 120
Telchin, Stan, 1924–
  Betrayed!, 4–5
Telecommuting
  Work@home, 239
Television. *See Also* Mass Media
  All God's Children and Blue Suede Shoes, 212
  All That Glitters, 210
Temptation
  Everyman's Battle, 117
Ten Boom, Corrie, 1892–1983
  The Hiding Place, 26
Teresa, Mother (of Calcutta), 1910–1997
  Something Beautiful for God, 33
Theater
  God Through the Looking Glass, 184–85
Theistic Evolution
  Coming to Peace with Science, 272
  Darwinism Defeated?, 273
  Evolution, 273–74
  Finding Darwin's God, 273
  God's Universe, 253
  The Language of God, 272
  One World, 254
  Pascal's Fire, 255
  Perspectives on an Evolving Creation, 273
Theologians
  The Confessions, 30
  Dietrich Bonhoeffer, 19
  Here I Stand, 18
  Jonathan Edwards, 22–23
  Milestones, 18–19
  The Original Memoirs of Charles G. Finney, 20–21

Theology. *See also* Attributes of God
    Catholic Christianity, 290
    Christian Beliefs, 289–90
    The City of God, 287
    Everything You Always Wanted to
        Know About God (But Were Afraid
        to Ask), 293
    Four Views on Hell, 288
    A Generous Orthodoxy, 291–92
    God of the Possible, 287–88
    God's Strategy in Human History,
        288–89
    The Great Divorce, 290–91
    Imagination, 217
    Letters to Malcolm, 59
    Mere Christianity, 158–59
    Pascal's Fire, 255
Theology – Reformed Theology
    Christian Apologetics, 164
Thinking. *See* Intellectual Life
Tithing
    Money, Possessions and Eternity,
        239–40
Tolerance
    Is God Intolerant?, 208–9
Tolkien, J. R. R. (John Ronald Reuel),
    1892–1973
    Tolkien: A Biography, 40–41
Tozer, A. W. (Aiden Wilson), 1897–
    1963
    In Pursuit of God, 25–26
Trapp, Maria Augusta, 1905–1987
    The Story of the Trapp Family Singers,
        38
Trapp Family
    The Story of the Trapp Family Singers,
        38
Trinity
    The Trinity in the Universe, 256
Trotter, Lilias, 1853–1928
    A Passion for the Impossible, 34
Tuskegee University
    Unshakable Faith, 14

UFOs
    Alone in the Universe?, 255–56
    Lights in the Sky and Little Green Men,
        254–55
Unplanned Pregnancy
    Life Interrupted, 133

Urban Missions
    Taking Our Cities for God, 65–66
Urban Renewal
    Renewing the City, 207

Vanauken, Sheldon, 1914–1996
    A Severe Mercy, 44–45
Virtue. *See Also* Character
    Raising Maidens of Virtue, 136–37
    TeenVirtue, 113
    Your Girl, 131–32
Visions
    Dreams and Visions, 84
    Visions Beyond the Veil, 5
Vitamins. *See* Nutrition
Vocation. *See* Work
Vocational Guidance
    In, But Not Of, 246–47
Von Trapp. *See* Trapp Family

War. *See* World War I; World War II
Warner, Kurt, 1971–
    All Things Possible, 39–40
Washington, Booker T., 1856–1915
    Unshakable Faith, 14
Watergate
    Born Again, 2–3
Wealth
    Rich Christians in an Age of Hunger,
        207–8
Wealth Transfer
    Splitting Heirs, 240–41
Wedding Vows
    The Complete Book of Christian Wedding Vows, 128–29
Weddings – Planning
    The Complete Book of Christian Wedding Vows, 128–29
Wesley, John, 1703–1791
    The Journal of John Wesley, 27
Whelchel, Lisa, 1963–
    The Facts of Life, 11–12
Wicca
    Wicca's Charm, 162
Wigglesworth, Smith, 1859–1947
    Wigglesworth, 27–28
Wilberforce, William, 1759–1833
    The Roots of Endurance, 24–25

Subject Index

Wilder-Smith, A. E. (Arthur Ernest), 1915–1995
   Fulfilled Journey, 14–15
Wilder-Smith, Beate, 1928–
   Fulfilled Journey, 14–15
Winner, Lauren, 1975–
   Girl Meets God, 45
Witchcraft. *See also* Occultism
   Wicca's Charm, 162
Wives
   The Excellent Wife, 126
   Singing Through the Night, 30
   When He Doesn't Believe, 125–26
Women. *See also* Wives
   And the Bride Wore White, 119
   Every Woman's Battle, 119
   Feathers from My Nest, 23
   The Feminist Mistake, 206
   Honey for a Woman's Heart, 99
   Moms Make a Difference, 24
   Secret Keeper, 115
   The Thrill of the Chaste, 118–19
   Wanting to Be Her, 115
Women – Health
   The Breast Cancer Care Book, 110–11
   A Woman's Guide to Good Health, 102
Women in Church Work
   Why Not Women, 288
Women in the Bible
   Why Not Women, 288
Women. *See also* Wives
Women's Issues
   After the Locusts, 151
   Chosen Vessels, 116
   The Christian Working Woman, 238–39
   For Women Only, 115
   Having a Mary Heart in a Martha World, 96–97
   Lies Women Believe and the Truth That Sets Them Free, 113–14
   Refuge from Abuse, 147
   She Who Laughs, Lasts!, 116–17
Women's Issues – Humor. *See* Humor
Word Studies. *See also* Greek Word Studies; Hebrew Word Studies
   Mounce's Complete Expository Dictionary of Old and New Testament Words, 281
   Strong's Exhaustive Concordance of the Bible, 281–82

Work
   Business Through the Eyes of Faith, 234–35
   The Call, 89–90
   The Christian Working Woman, 238–39
   Church on Sunday, Work on Monday, 236
   Created for Work, 237
   In, But Not Of, 246–47
   Loving Monday, 234
   Spirituality @ Work, 236
   Work@home, 239
   Your Work Matters to God, 237–38
Work – Bibliography
   The Marketplace Annotated Bibliography, 249
Work and Evangelism
   Going Public with Your Faith, 171–72
Working Mothers
   There's No Place Like Home, 134
World Religions
   God's Rivals, 291
World War I
   Sgt. York, 16–17
World War II
   Faith Under Fire, 17
   The Hiding Place, 26
   To End All Wars, 16
Worldview
   Discipling Nations, 178
   Fish Out of Water, 219
   A Francis A. Schaeffer Trilogy, 200
   Heaven Is Not My Home, 92
   How Now Shall We Live?, 210
   How Should We Then Live?, 194–95
   The Transforming Vision, 200–1
   The Universe Next Door, 163
   Total Truth: Liberating Christianity from its Cultural Captivity, 199–200
Worry. *See* Fear
Worship
   101 Hymn Stories, 72
   The Art of Worship, 73–74
   Here I Am to Worship, 71
   Restoring the Dance, 74
   to Know You More, 72
   The Unquenchable Worshipper, 73
   Whatever Happened to Worship?, 74
   The Worship Warrior, 72–73

Worship Leading
   The Art of Worship, 73–74
   Here I Am to Worship, 71
   To Know You More, 72
Writers
   Behind the Stories, 41
   The Collected Letters of C.S. Lewis, Volume 1, 43
   The Eyes of the Heart, 40
   Girl Meets God, 45
   The God I Love, 26
   Homestead, 42
   The Life You Save May Be Your Own, 41–42
   In Pursuit of God, 25–26
   Jack, 44
   Jane Kenyon, 44
   My God and I, 25
   A Severe Mercy, 44–45
   Surprised by Joy, 42–43
   The Power of the Powerless, 41
   The Seven Storey Mountain, 43–44
   Tolkien, 40–41
   Traveling Mercies, 42
Writing
   The Christian Imagination, 187
   The Christian Writer's Manual of Style, 186
   Christian Writers' Market Guide 2007, 187
   Walking on Water, 187
   Writing for the Soul, 186

Yankoski, Mike (Michael), 1983–
   Under the Overpass, 9
Yanomamo Indians
   Spirit of the Rainforest, 179
Yoga
   BASIC Steps to Godly Fitness, 109

York, Alvin Cullum, 1887–1964
   Sgt. York, 16–17
Youderian, Roger, 1924–1956
   Through Gates of Splendor, 31–32
Young Adult Interest
   And the Bride Wore White, 119
   Bruchko, 33
   Created for Work, 237
   Every Woman's Battle, 119
   GO Manual, 180
   Honey for a Teen's Heart, 227–28
   How the Bible Was Built, 285
   How to Be Your Own Selfish Pig, 159
   Is That Really You, God?, 31
   Money Matters for Teens, 241
   Preparing for Adolescence, 114
   Raising Maidens of Virtue, 136–37
   Real Teens, Real Stories, Real Life, 7
   Secret Keeper, 115
   TeenVirtue, 113
   Time for a Pure Revolution, 120
   Ultimate CORE, 80–81
   The Unusual Suspect, 10
Young Adult Literature
   Honey for a Teen's Heart, 227–28
Youth Culture
   Time for a Pure Revolution, 120
Yun, Brother, 1958–
   The Heavenly Man, 28–29
YWAM (Organization)
   Against All Odds, 34–35
   GO Manual, 180
   Is That Really You, God?, 31

Zacharias, Ravi K. (Frederick Antony Ravi Kumar), 1946–
   Walking from East to West, 29

About the Author

Photo by Tonja Rainey

David Rainey is senior bibliographer at the State Library of Louisiana. He also works in the young-adult section of the Bluebonnet Regional Branch Library in Baton Rouge. Mr. Rainey loves working in libraries, especially doing reference work and collection development.